Tudor Queens and Princesses

Tudor Queens and Princesses

Sarah Tytler

BARNES
&NOBLE
BOOKS
NEW YORK

M1688

This edition published by Barnes & Noble, Inc.

1993 Barnes & Noble Books

ISBN 1-56619-238-2
Printed and bound in the United States of America

M 9 8 7 6 5 4 3 2 1

CONTENTS

TUDOR QUEENS AND PRINCESSES

ELIZABETH TUDOR

A TUDOR BY BIRTH, AND QUEEN IN HER OWN RIGHT

PRINCESS ELIZABETH [1]

ELIZABETH TUDOR, the greatest of England's queens—in some respects the greatest of her sovereigns—was born at Greenwich Palace on the 7th of September, 1533. As the 7th of September happened to fall on a Sunday in 1533, the child's friends could claim for her the bountiful endowments which the homely old adage awards to a Sunday's child—

> "The bairn that is born on the Sabbath day,
> Is bonnie, and lucky, and wise, and gay."

It was farther remarked when her long reign was ended, and her title to that distinction which she proudly claimed for herself, "the Virgin Queen," was established for all time, that she was born on the eve of the Virgin's nativity, and died on the eve of the annunciation. Great store was set at one time on a third coincidence in connection with Elizabeth's birth. In the same year, on the same day, and at the same hour, a son was born to Sir John Dudley, who was named Robert,

---

[1] Agnes Strickland, Froude, Green, Brewer, Beesley, Camden.

and became the Earl of Leicester. According to the astrological superstitions of the generation—which Elizabeth shared in a large measure—this similarity of nativities produced a secret and invincible sympathy between the children, not only in infancy, but in after years, and wove together alike their natures and their destinies. If there is such a thing as "a prophecy fulfilling itself," the same may be said of a piece of superstition in a credulous age.

The sex of the child was a bitter disappointment to both father and mother; but Anne Boleyn was still in high favour with Henry VIII., so that he gave his little daughter a magnificent christening in the church of the Greyfriars, Greenwich. Miss Strickland has a glowing description of the church hung with arras, and strewn with rushes, the silver font, with its canopy of crimson velvet fringed with gold, &c.

Among the company were the Most Worshipful the Lord Mayor and his Council in their robes, who at the summons of Henry were rowed down the river to be present at the ceremony. A less imposing and more grotesque group consisted of gentlemen "in aprons, with towels round their necks," whose duty it was to guard the font. The aprons and towels marked off the gentlemen for their office, as rosettes on their coats distinguish the stewards at balls.

The child wore, in addition to a christening robe heavy and stiff with gold embroidery—recently exhibited among the relics of the Tudors—a royal mantle of purple velvet and miniver, with a train so long that it was borne up by a lady and two gentlemen. The one godmother was the baby's cousin, Frances Brandon, still only Marchioness of Dorset; the other, who carried the child, was her great grandmother, the Duchess of Norfolk; the godfather was Archbishop Cranmer. The Bishop of London, assisted by other bishops and abbots, baptized the princess.

The Howards, Anne Boleyn's kindred generally, mustered strong on the occasion, while Henry's relations were less liberally represented. It is on record that Elizabeth's sister, Mary, had been commanded to come to Greenwich, when the girl had mortally offended her father by refusing to call the infant anything save " sister," because the title of "princess" invalidated Mary's mother's claims to be the King's lawful wife, and robbed Mary herself of her birthright. But there is no mention of Mary's name among the christening company; she was at least spared that indignity.

The child of four days, with the gifts in gold cups and bowls, which her sponsors had presented to her, borne before her, was escorted back to the palace by a crowd of torch-bearers, amidst "flourishes of trumpets."

After all, the most singular and significant attribute of the company at Elizabeth's baptism was the tragic fate of so many persons who figured prominently in the ceremony. One, her godfather, Cranmer, was burned at the stake; four—the Marquis of Dorest, the Earl of Essex, the Duke of Norfolk, and Lord Rocheford, were beheaded; of the ladies, the Marchioness of Dorset had to mourn a husband and a daughter (Lady Jane Grey), who both perished on the scaffold; and the beautiful Lady Mary Howard, then plighted to the young Duke of Richmond, not only lost her husband in the morning of his days, she was forced to give such evidence at the trial of her brother, the Earl of Surrey, as helped to bring about his condemnation.

Princess Mary's "Lady Mistress," Lady Margaret Bryan, a good and kind woman, was transferred from Mary's service to that of Elizabeth, in order to preside over her household; and both princesses—the elder put beneath the younger until Anne Boleyn's downfall and death — dwelt together at Hertford Castle, Havering Bower, &c.

If there is any truth in an earlier episode, in which King Henry, Queen Anne, and their little daughter formed a melancholy group, which impressed itself on the popular imagination, the brief association must have been caused by the Queen's having sent for the child and tried to use her as an innocent charm and sweet instrument to disarm the King's wrath, and turn aside Anne's impending disgrace.

If the scene, said to have been described by interested watchers outside the palace, did occur, it must have been the last time that father, mother, and baby girl were together. Henry was observed standing moodily by a window; Anne Boleyn, leading the three years' old Elizabeth by the hand, was seen to approach him in a supplicating manner; but the King dismissed her with an irritable gesture, and continued to gaze out of the window. This was in May 1536; and a few hours afterwards a startling commentary was made on the incident by a distant report of the Tower guns, which announced that a prisoner of rank had been admitted, from a barge on the Thames, by the Traitor's Gate.

One or two curious and characteristic anecdotes of Elizabeth's early youth have been preserved. The first is the singular state of destitution into which her wardrobe had been allowed to fall after her mother's death. The Lady Mistress wrote to the Minister Cromwell, and made an urgent appeal to him to let her have the commonest necessaries for the King's little daughter. It was not merely "mufflers," mob caps, and kerchiefs that the child stood in want of; she had neither gowns nor petticoats, "nor no manner of linen"—a considerable contrast this to the royal mantle of velvet and miniver worn at her christening. But broad contrasts were the fashion of the day in that reign.

So soon as Elizabeth could put two ideas together, she was taught by Lady Margaret to be "circumspect." As a result, self-restraint alternating with violent impulses was, for the most part, a great feature of her character. There were other results not quite so desirable. To bring up a child to be always on her guard is hardly likely to develop a candid, ingenuous disposition. The early training given with the best intentions had something to do with the fact that "the Lady Elizabeth" was even in her girlhood an adept at concealing her real feelings, and at feigning any sentiments advisable for the occasion.

Without her sister Mary's blunt honesty, Elizabeth had inherited the same passionate, stubborn temper, so that, in spite of her circumspection, she was by no means easily managed either as a child or a girl. While she was still only "getting her teeth," her guardian had to protest against her charge's dining publicly at what was called "the board of estate," where the child saw "divers meats, fruits, and wine," which were not fit for her tender years; while it is clear that her small Grace had already a will of her own, which rendered it difficult for her governess to contradict her, especially in company. She was a beautiful child, the rosy cheeks and red-golden hair of the young Tudors being, in her case, united to fine aquiline features, which were still softened by the roundness of childhood. It goes without saying that she was full of subdued life, spirit, and wit from the first. Her earliest state appearance was at the age of four years, when, through the goodwill of gentle Queen Jane Seymour, not only the girl Mary, but the child Elizabeth, held a promient place at Edward's baptism. When Elizabeth was not with her sister, she was with her baby brother, and a remarkable attachment sprang up between them.

As a pretty illustration of their regard, the Princess of six presented the Prince of two on his birthday with a cambric shirt which she had made for him with her own hands.

The extraordinary energy and love of study which

beth exhibited throughout her life were shared by her years' younger brother. We are told that nothing could exceed the zeal and delight with which the wonderful pair of youthful scholars were accustomed to get up by dawn of day, in order to repair, of their own free will, to their religious exercises and lessons in languages and science. But it was not only her tutors whom Elizabeth fascinated; no one could come near her without being struck by her "charming manners." She received a messenger from her father with as much composure and "as great gravity as if she had been forty years old." The elder sister, whom the birth of the younger had dispossessed of her rights, tried magnanimously to say a word for her to their alienated father. Three stepmothers in succession, women as unlike as one can well imagine, all combined to make much of the lovely, lively little girl, with the curious amount of tact for her years, who, notwithstanding that tact, was as wilful as she was lively. Dull Anne of Cleves craved the bright child's company. Unhappy Catherine Howard called her "cousin," and assigned her the seat of honour next herself at court banquets. Motherly Catherine Parr never lost pride in the juvenile student's attainments.

Yet, by the time she was ten, Elizabeth gave her father sufficient offence, by some act of insubordination, for him to punish her by banishing her from court for a year; and it was only on the intercession of her stepmother, Catherine Parr, that the culprit was restored to favour. During her banishment, Elizabeth translated *Le Miroir de l'ami Pécheresse* from French into English, and in the end of 1544 presented the production to Catherine, to whom it was dedicated. Elizabeth also wrote to Queen Catherine a letter, still preserved, in which the writer begs the Queen to speak, or rather to write, to King Henry on her behalf. Surely the letter is couched in the very "tallest" language which a girl of eleven ever employed. It begins:

"Inimical fortune, envious of all good, and ever-revolving human affairs, has deprived me for a whole year of your most illustrious presence." The fact that the letter was written in Italian may have something to do with its grandiloquence. It was understood that Elizabeth could already correspond and converse with facility in French, Italian, Spanish, and Flemish. It is certain that she was very soon a good classical scholar, and well versed in history. She was also a very fair musician. In after years " Queen Elizabeth and her virginals " are synonymous, like " Queen Elizabeth, an aquiline nose, a farthingale, and a bushel of pearls."

During her father's lifetime she figured from her birth in schemes of marriages with august bridegrooms. After her mother's ruin the proposed bridegrooms were necessarily less august. It is needless to say that these projects fell to pieces from the beginning.

When King Henry's infirmities were at their climax, Elizabeth was at Hatfield, Hertfordshire, with her brother, sharing the instruction given him. Presently the two were separated, and she was sent to the manor-house at Enfield, and he to the castle at Hertford. The parting was a great grief to the boy especially, and the brother and sister took refuge in a learned and affectionate correspondence. They were again together at Enfield, where Edward was brought that he might be with his sister when the news of his father's death was broken to him. Elizabeth was then between thirteen and fourteen years of age, and Edward was about ten. Their grief was violent enough to touch the spectators, yet, with the old formality and pedantry of the day, in the epistle in which the boy subsequently replies to a letter of condolence which his sister wrote to him after they were again parted, he pauses to remark on her calmness of mind, and to commend "the elegance of her sentences."

By King Henry's will Elizabeth was, like Mary, entitled

to an annuity of three thousand and a marriage portion of ten thousand pounds. A far more dangerous bait to the ambitious and unscrupulous noblemen around her was supplied by the fact that she was named third in the succession to the throne, the two names before hers being those of a sickly boy and a delicate, fast-dying woman.

Speedy as was the wooing of the widowed queen by her former lover, the bold and blustering Thomas Seymour, it was confidently alleged that, four days before he was accepted by the mature Catherine, he made proposals of marriage to the girl Elizabeth. The audacity of such a proceeding can only be realised by the consideration that, though Seymour was the uncle of a king and the brother of a queen, and though his elder brother was about to take to himself the dukedom of Somerset and the protectorate of the realm, and to bestow on the aspirant to a royal bride the high office of Lord Admiral and the title of Lord Seymour or Lord Sudeley, not a Seymour of them all was anything better than the offspring of an obscure country knight. But the subject must be approached with caution, since the gentleman's instantaneous suit to Elizabeth rests chiefly on the manner in which he sounded the young king with regard to his views on Seymour's marriage, and on the garbled, conflicting testimony given later by Elizabeth and by her waiting gentlewoman, Mrs, Kate (or, as Elizabeth's accusers spelt it, " Kat ") Ashley.

Elizabeth, who, when a little older, was notoriously given to believing every man at her feet, said in substance to her gentlewoman, according to that gentlewoman, that, if Seymour had got his will, it would not have been Queen Catherine he would have married; while Mrs. Kate said to Elizabeth, according to Elizabeth, exactly the same thing, with a strong inference in either case. A still greater presumption against the story is, that Queen Catherine was said to have known of the overtures to her daughter-in-law on the part of the man whom the Queen herself consented to marry in the course of the next four days, and that some of Elizabeth's indignation at the unbecoming haste of her stepmother's fourth marriage was occasioned by the circumstance that Catherine was marrying the very man whom she had just advised Elizabeth to reject. The story, in its unpleasantness, does not hold well together, especially in relation to a woman like Catherine Parr.

Whatever the truth or falsehood of Seymour's suit to Elizabeth, she distinctly refused to quit the protection of the Queen, to whose care the Lord Protector Somerset and the Council had confided her; and in the refusal offended Princess Mary, who was deeply aggrieved by the impropriety of Queen Catherine's hasty nuptials, and offered her young sister a shelter with her. Elizabeth not only remained with her stepmother, after her marriage, at Chelsea and Seymour Place, she went with the Queen and the Lord Admiral to Sudeley.

In the household at Sudeley Elizabeth, by her own choice, got Roger Ascham, who had hitherto been her writing-master, for her tutor in Greek and Latin. She had also for her governess the gentlewoman, Catherine, or Kate Ashley, who was a kinswoman of Anne Boleyn's, for whom Anne's daughter conceived a strong and lasting affection. Mrs. Ashley figures among the learned women of the time; but her wisdom was not in proportion to her learning, though she had enough sense of propriety to cause her to remonstrate with the master of the house on his teasing, insolent behaviour, both in his wife's presence and in her absence, towards a royal ward, who was at the same time but a self-confident, giddy girl of fifteen.

With all Elizabeth's genuine love for her studies under the renowned Ascham, and her controversial interest in the religious exercises which prevailed in the house under the great Reformers, who were Queen Catherine's friends and chaplains, the girl was tempted to sigh for something approaching more nearly to the gaiety of youth.

The Admiral resented Kate Ashley's interference, and said, with an oath, that he would not alter his conduct, for he meant no harm, and it is almost certain he did not, in his interpretation of the words; but he lived to suffer for his folly.

The Queen, who had at first encouraged her husband's rough games, grew annoyed at the length to which they had gone. She was vexed at his lack of respect for the Princess. Catherine was also disturbed by Elizabeth's carelessness of what was due at once to high rank and modest girlhood, and sent her away with Mrs. Ashley to Cheston, where a separate establishment was formed for the Princess. A little later she went with her household to Hatfield and Ashridge.

Two letters of this date from Elizabeth to her stepmother are still in existence. In the first, while there is a great display of submission from her humble daughter to "the Queen's highness," there are some signs of injured feelings and rankling resentment. In the second, the two are again on perfectly cordial terms—how cordial may be guessed from the fact that Catherine approved of and desired a correspondence between her husband and Elizabeth.

On the Queen's deathbed, which was near at hand, she is said to have longed for the presence of the most beloved of her stepdaughters. It may be that some dim idea of recommending to Elizabeth's care Catherine's newly born child crossed the mother's disordered brain. It was believed that Catherine had a great opinion of Elizabeth's natural gifts, and entertained a strong conviction that she would yet be queen.

A special messenger sent by the Lord Admiral brought to Elizabeth the melancholy and unexpected tidings of Catherine's death, at the age of thirty-five. No mention is made of the young girl's grief for the loss of one who had been among her truest friends, only that she dismissed with scorn the messenger's statement that his master was a "heavy or sorrowful man;" and on Mrs. Ashley's taking it upon her to suggest that the Princess should write a letter of condolence to the widower, she answered indignantly, "I will not do it, for he needs it not." In all this, and in much that followed, the future Elizabeth stands revealed in her extravagant personal vanity, her boundless craving for admiration, her jealousy of rivalry, and the flashes of levity inherited from her mother, which stood out conspicuously even in those coarse, hard times, and fatally marred the nobler qualities of the woman and queen.

There is no question that although Thomas Seymour, Lord Sudeley, might have been well enough satisfied with the wife of whom he was unworthy while she lived, and although he might have been equally guiltless either of seeking to set her aside, or of practising on her life, she was no sooner in her grave than he sought to make Elizabeth her successor. He began by trying to overawe and cajole the people around her, and to flatter the young Princess herself.

A stir and murmur of gossip were got up indecorously and unfeelingly among the late queen's ladies and gentlemen and Elizabeth's ladies and gentlemen, with regard to the probability of a marriage between Elizabeth and the Lord Admiral, though the Princess was a girl in her early teens, and the gentleman was eighteen years her senior.

The desire to propitiate the great persons concerned, the fear of making an enemy of the young king's favourite uncle, the impression that Elizabeth was not averse to the match, the attraction of a state intrigue, seem to have turned the heads of all concerned. It was afterwards remarked that, though Elizabeth's household numbered as many as a hundred and twenty persons, not one was of sufficient rank either to attempt to control the young lady, or to exercise his or her judgment with no fear of offending the Princess and the Lord Admiral. Mrs. Kate Ashley, who had behaved herself with some spirit and discretion on a former occasion, now lent herself to support Seymour's secret suit; so did Parry, Elizabeth's "cofferer," or treasurer, and the two gossiped together in the most unwarrantable and unbecoming fashion over their mistress's concerns.

Kate Ashley and Thomas Parry in particular of Elizabeth's servants talked to her constantly of Seymour, introducing praises of his merits, and suggesting the advisability of the marriage, if the Duke of Somerset and the Council would give their consent. These untrustworthy and imprudent persons assailed the girl in her unguarded moments to ascertain what were her views and intentions. Happily for herself and them, Elizabeth, while she showed little feeling or delicacy in allowing the conversations, had not been taught caution from her infancy in vain; she declined to give any direct answer to their hints. Indeed, she seems to have taken a peculiar pleasure, from her very girlhood, in eluding and baffling any attempt to extract her real opinion on matters concerning herself nearly. Sometimes her haughty temper and her self-respect resented the unjustifiable liberty taken with her by her servants, when they sought to intrude into her confidence. She turned on a bedchamber-woman named Mountjoy, who was harping on the all-absorbing theme, and told her that she—the Princess—would have Mountjoy turned out of her presence if she did not desist. Elizabeth was so indignant at Seymour's presuming to offer her advice, through a servant, on the exchange of a house and land which formed part of her dowry, that she at first protested her incredulity with regard to his having been guilty of such presumption, and then declared passionately in reference to the advice he had given, "I will not do so, and so tell him."

Nevertheless, Elizabeth's attitude towards this daring adventurer was full of the coquetry which distinguished her manner to her favourite courtiers in future years. She encouraged his advances, if it were only to play with them, received him when he visited her in the sumptuous mourning which he wore for his wife and her stepmother, exchanged letters and messages with him, through Kate Ashley and Parry, and accepted the offer of a loan of his town-house—Seymour Place—when she should go to London to visit the young king. Elizabeth even had private interviews with the Lord Admiral through the same instrumentality, and appears to have been in his company when she and Mrs. Ashley were rowed one evening in a barge on the Thames. For this flagrant piece of indecorum Mrs. Kate was roundly rated by the ambitious wooer's sister-in-law, the Duchess of Somerset (Mary Tudor's "Gossip Nan"), who told the weak or designing governess, with much reason, that she was not fit to have the care of a king's daughter.

The excuses for Elizabeth in conduct which was not only undutiful, undignified, and unwise, but was singularly heartless when it had to do with the memory of poor Catherine Parr, were, that the girl was very young and wrong-headed, in spite of her superior mental powers. She had inherited her mother's tendency to flightiness and her hunger for men's praise; moreover, the Princess was surrounded by the worst of guides and advisers in a circle of foolish, intriguing, unprincipled candidates for place and power, in which Thomas Seymour was the most conspicuous figure.

Detection and punishment followed speedily. The Protector and the Council were warned of the plot for the disposal of Elizabeth's hand in marriage, and were highly incensed by the news. The Duke of Somerset, a more

honourable and humane man than could be easily found
among his contemporaries, tried at first, even while he was
well aware of his brother's disloyalty to himself, to defeat
the conspiracy without open scandal and violence.   He
arranged to send his brother, the Lord Admiral, much
against his will, on a mission to Boulogne, at the very
time when Elizabeth would be in London for the purpose
of visiting Edward.   After this mild measure was in-
effectual, the Protector saw himself compelled to take
an extreme course.

In the meantime Seymour was making a clumsy effort to
shelter himself behind the assertion that he "had thoughts
of the Lady Jane" for his next partner in life.   He had in
reality persuaded simple, stupid Thomas Grey, formerly
Marquis of Dorset, and now Duke of Suffolk (in the room
of his father-in-law, Charles Brandon), to entrust Seymour
and his mother with the other young girl who had been
reared in the household of Catherine Parr, and had walked
as chief mourner at her funeral.   But in all probability it
was to retain a hold on his nephew, King Edward, by
assuming the guardianship of his destined bride, and not
to keep Lady Jane as a second string to his own bow, and
a last resource for himself should the alliance with Elizabeth fail, that Seymour coveted and secured the keeping
of Lady Jane.   His ostentatious manœuvres, which were
constantly contradicted by his idle boasts, were of no
avail.

The Lord of Sudeley was thrown into the Tower in the
spring of 1549 on a charge of high treason, for having
conspired against his brother and the Council, compassed
the death of Queen Catherine, and aspired to the hand of
the Princess Elizabeth.   Mrs. Kate Ashley and her crony,
Parry, were arrested simultaneously, and subjected to a
severe examination, while Elizabeth was detained prisoner,
pending the inquiries at her house of Hatfield.

Sir Robert Tyrwhitt, the husband of Lady Tyrwhitt,

not only a bedchamber-woman and an intimate friend, but also a stepdaughter of the late queen's, who had waited on her deathbed, was sent by the Council to take order at Hatfield.

Sir Robert told Elizabeth that Kate Ashley and Parry, as well as the Lord Admiral, were, as a sequel to their examination, committed to the Tower. The information must have been a terrible shock to the Princess, since, in addition to her strong and constant attachment to her erring servants, she must have been sensible that her own fate hung in the balance. She had been guilty of sufficient insubordination and defiance of the Council to draw down upon her severe reprisals.

In spite of Elizabeth's customary self-control she cried bitterly, and was still more overwhelmed when Sir Robert told her, farther, that her servants had borne testimony against her in repeating the outrageous liberties which Seymour had taken with the Princess, in Queen Catherine's lifetime, together with her complacent reception of his advances after the Queen's death. Her maidenly modesty was never her strong point; but what she had of the quality to which she laid great claim in after years, along with her pride, received a sharp wound. Parry had been terror-stricken, and she called him "a wretch" for his arrant cowardice, and for his treachery in first having wormed out of Kate Ashley the coarse gossip, and then for being the person to retail it to the Council, thus doing Elizabeth's reputation a cruel, unmanly wrong.

But the girl's heart soon softened to her over-indulgent governess, her slain mother's kinswoman, while her quick wits were not long in recognising that her servants had said nothing which could seriously compromise either her or themselves—had given no hint of the existence of such a marriage contract as the Lord Protector and the Council dreaded to discover had passed between Elizabeth and the Admiral. In the absence of any convincing proof of this—the most common and the most fertile in misery of all the astounding follies of the day—it was Sir Robert's object, either by coaxing or threatening, to induce the Princess to make some direct statement which could be used against the wrong-doers.

But Elizabeth was not merely innocent of any heinous offence, she was in her element after she had recovered from the first effects of the blow, outwitting Sir Robert, and defending both herself and her servants who had displayed no very high standard of courage and truth. But their mistress was not going to escape blame on her own account by giving them up, knowing as she did that her youth and rank would be taken into consideration, while the subordinates would pay the full penalty of the misdemeanour. The magnanimity in her strong nature, which walked hand in hand with its selfishness, came already to the front. She wrote pressing letters "to my good lord the Lord Protector," not only stoutly asserting her own innocence, but warmly maintaining that of her servants. She turned the tables on the bewildered Sir Robert, who was striving with all his craft to beguile her into an admission of the faithlessness of Mrs. Ashley and Parry to their trust, if into nothing more. The Princess professed to be much in earnest, and very frank and sincere in seeking to call to mind everything that had happened : she would give the gist of all the conversations which had passed between her and her servants on the subject. But, in reality, she took up Sir Robert's time and attention with the repetition of a string of the merest trifles in speech and action, in confirmation of her unswerving declaration that Mrs. Kate and the cofferer had not committed any malpractices where their betters were in question.

One of Elizabeth's last biographers (Weissener) exclaims at the courage and astuteness of the girl in her teens, which could thus match and circumvent the wiles of the experienced statesman. He had the Protector and the Council at his back: she had only the silly waiting gentlewoman, who was at that moment separated from her and lodged in the Tower, to pay for her part in the transgression.

But Elizabeth's triumph was by no means unalloyed; she had to consent to have both Kate Ashley and Thomas Parry removed from her service; she had to submit to having Lady Tyrwhitt put at the head of the establishment at Hatfield—arrangements which called forth much angry opposition from Elizabeth. Neither as girl nor woman could she easily brook that her will should be thwarted, and that any control to which she was not well inclined should be exercised over her. She said that Mrs. Ashley was her "mistress," and she had not so behaved herself that the Council should need to put more mistresses over her, and that it would give a bad opinion of her behaviour to make her have another "governor."

When her protest served her nothing, either with Sir Robert or his wife, Elizabeth "wept all that night and lowered (frowned) all next day."

Poor Lady Tyrwhitt, if she did not possess sufficient experience in sickness to prevent her attaching much weight to the delirious utterances of Catherine Parr, was yet a devout and decorous gentlewoman, who had felt so little inclination for the trying office imposed upon her, that she had endured a rebuke from the Council for not undertaking it sooner. She and Elizabeth were by no means strangers to each other. They—and for that matter the culprit, Kate Ashley—were old acquaintances, who had been members of the same household in "Queen Catherine's" days. Elizabeth does not appear to have had any personal objection to Lady Tyrwhitt, with whom she had one taste in common. Sir Robert's wife and Lord Borough's daughter was one of the learned ladies who had gathered round Queen Catherine. In Lady Tyrwhitt's case learning had not altogether taken the place of common-sense and discretion. The love of study was a passion with Elizabeth from youth to age, and she was also quite capable of putting a proper value on prudence and honesty. It is not improbable that she had more respect for Lady Tyrwhitt than for the beloved, foolish Mrs. Kate, of whom her mistress never lost sight, for she was Elizabeth's servant, and that was enough.

The yoke against which the Princess rebelled petulantly did not sit very heavily on her. We soon hear, from Sir Robert's version of his wife's report, of the vehemence with which Elizabeth always defended Mrs. Ashley, and how, after a little interval of reserve, she could not hear the Lord Admiral " discommended " without being ready to make answer for him.

Any partisanship on Elizabeth's part, where the chief offender was concerned, was worse than useless. Seymour was executed on the 20th of March, 1549, according to one account, with letters containing desperate appeals to Mary and Elizabeth hidden in one of his velvet slippers. His death was taken quietly enough by those most interested in it. The deed was by the ordinance of the brother whose forbearance he had outraged, who was soon to follow him on the path to the scaffold. The Lord Admiral was said to be the favourite uncle of his royal nephew, whom he had flattered and courted. One of Seymour's bold plots was to get the young king on his side, and supersede the Duke of Somerset in the Protectorate. Yet the brief entry in Edward's austerely philosophic journal was, that on such a day Lord Seymour of Sudeley was beheaded, without a single word of regret or lamentation. The slain man had undoubtedly made an impression on Elizabeth's lively fancy. Like her father before her, she was very susceptible to personal beauty, and the Lord Admiral was still reckoned the handsomest man in the English court. He is described as " brilliant, magnificent, and audacious," in the middle of his bragging folly, and "so versed in allurements" as to be suspected of magic. He was not more than thirty-three years of age, having been two years younger than his wife. He was the first man who had worked on the huge amount of vanity which, at this date, overbalanced Elizabeth's keen shrewdness and cool, calm foresight.

Common humanity, the familiarity of use and wont, with any atom of affectionate remembrance for kindly, forbearing Catherine Parr, who had loved this man to the last, ought to have rendered the announcement of his violent death in the prime of manhood, on a charge which implicated her in his fate, a tremendous disaster to the girl of sixteen. But when the blow was dealt to her, in the presence of those who watched her every word and look, her self-command was perfect. " This day died a man with much wit and very little judgment," was her sole, half-disdainful observation.

"Impassable, impenetrable!" is Weissener's exclamation at the strange scene, half in horror, as at a prodigy, half in admiration as at a marvel.

But Elizabeth's acting in its flawlessness cost her something. Her generally vigorous health gave way under the frightful strain. She was sufficiently ill to excite the compassion of the Duke of Somerset, while some remorse for the cause might mingle with the compassion. (In a letter written by Elizabeth at a crisis of her life, years after the Duke's death and that of the Lord Admiral, she refers to the Lord Protector's having once told her, that if he had consented to grant his brother a personal interview, instead of listening to third persons, the fate of Thomas Seymour might have been averted.) The Duke's influence was at this time paramount with the Council, and enabled him to proclaim an amnesty in relation to Elizabeth. He sent back Kate Ashley and Thomas Parry to wait on the sick and suffering girl, and help to console her, by their

attendance and sympathy, for the indignities and trials
which she had been compelled to endure.

But Elizabeth's error was not entirely cancelled. In
spite of her entreaties, she was not permitted to appear at
court and visit her brother for more than a year. Apart
from Elizabeth's delinquency, Edward's tutors allowed him
to receive but few visits from his sisters, though he was
fond of both, and for a long time treated Mary as if she
were his mother. The tutors said that his sisters' visits
left the boy depressed and moody.

It is Weissener's opinion that a change now took place
in Elizabeth's character, and that her letters have, from
this date, the half manly, commanding, impetuous tone
which afterwards distinguished them; while the circumspection to which she had been trained from infancy did
not again forsake her to the same extent. She could hold
herself in check, and give play to her love of justice in
the abstract—where none of her own prerogatives were
invaded—to her devotion to the interests of the people,
her powerful judgment, penetrating sagacity, and her
occasional grand magnanimity. For many a year she
sought carefully to undo the consequences of the youthful imprudence — for which her servants were more to
blame than she was—which had yet cast a suspicion of
evil upon her. She continued to live in retirement with
Lady Tyrwhitt, giving herself up to study, chiefly of
theology, "the science of religion," which forcibly attracted not only all the more devout, but also all the
more inquiring minds of the generation. She displayed
a Puritanical plainness of dress, and such an indifference
to personal adornment, that for a period of seven years
she hardly so much as looked at, far less wore, any of
the rich jewels which came to her through a bequest of
her father's. It was in reference to this extreme simplicity of attire, and opposition to all forms of self-
indulgence, that her brother fell into the habit of calling

her, in a quaint conceit, his "sweet sister Temperance."

Elizabeth also exhibited a demure prudery of behaviour which, as it was difficult to distinguish it from maidenly modesty and discretion, recommended her especially to the members of the Reformed Churches. Their code on these points was then very strict, and they were fain to look to Elizabeth as, next to Edward, their great hope and stay.

In the March of 1551, when Mary was summoned to London to answer to the Council and to her brother for her practice of the Roman Catholic religion, Miss Strickland has pointed out that Elizabeth was also in London. She entered it on horseback in semi-state, with a distinguished following, the day before her sister's arrival; and the day after, as if by design, she came from St. James's Park (the way being strewn with sand for her and her cavalcade), while her reception at the court gate was marked by much respectful ceremony. Elizabeth was in her eighteenth year—a tall, fair, handsome girl, such as people loved to look upon.

It is uncertain, though it is very likely, that the sisters met on the visit which each paid to London. There was nothing of declared enmity between them then; but their relations, always difficult, and to be dealt with warily, were rendered still more complicated and hazardous by the manner in which the woman and the girl became mere puppets in the hands of the Spanish and French ambassadors, Renaud and Noailles. These gentlemen played off the one sister against the other, not for the princesses' honour and happiness, but for the benefit of the foreign countries whose representatives thus adroitly and unscrupulously employed every weapon on their sovereigns' behalf.

The downfall of the Duke of Somerset did not materially affect Elizabeth's position, unless by making way for the sway of the far more grasping and unprincipled Dudley, Duke of Northumberland. She refused Somerset's petition that she should intercede for him with her brother, on the plea that she had as little means of access to Edward as the imprisoned duke himself had. No doubt the excuse was true in the main, while it also reminded Somerset of the selfish precautions by which he had separated the young king from his sisters. But Elizabeth's action is also an example of the cool neutrality and inactivity which she adopted thenceforth, as her policy in all state affairs, till her time came.

It is said that as Edward lay dying in July, 1553, Northumberland made use of the same ruse to get Elizabeth into his power, which caused Mary to set out on the journey to Greenwich, under the belief that she was obeying the summons of her dying brother. If this was so, the younger sister, warned by her future great minister, Cecil, already her friend, stayed on quietly at Hatfield. If another statement is true, that Northumberland sought to bribe her by the offer of a large sum of money to acquiesce in Edward's settlement of the crown on his cousin, Lady Jane, thus disinheriting both his sisters, the plotter was foiled by the girl of nineteen, who gave him, and the commission in whose name he spoke, a warily temporising and eminently judicious reply, to the effect that they must first make their agreement with her elder sister, in whose lifetime she had no claim or title to reign.

There is no hint of grief for the death of her young brother and early playfellow on Elizabeth's part, unless it is to be found in the attack of illness from which she was reported to have suffered at this time. Many people thought it a mere feint to prevent Northumberland's seizing her person; but in fairness it is necessary to recall that, while Elizabeth was the reverse of Mary in having all the advantages included in the possession of a fine physique, and the enjoyment of excellent health, the proud imperturbability with which she had heard the news of the Lord Admiral's execution was followed by a similar fit of sickness. Poor young Edward's untimely death, together with the contents of his will, could not fail to produce in the girl a strife of conflicting feelings—lingering memories of childish fondness and kindred affection warring with indignant resentment at the manner in which he had abandoned her cause, no less than her sister's—an injury which Elizabeth was the last person in the world to forgive and forget. Elizabeth recovered in time to repair to her mansion of Somerset House the day before Mary's entrance into London as Queen. The Princess, with her train, went out as far as Wanstead to meet Mary, receive her gracious greeting, and ride, side by side with her, through Aldgate.

In this triumphal progress, when Elizabeth, it is not difficult to conceive, rather flaunted her youthful stateliness and beauty in contrast to Mary's small size and sickly, *passée* looks, even under the passing transformation wrought upon the Queen by a great spirit in the hour of its satisfaction, Michele, the Venetian ambassador, the most impartial of the contemporary witnesses of the spectacle, took notice of the manner in which Elizabeth showed off, among the other items of her charms, her beautiful hands.

In the contention which soon arose between the sisters on religious questions, Elizabeth was at once ready with her diplomacy, her professions of only following the faith which she had been taught, together with her willingness to receive fresh instruction, and her anxiety to express a modified conformity to the Queen's religion. Mary, in her honesty, was prepared to accept these concessions for more than they were worth, to take into consideration the age of her sister, and as a mark of satisfaction and trust, to bestow on her the gift of a jewelled rosary.

In all this it is advisable to keep in mind two things—
first, the extreme difficulty and even danger of Elizabeth's
position in the circumstances; and second, the fact of
her youth. Granted that what she said of herself afterwards was true even then, she had "a man's heart in a
woman's breast." It is also true that "she had a woman's
subtlety," the instinctive radical subtlety of some women
—of her cousin Mary Queen of Scots, for example, and
not the simplicity of other women—of her sister Mary or
her cousin Lady Jane. In conjunction with this duplicity, Elizabeth could lay claim to the reflective power of
a man. Elizabeth had no sympathy with Mary's bigotry;
on the contrary, she had an abhorrence of it. Mary, with
all her conscientiousness and uprightness, had it in her
from the first to be a female Robespierre; Elizabeth was
an Erasmus in creed, and would never have sacrificed a
hecatomb of victims to a system, a conviction. This is
not to say that she did not strive, like her father, to
bring about a certain uniformity of worship, as at once
a mark of homage to herself and a boon to the kingdom;
while her bye-laws with regard to nonconformists and
recusants were sufficiently severe in fines and imprison-
ments, stopping short, however, unless in rare instances,
of the sacrifice of life. She saw that her own claim to
the throne must stand or fall with the Reformed religion,
and she never lost sight of her interest. But it is also
true that her enlightened, cultured intellect, accepted and
approved, by preference, of the doctrines in which she
had been brought up; save only where they threatened
her royal prerogative, her right of private judgment, her
strong personal prepossessions. She would no more be
subservient to Geneva than she would be to Rome.

But even when Elizabeth was tempted to equivocate
and prevaricate in response to one side of her complex
nature, there is no real reason to doubt the sincerity
either of her Protestantism or her Christianity according

to her light. Possibly her religion—such as it was—
saved her from many a snare and stumbling-block in her
difficult path, though it was not of a nature to deliver her
from her weaknesses and blindnesses; and unmistakably
it was her refuge and support in days of darkness and
terror.

Elizabeth's character has suffered heavily, down to this
time, alike from her political friends and her political
foes, and almost as much from the one as from the other.
By the friends who hailed her as their deliverer, and
gloried in the solid benefits and splendid triumphs of her
reign, she was loaded with unqualified panegyrics, her
very faults twisted into virtues. She was "good Queen
Bess," the people's queen. By the more bitter Roman
Catholics, and her foreign enemies generally, she was
beset with unmitigated abuse, and stigmatised as a bold
hypocrite, a treacherous deceiver, a wanton and cruel
tyrant, whose sole merit was to be found in her commanding intellect and the penetration which enabled her
to select and bend to her purpose the greatest minds of
her country and era. It is hardly needful to explain that
the truth lay a long way between these two extremes.

The profound dissembler whenever dissimulation suited
the end she had in view; the dallier with suitor after
suitor; the coquettish and imperious mistress of Leicester
and Essex; the pitiless kinswoman of Lady Catherine
Grey; the gaoler and slayer, however reluctantly, of the
royal cousin who had fled to the Queen of England for
protection from her rebel subjects; the adept at deceit
who contrived to throw the odium of the death warrant
on the secretary Davison; the aged woman who refused
to own her years and infirmities, and declined to the last
moment to appoint a successor, lest she should live to
know herself forsaken, as she had known the dying,
broken-hearted Mary deserted for the Princess whom she
had fondled as a child, who was still in the hey-day of

life and strength and coming triumph—was no saintly
spirit—scarcely even a heroic figure in the highest sense
of heroism.

Again, the woman whom Burleigh served so faithfully;
before whom Sydney and Raleigh were content to bow
low; whose praises Spenser and Shakespeare sang with
enthusiasm; for whom Drake and Hawkins, Howard and
Greville fought; the mistress whose smile irradiated her
household "like sunshine;" the Queen who showed a
mailed breast and spoke with a patriot's tongue at Tilbury; whose humblest subjects called down blessings on
her head—was no mere false pretender.

In the precariousness of her footing after Mary's accession Elizabeth had no lack of suitors. It seemed one of
the offices of the manœuvring foreign ambassadors, as
well as of the Council, to suggest, now handsome, frivolous, vicious Edward Courtenay because of his Plantagenet
descent; now this prince, now that; Philibbert of Savoy,
whose proposals were destined to be repeatedly laid before
her; the heir of the King of Sweden; even strangest
suggestion of all, and likely to be extremely repugnant
to Mary, her own destined bridegroom, Philip of Spain,
her cousin, the Emperor's son. No doubt the last was
a mere subterfuge. Elizabeth would have none of them.
Her highest ambition was to be Queen of England; she
would not imperil her chance of succession by marrying
a foreign prince; neither was she disposed to share her
power with a subject, though her vanity and the strain
of lightmindedness, which was at this time kept in abey-
ance, might tempt her to trifle with a Leicester or an
Essex.

All the princely suitors, with the exception of Philibbert
of Savoy, fell into the background on the passing of the
Act of Parliament, which Mary obtained, asserting the
legitimacy of her rights, but failing to establish those
of Elizabeth. Mary's conduct immediately afterwards,

in giving her cousins, Frances Brandon and Margaret Douglas, court precedence before her sister, emphasised the omission, and so affronted the Princess, whose claims were thus seriously impaired, that she made a pertinacious request, at last granted, to be allowed, on the plea of her health, to withdraw from court, and reside at one of her country seats.

When Mary's marriage was announced and Wyatt's rebellion broke out, Elizabeth was at her manor house of Ashridge, in Buckinghamshire. Mary, doubtful, not without reason, of her sister's loyalty, despatched messengers, under the leadership of Elizabeth's grand-uncle, Lord William Howard, to bring her to court.

Elizabeth was ill at this crisis, as she had been on similar epochs in her life; and if mental anxiety had before broken her down, there was sufficient cause for the disaster now, for, innocent or guilty of conspiring against Mary, she stood then in deadly peril. Elizabeth's name and Courtenay's had been the rallying cries of the insurrection. She had managed, with her unsurpassable tact, not to commit herself—at least, to suppress every proof of her participation in the rising; but the presumption of her connivance was, and is to this day, so great that her innocence in any real sense is almost inconceivable.

Travelling by slow stages on account of her recent illness to obey her sister's summons, Elizabeth entered London in an open litter on the 23rd of February, 1554. As a sign of her innocence, she was dressed, in spite of the inclemency of the season, in white, like a "Fair Maid of February." But there the resemblance ceased. There was nothing of the pensive, meek grace of the first flower of the year about Elizabeth, whether well or ill, in prosperity or adversity. She had left such attributes to her little cousin, Lady Jane. Elizabeth's countenance "was pale and stern; her mien proud, lofty, and disdainful, by

which she endeavoured to conceal her trouble." Such
was the testimony of the ambassador Renaud, in a letter
to his master. A large company of the gentlemen of
Elizabeth's household and of the party of her friends, as
well as the guard sent by Mary, surrounded the Princess;
but they were as nothing to the great crowds gathered on
either side of the road to gaze upon her, many of the
spectators openly bewailing her destination. That morning the Duke of Suffolk, the husband of Elizabeth's
cousin, Frances Brandon, had perished on the scaffold;
not a fortnight before his daughter, Lady Jane, and her
husband, Lord Guildford Dudley, had been beheaded.
People thought that the terrible tragedies of Henry
VIII.'s reign were about to be even more fully repeated.
Some of the gazers could look back seventeen years, and
remember the spectacle of Elizabeth's mother, Anne
Boleyn, with her strange impassioned beauty, like that
of a lurid sunset, as she stood ready for the axe on Tower
Green. After all, no thought could be more piteous than
the simple consideration patent to everybody present,
that here was a beautiful, high-spirited girl of twenty—
princess or no princess, scornful or submissive, of one or
two things there could be no mistake—she was fatherless and motherless; there was none able and willing to
defend her, and she was advancing to meet her doom at
the hands of her nearest of kin—her own sister. Verily
the lion's cubs were preparing to rend each other.

Elizabeth was taken to Whitehall about four o'clock,
in the gathering blackness and darkness of the winter
afternoon. Her request to see the Queen was peremp-
torily refused. She was lodged, with a suite of six ladies,
two gentlemen, and four servants, in a well-guarded quarter
of the palace, and detained there in miserable uncertainty
as to her fate for three weeks.

When the divided parties in the Council at last agreed
to send Elizabeth to the Tower, and a deputation waited

upon her to acquaint her with their decision, she besought them "with something like a threat"—for she made them remember who she was—to alter it. Finding her petition rejected, half of her suite removed, a guard placed in the anteroom, the hall, and the garden beneath her windows —ominous tokens of what was in store for her—she spent the night in prayer. On the following morning—that of Palm Sunday—when two Lords of the Council arrived to tell her a barge was in waiting to convey her to the Tower while the tide served, she made a last desperate appeal to the Earl of Sussex, one of the two members of the Council, to take a letter from her to the Queen. His compassionate consent to do Elizabeth's errand brought down upon him Mary's hot displeasure; but it procured a brief delay in the execution of the sentence.

Here is the letter, beginning sententiously, "If any ever did try this old saying, that 'a king's word was more than another man's oath,' I most humbly beseech your Majesty to verify it to me, and to remember your last promise and my last demand—that I be not condemned without answer and due proof, which, it seems, that I am; for without cause proved, I am, by your Council, from you, commanded to go to the Tower, a place more wanted for a false traitor than for a true subject; which, though I know I desire it not, yet in the face of all this realm it appears proved. I pray to God that I may die the shamefullest death that any ever died, if I may mean any such thing." The Princess goes on in the same impetuous, forcible manner, to protest that she never "practised, counselled, nor consented to anything that might be prejudicial to the Queen's person or dangerous to the State." She therefore begs to be suffered to answer "afore" Mary's self, instead of being referred to the Council, and that "afore" Elizabeth went to the Tower. She tells what she has read, and within her own experience known (mentioning the case of the Lord

Admiral and his brother) of the loss to an accused person "for want of coming to the presence of their prince," or ruler, for the time, and prays God "that one sister might not be persuaded against another;" and all because of "false report." She ends by signing herself: "Your Highness's most faithful subject, that hath been from the beginning, and will be to my end, Elizabeth." Then follows one more piteous entreaty for "but only one word in answer from yourself."

Something has been already said of the beautiful handwriting of this letter, in which there is not a sign of agitation or tremor. Weissener gives additional details, describes "the elegant and measured flourish" which accompanies the signature, and instances the curious fact, that on a portion of paper uncovered by writing at the end of the letter, to which a forged addition might thus have been added, Elizabeth had taken the precaution of drawing a number of fine strokes (with scarcely a shake in them), and so filling up the blank as to render it impossible to write upon it. Weissener dwells on the singular alertness and prudence which could at such a moment foresee every contingency, and guard against it.

Mary was either too incensed or too doubtful of her own firmness to grant the prayer. She refused with vehemence either to see or write to her sister. Elizabeth was rowed to the Tower so early, that all London was still safely bestowed in the churches decked with palms —emblems of victory and rest; but so late where the tide was concerned, that difficulty and danger had to be met in passing London Bridge, where the barge hung in the tidal wave long enough to startle and alarm the occupants of the bridge houses for the safety of the passengers it carried through. None save her escort was acquainted with the identity of the Princess.

At the Traitor's Gate, which was opened to admit prisoners arriving by the Thames, Anne Boleyn's daughter

was sufficiently overcome to draw back for a moment—
still more from the cruel memories of the past than from
the frowning walls above her. She refused to land, in
a resistance which was practically useless. She said
pettishly, first, that it was the name of the gate which
she could not endure, and next, that she did not wish
to wet her shoes. Not only was the river water lapping
the stones beneath her, the grey clouds overhead, obscur-
ing the sky on the wild March morning, were dissolving
in rain. A member of her escort offered her his cloak,
but "she dashed it from her with a good dash," and set
her foot on a step, saying, "Here lands as true a subject,
being prisoner, as ever landed at these stairs. Before
Thee, O God, I speak it, having no other friend but
Thee above." One of the company in the barge was
guilty of the disrespect and want of feeling of replying
to the forlorn protest with the cool taunt, spoken only
half aside, "If it were so, it were the better for her."

Again Elizabeth stopped short. These grim towers,
with their bloody annals, were too much even for the
high spirit of one who was yet throughout her life a
consistent hater of bloodshed. She sat down on a wet
stone by the water's edge.

It is Weissener's impression that, valiant as the Princess
was, and great as were her powers of self-command, she
was not so wholly dauntless as Mary showed herself, and
that Elizabeth was subject in seasons of difficulty to fits
of hesitation and apprehension, which were perplexing
and discomfiting to her followers. But this may be only
to say, by anticipation, what the biographer himself remarks the next moment, that Elizabeth's judgment far
exceeded that of Mary. The younger sister was qualified to foresee objections and consequences which were
not apparent to the elder, and so could not, for a second,
quell and disarm her.

The Lieutenant of the Tower, Brydges, entreated the

Princess to take shelter, and said the place where she sat was unwholesome; to which Elizabeth answered, with quite as much temper as despair, "Better sit here than in a worse place, for God knoweth, not I, whither you will bring me."

But when her gentleman-usher burst into tears, the girl of twenty was impatient of his weakness, pulled herself together, and chid him roundly for taking away her courage instead of doing his best to maintain it. She seemed to recognise the vain, and therefore undignified, nature of the altercation, and resolutely passed within the gloomy portal. When the rattle of the bolts and bars around her ceased, she stood firm, with her book in her hand, in the centre of her handful of attendants, and prayed to God to give her His grace to build not on the sand, but on the rock.

Elizabeth was always ready with her public prayers— rhetorical, figurative, and, as a rule, highly denunciatory —calling down freely curses, instead of blessings, on her enemies. We may be permitted to question the Christian spirit of these petitions, and even the perfect candour and single-mindedness of the petitioner; but it is not necessary to doubt her sincerity within certain bounds, and in the light in which she viewed all that happened to herself. Totally unlike her sister Mary in this, as in so many respects, Elizabeth was even in girlhood radically untruthful, capable of profound and prolonged dissimulation; but it was, to begin with, at least, the untruthfulness of casuistry, and a double nature which deceived itself, rather than that of a girl or woman who set herself knowingly and deliberately to tell lies. Elizabeth's specious metaphysical intellect and far-reaching ambition blinded her to simple honesty and integrity, so that she could call on the righteous God to help her in double dealing without any conscious sense of hypocrisy. It is a somewhat awful thought, but it is desirable to bear it in mind in considering the mightiness and meanness of the great Queen's character; its two sides, the one splendid in courage, wisdom, and justice; the other sordid in selfishness, light-mindedness, and a furious temper, and, above all, in endless treacherous craft.

For the first month of her imprisonment, Elizabeth "never set foot outside her room," was compelled to hear Mass, and was systematically persecuted by the Governor Gage. Two of her ladies—Mrs. Sandys and Isabella Lady Harrington, a young bride—were, in the case of the first, removed from attendance on the Princess, and in that of the second, imprisoned along with her husband (who had been committed to the Tower for a previous offence), because of their Protestant faith, and their unconditional refusal to conform to Roman Catholic rites. Elizabeth had little ground to look for redress or mercy; and if what she said long afterwards to the French envoy, Castelnau, was a correct representation of her feelings, "she gave herself up for lost," and she meant to make only one request, that she might be slain by the sword, as had become the custom in France, and not by the axe, and that a swordsman might be sent for from France to despatch her (as a headsman was sent for to behead her mother).

In the course of this month Elizabeth was examined before the Council, headed by her bitter enemy, the Lord Chancellor, Stephen Gardiner. She defended herself with great presence of mind and animation, not only on the general accusations of her complicity with Wyatt, and of her being in alliance with the French, but on such details as her removal from one of her houses (Ashridge) to another (Donnington), as was believed with the purpose of her reaching a spot where her communications with the rebels might be easier.

So great was the fascination of her youth, beauty, and wit, together with the peculiar blending of a frank address and a majestic carriage, which she was said to have inherited from her father, King Henry, that after she had borne unfalteringly the humiliation of being confronted with one of her servants as to the true meaning of her "remove from Ashridge to Donnington," not only did the servant (Sir James Crofts) fall on his knees to confirm her assertion of innocence of evil intention, the Catholic Earl of Arundel, understood to be keenly opposed to her, knelt in his turn, stated his conviction that her Grace was speaking the truth, and expressed his regret for having troubled her about such small matters.

In the meantime the great Emperor was clamouring for her death, as the daughter of Anne Boleyn and the dangerous rival of his cousin Mary ; and the utmost which Elizabeth's friends could do on her behalf was the clumsy device of hiding a girl in the hollow of a wall and setting her to speak unseen, praising Elizabeth and abusing the Mass.   Crowds of Londoners came in a great ferment to listen to "the talking stone."   But the Council had only to send a few masons to pull down a portion of the wall in order to reveal the fraud.

Mary shrank from imbruing her hands in her sister's blood, and cooled and softened a little as the weeks went on.   She began to let fall in conversation the words, "my sister," which had not crossed her lips for some time, and permitted Elizabeth's picture to be replaced on the palace wall, from which it had been removed.

At the Tower, in the lengthening spring days, Elizabeth was allowed more of the liberty for which she had pleaded, on the ground that her health was suffering from the closeness of her confinement.   She was granted a gradual relaxation of the severity with which she had been treated. She could take exercise in the Queen's rooms, on condition that she did not show herself at any of the closed windows, and was attended through the rooms by the Lieutenant of the Tower, the Lord Chamberlain, and three of the Queen's ladies; an imposing cavalcade, the assembling and marshalling of which made the indoor walk a very formal and ceremonious proceeding. Afterwards she was suffered to walk in a little garden, surrounded by a high palisading, with the proviso that nobody was to appear at any of the windows of the Tower which looked into the garden while the Lady Elizabeth was taking her exercise.

Notwithstanding all these precautions, Elizabeth found company in the garden, where some of the warders' children—innocent little birds for such a cage—were accustomed to play. One wonders if they played at beheadings, as other children will play at funerals, and if Elizabeth saw in their games a rehearsal of her own doom, or a revival of the execution of her mother—that mother of whom she never spoke, though she seldom failed to show kindness to any Boleyn or Howard who crossed her path.

Elizabeth, like her sister, was fond of children; indeed, she was fond, in a way, of any helpless dependent on her bounty. She made friends with two of the Tower children. Tradition tells something of these small playmates. One of them was a little girl of three, named "Susannah;" she had heard, from the talk of the grown-up people round her, that the Princess was locked up, and offered her some small keys which had come into the child's possession, telling the lady, in sweet babble, that she might open the gates, and need not stay there any longer.

Another story—and this is authenticated—refers to a boy of four. He brought the prisoner flowers, and received sweetmeats and toys from her in return. So jealously was Elizabeth guarded that even this simple intercourse was noticed, and put a stop to. It was thought that the boy might be made a means of communication between Elizabeth and the other prisoners. Among the most dreaded occupants of these dismal lodgings were two handsome, unscrupulous young noblemen, Edward Courteney, Earl of Devon, deeply embroiled in Wyatt's rebellion, and Lord Robert Dudley, whose father, the Duke of Northumberland, and his brother, Lord Guildford Dudley, had lately been beheaded, along with a more innocent victim, for the attempt to seat Lady Jane Grey on the throne. One of Northumberland's hairbrained, unprincipled projects was said to have included both Elizabeth and Mary, as well as Lady Jane, in its aim. He would, if he had got his will, have wedded all his three sons to women of royal blood, so that one at least could hardly fail to secure the crown of King Consort. Ambrose he would have wedded to Mary, Robert to Elizabeth, and Guildford—the only part of the programme which was fulfilled—to their cousin, Lady Jane. It is a striking commentary on the lack of reverence with which the marriage tie was then viewed, that Northumberland was in no way deterred from his triple scheme by what would in another generation have been a serious obstacle, that of his three sons, two — Lord Ambrose and Lord Robert — were already married.

The near neighbourhood of Courtenay, with his strain of royal blood, his familiarity with the Tower and its officers, and his feather-headed ambition, was a source of grave anxiety to the authorities.

There is not an atom of proof that either Courtenay or Dudley so much as attempted to communicate with Elizabeth—whether in the spirit of the romantic chivalrous notions which were becoming a feature of the period, whether in a temper of more sordid calculation. Such an attempt would have been as much as the bold man's head was worth. But on the mere apprehension of an adventure of this kind, it is on record that the little man who had taken it upon him to present the flowers, and his father the warder, were subjected to a sharp cross-questioning and a severe reprimand, and were sternly forbidden to be guilty of any approach to royalty in future. These hard lines did not hinder the little fellow, as the story goes, from looking through a hole in the enclosure of the garden, and naïvely informing Elizabeth, "Mistress, I can bring you no more flowers now!"

On a morning in May, after Elizabeth had been in the Tower for two months, while Mary was eating her heart out at Westminster and Richmond on account of the non-arrival of her bridegroom, Philip of Spain, Sir Henry Bedingfield—a Norfolk gentleman of honourable antecedents and sober years, who was well known for his strict Roman Catholic principles—arrived with Mary's commission, and a hundred soldiers of her guard, to take Elizabeth from the Tower, and at the same time to detain her in safe keeping. Without direct evidence of her guilt, it was found impossible for any English Court to try and convict Elizabeth of high treason; at the same time she was not to be left at large.

Sir Henry Bedingfield, like Lady Tyrwhitt of earlier days, had no great mind for the perilous undertaking. But his part was to obey his Queen's orders. There had been some uncertainty as to where Elizabeth should be established—at Pontefract or Woodstock. Mary was incapable of feeling the public's pulse as Elizabeth afterwards felt it. The elder sister was singularly obtuse on such points, but she was not totally insensible to the effect which such ghastly associations as those with Pontefract [1] would be likely to have on the people in connection with the disposal of their idol. Thus Woodstock was finally selected as the scene of the Princess's banishment, while almost contemporaneously with her departure, Courtenay was transferred from the Tower to Fotheringay, whose halls were not yet darkened by a royal tragedy.

Elizabeth did not know her destination, and either was, or professed to be, much alarmed by the appearance of Sir Henry and his men-at-arms. She demanded first,

[1] Where Richard II. was imprisoned, and in all probability assassinated.

whether Lady Jane's scaffold had been removed; and
second, what sort of man Sir Henry Bedingfield was—if
he were a man who would commit a secret murder?

On the 19th of May Elizabeth quitted the Tower, and
went in a barge, under the escort of Sir Henry Bedingfield, as far as Richmond. On their way the first sound
of cheer from the world without greeted her. Three
cannon shots were gallantly fired from the office of the
Hanseatic League by the Protestants met there, in honour
of the Princess's deliverance, with which they had become
acquainted. It is likely that she guessed the import of
the salute, and took heart from it. The boom of the
cannon reached the ears of Mary in the palace of Westminster, and filled her with resentment, while the barge
thus hailed passed on without stopping.

At Richmond, where Elizabeth rested for the night, the
most of her servants were withdrawn from her. She took
leave of them with great mournfulness, "for this night I
think I must die," she said, a conclusion for which there
was no reasonable warrant, unless that a French messenger, imprudently sent to get tidings of her by the ambassador Noailles, under the pretence of making her a present
of apples, was seized, searched, and sent adrift. On
setting out next day, in the Queen's litter, for Windsor,
Elizabeth saw some of her dismissed attendants watching
her progress from a little distance, and sent a gentleman
to them to say from her, "like a sheep to the slaughter,
for so am I."

But it was in anything rather than a lamb-like spirit,
or the temper of a victim anticipating speedy death, that
Elizabeth proceeded to pursue her journey, and comfort
herself during her banishment. It was as if she set
herself deliberately to vex and annoy her unfortunate
guardian in a manner that would have better become a
country wench than a mighty princess. On the arrival of
the party at Windsor, she declined to accept the room

assigned to her, and dragged Sir Henry all over the Castle in search of another more to her mind. It is difficult to see why, when she was reassured as to her personal safety, the expedition in the opening summer, along pleasant country roads, through quiet country towns, the population of which streamed forth not merely to gaze upon her, but to do her cordial homage, should not have been a welcome change from her residence in the Tower. Elizabeth loved the face of the country, as she also loved the faces of the people on whom she was wont to bestow her most gracious smiles, receiving praises and blessings in return. King Henry's bluffness was in Elizabeth a winning affability, while her mother's careless suavity and undue familiarity with her attendants had taken the form, when the daughter was in the humour, of a gay, yet dignified, good nature.

She is thus described by a contemporary :—" She was of personage tall, of hair and complexion fair, and therewith well-favoured, but high-nosed ; of limbs and features neat, and which added to the lustre of these exterior graces, of stately and majestic 'comportment,' participating of this more of her father than of her mother, who was of an inferior ' allay ; ' plausible, or, as the French hath it, more *débonnaire* and affable—virtues which might well suit with majesty, and which, descending to the daughter, did render her of a more sweeter temper, and endeared her more to the love and liking of her people."

There was one respect in which Elizabeth resembled her sister rather than her mother—both King Henry's daughters had loud, harsh men's voices.

Elizabeth was treated with all possible respect by Sir Henry Bedingfield; while his coadjutor, Lord Williams of Thame, at whose house she stayed for a night, went the length of inviting a large party of ladies and gentlemen to meet the Princess, and she walked with the rest of the party in the gardens and park, in no sense like a prisoner.

As she journeyed, the countrywomen came with cakes and nosegays, flinging them into the litter, till she had to beg of their good-will not to smother her with their kindness. At Aston, the ringers took it upon them to ring the church bells (for which the ringers were arrested and imprisoned; but of that Elizabeth was ignorant at the time). At Islip, a pageant had been hastily got up, with women singing in parts. It was more like one of those triumphant royal progresses, in which Elizabeth took delight in after years, than the passing along of a prisoner, though the object of all the attention refused to be reconciled to the situation. Woodstock was reached before soldiers' halberds and high castle walls appeared behind the shouting crowd.

Elizabeth was not lodged in the castle, but in a long, low building connected with it, called the Gate House. There she was to occupy a suite of rooms, hung with arras for the occasion. Both she and Sir Henry had reason to complain of the condition of the dwelling assigned to her, for the walls were dilapidated, the roof leaky, and the number and locality of the doors rendered the guarding of them a difficult matter. Another cause of insecurity was that, reduced as the number of Elizabeth's retinue was, accommodation could not be found for the whole of them in the house; some of the servants had to lodge in the town of Woodstock, at an inn named "The Bull," where the old, untrustworthy retainer, Thomas Parry, dismissed for a second time by the Council, had taken up his quarters. With or without Thomas Parry, the servants were very liable to be tampered with at the inn.

There was no diminution of the closeness of the watch kept over Elizabeth, though she was removed to some distance from London, and placed in hands Mary could trust. Sir Henry's orders, which he was too faithful to disobey or evade, were stringent. Sixty soldiers guarded the building by day—forty by night. Elizabeth had the use of four rooms for herself, her ladies, and servants. Into these rooms none could enter save Elizabeth, her attendants, and certain of the Queen's servants; but out of her rooms the Princess could not go, unless she was accompanied either by Sir Henry Bedingfield or Lord Chandos, who unlocked and locked the doors for her, retaining the keys, and escorting her while she was out of doors. She could receive neither messenger nor message, unless in the presence of Sir Henry. Her very linen, in going to and coming from the laundress, had to pass through the hands of the Queen's servants, who searched it before it was delivered. She could walk either morning or afternoon in the garden, but always with the escort referred to.

Nothing could have been more irksome and galling to a young woman of Elizabeth's temper than the restraints imposed upon her. We are ready to pity her; but we also pity Sir Henry Bedingfield, on whom she did not hesitate to vent her wrath and *ennui*. After her arrival she shut herself up in her rooms, and only appeared to take leave of Lord Williams of Thame, and the ninety cavaliers who had ridden with her on the last stage of her journey, and had lain, as best they might, at the lodge in the park for the first night of her stay.

Elizabeth was left, by the command of the Queen and Council, with neither books nor pens and ink. It is easy to understand why pens and ink were prohibited, but the interdiction of books seems to have been accidental. Naturally, she petitioned for books, and, hard as they were to come by in those days, Sir Henry was presently instructed to provide the Princess with "any good and pleasant book," with the single reservation that it was not to be written upon, when she declined for a time to avail herself of the concession. Her favourite lady-in-waiting, Mrs. Sandys, who had been removed from attendance on the Princess in the Tower, was again dismissed for her

Reformed doctrines.   Elizabeth's defiance to this order
was to ask Sir Henry Bedingfield to furnish her with an
English Bible—a request which savoured of rank heresy
to a zealous Roman Catholic, the officer of a fanatical
Roman Catholic Queen.   He offered her a Latin book
instead, with a compliment on her learning; but she
scouted both book and compliment.   Eventually an
English Bible was supplied to her.   The Psalms of David
in Latin, and a copy of Cicero, were brought to her by
the steward's son; but as he also brought three letters for
Elizabeth, the whole were sent back.   In like manner,
Lord Williams' son-in-law desired to make a gift of fresh-
water fish and game for the Princess's table; but stout
Sir Henry could not permit such a piece of courtesy, even
from the near relative of his fellow - official, when the
gentleman was guilty of staying a long time about the
place, talking to Elizabeth's servants.   Certainly the charge
of an unruly Princess is no slight obligation.

In those perfunctory walks which Elizabeth took in the
long summer days with her keeper, sometimes she preserved a morose silence, sometimes she pressed and
" flouted " him the whole time, with arguments against
her incarceration, and urgent pleas for him to interpose
on her behalf, where the Queen and the Council were
concerned—a line of conduct which he really did pursue
as far as he dared, but which, to have conducted in the
summary fashion which she proposed, might have been
fatal to both of them.   When one thinks of all the
resources of a woman's wit, and of Elizabeth's in particular, and of the positively malicious ingenuity which she
displayed in circumventing Sir Henry's ponderous efforts
to keep the peace, while he did his duty, there is a
dry humour (which might have been perceived by the
prisoner) in the situation.

The solemn daily walks in which the formal, harassed
gentleman had to bear his part; the very varying moods

of the brilliant young lady who was his distinguished
companion ; the sore provocation he received, under which,
honourable gentleman as he was, and sister of his mistress
the Queen as she was, he could not always resist complaining of her arrogant bearing to his employées ; the exasperation with which he styled her " the grand lady," and
metaphorically shook himself free of her—all the details
lend themselves to satire.

But though the scenes may have their spice of amusement for us impartial spectators contemplating them at a
distance of upwards of three hundred years, the passages-
at-arms were no joke, or else a very grim joke at the time,
to Sir Henry Bedingfield and Elizabeth.

The manner in which the Princess tried the feelings
and nerves of her guardian to the utmost extent was in
connection with an attack of illness which was brought
upon her either by mental vexation, her limited amount
of exercise, or the insalubrity of the Gate House. She
had swellings in the hands—and we have heard what store
she set on her hands—arms, and face, together with other
uncomfortable symptoms. She availed herself of the circumstance to crave the attendance of one of the court
physicians, whom she would, without doubt, have tried to
use for her own purposes. The Queen and the Council,
suspicious of her double object, either could not or would
not grant her request for some time, but offered to let her
have the services of a learned doctor from Oxford. She
haughtily rejected the proposal, saying " she did not care
to speak to strangers about her health," and remained for
an interval without medical attendance ; both she and
everybody else being well aware that if she sickened further, or came to die without a physician's help while in
Sir Henry Bedingfield's care, it would be the greatest
misfortune which could befall Sir Henry.

When Elizabeth at last gained her ostensible end in
having court physicians sent down to prescribe for her,

she is said not to have been disappointed in securing their good offices for more than her health. She did not fail to declare herself satisfied with the gentlemen's professional efforts. She announced herself relieved by the doctors' resort to the great panacea for physical evils in the sixteenth century—bleeding in the hand and in the foot. So Sir Henry Bedingfield was delivered from a haunting apprehension.

Mary had at last consented to receive a letter from her sister, though the Queen would only reply through Bedingfield. In this reply she refused to pardon her sister. Sir Henry could not venture to show the Princess more than an abstract of the letter, which, as he was no scholar, he had prepared with some labour for her inspection. He offered to give it to her when she spoke to him after he had been hearing Mass in her rooms, a celebration at which she did not decline to be present. With her usual caprice she refused to look at the paper till she had dined. After dinner he read it to her, kneeling as he read. She reiterated her imperious demands that he should appeal to the Council for her, both then and in the next walk the couple took; and when he still objected, she cried out that she was worse treated than the worst prisoners in the Tower and in Newgate, since the first could speak to the Lieutenant of the Tower and he wrote to the Council for them; and the second were allowed to have friends to plead their cause.

Sir Henry was struck by the truth of the statement, while he was ready to be thankful for the rain which made Elizabeth break off with the words: " It waxeth wet, and therefore I will depart to my lodgings," and delivered him from farther importunity. He did his best; he took it upon him to forward a copy of the conversation to the Lords in Council, who in their turn were sufficiently touched to grant her permission to write to them.

Sir Henry believed he was bringing her gratifying news

when he laid the permission before Elizabeth. But she, in the spirit of contradiction which seems to have taken possession of her at this time, received the tidings in a manner calculated to baffle and mortify their bearer. She did nothing in the way of availing herself of the permission which he had procured for her with much risk of misconception and censure. She took a species of revenge upon him by hugging her privations, and adopting no means to relieve them, and by addressing to him such taunts as, "that she knew the Lord Chamberlain would laugh in his beard when he found how far Sir Henry carried his scruples."

Then on Sunday, August 26, 1554, she sent for Sir Henry Bedingfield, for another gentleman in the Queen's service, and for the Queen's principal woman-servant. They were at a loss to know what she could want with them, and knelt down to receive her orders. Whereupon she made a loud protestation that she had done nothing to endanger the Queen and the State, as God was judge, and immediately afterwards received the Host. She had already confessed to a priest. In whatever manner Elizabeth might explain away, in her tortuous mind, her declaration of having done nothing to imperil the Queen and the State, together with this plain act of conformity to the Roman Catholic form of belief, it is sufficient to give an example of how little real sympathy she had with the creed which she was thus ostentatiously professing. She was at that time secretly sending money from her privy purse in aid of the prisoners ready to suffer for the Reformed doctrines, who were in sore straits no farther away from her than Oxford. Besides Bishops Latimer and Ridley, Archbishop Cranmer, her father's trusted adviser, her own godfather, her brother Edward's chief guardian, was lying in desperate need in the common Bocardo prison. It was not mere humanity which actuated Elizabeth's charities, in which she was not stinted, since want of money was not one of her hardships; in fact, she was called upon to pay not only her own expenses and those of her household, but the debts incurred by Sir Henry Bedingfield during her compulsory stay at Woodstock. The fact was that the martyrs for the truth were the teachers whose faith she really held. But the long-believed and fondly-cherished story of her constancy to her creed under persecution is now " completely disproven." The tale was credulously promulgated by Strype, Holinshed, and Foxe, all fain to invest their Protestant Queen with every virtue under the sun. The love of her partisans and subjects carried them away.

So far from making any approach to treading the steep and thorny path of martyrdom which Anne Askew's unswerving feet had traversed, Elizabeth committed more than one deed of apparent apostasy to disarm the Queen's resentment, in which she was more or less successful.

But we are told by Miss Strickland that Mary had her doubts of so complete a submission. She requested that Elizabeth might be questioned as to her views on transubstantiation; when the Princess, a mistress of every style of equivocation, got rid of her embarrassment by repeating the rhyming lines which committed her to nothing—

> " Christ was the Word that spake it ;
> He took the bread and brake it ;
> And what His Word did make it,
> That I believe and take it ! "

How little dependence Sir Henry Bedingfield put upon Elizabeth's sincerity and the permanency of the change in her opinions may be guessed by his waiting three weeks before he reported her act to the Council. The Princess had, however, ingratiated herself in a measure with the Queen, who was incapable of false pretences, so that Mary followed the example of the Council in giving her consent to Elizabeth's appeal to them.

Once more Sir Henry was staggered in his honest gratification at the announcement. Elizabeth received it coldly and indifferently; she did not so much as ask for writing materials till a whole week had passed. In the end, during a walk on a Sunday afternoon, she condescended to request that she might be furnished with the necessary materials, and Sir Henry solemnly entrusted to one of the Queen's women, on the Princess's behalf, an ink-bottle, five pens (of which she took care to return only four) two sheets of good paper, and one of inferior quality, to enclose the other. This was done on condition that Elizabeth should write the letter under the eye of one of the Queen's women. The Princess consented, but put off the letter till another day on the plea of headache. Presently she bathed her temples, changed her mind, and as a climax to her perversity, suddenly declared that she could not demean herself to write with her own hand to the Council, therefore she sent for Sir Henry Bedingfield, and imperiously commanded him to fill the office of her secretary.

In vain he sought to escape from the commission imposed upon him. He had not Elizabeth's adroitness at evasion, and the troubled gentleman could only urge the schoolboy's plea of his bad handwriting, which did not avail him. She constrained her keeper to "write at her dictation, while she kept the rough copy of the letter turned towards her." After he had finished by writing the date, she added a few lines in her own hand, and would not tell him what she had written. She made him seal, close, and address the letter, and entrusted it to him to place in the hands of the Lord Chamberlain. No teasing, mocking schoolgirl could have behaved with more exasperating arrogance and impertinence than did the royal maiden who was woman grown in her twenty-second year.

On another occasion, when she stormed at Sir Henry

as her gaoler, and he defended himself by telling her
that he was but one of the Queen's officers, doing his
duty to his sovereign, as he would, in the same circumstances, have done it to Elizabeth, she cried disdainfully,
"God bless the Queen, and from such officers, good Lord
deliver me!"

It is a relief to find that Elizabeth did not spend the
whole of the seven months which she passed at Woodstock in "systematically harassing" her unlucky guardian
and victim. She practised, when she was in the humour,
the art of embroidery. She was "a needle-woman, royal
and renowned." There is still preserved in the Bodleian
Library her black-letter copy of the epistles of St. Paul,
with the cover worked by her own hand, in delicate
devices in gold, during her stay at Woodstock. On a
blank leaf is written one of the allegorical conceits in
which she took pleasure :—

"August. — I walked many times in the pleasant
fields of the Holy Scriptures, where I pluck up the
goodlisome herbs of sentences by pruning, eat them by
reading, chew them by musing, and lay them up at
length in the high seat of memorie by gathering
them together; that so, having tasted their sweetness,
I may the less perceive the bitterness of this miserable
life."

Elizabeth is said to have also illustrated her theory
of government by what she noticed with regard to the
great trees in the park, that they overshadowed and injured the underwood by depriving it of light and air. In
a similar manner the nobles obstructed the growth of
the people, and in her judgment the prerogatives and
privileges of the higher class ought to be diminished in
order to permit the rise of their social inferiors. This
was the policy which had already recommended itself to
Henry VIII., and in thus advocating it there spoke the
future queen of the people, the vindicator of their rights

and protector of their persons, as she said of herself, "the most English woman in her kingdom."

Elizabeth's old house of bondage, together with the Castle of Woodstock, of which it was an appendage, has long ago perished; but while it remained two relics of her survived, according to eye-witnesses. On a pane of glass in a lattice window she had written with a diamond the sarcastic commentary—

> "Much suspected, of me
> Nothing proved can be,
> Quoth Elizabeth, prisoner."

And she is said to have also written with a piece of charcoal on a shutter a more ambitious and elaborate protest, beginning—

> "Oh ! Fortune, how thy restless, wavering state
> Hath fraught with cares my troubled lot,"

ending with her customary vigorous denunciation of her enemies :—

> "So God send to my foes all they have brought,
> Quoth Elizabeth, prisoner."

The well-known episode of the milkmaid is said to have occurred at Woodstock. The Princess, sick with hope deferred, crushed by the intolerable irksomeness of her captivity, perhaps no longer caring to take refuge in proud sullenness and idle petulance, heard a milkmaid singing in rustic freedom and content as she carried her pails along a path behind the garden wall. Then the daughter of kings exclaimed in her weariness and soreness of heart, that she would she could change places with the peasant's daughter. It was well that the wish was not granted, for the woman who was destined to be a great Queen would have made, unless she had undergone another transformation than that of rank, but a sorry milkmaid !

Outer forces were compassing Elizabeth's deliverance. Mary, in her brief married happiness, was disposed to be more favourable to her sister, especially when Philip exerted himself to plead her cause. The reason of Philip's persistent friendliness to Elizabeth at this date is totally inexplicable to modern historians. It was certainly from no innate humanity or kindliness of disposition. It may have been in an ill-natured effort to thwart Renaud, who had strongly advocated Philip's detested marriage. On the other hand, there was an impression that if Philip was to find a bride in England he would have greatly preferred the handsome, high-spirited younger sister, his equal in years, to the faded, sickly, and, alas! too devoted Mary.

It has been thought that in his heartlessness he calculated on his wife's speedy death, and did not wish to prejudice his chances as Elizabeth's suitor when he should be free. Elizabeth, with her rampant personal vanity, took this view of his conduct, and upheld it in after years. But she is by no means an impartial witness, and his long-continued support of the suit of Philibbert of Savoy for the hand of Elizabeth, is an argument against the idea that Philip then thought of her as a wife for himself.

Whatever its origin, Philip's maintenance of Elizabeth's claims caused her to be invited to Hampton Court for the festivals at Christmas, 1554. She was escorted to and fro by Sir Henry Bedingfield.

A very comical anecdote is preserved in the Harleian MSS. of the earlier part of their progress. " As she came to Ricot, the wind was so high that her servants had much ado to keep her clothes about her, and her hood was blown twice or thrice from her head, whereupon she desired to retire herself to a gentleman's house to dress up her head. Sir Henry would not permit this, and she was fain to alight under a hedge and trim herself as she best could." If Elizabeth had to perform her toilet " under a

hedge," Sir Henry was not without his reason. Either
he distrusted her motives, or he had ground for condemning the politics of the house to which she wished to repair.
Unquestionably she was allowed so much of her state as
a princess, that sixty of her suite were suffered to rejoin
her before she arrived at Court. *Apropos* of her suite,
one member to whom Dr. Dee refers a little later is
"Thomasine the Dwarf." The classification sounds like a
pendant to that of "Jane the Fool," who figured in Mary's
household.

Elizabeth's reception was still dubious enough. She
was not allowed to forget that, though a guest, she continued a prisoner. She was kept under guard, and she
had repeated interviews with Gardiner and other members
of the Council, who urged her to confess her wrong-doing,
as a justification of their treatment of her, and as a step
to receiving the Queen's pardon. Elizabeth was not to be
betrayed into criminating herself. Poor Wyatt's speech
on the scaffold had failed to inculpate her, and she preserved an undaunted, defiant front to her assailants. She
took her stand on having suffered wrong from having
been unjustly kept in durance, and utterly repudiated
the notion that she had done anything to deserve imprisonment. After the lapse of a week, she was conducted one night across the garden to Mary's "lodging."
There the two sisters had the famous interview at which
Philip is rumoured to have assisted behind the arras.
If so, it was the first time he saw Elizabeth. A bench
of judges and bishops, nay, a headsman and his axe,
would not have sufficed to shake her on the high ground
of injured innocence which she chose to take up. Naturally, a gloomy, unconvinced sister, simply seeking to
do right in her pain and perplexity, failed to wring
anything from the unconvicted offender. Elizabeth had
the victory; and though Mary would not own herself
satisfied, her sister was at least partially restored to her

place as Princess.   She shared in the royal festivities, she
sat at the Queen's table, and in the royal gallery at the
joustings held in honour of Philip and Mary's marriage.
She heard matins in the Queen's closet.   Either out of
policy or bravado, she renounced the extreme simplicity
of dress, for which she had been hitherto distinguished,
and appeared in the dainty magnificence of white satin
and pearls.   It was understood that Philibbert of Savoy,
who was expected on a visit to his friend, Don Philip, had
been invited with the intention of promoting the union
with Elizabeth to which she was wholly disinclined; but
the wooer was delayed by stress of weather and sickness,
and came too late for the festivities.

It is known that Elizabeth returned to Woodstock, while
it could hardly have been of her free will; but the dates
of her return and of her final departure are both uncertain.
Her first stay was of seven months' duration; her second
could not have lasted above three months.   She was in a
different position latterly (when her granduncle, Lord William Howard, visited her), and was granted much more
freedom of action; and just as there had been inevitable
reports of plots for her assassination in the beginning of
her captivity, there were rumours towards the close that
she was practising magical arts against Queen Mary, with
the assistance of no less a person than the Welsh scholar, Dr.
John Dee, who was then residing at Oxford, and figuring as
an astrologer.   There can be no doubt that Elizabeth, in
spite of her strong sense, had a great hankering after the
romantic mysteries of astrology.   When she was the young
Queen, she had frequent confidential consultations, on the
most private matters, with the fantastic dreamer and dupe
of his own learning.   She not only summoned him to her
palaces, she visited him on more than one occasion at his
house at Mortlake, an honour of which he has left minute
accounts in his private diary.   She was not singular in her
inclination.   One has only to read Dr. John Dee's Diary

to marvel at some of the names simply and familiarly given as those of his clients. The owners of the names came not only to examine the rare collection of mathematical instruments he had brought from the Low Countries, but to have their horoscopes drawn out, and the favourable days selected for the gentlemen to start on important enterprises. Among these clients were the Secretary Walsingham; the future Chancellor, Sir Christopher Hatton; Raleigh's half-brother, "Sir Humphrey Gilbert;" and "young Mr. Hawkins, who was then at sea with Drake."

It is a pleasure to find, in relation to Elizabeth's nobler qualities, that when she did quit Woodstock, she and Sir Henry Bedingfield parted in amity after their protracted warfare. Not only did Elizabeth bear no malice against her "gaoler," whom she had tormented with great skill and success; she recognised his trustworthiness, and showed her recognition, in the days of her power, by promoting and employing him, zealous Catholic as he was.

Elizabeth was at last permitted to go to her own house of Hatfield, and stay there, with some royal surroundings, as she had dwelt formerly. But she was not left solely to her own devices; she had to accept the presence of Sir Thomas Pope, as a kind of comptroller of her household— an office to which he was appointed by Mary, in order to prevent further political intrigues on her sister's part. In other respects, Sir Thomas discharged the duties of a courteous and well qualified chamberlain, with whom Elizabeth was on the best of terms. She accommodated herself to his company, and he, in his turn, made it acceptable to her by ministering to her love of splendour and romance, by getting up—sometimes at his own cost—such masks and pageants as she delighted in. Now it was a mask in her hall—to contribute to which twelve minstrels were "anticly disguised," and forty-six gentlemen and ladies presented themselves "apparelled in crimson satin, garnished with borders of hanging pearls." Now it was an open-air pageant, that Elizabeth might "hunt the hart," as if in an enchanted forest. Her retinue consisted of twelve noble ladies in white satin, and twenty yeomen in green, all on horseback. She was met by "fifty archers in scarlet boots and yellow caps, armed with gilded bows." One of the archers presented her "with a silver-headed arrow, winged with peacocks' feathers." At the close of the sport, her Grace was gratified with the privilege of cutting the buck's throat," a compliment of which she was not unlikely to avail herself, Agnes Strickland remarks drily. Yet Elizabeth was not bloodthirsty.

Elizabeth was not always indulging herself in such sports. In Mary's misery, on the departure of Philip, in 1555, her sister was with her at Greenwich, and sedulously recommended herself to the bereaved and desolate woman by emulating her fasts, confessions, and attendance at mass. Elizabeth also resumed her studies under Roger Ascham, reading with him Greek (the orations of Æschines and Demosthenes), both at Greenwich and when she returned to her own house of Hatfield. Her gifted tutor, who had known many of the accomplished women of the day, notably Elizabeth's young cousin, Lady Jane Grey, entertained an immense admiration for the Princess, not merely for her wonderful mental powers and attainments, but also for the gentle and amiable tone which it was her pleasure to adopt to him. His high-flown compliments were better warranted and more sincere than many of a similar character which were addressed to Elizabeth. Ascham was not the only old friend whom Elizabeth recalled. With her tenacious will and retentive affections, whether they were well or ill-bestowed, she summoned back others who were not desirable associates, among them Mrs. Kate Ashley and Thomas Parry, an unwise proceeding, with regard to which Mary had still enough interest in what was passing around her to testify her displeasure.

In spite of the small amount of cordiality that existed between the sisters, they continued to exchange visits at Hatfield and Greenwich. Of the principal visit which Mary paid to Elizabeth, Miss Strickland has furnished us with some details. Elizabeth had the State apartments hung with new and magnificent tapestry in the Queen's honour, while a play was acted by the choir boys of St. Paul's for her delectation. The hostess herself played on the virginals, in order to accompany the singing of a specially sweet-throated chorister.

Elizabeth was still beset at times, not only by Mary, but through Mary, by Philip, with overtures of marriage from her persevering wooer, Philibbert of Savoy. Yet the gentleman was credited with so little sincerity in his pursuit, that he was said to have been seen "making love" from his window in the palace to another princess. This interloper was Philip and Mary's beautiful twice-widowed cousin, Christina of Lorraine, who was also on a visit at the English Court.

Elizabeth's house of Hatfield was not more than twelve miles from London, to which she now went occasionally, attended by a goodly company of lords, ladies, and gentlemen, and hailed with vehement expressions of regard by the citizens.

In the winter of 1558, Mary was evidently dying. In obedience to her sense of justice, and at the request of her absent husband, whom she had vainly proposed as her successor, she was ready to appoint Elizabeth her heir. But, as might have been expected, she sought first to obtain from her sister an assurance on the subject which was nearest to Mary's heart—the continuance of the Roman Catholic religion, as it had been re-established in England by her means. Very different and entirely conflicting testimony is given with respect to Elizabeth's reception of the Queen's requirement. According to one of the Princess's friends, she replied with great dignity and

intrepidity. She expressed her regret for Mary's illness,
but declined to owe her any obligation for the succession
to the Crown, as it was hers—Elizabeth's—by right. She
announced that she would hold herself as much at liberty
to choose her councillors as Mary had been to choose hers.
She promised not to change the religion of the country,
inasmuch as it could be proved by the Word of God. She
undertook to pay Mary's debts, since they were a primary
claim on her successor.

There is this to be said for the authenticity of the account,
that the sentences have the ring of Elizabeth's speeches.

According to Elizabeth's enemies, her behaviour was
very different. The chief witnesses are the De Ferias.
Count de Feria was at this time Philip's ambassador. The
Countess de Feria, whom he married not long afterwards,
was Mistress Jane Dormer, one of Mary's ladies. She
alleged that Mary sent her with the Crown jewels to Elizabeth, asking from her a pledge for the preservation of the
Roman Catholic religion. Then Elizabeth, calling down
upon herself a peculiarly awful punishment (that the earth
might open and swallow her up), if she were not a true
Roman Catholic, bound herself to comply with the Queen's
wishes.

The truth probably lies between these two versions of
the story. Elizabeth had so long trimmed her sails to
suit the policy of the moment, that it is hardly likely that
before Mary's death was *un fait accompli*, she should burst
out into a declaration of independence. Neither was she
by any means the person to be swayed by a dying woman's
last prayers. She knew that, provided Mary died, as she
was expected to do, the course was clear for her successor.
She had only to wait for a sign of how the wind of public
opinion in the masses blew, to steer her bark on that middle
course between extreme Roman Catholicism on the one
hand, and extreme Protestantism on the other, which was
so dear to her philosophic, temporising mind.

One thing was plain. Crowds of courtiers were flocking along the twelve miles of road to Hatfield to hail the coming Queen, while Mary lay dying among her few remaining friends at St. James's Palace. Although the sisters had been on fairly good terms for years, there is not the slightest hint that Elizabeth made any movement to see the Queen and bid her farewell. The Princess is said with her usual astuteness to have employed Sir Nicholas Throckmorton to bring her certain news of Mary's death, by asking from one of the Queen's ladies, who was friendly to Elizabeth, a particular token of the event, in the shape of a black enamelled ring, one of Philip's gifts, which poor Mary had been in the habit of wearing day and night. But before Throckmorton could do his errand, a deputation from the Council reached Hatfield. They came to announce the Queen's death, and offer Elizabeth their homage. She appeared greatly overcome. She fell upon her knees, and with the tendency which she so often showed to wrest Scripture to suit her circumstances, cried, "This is the Lord's doing! It is marvellous in our eyes."

On that November day Elizabeth had attained the age of twenty-five years and two months.

THE YOUNG QUEEN. [1]

"The bells which had pealed merrily for Mary, pealed as merrily for Elizabeth," writes Mr. Froude. "Through the November day steeple answered steeple, the streets were spread with tables, and, as the twilight closed, blazed as before with bonfires." And the bells of Westminster, ringing for Elizabeth's succession, were probably the last sounds heard by Mary's friend, Reginald Pole. If he heard and identified them, he must have recognised in the sound the knell of his hopes and efforts. His death saved him from imprisonment or banishment, for

---

[1] Agnes Strickland, Froude, Green, Camden, Hayward.

he was as obnoxious to Elizabeth as he had been dear to
Mary. Heath, Archbishop of York and Lord Chancellor,
announced Mary's death and Elizabeth's succession in
Parliament, and was met by glad shouts of "God save
Queen Elizabeth!" In the meantime Elizabeth remained
in retirement at Hatfield, where she held her first Council.
It was then and there she achieved the master-stroke of
her future wise government—she appointed William Cecil,
conspicuous for his sagacity and patriotism, her secretary.
He had long been her friend, and had already, within an
hour of Mary's death, written Elizabeth's proclamation,
changed the guard at the Tower, despatched envoys to
the principal foreign courts, and chosen who was to preach
the following Sunday at St. Paul's Cross. Cecil's brother-
in-law, Sir Anthony Bacon, another upright man, was
made Lord Keeper. Cecil and Bacon were leaders of
the Protestant party, and their wives, the learned daughters of Sir John Coke, who had found places in Mary's
household because of their friendship with Catherine Parr,
and the tastes they had in common with her and her
step-daughters, were in strong sympathy with the Reformed Church. Elizabeth's own household had always
been deeply tinged with the so-called heresy in which
she was reared, while her opinions were more or less an
arbitrary jumble of intellectual prepossessions and individual biases. She inclined more to the doctrines of
Luther than to those of Calvin, her inclination being in
opposition to the bent of the English Protestantism of
the time. She had a distinct aversion to the views of
John Knox, and a rooted dislike to the man. She did not
forgive his "Monstrous Regiment of Women," a treatise
directed against the practice of sovereignty being placed
in the hands of women. She was regarded as the champion
of liberty. Neither was it in her nature to reckon "an
opinion a crime." Not only were her political interests,
and the cause of the mother whose name she never men-

tioned, bound up with Protestantism; she had not forgotten what she herself had endured in the conflict, and she could feel for and with those who had borne a clearer testimony, and fought a harder battle. It is said of her that, unlike her sister Mary, her safety and strength lay in her remarkable capacity for ascertaining and responding to the national pulse; and at the succession England's most passionate heart-throbs were for the hecatombs of martyrs, the victims of the dogmatism and bigotry of Mary and Pole. Elizabeth was not honest enough to be either dogmatic or bigoted, but she desired with all her heart to be fair, and her common-sense told her that her strength was to be found in fairness. Her scholarly instincts tended to a temporising middle course, and she was confirmed in it by her share of "the free, proud spirit of the educated laity which declined to be dictated to by priests"—whether of Rome or Geneva.

Elizabeth came to London on the 23rd of the month, six days after Mary's death. She was the centre of a magnificent company, and was met by vast crowds journeying out of the city to welcome her. Hayward has an enthusiastic description of her bearing on the occasion :—"If ever any person had the gift or the skill to win the hearts of the people, it was their Queen, and if ever she did express the same it was at that present, in coupling mildness with majesty, as she did, and in stately stooping to the meanest sort. . . . Her eye was set upon one, her ear listened to another, her judgment ran upon a third, to a fourth she addressed her speech. . . . Some she commanded, some she pitied, some she thanked, at others she pleasantly and wittily jested."

The exception to this universal graciousness was in the case of Bishop Bonner. When Mary's bishops knelt by the wayside to offer the new Queen their homage, she received them graciously. But she de-

clined to let Bonner kiss her hand.   Those lips which
had passed many a brutal sentence should never touch
her fingers.

In fact, Elizabeth, "the people's idol," was in her glory
in this cheering, swaying multitude of great and small.
Yet there was not a more lonely young woman in England
than she was that day.   Of near relations she had not
one.   Her nearest surviving relation in point of law was
her life-long rival, Mary Queen of Scots, who had already
assumed the arms of England; while the cousins had
never met, and were never destined to meet.   Elizabeth's
position was perilous in the extreme.   She was hedged
about with stumbling-blocks and pitfalls.   She had many
advisers, but few friends.   Among the advisers were such
insiduous councillors as the Count de Feria, Philip II. of
Spain's ambassador,—the husband of Mrs. Jane Dormer,
one of the late Queen Mary's ladies, a potent person with
the Catholics.   Suitors, led by her dead sister's widower,
Philip, were coming round her in swarms; and neither
adviser nor suitor doubted that Elizabeth would be
governed by him, and would become little better than
a puppet in his hands.   Nobody, unless it were Cecil,
guessed that Elizabeth had not only a mind of her own,
it was so great a mind that it could carve out an original
course for a sovereign of England; it could rule by the
sheer force of a splendid judgment, and a burning zeal
for the welfare of her people.

Hayward has a personal description of Elizabeth at this
time which, if allowance be made for an excess of dazzled
laudation, is graphic and fairly lifelike :—" She was a lady
on whom Nature had bestowed, and well-placed, many of
her favours.   Of stature ' meane ' (middling), slender and
straight, and amiably composed of such state in her carriage as every motion of her seemed to bear majesty; her
hair was inclined to pale yellow; her forehead large and
fair—a seemly seat for princely grace; her eyes lively

MARY, QUEEN OF SCOTS.
(From the Original Painting by Zuccero.)

and sweet, but short-sighted;[1] her nose somewhat rising in the midst; the whole compass of her countenance somewhat long, but yet of admirable beauty, not so much in that which is termed the flower of youth, as in a most delightful composition of majesty and modesty in equal mixture."

Elizabeth lodged that night at the Charterhouse. Next day, according to Hayward—five days later, according to Miss Strickland—she was met at the Charterhouse gate by the Lord Mayor and the City dignitaries. As she rode in great state, Garter King-at-Arms carrying a sceptre before her, she wore a purple velvet riding dress, which suited her fine figure. Her evil genius, Lord Robert Dudley, whom she had already named her Master of the Horse, rode by her side. His sole claim to the honour was his handsome person, his soft tongue, and the fact that he, along with poor Edward Courtenay, had been a prisoner in the Tower when she was in the same evil plight. She entered Cripplegate, and passed by the wall at Bishopsgate. " This gate was richly hanged, and thereupon the waits of the City sounded loud musick." When she reached " Martlane," a peal of ordnance began at the Tower, which continued for half an hour. As she entered the Tower gate she made a speech, according to her invariable custom. " Some have fallen from being princes in this land to being prisoners in this place"— (were her thoughts of her unhappy mother when she said these words ?)—" I am raised from being a prisoner in this place to be a prince of the land. *That* dejection was a work of God's justice : *this* advancement is a work of His mercy ; as they were to yield patience for the one, so I must bear myself to God thankful, and to men merciful and beneficial for the other."

[1] Short-sightedness was present also in Elizabeth's sister, Mary Tudor's singularly penetrating brown eyes. Like the loud deep voice which distinguished each of Henry VIII.'s daughters, short-sightedness was a defect common to both.

The speech is almost suspiciously appropriate and antithetical, but its occurrence is in harmony with Elizabeth's passion for delivering speeches, while its tone agrees with her love of pointing a moral, drawing sharp contrasts, and appealing to Heaven, not only in acknowledging the Divine goodness where she was concerned, but also in illustration of the position which she claimed as God's chosen servant.

Poor Queen Mary had not been more possessed with the idea, at the beginning of her reign, that she was favoured by Heaven, than Elizabeth professed to be convinced that she enjoyed the same exalted dignity.   Elizabeth, however, spared no worldly means to make her position secure.

Miss Strickland quotes the tradition that the Queen went straight to the room in which she had been imprisoned, and, falling on her knees, added to her speech an extemporaneous prayer, in which she likened her deliverance to that of Daniel from the lions' den.

Mass was said at Mary's funeral, which Elizabeth attended; but when White, Bishop of Winchester, proceeded in a Latin sermon to eulogise the late Queen, and to indulge in slightly-veiled comparisons and inferences disadvantageous to Elizabeth, she was highly incensed. She ordered him to be put under arrest; he threatened her with excommunication; but there the matter ended, for she was not naturally a persecutor.

It is said that on the first Christmas-day after her succession, Elizabeth, with her train, quitted her closet after the reading of the gospel before the celebration of Mass, which she thus repudiated.   Her next step was the proclamation that from the following New Year's Day, 1559, the Epistle and Gospel were to be read in English in all churches throughout the land.   The last was, with reason, a most welcome and popular measure where Protestants were concerned.   "The first morsel of prayer and Scripture in the English tongue was most sweetly swallowed."

At the same time Elizabeth's reforms in religion were moderate and gradual. Her own convictions were hazy and vague, to say the least. She was offended by any violent excess—such as the tearing down of the crucifixes in the streets and the hustling of priests into the kennel —into which the mob were apt to fall. She wished to retain crucifixes in the churches, and strongly upheld the celibacy of the priests. She was content, in the beginning, with the re-establishment of the Royal supremacy in Church as in State, the setting aside of Mary's decrees where religion was concerned, and the revival, in another form, of the Act of Uniformity requiring a modified harmony of worship in public.

On the 12th of January, Elizabeth paid her second visit to the Tower, in anticipation of her coronation. She went on this occasion by water, sailing from Westminster in her barge, escorted by a magnificent fleet of barges, including those of the Mayor and the different guilds. She did not now land at Traitors' Gate, but at the private stairs reserved for the Sovereign on Tower Wharf. The 15th of January had been appointed for her coronation, the stars in their courses having declared it a highly fortunate day for the ceremony, according to the mathematician and astrologer, Dr. John Dee—Elizabeth's old ally during the last months of her stay at Woodstock, when he was a resident of Oxford. Dr. Dee was now the occupant of a house at Mortlake, and was at the height of his fame—full of business in drawing up the horoscopes of the principal nobility and adventurous sailors and soldiers of the day.

On the afternoon of Saturday the 14th, Elizabeth started from the Tower to make the grandest of all her grand processions through the city to Westminster. The scene was one of unparalleled rejoicing; the pageants were a succession of triumphs; the people were half mad with joy; the dark days of the late reign, with its persecutions at home and losses abroad, were ended, and in a fair way to be forgotten, though one of their disastrous consequences was the poverty of the royal exchequer. Mary had been raising money from Flemish money-lenders at an enormous interest. The last bonds, lying in her death-chamber waiting for her signature, were used by her women to " cere her corpse." Had not Cecil sent out the princely merchant, Gresham, to appease these importunate creditors, and obtain better terms from them, Elizabeth's ill-filled purse would have been still emptier. But what she lacked of means to contribute to the great shows she made up by the exceeding graciousness and cordial animation of her demeanour. Never was Queen more enthusiastic in responding to the passionate loyalty of her subjects. Sitting in her crimson velvet-lined coach, she had smiles, waving of her hands, frank words for rich and poor alike. Again and again she made her coach be stopped, that she might the better see, hear, and answer the ingenious allegories and grandiloquent addresses got up for her delectation. There was a great rose pageant, mocking the wintry season, at the end of Gracechurch Street. Gentle, beautiful Elizabeth of York sat in the centre of a white rose, while her cautious, long-faced partner, Henry VII., the son of the Venerable Margaret, was the heart of a great red rose. On another storey of the pageant their son, bluff King Hal, emerged from a red and white rose, and by his side—represented there for the first time since her execution—was Anne Boleyn. On the third and upper storey was Elizabeth, in solitary majesty, surrounded, like all the others, with garlands of red and white roses.

When " Time and Truth " was played in Cheapside, " Time," exclaimed the Queen, of the old man with the scythe and hour-glass, " Time has brought me here ! " The figure of Truth held a Bible, which was let down by a string into the coach. The Queen caught it, kissed it, clasped it to her bosom, and promised to read it diligently. At the upper end of "Chepe," with its gorgeous banners and rich tapestries, the Recorder of London, in the name of the Lord Mayor, offered for her Majesty's acceptance a crimson satin purse, curiously wrought, holding a thousand gold marks. This the Queen took between her hands, thanking the givers, assuring them that she would not only spend every coin she possessed, she would shed every drop of her blood, if need were, for her people; and pledging herself to be as good to them as ever queen was. Neither did she neglect smaller gifts. She received nosegays and flowers from the poorest. A woman gave the Queen a sprig of rosemary in Fleet Street, and Elizabeth was still seen to retain it at Westminster. When verses were sung in her honour at Temple Bar she requested the people to say "Amen," as she did, at the end of each verse. When they wished her prosperity she thanked them and wished them the same. She twisted every omen, good and bad, to fit in with her exultant humour. When one old man turned aside his face and wept, she cried, "I warrant it is for joy." When another proclaimed that he remembered "old King Harry," she laughed with pleasure, as if the association with her father was the pleasantest and most propitious that could arise.

At her coronation, on the 15th of January, 1559, only one bishop, Oglethorpe of Carlisle, officiated. There was no Archbishop of Canterbury, and the Catholic bishops stood as much aloof as they dared. Little wonder that the ceremony was less impressive and more shorn of splendour than it had been wont to be. It was conducted according to the Roman Catholic form, though it was installing a Protestant Queen on the throne, and it was the third coronation which had taken place within the last twelve years. Elizabeth herself, with the rampant critical faculty and the levity which was present with her, even at the most solemn moments, remarked to her maids of the anointing oil that it was "grease, and smelt ill."

Her coronation robes consisted of a train and mantle of cloth of gold, furred with ermine. She was girded with a sword before the crown was put on her head and the sceptre in her hand. She made the usual offerings, including her crown, robes, and regalia, and reappeared for the banquet in Westminster Hall dressed in violet velvet, and wearing the crown of state while she dined. Her champion rode up the hall and flung down his gauntlet. Miss Strickland quotes the Queen's title, which Sir Edward Dymoloe was there to defend; and it was sufficiently curious and open to question. It was "That of the most high and mighty Princess and dread Sovereign Lady, Elizabeth, by the grace of God Queen of England, France, Ireland, defender of the true, ancient, and Catholic faith, most worthy Empress from the Orcade Isles to the mountains of the Pyrénée."

The Easter and the summer following the Queen's accession were naturally full of rejoicing. In fact, she had already given every assurance for the peacefulness and prosperity of her reign. She had, with the felicity of choice which was one of her crowning gifts, appointed such a Council of wise and noble-minded men as has never been equalled in the annals of her successors. She had nominated to the See of Canterbury Archbishop Parker,[1] whose moderation equalled his learning. His power of organisation restored something like order to the divided and distracted Church, and his firmness to his convictions enabled him to hold in check the lion Queen on the questions of crucifixes in churches and the celibacy of priests. In the last contention Elizabeth revenged herself by behaving with scant courtesy to the wife of the Archbishop at the close of a banquet at which both were present. Married ladies were addressed then

[1] "Painful Parker," the translator of the Psalms into English metre.

as "Madam," unmarried as "Mistress." When Mrs. Parker advanced at the close of a sumptuous entertainment at Lambeth, to take leave of the Queen, Elizabeth feigned a momentary hesitation. "Madam," she said at last, "I may not call you, and Mistress I am loth to call you, but I thank you for your good cheer."

In her first speeches, both to her Parliament and her judges, Elizabeth showed the noble side of her strange, complex nature. "Nothing," she said to her first Parliament in words of unwonted fire—"Nothing, no worldly thing under the sun, is so dear to me as the love and goodwill of my subjects;" and, adds Mr. Green, "the love and goodwill which were so dear to her she fully won." To the judges she said, "Have a care over my people. You hear my people—do that which I ought to do. They are *my* people. Every man oppresseth and spoileth them without mercy. They cannot revenge their quarrel, nor help themselves. See unto them, see unto them, for they are my charge."

One of those later biographers of Elizabeth who have painted her subtle character, contradictory to its core, with masterly touches, has argued that she neither loved nor hated, and was as incapable of vindictiveness as of enthusiasm. She scorned to punish, or even to remember, as a Queen, the slights she had received as a Princess. But the verdict does not hold good in relation to women. Elizabeth's nearest female relations, after Mary Queen of Scots, were Margaret Countess of Lennox and Frances Duchess of Suffolk, her cousins, leaving out of count Frances's younger sister, Eleanor Brandon, a less prominent person. Margaret was the mother of two sons, Henry Lord Darnley and Charles Stewart. Frances was the mother of three daughters, Lady Jane, Lady Catherine, and Lady Mary Grey. After the execution of her husband and eldest daughter the Duchess married again, with unseemly rapidity, a young member of her household, Adrian Stokes. When Elizabeth heard of the *mésalliance* she exclaimed contemptuously, "What! hath she wedded her horsekeeper?"—a sarcasm to which William Cecil dared to answer, with the candour of the time, "Yes, madam, and she says your Majesty would like to do so too"—alluding to the post of Master of the Horse held by Lord Robert Dudley, and to the fear entertained by Elizabeth's friends from the day that she came to the throne that she would stoop from her high estate and marry him.

Certainly Elizabeth had not forgotten the fact that Queen Mary had made use of the Duchess of Suffolk and the Countess of Lennox to humble Elizabeth by causing them to take precedence of her in Court ceremonies. The mercurial Duchess soon passed beyond the reach of the Queen's approval or disapproval, since within a year of her second marriage she died in childbirth, at the age of thirty-five—the same age at which her mother, the Queen Dowager of France, had died. Elizabeth loved the Duchess's daughters no better than the Duchess, and very soon after the Queen's accession Count de Feria communicated to his master, Philip, that Lady Catherine Grey had confided to him how little Elizabeth liked her, how different was the treatment she received from Elizabeth from that she had been accustomed to receive from Queen Mary, who had been kind and friendly, though their faiths had been different, while the very circumstance that Lady Catherine, by King Henry's will, stood next to Elizabeth in the succession to the throne caused the Queen to look askance at her kinswoman. Elizabeth had as little consideration and forbearance for Lady Lennox when her troubles overtook her, nor was the personal grudge likely to be lessened if Elizabeth knew that in the Lennox household the birthright of Anne Boleyn's daughter was spoken of with scorn, and even the family fool was permitted to jest over it.

To men Elizabeth was more magnanimous. She was especially gracious to Sir Henry Bedingfield, though she called him in jest her "gaoler," and she paid him the compliment of visiting him at his house at Oxburgh Hall, Norfolk.

Elizabeth's Parliament and people prayed her to marry, dreading, as they did, the disputed succession that was sure to arise in case of her death. Her reply was to point to her coronation ring, as Mary had pointed to hers, to affirm that she was wedded to her realm, and that she would live and die a virgin queen. Her resolution was not caused by any lack of suitors. They and their proposals were legion. Philip of Spain, her brother-in-law; the Archduke Charles, remarkable for his huge head, son of the Emperor Ferdinand; two French princes, Anjou and Alençon—Alençon, with the reputation of being the ugliest man in France—sons of Catherine de Medicis; Eric of Sweden, Casimir of Poland, the Scotch Earl of Arran, the English Earl of Arundel, and Lord Robert Dudley, possibly, also, her Chancellor, Sir Christopher Hatton, all made their suits in turn. With all she dallied, partly in accordance with the coquettish levity which she had inherited from her mother, and partly, where the foreign princes were concerned, from her favourite policy of procrastination and profound dissimulation, using each man's offer, as she used every public event, as a means of safety and prosperity for England, which she had found on her accession defeated and impoverished. Above all things she shunned war. It was abhorrent to her, from her natural dislike to bloodshed, and from her perfect comprehension that in the condition of her country it would be simply ruinous. No false dreams of glory, or of inordinate personal ambition, blinded her reason—she laughed them to scorn. She refused the sovereignty of the Netherlands, and scouted the idea of being the leader of the Protestants of Europe. But by consummate prudence she would raise her England to a

high place among the nations.   Therefore she shouted at
the council-board, "No war, my lords, no war!" and
therefore she played with her lovers, played them one
against each other, deluded them and the governments
they represented with false hopes, keeping them quiet and
winning favours from them till she gained her purpose.
It was by no means a noble policy, neither did the end
justify the means; but this much must be allowed to
Elizabeth, and it was this which, in spite of her falseness,
made her great, and distinguished her honourably from her
contemporaries—that before all else, before her own headstrong will and passion even, she held the solid welfare of
her people.   For them she could deny herself on every
side.   With her mother's sensuous love of luxury and
pleasure, Elizabeth was the thriftiest of English sovereigns;
her fare was of the simplest and most temperate kind.
She worked hard, she subdued her pride, and submitted
to be thwarted and mortified when it fitted into her great
hope of serving her people.

Still, while Elizabeth was the young Queen, the extraordinary influence exercised over her by her favourite,
Dudley, kept their probable marriage an imminent danger
for many a day.   The infatuation was unaccountable
enough to cause the superstitious to attribute it to magic,
to the irrestible motions and attractions of the stars.
Dudley lacked every quality that one would have expected
Elizabeth to prize above all others.   He is said to have
been "without courage, without talent, without virtue,"
a mere handsome, sleek-mannered courtier.   His very attractions were in direct opposition to the Queen's daring,
her intellect, and what Mr. Froude calls her "high, conscientious devotion to duty, that great sovereign nature
which shone out in her grander moments—dashed with the
taint which she inherited with her mother's blood."

In addition to every other disadvantage, Lord Robert
Dudley's reputation was soon clouded with the suspicion

that he was concerned in the violent death of his wife, which happened at Cumnor Place, near Oxford, within two years of Elizabeth's accession. We are most of us familiar with Sir Walter Scott's great tragic novel of "Kenilworth," by which the name of Amy Robsart is embalmed in English literature. There are only a few particulars in which the facts differ from the fiction. The ages of the principal persons concerned are recorded differently. The victim, Amy, was indeed beneath Dudley in rank, but their "love-marriage" was not a private one. The date is given in King Edward's "Journal," and the boy-king indulges in a nearer approach to boyishness than was common with him, when he proceeds to describe some of the more striking rejoicings on the occasion. However, Dudley was only a lad in his teens; and although the circumstances of his marriage was well known, he was understood not to be happily married to the wife whom he neither brought to Court, nor appeared with in public. When she was found dead at the foot of a staircase on a day when her servants were absent at Abingdon Fair, the irregularity and opportuneness of her death immediately awoke a rumour of foul play. Dudley met it by giving the poor lady a sumptuous funeral. She was buried with great ceremony before the altar of the stately Church of St. Mary the Virgin, Oxford (in which Cranmer spoke his recantation) and in empowering a commission, in which some of the dead woman's relations took part, to inquire into the cause of her death. But his own absence from the commission, and various inconsistencies in its report, together with the widespread belief that the Queen would one day wed the widower, led to an equally widespread conviction, that if Dudley did not take an active part in the murder of his defenceless wife, it was the work of some of his followers, with the object of promoting the ends of his ambition. It will be remembered that Sir Walter Scott uses this theory in the machinery of his novel.

Altogether it is not unreasonable to conclude that Elizabeth's extravagant regard for Dudley was more like "a violent fancy which would not brook contradiction," than like worthy love. Certainly she played with him and his lover's suit very much as she played with other suits and suitors, though, after her mother's unhappy fashion, and in accordance with the free manners of the time, she allowed him to take undesirable liberties with her, and made a point of exhibiting her fondness for her chosen Squire "Robin" in public. She took a malicious delight in astonishing and mystifying her circle. Mr. Froude relates that when Dudley's patent of nobility in connection with the earldom of Leicester, which the Queen had conferred upon him, was drawn out, she cut it to pieces with a penknife, instead of signing it, saying the Dudleys had been traitors for three generations. Again, on a reconciliation after a lover's quarrel, she cried out, clapping "Robin" on the cheeks, "No, no; the bear and ragged staff is not so soon overthrown." Once more, when her courtiers said in effect, "Marry him, then," she would "puff out her lips," and declare that she would not marry a subject or make him a king. Truly it was not in her Council alone that Elizabeth tormented her audience with exhibitions of the curious engrained irresolution that balanced her audacity. She was tenacious enough in maintaining her point when she had taken a determination; but she had not her sister Mary's singleness of heart, which caused her never to falter or to flinch in any course, right or wrong; and it would have been a wise man indeed who could have told, from the signs on the surface, whether Elizabeth's irresolution was real or assumed.

The royal progresses, in which Queen Elizabeth took great delight, that were a marked feature of her reign, began with its very commencement. Those magnificent pageants were sometimes on the waters of the Thames, where the Queen's barge disported itself in the centre of a gorgeous crowd of attendant barges, sometimes on land in "gilded and silken tents" in Greenwich Park, to which she invited her loyal subjects, sometimes in superb processions into the City, or into the country from town to town, and castle to castle, throughout the length and breadth of her pleasant land. Each and all owed its origin to two sources—to Elizabeth's passion for splendour and social entertainments, in which she resembled her father, and to her shrewd guess that nothing kept her stout citizens in better humour, after the innumerable proofs she gave them of attending sedulously to their material interests, than to afford them amusement by furnishing them with a succession of majestic and dazzling spectacles. It must be always borne in mind that Elizabeth was preeminently the people's "Good Queen Bess." The flower of the English nobility—Catholic as well as Protestant—gathered around her, charmed by her wit and wisdom, her sound learning, her brilliant accomplishments, her wide sympathies with her soldiers and sailors, her knightly adventurers like Raleigh, her wits and dramatists like Spencer and Shakespeare—even her alchemists and astrologers like Dee; but she had her father Henry's resolution to rule for the people. She never forgot the little parable she had spoken of the growth of vegetation in the park at Woodstock when she was a prisoner there—how the tall trees must be thinned out and kept in subjection, so that the sweet, fresh air and sunlight might reach the undergrowth of bushes, and preserve them also in wholesome health and well-being.

Miss Strickland gives a lively description of the manner in which Elizabeth kept her Maundy-Thursday at Westminster Hall in 1560. She washed the feet of twenty poor women, and then gave gowns to every woman—to one woman the gown her Majesty had worn on the occasion. She drank to every woman in a new white cup, and then gave her the cup. The same afternoon, in

St. James's Park, she gave alms of twopence (from six-
pence to eightpence in our money) to each of upwards
of two thousand poor men, women, and children, "both
whole and lame."

Elizabeth, by an act of great justice and judiciousness,
called in the worn old gold coins and re-issued a fresh
coinage of full weight. One of her gala visits was to the
mint, where she coined several of her gold pieces. When
she passed with her train, on these State occasions,
through the streets of the City, "they were freshly
sanded and gravelled, and the houses hung with cloth
of arras, rich carpets, and silk, but Cheapside, then pro-
verbially called 'the Golden Chepe,' made a display of
magnificence in honour of the passage of the sovereign
which we should vainly look for in these days of flimsy
luxury, being hung with cloth of gold and silver, and
velvets of all colours."

Elizabeth had soon to mourn a loss to her town of
London of what was one of the glories of its architecture.
On the 4th of June, 1561, the beautiful spire of St. Paul's
was set on fire by lightning. From the windows of her
palace at Greenwich Elizabeth saw the smoke of the
burning, which soon extended to the church. Young
Admiral Winter and his sailors stopped the fire, and saved
the bishop's palace, but the Cathedral itself was left a
roofless ruin.

In the same year Lady Catherine Grey was sent to the
Tower by her cousin the Queen for the enormity of having
married the Marquis of Hertford, son of the late Lord
Protector Somerset, without the knowledge and authority
of Elizabeth. The bridegroom was sent, after the bride,
to the same dismal lodging. Their first-born son and a
second child were born within its walls, and after a lingering imprisonment of seven years poor Lady Catherine, a
devout and accomplished scholar, like her elder sister,
died within a stone's throw of the spot where Lady Jane

and her husband, Lord Guildford Dudley, and her father, the Duke of Suffolk, had suffered. Relationship to royalty was a doubtful boon in the reign of the maiden Queen. There was yet one of the Ladies Grey left—Lady Mary, less in stature than Lady Jane, the smallest lady at the Court. Sickened with splendour that was dashed with blood, and darkened by the shadow of a prison, or rendered reckless and desperate by what had gone before, Lady Mary disposed of herself in her own foolish way. She got a drunken priest to marry her to the biggest man about Court—whose size, however, was his principal recommendation, unless indeed the obscurity of his position counted for something, since Thomas Keys (appropriate name) was nothing better than a sergeant porter. The alliance was so incongruous and absurd that it only excited laughter. It was annulled, indeed, by the powers of Church and State, but no further punishment was administered to little Lady Mary and her large partner than temporary imprisonment.

Already the royal lady, who was from first to last a sharp thorn in the sensitive flesh of Elizabeth, began to appear prominently on the scene. Mary Queen of Scots, a widow at eighteen, was on her way back to her native kingdom from France, the scene of her education and of her brief wedlock to King Francis II., the eldest son of Catherine de Medicis. A safe conduct was asked for her from her cousin, Queen Elizabeth, which she refused, just as she had declined to permit John Knox to pass through any territory of hers. Mary was younger and more beautiful. She was invested with the tender grace of her recent widowhood. If she was not more learned and accomplished, she also was no mean scholar, in that generation of scholarly women, and she was still better versed than Elizabeth in those arts and graces which blind men's judgments, and dazzle their imaginations. The maiden Queen, who likened herself to a lion and a

lion's cub, was on that baser side of her which was in-
ordinately vain and covetous of admiration, furiously
jealous of Mary. She not only dreaded her as a rival
queen who claimed the throne of England, and disputed
Elizabeth's title to the succession, and as the sworn ally
of France, who might well aid in shattering that peace
which was so necessary for the recovery of the drained
and exhausted forces of England; Elizabeth also detested
Mary with a giddy, arrogant, woman's passionate dislike
to a formidable invader of her woman's kingdom, a con-
tester of her right to be regarded as the first in beauty
and grace, no less than the first in sagacious statesman-
ship.

Mr. Green's description of Elizabeth's rival, Mary, is
very striking :—"She was hardly inferior in intellectual
power to Elizabeth herself, while in fire and grace and
brilliancy of temper she stood high above her. She
brought with her the voluptuous refinement of the French
Renaissance. She would lounge for days in bed, and rise
only at night for dances and music. But her frame was
of iron and incapable of fatigue. She galloped ninety
miles after her last defeat, without a pause save to change
horses. She loved risk and adventure and the ring of
arms. As she rode in a foray against Huntley, the grim
swordsman beside her heard her wish she was a man,
'to know what life it was to lie all night in the field, or
to watch on the cawsey with a Glasgow buckler and broad-
sword.' But in the closet she was as cool and astute a
politician as Elizabeth herself, with plans as subtle, but of
a far wider and greater range than the Queen's."

When this is said, it had better be added that these
plans were for the re-establishment of the Catholic religion
in Scotland, England, and France, where the Huguenots
were then a formidable political party, and for her own
personal power and glory. She lacked utterly Elizabeth's
wise moderation and devotion to her people. Except for

the briefest interval Mary and her people were at hopeless variance. " Whatever policy is in all the chief and best practised heads of France, whatever craft, falsehood, and deceit is in all the subtle brains of Scotland, is either fresh in this woman's memory or she can fetch it out with a wet finger," wrote an English contemporary of Mary. In conclusion :—" Her beauty,[1] her exquisite grace of manner, her generosity of temper and warmth of affection, her frankness of speech, her sensibility and her gaiety, her womanly tears, her man-like courage, the play and freedom of her nature, the flashes of poetry that broke from her at every intense moment of her life, flung a spell over friend and foe which has only deepened with the lapse of years."

There is little question that Henry Stewart, Lord Darnley, brought up a strict Catholic by his mother, Lady Lennox, was from the first destined by his kindred to be Mary's husband. The marriage would unite two claimants to the English throne, and make their double claims all the more weighty. Mary claimed through her father's mother, Margaret Tudor ; he claimed through his mother's mother, the same Margaret Tudor. The Greys, of course, claimed through their mother's mother, Mary Tudor, the younger sister of Margaret. The Greys also claimed through the wills of Henry VIII. and Edward VI., which had passed over Margaret and her children. Both Lord Darnley and the Greys had the additional chance in their favour that they were born and bred in England, while Mary was alien born. The first whisper of the intended marriage between Darnley and Mary naturally aroused Elizabeth's alarm and indignation. Forthwith she proceeded to send her cousin, Lady Lennox, to the Tower for a time, on the charge of having been privy to the purpose

[1] No existing portrait of Mary gives any idea of her brown-haired peaked-faced beauty, which must have owed much to constant play of expression and charm of manner.

of marriage. It was not the lady's first, neither was it her last, experience of Tower lodgings, and, as it happened, it was always in relation to weddings projected or completed that the incarceration took place. In her youth, in the reign of her uncle, King Henry, Lady Margaret had been guilty of receiving overtures of marriage on her own account. Now it was the question of her son's marriage, later it was her granddaughter, "the Lady Arbel's," rash venture in matrimony which produced the recurrence of the unpleasant experience.

In 1652 Elizabeth, when residing at Hampton Court, was seized with small-pox, and was for a few days in danger of her life, to the horror and distress of her country. The Council showed their anxiety by keeping watch in her sick room during the hours when she was at the height of her peril—a piece of attention which might have been fatal to the patient. In her weakness Elizabeth talked of Dudley, and of her love for him, and recommended him as Lord Protector of the kingdom. On her recovery, her Parliament renewed their urgent entreaties that the Queen would marry; or, if she did not marry, that she would name her successor. It is hardly necessary to say that she ingeniously evaded giving a promise to comply with either request. As to Elizabeth's suggestion that her favourite courtier, Dudley, should be accepted as a suitor by Mary Queen of Scots, it is hard to know what to make of it. Elizabeth was quite capable of offering the suggestion in a spirit of malicious mischief to baffle the curiosity of her Court, to torment Dudley, and to mortify Mary. On the other hand, it was a suggestion persisted in and renewed, as if she had a serious intention in it. She even offered to name Mary as her successor if she would marry Dudley. Is it not possible that Elizabeth in her cooler moments desired to give what might be considered an honourable dismissal to Dudley by proposing him for the husband of the sister Queen, and that she also sought to remove out of her own path a temptation which, while she would not stoop to wed him who was her subject, certainly rendered her unwilling, in her dalliance with a forbidden inclination, to engage in a more suitable alliance?

However, one may draw a different inference from Elizabeth's unblushing remark to Mary's ambassador, Melville, that it was a pity Dudley's elder brother, Lord Warwick (a worthier man) had not the "sweet delicacy" of Lord Robert, "else she and Mary might each have had their own."

One of Elizabeth's most triumphant progresses was to the University of Cambridge, which she visited in 1564. She went at the request of Cecil (who was Chancellor of the University), but his share in the ceremonial was cut short by what was quaintly styled by the old chroniclers "an unhappy grief to his foot"—probably gout. The Mayor and Corporation met her at Newnham, delivering to her the mace and "a fair standing cup, containing twenty gold angels." Her Majesty returned the mace to the magistrate, and handed the cup to one of her footmen. After she had changed her horse she and her ladies, with their escort, rode into Cambridge. Elizabeth's riding-dress was of black velvet. She had a "caul" or cap on her head set with pearls and precious stones, and a hat spangled with gold, having a plume of feathers. She entered Queen's College, all her train alighting, the Queen alone remaining on horseback. Sir William Cecil, in spite of the "grief" in his foot, knelt to welcome her. He took the staves which the beadles of the college kissed and handed to him. He kissed the staves in his turn, and presented them to Elizabeth, there being so many that the beautiful hands, which she was so fond of displaying, could hardly encircle them. She re-delivered them to their custodians. With a merry jest she enjoined all the magistrates of the University to administer justice uprightly, or she would take the staves into her own hands, and see to it; and added, "that though the Chancellor halted his leg by being sore, yet she trusted that justice did not halt." When the orator of King's College praised her virtues, she cried out, "*Non est veritas.*" In her sudden fit of modesty "she bit her lips and fingers." She also said coyly that she would have answered him again in Latin but for fear she should speak false Latin, and then they would laugh at her.

The Queen lodged with her ladies at King's College, her stay at Cambridge lasting four days. On Sunday she attended the college chapel in state, four doctors of divinity bearing a canopy over her head. She bade her chamberlain tell the preacher that his Latin sermon was the best she had ever heard or was likely to hear. At the same time she had not hesitated to interrupt him in the middle of his discourse by sending him a gracious message that he was to put on his cap. Elizabeth was entertained in the evening with a play from Plautus performed in the same chapel.

In St. Mary's Church the Queen listened to a disputation of learned doctors. She paid great attention to the arguments; when a speaker mumbled she called out, "*Loquimini altius.*" But finding this did no good, in order to get nearer to the speaker she rose and stood at the edge of the platform erected for her accommodation.

Although the learned Queen still kept up a pretty pretence of humility with regard to her own attainments before the assembled scholars, she delighted them by replying to the public orator in Greek, and by at last consenting to address the University in Latin, while she did not forget to apologise coquettishly for paining the listeners' ears, and to express her hearty wish that all those who heard her had drunk of Lethe. "*Vivat Regina,*" shouted the scholars; "*Taceat Regina,*" responded Elizabeth.

An unfortunate incident somewhat marred the harmony of the visit. Various plays had been acted by the students for her amusement, and when she found that, after she had left Cambridge and gone as far as the Bishop of Ely's palace of Stanton, a party of lads had followed her with an unacted play still on their minds, she consented, in spite of her fatigue from the heat of the weather, to come forth from her chamber to witness the performance. Cambridge was then ultra-Protestant, and in an unlucky moment the youthful performers had fixed on a representation which should express their sentiments with little taste and discretion, and with still less regard for the feelings of thousands of their countrymen. The Cambridge students chose to act a burlesque of the most cherished Roman Catholic tenets, introducing and parodying not only the distinguishing doctrines, but the leaders among the priests and bishops. Bonner was portrayed carrying in his arms a lamb, at which he gnashed his teeth; a dog followed, with the Host in his mouth. Elizabeth, half a Roman Catholic at heart, and consistently opposed to gratuitous outrages of any kind, indignantly left the room, while the discomfited players had to bring their piece to a summary conclusion,

Another instance occurred in the following year of the degree to which the Queen was offended by any public attack on the Roman Catholic Church. She had gone to Paul's Cross to hear a sermon preached by Dr. Nowell, Dean of St. Paul's. In the course of the sermon the preacher thought fit to inveigh against the worship of images. The Queen stopped him without ceremony. "Leave that alone. To your text, Mr. Dean: we have heard enough of that," she cried. The unfortunate Dean stammered, unable to go on, while many of the Protestant congregation were in tears.

Little wonder that some of the Reformed Churchmen retaliated, and that one of them spoke of Elizabeth in the

pulpit to her face as having fallen away from her early
promise, and degenerated into "an untamed heifer"—an
example of plain speaking of which Elizabeth showed her
opinion by quitting the church.

Elizabeth did not always resent plain speaking ; on the
contrary, she encouraged it in those who came near her,
even though they were the meanest of her subjects, and
enjoyed, above all things, holding her own, and disarming
her companions by sheer force of wit. She was frank and
free of speech, like her father King Henry, though also,
like King Henry, she could still retain her majesty of
demeanour, and in some moods it was playing with fire
and venturing within the lion's jaws to thwart and pro-
voke her. When Sir James Melville, Mary's envoy, was
on a diplomatic errand at Elizabeth's court, chiefly to get
Lord Darnley to go to Scotland that his marriage might
be arranged with Mary, Elizabeth professed to Melville
that she would never marry unless the Queen of Scots'
behaviour compelled her to, upon which the ambassador
swore roundly, "Madam, ye need not tell me that. I
know your stately stomach. Ye think gin ye were
married ye would be but *Queen* of England, and now
ye are baith King and Queen ye may not suffer a
commander."

Elizabeth scouted "that long lad Darnley," as a husband
for Mary, and pressed the trusty envoy with questions
respecting her beauty—whether his Queen's hair or hers
was the best, which of the two was fairest, which of them
was of the highest stature. The bated man tried to get
out of the difficulty by replying with dry humour that
the fairness of both was not their worst fault, that
Elizabeth was the fairest Queen in England, and Mary
the fairest Queen in Scotland, &c. When he avowed
that his queen was the tallest, Elizabeth remarked with
what one is compelled to call regal pertness, "Then she
is over high, for I am neither too high nor too low."

The Queen took every means of impressing her cousin's messenger with her own personal attractions. Having told him that she had "weeds" or costumes of every country, she appeared in a fresh one each day, asking him which became her most. She contrived that he should, as if by accident, hear her play on the virginals, just as she had contrived, three years before, that one of the Guise princes, then in England, should see her dance. After Melville had heard her play, she urged him to say whether she or the Queen of Scots played best, and had the satisfaction of hearing the honest arbiter admit that Elizabeth was the best musician. She spoke to him in Italian and Dutch (German), in order to display her skill in languages. She wound up the exhibition by dancing before him, after she had detained him two days, according to his account, till she could find an opportunity; she then asked him whether she or his queen danced best. The gentleman answered with a "canny" reservation that his queen danced not so highly and disposedly as Elizabeth danced. The Queen, who thus displayed the aggressive unbridled vanity of the silliest, most forward chit in her kingdom, was then in the dignified prime of her thirty-first year. Moreover, she was ruling England with the wisdom of Solomon, and eclipsing all the statesmen in Europe by the subtlety of her Machiavellian policy.

In the meantime Mary Queen of Scots, with whose fortunes those of Elizabeth are inextricably mingled, was pursuing her disastrous course. Mary began by taking the hearts of her subjects by storm with her youth, beauty, and endless fascinations; but she soon alienated her people as completely. A gulf divided their religious principles and practices from hers. She had a high spirit, which did not easily brook control, and an extravagant love of pleasure. Her uncles, the Guises, exercised as prejudicial an influence over her as that by which they had swayed her mother. The younger Mary's self-will and estranged sympathies—for she was in everything French, not Scotch —speedily formed a strong party against her, a party which was led before long by her ambitious but patriotic and enlightened half-brother, the Earl of Murray.

Mary braved the wrath of Elizabeth and married Darnley, the most suitable husband that could be found for her; yet never was marriage more ill-fated, or a surer stage on the road to ruin. Darnley, not yet twenty, was a vicious, ill-mannered young fool, whose excesses, together with his rude arrogance, disgusted his high-bred, brilliantly-endowed wife. Only one bright spot broke the gloom of the wretched marriage. This was the birth of Mary's son, James VI., on the 19th of June 1566. The news was brought by Sir James Melville to Elizabeth at Greenwich. She was dancing, after supper, when the envoy arrived, and Cecil whispered into his Queen's ear the momentous tidings. Suddenly the music and dancing ceased, while Elizabeth flung herself on a seat, laid her head on her hand, and complained bitterly to the ladies nearest to her that the Queen of Scots had a fair son, while the stock to which she belonged was barren. When advised to mask her annoyance, she did it so effectually that she received Melville with a girlish skip of apparent delight at his news, overwhelmed him with congratulations, consented to stand as " cummer," or godmother, at the prince's christening, and sent down to Scotland, as her gift, a golden font, which cost a thousand pounds.

In the August of 1566 Elizabeth honoured the University of Oxford, as she had honoured Cambridge, with a visit, and the stay at Oxford was even a greater success than that at Cambridge, for at Oxford no violent Puritan demonstration was likely to disturb the peaceful rejoicings, notwithstanding Elizabeth did not scruple to twit Dr. Humphreys, the acknowledged head of the Puritans at Oxford, with the gay jest, " Mr. Doctor, that loose gown becomes you well. I wonder your notions should be so narrow."

Elizabeth had journeyed by her old prison of Woodstock, in which she had spent so many weary days twelve years before. At Wolvercote she was met by Leicester, the Chancellor of the University, the heads of houses in their hoods and gowns, and the magistrates in their robes. The city mace was given up, and given back; the silvergilt cup, with old gold pieces, was received. She then approached the city of towers by the north avenue "in the glow of an August sunset." Her carriage entered by the north gate, and she had before her, Mr. Froude points out, "the black tower of the Boccardo prison, in which Cranmer had lain, and the ditch where he had died." She drove up the Corn Market between rows of shouting students, calling "*Vivat Regina*," to which she replied, "*Gratias ago, gratias ago.*"

Then at Carfax, where, forty years before, Bishop Longlands burnt Tyndal's Testaments, an orator addressed her in Greek, and she answered in the same language. She was lodged in Christchurch, and entertained, as at Cambridge, with plays and disputations, to which she listened with equal zest. Two comical incidents are recorded as happening when the Queen was at Oxford. In one of the plays the cry of hounds in full chase was introduced. It was caught up by the young scholars in the windows of the hall and in the quadrangle below, accompanied with shouts, "Caught! He's caught!"

" Oh, excellent ! " cried the Queen from her box; "the boys, in very truth, are ready to leap from the windows to follow the hounds."

At the disputation in St. Mary's Church, a learned doctor prolonged his discourse to so great a length that Elizabeth, who was in general the most interested of listeners, sent a peremptory message to him to end without delay. In spite of it, the orator continued to declaim for half an hour longer. The Queen was the more annoyed because she had meant to speak herself, and had to put off her speech till next day. She sent another message to demand angrily how the speaker could presume to go on when she had told him to stop. Whereupon the poor man had to confess humbly that, as he was delivering a harangue learnt by heart, he dared not leave out any part lest he should "lose his cue" and be brought to shame before the University and the court. Elizabeth was immediately appeased, and laughed heartily, while the lesson which she proceeded to administer to the fettered man was by example, and not by precept. In the course of the Latin oration which she made to the whole University, she interrupted herself in order to direct one of the attendants to bring a stool, that Cecil might not need to stand on his lame foot. Presently she resumed her discourse, with the same eloquence that had distinguished it from the beginning.

Elizabeth stayed five days at Oxford, sumptuously entertained to the last day. She was begged by the Commissary and proctors to accept "six pairs of very fine gloves." It is said the very town walls were papered with verses in her honour. After dinner on the last of "these bright days, Elizabeth heard one more oration, a farewell one this time," and rode away over Magdalen Bridge. As she crested Headington Hill, she reined in her horse and looked back. There lay the city and its spires, among clustering masses of college elms. There wound the silvery lines of the Cherwell and Isis. "Farewell, Oxford!" she cried; "farewell, my good subjects here! farewell, my dear scholars, and may God prosper your study! Farewell, farewell!"

While Elizabeth was thus adding to her peaceful triumphs, and winning more and more the love and admiration of her people, in Scotland Mary's affairs had arrived at a fatal crisis. Who does not know that sombre and piteous tragedy, sombre by reason of the guilt of the victims; piteous because of the youth, beauty, and rank of the unhappy Queen? Before the birth of her child, Darnley had inflicted on his wife the gross insult of being one of the conspirators who engaged in the brutal murder of her secretary and musician, David Rizzio. Mary, in her turn, had taken a cruel revenge, culminating, in February 1567, in the blowing up of Kirk-on-Fields, in which Darnley lay sick. It is hardly possible to believe that she was not cognisant of the deed when she married within three months, whether coerced into the marriage or of her free will, his murderer, Bothwell, the boldest and worst of her nobles on whom she had showered favours.

Then followed, in quick succession, the rising of her incensed subjects, the proclamation of her infant son, James VI., her defeat in the battle of Carberry Hill, the flight and disappearance of Bothwell, her imprisonment in Loch Leven Castle, her romantic escape, her second defeat at Langsyde, and her flight into England. She was then twenty-five years of age—the age of Elizabeth when she ascended the English throne. There can be no doubt that Mary's arrival in England was unwelcome to Elizabeth, that it filled her with extreme alarm, and that she placed her from the first in custody because she did not know how to dispose of her sister queen and cousin otherwise. Elizabeth had already been scandalised by the news of the death of Darnley, who was her kinsman and subject, and by Mary's marriage with Bothwell. The Queen had shown sufficient feeling for the murdered man's mother, her cousin, Lady Lennox, to cause her to be released from the Tower, and to express friendly sympathy with her. On the other hand, cordially as Elizabeth detested Mary, her *esprit de corps* was outraged by the knowledge of a contemporary sovereign's degradation, and the fact that she had been driven from her throne and kingdom by her insurgent subjects. Accordingly, when Lord and Lady Lennox demanded vengeance for the murder of their son,

and urged that Mary should be brought to trial as accessory
to the crime, Elizabeth answered coldly and haughtily.
Old Camden remarks warily: "Queen Elizabeth seemed
—for who can dive into the secret meanings of princes,
and wise men do keep their thoughts locked up within
the closets of their breasts—seriously to commiserate the
most afflicted princess, her kinswoman." Nevertheless
she answered the countess's cry for vengeance with the
stern reminder that "Lady Lennox should not charge a
crime on so great a princess, her (Elizabeth's) near kinswoman, which could not be proven by certain evidence."

Well did Elizabeth know that Mary's presence in England was that of a deadly enemy, and she did her best to
get rid of her honourably in the first place. She urged
in vain on Mary's half-brother, Regent Murray, to suppress the graver charges against his sister, and reinstate
her on her throne, and she also urged, in vain, on Mary to
abdicate in favour of her son, and to leave Murray in
possession of his power as Regent, while she was permitted
to return to Scotland in safety.

When everything else failed, Elizabeth had no choice
save to detain Mary in custody, though the Queen of
Scots did not hesitate to say that "if they kept her a
prisoner they should have enough to do with her." What
she asked was either help in money and arms, to restore
her to her throne, or a free passage to France. Both demands were not in Elizabeth's power to grant with any
prospect of peace. Mary would not submit to a legal trial
of her guilt or innocence. Elizabeth had no right then,
though she assumed it later, to bring her to trial, while to
send her to France was to raise the French Catholics in
her favour, and promote a French invasion of Scotland.
The third alternative, of letting her loose in England, was
to make her the centre of a hundred Catholic plots—a far
more dangerous presence in the kingdom than the presence
of Catherine of Aragon's daughter, Elizabeth's sister Mary,

had been in Henry VIII.'s day. Mary Queen of Scots free
in England, Elizabeth's crown would not be secure on her
head for an hour. So untenable was the position, that
though Mary could not have anticipated Elizabeth's course,
and probably trusted a good deal to a personal interview
and a cunning, wily tongue, it is scarcely conceivable that
so crafty a politician could have expected her requests to
be granted. She sought to temporise, to gain time, while
she had escaped for the present from her furious enemies.

There was little leisure, in the troubles of the time, for
Elizabeth to mourn for her former tutor, Roger Ascham,
who died in 1568, yet she took breath to say of him that
she would rather have lost ten thousand pounds than her
schoolmaster. In spite of her patronage, Ascham died
poor, and one learns with wonder and regret, from Camden, that the great scholar lost his means by indulgence
in the practices of cock-fighting and "dicing."

The Roman Catholics in England allowed Mary's misfortunes to cancel her crime, and rose on her behalf in
1569, under the Earls of Northumberland and Westmoreland. The insurrection was speedily put down, but it was
a sign of the times, which did not increase Elizabeth's
charitable inclinations towards Mary. Accordingly there
began for the Queen of Scots that series of detentions in
the castles of trusty servants of Elizabeth, by whom the
prisoner was kept under strict watch and ward for so
many years. The Pope excommunicated Elizabeth, and
Regent Murray was assassinated without any material
change in the attitude of the contending parties.

Elizabeth was still trifling with her suitors, shrewd
enough to make up her mind to marry none of them, yet
politic and coquettish enough to leave them doubtful of
her ultimate purpose.

She kept the Archduke Charles dangling after her for
seven years, and was exceedingly indignant when he married at the end of the term. In fact, she always resented

the marriages of her former suitors. Like the fox which lost his tail and wished the loss to become the fashion, she desired that her spinsterhood should be duly honoured by the corresponding bachelorhood of her lovers. One only fulfilled the condition—Sir Christopher Hatton, whose nimble dancing of the "brawls" is said to have procured for him from his sovereign the Lord Chancellor's seals, which he used wisely and worthily enough. Light-footed Sir Christopher is reported to have been the only one of Elizabeth's many lovers who lived and died a bachelor for her sake.

For some years, about this time, a marriage between the Queen and one of the French princes, Henry of Anjou, afterwards Henry III. of France, was much discussed. With her ineradicable craving to be at least equal in all things to her royal prisoner Mary, Elizabeth showed more liking for this match than for most of the others proposed to her. Perhaps after all it was because of her restless spirit of contradiction, since she knew that her Council were not likely to agree to a union with France.

When Anjou, to Elizabeth's great disgust, withdrew his pretensions to her hand, his mother, Catherine, brought forward her youngest son, Alençon, who was understood to be more complacent in the matter of adopting the Protestant religion; but he was a mere lad of seventeen, while Elizabeth was a woman of thirty-eight, and the comment was at once made that the couple would look like mother and son. In addition, Alençon was a little fellow, grotesquely ugly. However, Elizabeth, as usual, professed to give careful consideration to his suit. Certainly Leicester's star was not then in the ascendant. There were coolnesses between him and the Queen. He was mixed up with the Duke of Norfolk's designs of liberating and marrying Mary Queen of Scots. Letters on the subject, concealed in beer-bottles, were said to pass between the Duke and the Earl. When Elizabeth's suspicions were aroused, Leicester is reported to have undergone a violent panic lest his connection with the project should be brought to light. Norfolk was the first Catholic nobleman in the kingdom; he was also Elizabeth's connection through her mother's mother, who was a Howard. The Queen always showed kindness to the Howards, and she did not suffer her Council to descend on Norfolk without giving him warning. Let him take care on what pillow he rested his head, she told him, meaningly; but the man was doomed! The proofs of his plots on behalf of Mary were beyond question. He was arrested, and tried by his peers. He walked to the place of trial with the executioner's axe carried before him, the sharp edge turned outwards; he came back with the edge turned inwards, the signal of his condemnation. After signing his death-warrant, Elizabeth revoked it no less than four times, and the struggle she passed through cost her a dangerous illness, during which Leicester, restored to her good graces, and Cecil, now Lord Burleigh, watched three whole nights by her bed. Eventually the Queen was restored to health, and Norfolk was executed on Tower Hill—as his father had been before him—in 1572.

In the meantime, Elizabeth's England was, under her fostering, unslumbering care, flourishing on every side, and recovering more than its former might. Scotland, on the contrary, ravaged by civil war, was, but for its staunch Protestantism, and its heroic reformer, John Knox, a scene of desolation. The result was, in either case, largely the work of a woman—the consequence of Elizabeth's superb sense, strong curb on her nature, and high conception of duty, where the welfare of the nation was concerned, and of Mary's undisciplined spirit, reckless self-indulgence, and unbridled passions. In England, vagabonds and beggars had been put down by royal statute as they had never been restrained before. The land was under constant cultivation. Manufactures, especially the woollen

manufactures, received steady support, and throve apace.
" Every little harbour sent out its fleet of fishing-boats,"
and trading ships began to extend the commerce, which
had hitherto prevailed chiefly with Flanders, as far as
Archangel, the Indies, Guinea, &c. Though young Raleigh
and Sir Humphrey Gilbert had not yet started in search
of El Dorado, Sir Thomas Gresham had found a model
for his Bourse in Antwerp, and thought to console himself for the death of his only son by building its fellow on
Cornhill, and presenting it as a gift to the merchants of
London. Elizabeth loved " my merchant," as she called
him, in his peaked cap and furred gown, and graced " the
festival of the Bourse " at its opening with her regal presence. She first dined with Sir Thomas Gresham at his
house in Bishopsgate Street, and then went in the evening, when the building was brilliantly illuminated, and
inspected it with the greatest interest, bestowing on it the
name of the Royal Exchange.

The habits of the people were undergoing a refining
change under the sunshine of prosperity in which the
whole country was basking. Mr. Green calls attention to
the march of progress. Houses of stone took the place
of the old wattled houses, pewter superseded wood for
trenchers. Meat was taken frequently in the room of
stock-fish. Carpets were laid down where rushes had
been strewn. In great houses "costly wainscoting, the
cumbrous but elaborate beds, the carved staircases, &c.,
marked her increase of wealth and taste." The prodigal
use of glass became a new feature in this changed England. So did the rich stuffs employed in dress, and the
increased cost of living. Elizabeth had no less than three
thousand robes, and we are told they were rivalled in
their bravery by "the cut velvets, the ruffs, the jewelled
purpoints" around her. But while masques and pastorals
were paving the way for English plays, and the new old
learning of Greece and Rome was beginning to be spread

by the grammar schools broadcast over the country, and the Bible in the English language was exercising a still more marvellous influence on the intellect as well as on the religious standards of the people, the giants in literature who have made Elizabeth's reign famous had still to appear. Shakespeare was simply the wool-stapler's son at Stratford-on-Avon. Spenser was still a lad, and not a particularly promising lad, at Cambridge. Ben Jonson, the youngest of the three, had not begun his scramble for education at Westminster School. Even Elizabeth's two sworn knights, the pink of courtesy and gallant adventure, Sir Walter Raleigh and Sir Philip Sidney, had barely come into view. Raleigh, at the age of twenty-six years, was on the point of returning from a prolonged campaign in the Low Countries. Sir Philip Sidney, Leicester's nephew, at the age of twenty-two, was spending his two years of leave to travel in France. Mary Sidney, his dearly-loved sister; Penelope, Lady Rich, who was to be the "Stella" of his *Asphodel;* Frances Walsingham, who was to be the "Pastorella" of Spenser's *Faëry Queen,* and Sidney's future wife; Elizabeth Throckmorton, for whom Raleigh was to be thrown into the Tower, were but a cluster of young girls, strangers to Elizabeth's brilliant court.

THE OLD QUEEN.[1]

Mr. Froude has given us a vigorous though somewhat startling description of Elizabeth as she approached middle life. She was hard of feature and harsh of voice. Her humours had not grown weak with age; but she was free of access, quick-witted, familiar, and frank with men of all degrees. She was familiar in act also. She collared her Chancellor, Sir Christopher Hatton; she boxed the ears of other offenders; she gave Gilbert Talbot, the Earl of

[1] Agnes Strickland, Froude, Green, Beesley, Brewer (Essays), Camden.

Shrewsbury's son, "a fillip on the forehead "the first time
she met him after he had walked early in the tilt-yard, and,
looking up to the Queen's window, had seen her standing
there in her night-cap.   She stooped down and kissed her
youthful suitor, the Duc d'Alençon, when walking with
him, in the presence of the French Ambassador and other
witnesses, in the gallery at Greenwich.   "She rode, shot,
jested, and drank beer,[1] spat, swore upon occasions—
swore, not like 'a comfitmaker's wife,' but round, mouth-
filling oaths, . . . yet with the queenly dignity never so
impaired that liberties could be ventured in return."

Rough and coarse as Elizabeth's manners were, the
queen and woman was invested with a certain fantastical
idealisation and glamour of stateliness and grace handed
down from the days of chivalry. She loved to be addressed
with the most high-flown compliments, to which she replied in the same strain.   Her courtiers were perforce her
humble adorers; and while in one light she laughed at
them and their professions, in another, that of her inordinate vanity, she was still well pleased to view them as
so many despairing heart-broken lovers—victims to her
irresistible charms of person and mind.   These she grew
to regard as almost superhuman.

With Elizabeth's great statesmen she was no fool, though
she was not unwilling that even they should flatter her.
She was clear-headed and plain-spoken.   Her highly successful policy might not be very creditable, for it was that
of a trimmer and temporiser, who played off France against
Spain, and Scotland and the Netherlands against both;
but it was an exceedingly shrewd and consistent policy.
The worst of it was that it was steeped in duplicity.   It
was "both dishonourable and dangerous," Walsingham,
her secretary, complained, for she never kept a promise
which was inconvenient to her, and in turn all who dealt

---

[1] She was unwilling to drink wine unless it was largely mixed with
water. She was still more temperate in age than in youth.

with her distrusted her. Her vacillation is said to have been caused by her absolute personal impartiality to the actors and events which were her environment. Her parsimony was exhibited in her disposition to grudge every penny that was spent on the public expenses. All the same, never queen had better servants than she possessed, men so faithful in the discharge of their duties, so jealous of her honour, so attached to her individually. Burleigh wept for incurring her displeasure ; Walsingham ruined himself to spare her purse, and, according to Camden, was buried at night because he had died so poor that his family could not afford the expense of a public funeral. Her poets, philosophers, great sea-captains, in the foremost ranks of their fellows in all lands and ages, lavished on her their homage.

Even among those whom one of Elizabeth's later biographers has defined as her "human playthings," "lapdogs," and "tame cats"—Leicester, Hatton, Raleigh, Harington, Essex, Mountjoy—the two last young enough to be her sons, with whom she was foolish and reckless; whom she nicknamed by absurd pet names her "sweet Robin," her "sweet liddes," her "sheep;" on whom she squandered her favours and her revenue—there were men who loved her truly after their fashion—Hatton, her godson Harington, possibly the ill-fated Essex, in spite of his violence.

It is right to say here that modern historians have sifted contemporaneous scandals, gross with the grossness of a coarse, unscrupulous generation, and have arrived at the conclusion that Elizabeth's deadliest enemies, the ambassadors and envoys of Philip of Spain, were compelled at last to relinquish the hope of finding in her heedless levity and high-handed wilfulness any trace of the vice and crime which were brought home to her brilliant rival Mary Queen of Scots, so that only the most strongly biassed or credulous of partisans can doubt their existence.

The last royal suitor whose suit Elizabeth entertained

was still the Duc d'Alençon, youngest son of Catherine de Medicis and Henri II.; she was forty-six, he was half her age. Time had not dealt kindly with her. It had accentuated her aquiline features, withered her fair skin, and rendered her yellow wigs out of keeping. But sharpened as her pointed nose and chin were, and spare and angular her once fine figure, she was still a woman majestic even in her increasing masculineness.

Here is the parallel picture by Froude of Alençon, or Anjou, as he became afterwards : " A small brown creature, deeply pock-marked, with a large head, a knobbed nose, and a hoarse, croaking voice." Elizabeth called him her " frog."

Alençon came to England, and was received by Elizabeth with the greatest attention and apparent satisfaction; in fact, she represented herself as enchanted with him. Her councillors and people, who had so often urged her to marry, were keenly opposed to the match. Not only was the fate of Mary Tudor in their minds; they wished no alliance with a Roman Catholic and a Valois. Nobody had forgotten the terrible livery, " turned up with crimson," bestowed on the Huguenots when they went with the young King of Navarre to Paris that he might wed Margaret of Valois, and the wedding was signalised by the hideous massacre of St. Bartholomew. But Elizabeth was the soul of perversity, above all when she was not obliged to stand by her waywardness, but could display it as a passing freak, pardonable by way of variety in a charming woman and mighty queen. Besides, her heart was sore and bitter at the time. It was not long after she had made the royal progress to Kenilworth, which Sir Walter Scott has immortalised. She had honoured her Master of the Horse by becoming his guest for several days, and he had responded to her graciousness by the magnificent reception he had prepared for her, and the large sums of money he had spent on gorgeous masks and

pageants for her entertainment. The days of her early
excessive partiality for the Earl, with the probability of
her giving her hand to her subject, were past; so was the
pathetic little tragedy connected with his first wife, Amy
Robsart, who, whatever Sir Walter might say in future,
had lain for years at rest in her grave before the altar in
St. Mary the Virgin, Oxford. But the terms on which the
Queen and her Master of the Horse stood, still pointed
to the most sentimental of friendships, which had lasted for
more than twenty years. If time had touched her, it had
not spared him. He was growing bald, white-bearded,
and red-faced, though still stately in figure, and imposing
in presence, in the rich, picturesque dress of the day.

Elizabeth could not brook a rival in these sentimental
friendships, which she cultivated extensively. She hated
the mention of marriage among her ladies and gentlemen.
Her example ought to be enough for them. The slightest
mark of her regard should be worth more than family
affection and domestic ties. Yet she was forced to listen
presently to floating rumours—unfounded in the one case,
but proved beyond doubt in the other—that Sir Christopher Hatton and Lord Leicester had both married without
her permission. Hatton was found innocent of doing
anything save dangling, moth-like, round the light of his
eyes in the person of his royal mistress. Robert Dudley,
Earl of Leicester, was shown to have married secretly a
thoroughly unprincipled woman, Lettice Knollys, widow
of Walter Devereux, Earl of Essex. She was, through
her grandmother, Mary Boleyn (sister to Queen Anne),
Elizabeth's cousin once removed.

Nay, there was a suspicion that, in addition to his
marriage with Amy Robsart, which was public, and his
private marriage with Lettice Knollys, he had, in the interval between, entered into one of the miserable secret
contracts, which he did not hesitate to break, with another
cousin of Elizabeth's on the Howard instead of the Boleyn

side of her house.   Camden alludes warily, and not without a touch of humour, to this reported second marriage.
After saying that the earl had in his youthful days been
very complaisant to ladies, the old historian adds, that when
Leicester grew almost past it, he "expressed a strange
fondness for marriage."

Penetrated by what was to the Queen the base ingratitude still more than the treachery of the act, Elizabeth
made a feint of compelling herself, with floods of tears, to
sign the passport for Alençon's journey to England, which
was understood to be the first step to their marriage.   Yet
when not only Hatton, with genuine tears in his eyes, but
Leicester, with sarcasm on his lips, ventured to enter her
presence-chamber and appeal to her as to the truth of
her intentions, she simply laughed at the fright she had
given them, and said she would never marry Alençon or
any man.

A still stranger contradiction came to pass where the
Alençon marriage was in question.   Elizabeth acted in a
manner quite opposed to the usual absence of vindictiveness in her character.   For it could be said of her, that
"she neither remembered an injury nor suspected a treason," so confident was she in her unshaken supremacy and
unbounded self-esteem.   She could fly into a passion like
her father, King Henry; but as a rule she did not know the
meaning of the word "vindictiveness."   However, on the
point of her marriage with Alençon—a piece of mockery
which she never intended to turn into earnest—she was
guilty of a deed of revengeful cruelty.   The well-known
Puritan, Stubbs, wrote a pamphlet against the marriage,
and had it printed and circulated.   In the pamphlet he
not only attacked the whole house of Valois, and denounced
Alençon as depraved; he referred in the most uncourtly
terms to the delicate subject of Elizabeth's middle age.
She had Stubbs, his bookseller, and printer arrested.   It
is believed she would have hanged them if she could.

Failing that extreme measure, in which the law would not support her, she consented to the sentence by which Stubbs's right hand and that of his bookseller were struck off with a cleaver. One of the undaunted men cried, "There lies the hand of a true Englishman!" The other, Stubbs, waved his hat above his head with his left hand, and led the shout, "God save Queen Elizabeth!" till he fell fainting from loss of blood.

It is a relief to view Elizabeth in another light—that of the cordial admirer and liberal rewarder of her sailor Drake, who was to pay back her favours a hundred-fold. Drake, in his voyages to the West Indies, had already begun to "singe the King of Spain's beard." It must be admitted that even in holding the Queen's roving commission, which she gave him in 1572, his mode of warfare would now be considered decidedly buccaneering and piratical. England was not at war with Spain, yet Drake not only engaged every rich galleon he encountered; he landed, captured, and plundered many of the towns on the Spanish main, both in the islands and on the coast of South America, returning in 1573 laden with spoil, and naturally pursued by the complaints and threats of King Philip. Cautious as Elizabeth was of giving provocation to her neighbours, she could not resist acknowledging the prodigies of valour performed by Drake and his little fleet. Later, she not only went so far as graciously to accept the offerings he made to her on his return from his voyage round the world in the *Pelican;* she went from her palace at Greenwich to Deptford in order to dine with him on board his ship, and confer on him the distinction of knighthood. One of her gifts to him was a sumptuous piece of goldsmith's work in the form of a silver ship.

Elizabeth was deeply concerned in the struggle going on in the Netherlands between the Dutch Protestants on the one side, and on the other Spain's representatives, the terrible Alva and the Prince of Parma. It was the

prompting alike of her policy in seeking to preserve the
balance of power between her natural enemies in other
European states, and of such sympathy as she had with
the fairness of granting a certain amount of political and
religious freedom to the people, to do what she could for
foreign Protestants.   She helped the Huguenots in France,
and probably helped them more effectually by doing it
diplomatically instead of by coming to an open rupture
with the Catholics.   In the same way she aided the Dutch
by her treaties with France and Spain while still at peace
with Philip, and when the gauntlet was thrown down, by
both money and troops.   But she was far too sagacious,
too concerned for the welfare of England, to be tempted
by the lure of the sovereignty of the revolted states in the
Low Countries, which the Prince of Orange was empowered
to offer her.   Had she caught at the crown of the same
wealthy trading states which had been settled on her
sister Mary at her marriage with Philip, she would have
entangled England in an endless contest; for Spain,
which had been till then the greatest power in Europe,
would not have tamely yielded her richest possessions.
Elizabeth would also have defeated her own purpose of
so consolidating and developing the resources of her
kingdom as to raise it to a high place among the nations.
Vulgar personal ambition, the mere desire to add crown
to crown, and to figure as the ruler of more countries than one, was beneath Elizabeth.   When war was
eventually declared between England and Spain by the
expulsion rather than the withdrawal of the Spanish
ambassador, the Queen was at liberty to pursue a more
honourable course than that which had expressed itself in
holding out fresh hopes to Alençon in order to secure an
alliance with his brother, Henry III. of France, against
Spain.   The immediate result of the manœuvre was the
speedy death from consumption of the cheated and mortified would-be bridegroom.   At this catastrophe, Elizabeth

shut herself up, put the court into mourning, and assumed the tone of an inconsolable widow.

When this phase passed, an English force was in Holland under the command of no less a personage than the Earl of Leicester. He was destitute of military skill, and he has been accused of cowardice; but he showed no want of patriotism on the occasion. He not only defrayed his own expenses, mortgaging his estates for the purpose, he laid out large sums on his army. According to Elizabeth's latest historian, Professor Beesley, Leicester was not so unsuitable a person for the office he held as has been supposed; neither was his appointment solely owing to one of the freaks of a woman's fancy. Leicester had become, by his Queen's favour, a great English nobleman. He was known to have her confidence. He was also understood to be trusted by Burleigh and Walsingham. In many respects he was acceptable as her representative—not only as lieutenant-general of her troops, but as governor-general of the provinces, the post which was immediately offered to him by the Dutch states. His acceptance of it—with the concurrence of Elizabeth's Council, it is supposed—but without consulting the Queen, seriously angered her, and his rule was neither wise nor successful.

In the course of the fighting in the Netherlands, a far nobler life than Leicester's was laid down. It was that of his nephew, Sir Philip Sidney, who held a command under his uncle. Sir Philip, the flower of English knighthood, had not reached his thirty-second year, but he had already formed fast friendships with Languet, one of the learned leaders of the French reformers, and with William of Orange, the staunch champion of Protestantism. Sidney had loved and wooed in vain the "Stella" of his sonnets, Penelope Devereux, the daughter of Elizabeth's cousin, Lettice Lady Essex, whom Sidney's uncle had married. In this case it was "like mother, like daughter." "Stella" was more of a bane than a boon to the lover of her youth.

She was reputed the most beautiful woman of her day. Her red blood was said to be like rich wine under her skin. Her eyes, like those of another beauty, Madame de Sévigné, were *bizarrês*—they did not match in hue.   She married, while still very young, Sir Robert Rich.   Sidney had been now smiled upon, now frowned upon, by Elizabeth, who was by turns charmed with his gifts and virtues, and offended by his strenuous efforts to get her to act more decidedly in favour of the foreign Protestants, and by his unqualified protest against the marriage with Alençon.

It was while under a cloud at court that Sidney withdrew to Wilton, the seat of the Earl of Pembroke, the husband of Mary Sidney, Sir Philip's dearly loved sister. She is immortalised in Ben Jonson's famous epitaph :—

> " Underneath this sable hearse,
> Lies the subject of all verse—
> Sidney's sister, Pembroke's mother.
> Death, ere thou hast slain another
> Learn'd, and fair, and good as she,
> Time shall throw a dart at thee."

Camden writes of her quaintly as "a lady much addicted to poetry, and other pleasant studies."

In such congenial society Sir Philip wrote his prose romance " Arcadia," and called it " The Countess of Pembroke's Arcadia."   He married Frances Walsingham, only child of Sir Francis, and the " Pastorella " of Edmund Spenser.   The compliment may be explained by the fact that Sidney and Spenser were friends, and it was to Sidney that Spenser dedicated his " Shepherd's Calender."

When with his uncle in the Netherlands, Sir Philip was wounded at the capture of Zutphen, where he led the charge in three different attacks.   As he was carried off the field the incident occurred which is recorded by his friend from boyhood, Fulke Greville.   Being thirsty from excess of bleeding, the wounded man called for drink.   As he was putting the bottle to his mouth he saw a soldier in extremity looking eagerly at it. Without drinking he passed the draught to his comrade, saying with unselfish consideration, "Thy necessity is yet greater than mine."

Sir Philip was taken to Arnheim, where he survived for five and twenty days, cared for by Leicester, who had never failed in affection for him, and devotedly nursed by his wife and his brother Robert. There, in Mr. Froude's eloquent words, "in musical discourses on the immortality of the soul, on poetry, Plato, and the Bible, and the vanity of the world, his spirit sang itself swan-like away." Elizabeth was so concerned to hear of Sidney's danger that she sent a messenger to the Low Countries for the express purpose of conveying her sympathy and ascertaining his state.

One of the great crises of Elizabeth's life was at hand. Her position with regard to her rival, Mary Queen of Scots, a prisoner in England, was getting absolutely untenable. It had lasted nearly eighteen years; but towards the end of the time it was viewed with utter distrust and growing alarm amounting to panic by Elizabeth's wisest and most faithful councillors, and by the mass of her Protestant subjects. Year by year, almost month by month, it was rendered clearer that the situation must end in the death of one of the Queens. Not only did Spain pronounce its opinion that it would be a saintly deed to take Elizabeth's life ; the Pope directed a crusade against her. The plots of the English Catholics for the assassination of the Queen followed thick and fast on each other. Somerville, Throckmorton, Babington, were arrested not an hour too soon. The whole of Protestant England was wild with dismay. So convinced were the Council of the probable murder of Elizabeth while no successor to the throne was appointed, and of their being confronted with Mary and her claims as next in the order of succession, backed by the whole body of English and Scotch Catholics, and by the combined powers of France and Spain, that an extraordinary

step was taken. The Council drew up a bond of association which became afterwards an Act of Parliament,
authorising them to resist and pursue to death any conspirator aiming at Elizabeth's life, or any person in whose
behalf the conspiracy was organised. The last clause was
a bold attempt to secure the English statesmen from being
compelled to submit to Mary and acknowledge a right
bought by the most sinister bloodshed.

Elizabeth was less disturbed than her Protestant subjects. In her overweening confidence she was careless of
her personal safety. In spite of plot after plot brought
home to the conspirators, with more or less proof of Mary's
cognisance and support of them, the English Queen rather
scouted the danger she ran. She could make her plaint
to the French envoy, " her features working with passion,"
that the Queen of Scots had three times attempted her
life, and that she—Elizabeth—was " a poor, lone woman,
surrounded by enemies." But in another and much more
characteristic mood she bandied grim jests with her
ministers, and declared she would come back after she
was dead and see the Queen of Scots "making their
heads fly."

The archbishops and bishops of the English Church
sought an interview with Elizabeth, to lay before her their
unanimous opinion that it would be no crime, but the reverse, to cause justice to be done on Mary Stuart. They
instanced, as examples in point, the deaths of Jezebel and
Athalia, and the ruin brought on Saul by his refraining
from taking vengeance on Agag.

The Queen put her advisers off with evasive answers.
Parliament made their prayer in the same strain, and she
begged, after three days' consideration, that they would
find "another way." Her declaration afterwards was, that
for fifteen years she, and she alone, at the peril of her life,
had stood between the Queen of Scots and death ; and the
truth of the assertion is now generally admitted. There

is no greater instance of irony in history than the popular delusion which long condemned Elizabeth—not as the crafty and double-tongued politician; not for the levity inherited from her mother; not for the sudden fierce blazes of passion which burst out on any check to her will, and were for the most part as short-lived as they were violent; not for the ill-judged thrift which grudged money for the maintenance of her government, and the equally ill-judged liberality which squandered it upon her idle and luxurious courtiers; but as the wanton slayer of the rival Queen, her kinswoman, who had come to her for aid. Whatever Elizabeth's faults may have been, she was innocent of any desire to compass Mary's death, and she struggled against the necessity to the last. She protested that she could not kill the bird which had flown to her for refuge from the hawks. It went against the grain with the woman who was described as having "no gall," who was personally, with hardly an exception, the least revengeful and bloodthirsty of human beings.[1] The women were rivals in every light, as they have continued to be in men's minds to this day. Elizabeth, in her transparent personal vanity and jealousy, was constantly exposing her feelings with regard to the royal cousin, who was so much younger, fairer, and more potent to steal men's hearts. But even the height of womanly jealousy is altogether different from the deliberate planning of murder, unless, indeed, in the nature of a woman at once so passionate and so callous as Mary Stuart had shown herself. Elizabeth was not passionate in that sense; she had gusts of temper, but they passed to a great extent innoxiously; she had not even her sister Mary's dogged determination and fatalistic insistence. It was pain to Elizabeth to form a decision which implied war or death.

[1] This was true of Elizabeth the woman. Elizabeth the Queen punished rebels and malcontents against the royal jurisdiction and government with a heavy, unsparing hand.

Elizabeth at last consented that a commission should be appointed to try Mary, not in connection with the murder of Darnley—which, although a much earlier commission had already sat on the question at York and at Hampton, was really out of the jurisdiction of Elizabeth and her Government—but for Mary's complicity in the plots to assassinate the Queen in England. The commission went down to Fotheringay, where Mary was then lodged, and sat two days there, examining evidence. Mary at first refused to appear before the commissioners, denying, as she had always denied, their right to arraign her; but when she saw opposition was useless, she not only faced her judges, she met them with a masterly defence. Elizabeth herself had never been more intrepid or quicker at catching at every advantage which presented itself, or bolder in dissipating the effect of prejudicial testimony. This meant a great deal more than such suspicious circumstances and confirmatory details as cropped up in Elizabeth's examination after Wyatt's insurrection. It had to do with what Mary must have strongly suspected was the clearest and most incontestable proof held against her by Burleigh. The forlorn woman, who had entered the hall in no robes of state, but "in the grey gown, her usual wear," calmly seating herself, and glancing round with interest at her accusers, was a match in courage and shrewdness for the wisest there. It is supposed that even to the end she could not conceive that Elizabeth and her Government would dare to condemn her, and Elizabeth would fain have saved her kinswoman from paying the last penalty. The royal prerogative was dear to all the Tudors, and Mary was royal. Elizabeth dreaded, with reason, the obloquy which Mary's execution would draw upon her rival. She would not accede to Mary's well-nigh insolent demands under the circumstances. She could not send the next heir to the English crown to France, to let loose the French Catholics on both England and Scotland; she could not invade Scotland, and bring her allies the Protestant Scotch, and latterly their sovereign James, upon England ; she could not set Mary at liberty in England, to become the centre and rallying-point of the English Catholics.

Elizabeth had done what she could all along. She had tried to get the Earl of Murray, while yet alive and Regent, to suppress the worst charges against his sister, and to suffer her to return to Scotland. She had sought to induce Mary to renounce her claim of succession to the English throne, which would have simplified matters. When James was old enough to be dealt with, Elizabeth had endeavoured to procure his consent to reigning jointly with his mother on the same conditions. She would have been only too glad if Mary would have submitted. But neither submission nor confession entered into Mary's thoughts, and she indignantly declined to relinquish the right she had forfeited.

Murray's personal ambition had stood in the way of the reconciliation of the conflicting parties through him, and he had not had the slightest faith in Mary's becoming harmless. James I. of Scotland, "the old young man," as a French authority cleverly defined him, had been separated from his mother in his infancy, when he was crowned in her stead, and his standard was unfurled against her in the field. He had been brought up to detest her as presumably concerned in his father's murder, and certainly the woman who had married the murderer within three months of the crime. She was the skeleton in James's cupboard, the blot on his escutcheon. She had threatened him with her curse ; she was ready to disinherit him, so far as her word could do it. He was willing that she should remain in England, in solitary confinement, for the rest of her life. There is a still more repulsive indication of his utter revulsion from her. He let it be known by his envoys that though common feeling would prevent him from taking any active step in the business, he would not

refuse to consent to the fulfilment of the long-delayed
punishment, provided his position as the next heir to
the English throne was more directly acknowledged, and
the income settled upon him as heir-presumptive was
increased.

If Mary's own son was thus hostile, France and Spain,
to which she trusted, were growing weary of the complications arising from her offences and injuries.   Even the
Pope, who had gone far in signifying that killing was no
murder when it had to do with Elizabeth, began to be more
wary in pleading the wrongs of the erring daughter of the
Church.

Mary's bitter end caused a reaction in her favour, and
stirred up her old kindred and allies to revenge her death;
but while she was still alive, though France remonstrated
and Spain threatened, no decisive action was taken to stay
the inevitable result.

The Commissioners, after sitting for two days at Fotheringay, returned to Westminster, and there delivered their
verdict, which did not, however, become public at once.
When it was announced as a verdict of guilty, with the
sentence of death pronounced, nothing could exceed the
public exultation.   The bells of all the churches pealed
forth their noisy congratulations, and the streets of
London were alight with bonfires.

Elizabeth's signature was still needed for the execution
of the death-warrant, and this no entreaties of her ministers could draw from her during two whole months—
those of December, 1586, and January, 1587.   At times
she assumed an air of carelessness and gaiety; on other
occasions Camden describes her as sitting in solitude
muttering the Latin phrases which find an equivalent in
the English words, "Either bear or smite;" "Strike, lest
thou be stricken."   At last, unable to help herself, Elizabeth signed the warrant along with other state papers,
throwing them on the ground, and forbidding her Council

to trouble her again in the matter. It was not Walsingham, but his colleague Davison, who had the interview
with her, and according to his account the Queen declined
to give him the necessary authority to forward the warrant,
while she hinted broadly she would prefer it should be put
in force without her appearing further in the transaction.
She even suggested that Sir Amyas Paulet and Sir Drew
Drury, in whose custody Mary was, might see the warrant
carried out on their own responsibility. This conversation
rests solely on the word of Davison. Even if it were
correct, the hypothesis that Elizabeth implied the assassination of her enemy is no longer held. The question is
understood to have turned on the manner in which the
warrant was to be executed. Indeed, the further recommendation given by the Queen, which is also in
Davison's statement, that the hall of Fotheringay was
preferable to the court-yard or to the Green for the block,
ought to be conclusive. But undoubtedly Elizabeth's
conduct was marked by the wily craft which so often
marred her nobler qualities. In this instance at least she
overreached herself. She had yielded, and might be jus-
tified in yielding; but she would not, if she could help it,
take the blame of her decision—she would throw it on
other shoulders. She would reserve for herself the excuse
which she could make to France and to Scotland, that she
had not despatched the warrant; that she had kept it
back for the chance of being able to change her mind;
that, in fact, its execution was a kind of disastrous accident
over which she had not possessed any control.

Whatever Elizabeth's motives, she did her reputation
great injury by giving them play. Her manifest lack of
straightforwardness in the end drew down upon her the accusation of having played an odiously hypocritical part from
the beginning. It is of comparatively little consequence
that the rash conclusion is amply disproven to all careful
students of history who examine the whole bearings of

the case. The careless, prejudiced portion of the public, prone to leap at conclusions, will not stop to reason.

Neither Davison, nor Walsingham, nor Paulet, nor Drury would take the responsibility which belonged to their mistress, well aware, as they all were, that if the temptation presented itself, she would not hesitate to make one or other of them the scapegoat. She might not sacrifice her servant outright, but she would not scruple to cause him to suffer so far in her stead.

Burleigh put an end to the difficulty when the signed warrant was carried in a panic to him, though Elizabeth had forbidden Davison to make public what had taken place. Burleigh assembled such of the Council as he could gather together in his room in the palace at Greenwich, told them that the Queen had done all which could be expected from her, and that they ought not to trouble her further, but act at their own discretion. Thus the warrant, with instructions for its fulfilment, was forwarded to the Earls of Kent and Shrewsbury, members of the Council, who happened to be then in the neighbourhood of Fotheringay.

At last Mary's eyes were opened to her danger, and she met it with native courage and dignity. Mr. Froude's opinion is, that when she was sensible that her position was desperate, she set herself to die in the full odour of Roman Catholicism, posing, as it were, in the character of a martyr to her faith. In doing so, she took the surest means to draw down on Elizabeth the vengeance of every papist in Europe. With all deference to the historian, it is not necessary to endorse this opinion. Mary was a woman of lively imagination and strong sympathies. There is no real reason to doubt her devotion to the Church of which she was a bigoted adherent. She had been brought up to look upon what was orthodoxy to her as a cardinal merit, which covered a multitude of sins, and to count as venial, by comparison, the stormy passions and fierce crimes which marked her career. When every other refuge failed her, she was certain to cling to her Church, and to deceive herself as well as her neighbours into the belief that she suffered not for her follies and unbridled self-indulgence, but for her fidelity to its teaching. She could in this mood rise into a state of exaltation of spirit.

Mary was beheaded in the hall at Fotheringay, with all the sad ceremonies usual on such an occasion, on the 7th of February 1587, in the forty-fifth year of her age, and the nineteenth of her captivity. Confinement had told upon her. She was grey-headed beneath her wig, and her limbs were stiff with rheumatism.

Elizabeth was probably more of an actor than the Queen of Scots had just been. When the news of the death reached the English Queen, even though there might have been a grain of truth in her outcry that her hand had been forced, and that the power of decision had been finally wrested from her, she stormed at everybody, threw Davison into the Tower, fined him, and suffered him to die a prisoner. She rated her offending Council, though they were, as Burleigh had astutely calculated, too many to be punished in a body.

Calm was restored in time to enable England to engage in the requisite preparations for the arrival of the Invincible Armada, which Philip of Spain fitted out. He was armed, in addition, with the Pope's anathema on Elizabeth, sent to overwhelm her. He was resolved to deal death and destruction all around, and to place himself, whom Mary had named as her heir, on the English throne. He claimed as the nearest Roman Catholic in the line of succession, founding his claims on his descent from two English princesses, Philippa and Catherine Plantagenet, daughters of John of Gaunt, who were respectively Queen of Portugal and Queen of Castile.

In England, Queen and people responded nobly to the

call.   The great upholder of peace was found ready for
war when it came, and in the moment of deadly peril
Elizabeth and her subjects were united as they had never
been before.   For not only did the Protestants raise troops
in every direction, the Roman Catholics, heedless of the
papal anathema, forgot all difference of creed, remembered
only that they were Englishmen, and rallied round the
royal standard.   Elizabeth was not to be outdone in
generous trust.   With a magnanimous confidence, which
proved a splendid stroke of policy, she insisted on appointing a Catholic, her kinsman, Lord Howard of Effingham,
to the post of Lord High Admiral, which his father and
his grandfather had filled with honour before him.   Drake
was summoned, to help to receive the foe, from the Tagus,
where he was doing all the mischief in his power, and
where he would fain have struck a blow at the Armada
without waiting for its arrival on the English coast.   He
was named Vice-Admiral of the Fleet.   Other great cap-
tains, Hawkins and Frobisher, with adventurous young
nobles such as the Earl of Cumberland, were in the ships.

The land forces were commanded in the first place by
the Earl of Leicester, with Sir John Norris under him.
Another detachment of troops, designed specially to
guard London, was led by Elizabeth's cousin, Carey, Lord
Hunsdon.   The soldiers armed themselves to fight with
the stouter hearts that it was on English soil they were to
encounter their old enemy in the Netherlands, the Prince
of Parma.

In the middle of these warlike arrangements for mutual
destruction, one wonders whether Philip and Elizabeth
ever found leisure to look back to the relations of other
days; whether Philip remembered the blooming young
princess whom he first saw under a cloud of disgrace,
when she was barely suffered to come from Woodstock to
Hampton Court to be present at the Christmas festivities
there ; whether Elizabeth ever realised in her mortal

enemy, the King of Spain, her unhappy sister Mary's idolised husband, Elizabeth's friend and champion in those days, her suitor a little later.

Elizabeth held herself as the supreme head of the army. She went to Tilbury to review the principal body of her troops, and appeared before them attended by the Earl of Leicester, &c. She was on horseback, with a field-marshal's baton in her hand; a page followed her, carrying her white-plumed helmet. Miss Strickland tells us farther, the Queen wore a corselet of polished steel, reaching down to her huge farthingale. She rode bareheaded down the lines amidst the ringing cheers of the men, to whom she made the stirring speech which rang in their ears like the blast of a trumpet. She said she had come to live and die among them, to lay down, for her God, her kingdom, and her people, her honour and her blood, even in the dust. For though she had the body of a weak, feeble woman, she had the heart and stomach (courage) of a king, and a king of England. She thought it foul scorn that Parma, or Spain, or any prince of Europe, should dare to invade the borders of her realm. Sooner than any disorder should grow by her, she would take up arms; she would be their general and judge. She promised them a famous victory over the enemies of her God, her kingdom, and her people.

In point of fact, the great naval victory had even then been won; but in the slowness with which news travelled in those days, the Queen and her ministers were not apprised till later of what it concerned them so much to know.

On July 29, 1588, the sails of the Armada were seen from the Lizard Point. Already they had been descried out at sea in the bright moonlight of the previous night.

" It was about the lovely close of a warm summer day,
There came a gallant merchant ship full sail to Plymouth Bay ;
Her crew hath seen Castile's black fleet beyond Aurigny's isle
At earliest twilight on the waves lie heaving many a mile.

At sunrise she escaped their van, by God's especial grace,
And the tall *Pinta* to the noon had held her close in chase.
Forthwith a guard at every gun was placed along the wall,
The beacon blazed upon the roof of Edgcumbe's lofty hall.
Many a light fishing-bark put out to pry along the coast,
And with loose reins and bloody spur rode inland many a post.
With his white hair unbonneted the stout old sheriff comes,
Behind him march the halberdiers, before him sound the drums.
His yeomen round the market-cross make clear an ample space,
For there behoves him to set up the standard of Her Grace.
And haughtily the trumpets peal, and gaily dance the bells,
As slowly upon the labouring wind the royal blazon swells.

   .   .   .   .   .   .

Night sank upon the dusky beach, and on the purple sea,
Such night in England ne'er had been, nor e'er again shall be ;
From Eddystone to Berwick bounds, from Lynn to Milford Bay,
That time of slumber was as bright and busy as the day.
From swift to east and swift to west the ghastly war-flames spread,
High on St. Michael's Mount it shone, it shone on Beachy Head ;
Far on the deep the Spaniard saw, along each southern shire,
Cape beyond cape, in endless range, those twinkling points of fire."

As the Spanish ships came into view at Plymouth,
Drake was playing his never-forgotten game of bowls on
the Hoe, and coolly announced that he should have time
to finish his game before he engaged the enemy. The
enormous fleet sailed slowly in the shape of a crescent into
the Channel. It was commanded by the Duke of Medina
Sidonia. Lord Howard of Effingham and his ships already
hung like bull-dogs on the Spaniards' rear.

The English ships were tremendously outnumbered and
outweighted. The Spanish galleons, turreted vessels of
great size, appearing "like castles in the sea," were one
hundred and thirty in number. The English ships, many
of them no larger than modern yachts, were not above
thirty fully equipped Queen's ships, with some fifty
more irregularly fitted-out vessels. The Spanish galleons
held upwards of twenty thousand soldiers, many priests,

[1] Macaulay.

and eight thousand mariners. Two thousand five hundred cannon were on board, and immense stores of provisions. The English ships were manned by nine thousand able-bodied seamen, and had, as far as can be known, one thousand guns.

The advantages on the side of the English ships were, that they could, not only from being better sailed, but from their very inferiority of size, sail two feet for the Spaniards' one, and fire four times for the Spaniards' two; and the crowded decks of the vast hulks caused terrible carnage from the English fire into the Spanish ranks, while the skilfully handled, nimbly sailing English vessels suffered little comparatively from the lumbering broadsides of the enemy. "The high-towered broad-bowed galleons moved like Thames barges piled with hay, while the sharp, low English ships . . . shot away as if by magic in the eye of the wind." One of their first feats was to sail rapidly along the Spanish line, firing into each galleon as they passed, turn, and retrace their course before the Spanish commanders could recover from their surprise at the sharpness of the manœuvre. The English did not venture at first to come to close quarters with their Brobdignaggian adversaries, but dogged and pressed upon them in a running fight, which lasted for eight days, in the Channel. The weather broke, and was squally, and the Spanish squadrons were huddled together. On the second evening a galleon " carrying the flag of Don Pedro de Valdez," "fouled another galleon, the *Santa Catalina*, and both were much damaged." "Don Pedro was the only officer of high rank in the fleet who was well acquainted with the Channel; he was himself of more importance than his ship, and the Duke (Medina Sidonia) despatched boats to bring him off with his crew. But he would not leave his charge, and was left to his fate.[1]

[1] Froude.

Whatever criticism might be passed on the Spaniards' maritime skill, there was no fault to find with their courage and devotion. Fresh misfortunes befell the invaders, while the English were only troubled by their stock of ammunition running low.

The knowledge of the gallant struggle in the Channel had reached all England. "Cliffords, Veres, and Percies, took their place beside the Raleighs and the Cecils of the new era, and from Lyme, and Weymouth, and Poole, and the Isle of Wight, young lords and gentlemen came streaming out in every smack and sloop they could lay hold of, to snatch their share of danger and glory at Howard's side. The strength they added was nothing; but they brought enthusiasm. They brought to the half starved and neglected[1] crews the sense that every heart in England was with them."

The warfare was so harassing and hopeless that the Spaniards grew disorganised and disheartened. In the English sailors' graphic words, "the feathers of the Spaniards were plucked one by one. Galleon after galleon was sunk, boarded, or driven on shore."

Then Howard sent eight lit fire-ships at midnight to be driven by the tide into the Spanish lines. The device succeeded, the fleet cut their cables, and stood out to sea in the direction of Gravelines, when Drake took them in hand and closed with them, till the ammunition of his ships was all but spent, and not in vain. "Three great galleons had sunk," writes Mr. Green; "three had drifted on the Flemish coast; but the bulk of the Spanish vessels remained, and even to Drake the fleet seemed 'wonderful great and strong.' He was soon to find the leaders were in despair and their men cowed. Four thousand had fallen, while the ships' sails were torn, their masts shot away, and their decks slaughter-houses. In a Spanish council of war it was determined that the battered rem-

---

[1] Elizabeth's army and navy were ill-paid, ill-clad, and ill-fed.

nant of the Armada should retreat to Spain, by making a circuit of the Orkney Islands. In the northern seas a new terror awaited the doomed expedition. A great storm arose, and scattered and wrecked the last of the fleet. Out of the hundred and thirty galleons which had sailed for England, only fifty succeeded in gaining Corunna: out of the twenty-eight thousand men of war, only ten thousand, stricken with pestilence, returned to Spain. On the Irish strand, near Sligo, an English captain counted eleven hundred corpses cast up by the sea. The wreckers of the Orkneys and the Faroes, the clansmen of the Scotch Isles, the kernes of Donegal and Galway, all had their part in the work of murder and robbery."

In contrast to the horrors described by Mr. Green, there is a well-authenticated incident of Christian chivalry and humanity which happened on the Fife coast in connection with a ship of the Armada. One of the smaller vessels of the Spanish fleet, the captain and crew of which were spent with many days and nights of fighting and of battling with the winds and waves, found themselves in strange waters. The sailors were ignorant of their bearings, and famine was added to their troubles. The ship took refuge during the night—or early in the autumn morning—in Anstruther harbour. The worthy townspeople awoke in amazement and alarm to discover a ship of their dreaded enemy, with the crew as it turned out, in their exhaustion and misery, as helpless as the tempest-tossed vessel, lying belated in the middle of the town.

The Provost and Bailies hastened to their great referee in all public matters, their minister, James Melville, nephew of the famous reformer Andrew Melville, as great as Andrew in piety, and only second to him in learning.

Should they haul the captain and crew of the Spanish ship to the Tolbooth, and make short work of them there?

cried the sons of thunder in the town council to the
minister of peace.

But James Melville had not so learned the Gospel.
He replied to the effect, "What! Imprison or hang defeated, shipwrecked men who were at the town's mercy?"
If they had come on an evil errand, they knew no
better, and were acting in obedience to their king; and
the minister did not fail to remind his excited hearers
of how Elisha had dealt with the messengers of the
King of Syria when, struck with blindness, they were led
unwittingly into the centre of Samaria.

James Melville's teaching to his people had not been
such that their practice should be inferior to that of the
Israelites of old. Take the Spaniards to the Tolbooth by
all means, because there they could be safely lodged, and
then relieve their wants. So by the minister's direction,
seconded by those of the members of the town council, the
strangers were supplied with food and drink and whatever their forlorn condition required. When their ship
had undergone the necessary repairs, the men were permitted to set sail for Spain. They were not forgetful of
the kindness which had been shown to them in their
extremity. After peace was restored, and Anstruther
trading ships lay once more in the Spanish port from
which the galleon in question had sailed, the Fife skippers
were treated with distinction, and loaded with bounties
by the authorities. The story survives in local tradition,
and in its main points is confirmed by James Melville's
printed diary, which may be read by whoever cares to
study the quaint original.

When Elizabeth returned to St. James's Palace, she
was received with great public rejoicing. She went in
state to St. Paul's to offer thanksgiving for her victory.
She was drawn by white horses in a car surmounted by
a canopy resting on pillars—two of them bearing a lion
and a dragon, the supporters of the English arms. The

Queen sat alone, while she was attended by the officers of state, the judges, and a great company of ladies and gentlemen.

She had in the hour of danger composed a prayer for deliverance to be read in all the parish churches. With her old habit of applying the words of Scripture to her circumstances, it is probable that she chose the text of the sermon which the Bishop of Salisbury preached before her in St. Paul's—"Thou didst blow with Thy breath, and they were scattered."

It was on Elizabeth's return from this ceremony—which took place in the month of November—that she is said to have eaten of a Michaelmas goose, and commanded all her faithful subjects, while England remained a kingdom, to celebrate the anniversary by following their Queen's example.

Elizabeth commemorated her triumph in another way by having medals struck, one of them bearing the inscription in Latin, "It came, it saw, it fled;" and another, "It was done by a woman."

It is a grievous commentary on such display to learn that the brave sailors who bore the brunt of the strife were afterwards shamefully abandoned to poverty, many of them dying of want rather than disease. Elizabeth's invariable impression was that whoever had to pay the expenses of the government, the army and navy, she and her exchequer ought not to be expected to defray the costs in full, or in any other than a stinted measure. There is this excuse for her with regard to the exceptional charges of resisting the Armada, that, grudge and withhold as she might, her cherished exchequer never recovered from the effects of the sums she had to disburse. Her favourite dream of a surplus was not again fulfilled. Indeed, latterly some of her jewels had to be sacrificed to cover the deficit.[1]

[1] Beesley.

Already a private sorrow had dimmed the lustre of Elizabeth's public triumph. Within six weeks of her visit to Tilbury, the Earl of Leicester died, at the age of fifty-five—that of his royal mistress—of fever caught in the Essex marshes. He had ceased to be her lover; but he had continued to be the foremost of her friends. The Queen and her courtier were growing old together; they were bound to each other by a thousand familiar associations and social ties. She received the unexpected information of his death with a burst of tears. Camden has a cautious and apparently correct summing-up of Leicester's qualities:—"A person of exact neatness; a generous patron of arts and arms—one who knew how to nick a juncture and manage a turn to his best advantage. Besides, he was of a temper pleasant and popular . . ." Then the historian proceeds to refer to "the libellous pens" and "infamous and false reflections" which busied themselves with the Earl, so that "the crowd caressed him in public, and in private used quite another language."

It was the custom of the time to attribute the death of every distinguished man and woman to the administration of poison by an enemy. Camden himself is not free from such suggestions, though he does not indulge in them in the case of Lord Leicester. In recording the sudden illness and death of the young Earl of Derby, the old writer not only notes some signs of foul practice, he gravely mentions the fact that a wax image was found in the nobleman's bedchamber with the body stuck full of hairs of the same colour as Lord Derby's hair. If Camden was silent, his gossiping contemporaries unhesitatingly mixed up Leicester's name with charges of poisoning. According to these credulous informants, he was both poisoner and poisoned. He was an adept in the art. He made away with Sir Nicholas Throckmorton, and Walter, Earl of Essex—of which there is not a particle of proof. Equally unsupported is the prosaically fantastical legend which attributes his death to a draught which he gave to his wife Lettice, for the purpose of compassing her death; but she suspected his design, and not only did not swallow the draught, she contrived to transfer it to the donor as a prescription for the cure of indigestion! Lettice Knollys, in her buxom maturity false to Leicester—as in her youth she was false to Essex —married for the third time Sir Christopher Blount, who had been Leicester's Master of the Horse.

Miss Strickland has given a selection from the many costly gifts with which Leicester—enriched by the Queen's bounty—was wont to greet her on festive occasions. Among his offerings were several watches or "round clocks," which were then greatly prized. One was "in a green enamel case, to imitate an apple." Other gifts bore in gold, amidst encrustations of diamonds and emeralds, "the bear and the ragged staff," which formed the device on the privileged courtier's coat-of-arms. It was very gallantly exhibited on the gift, described as follows:—"A fan of white feathers, set in a handle of gold, garnished on one side with two very fine emeralds, fully garnished with diamonds and rubies; the other side garnished with rubies and diamonds, and on each side a white bear and pearls hanging, a lion rampant with a white muzzled bear at his feet."

Leicester died so poor, that his effects were put up to public sale in order to defray a debt to the State. Elizabeth has been blamed for allowing this indignity. Camden's comment is, "For however gentle the Queen might show herself in other respects, yet did she very rarely remit what was owing to her treasury."

It was when England was in the full glory of her success over Spain, with the respect and awe which the triumph of her arms inspired in other foreign nations, that the unexampled prosperity and distinction of Elizabeth's reign were displayed in their brightest colours.

Town and country vied with each other in tokens of
wealth and luxury. Then broke forth that exuberant
burst of intellectual activity and splendour like a chorus
of full-throated song, which the nation has not so much
as equalled again. Many causes—notably the culture
lent by the French Renaissance, and the inspiration supplied by the Reformation—have been suggested for the
wonder; but unmistakably the wisdom of Elizabeth's rule,
and the peace and freedom in the main which she secured
for her subjects, had much to do with it. Young Francis
Bacon was already planning his system of philosophy
which was to culminate in the *Novum Organum*. Spenser
was introduced by Sir Walter Raleigh to the Queen in
the year after the defeat of the Armada, and read to
her portions of his *Faerie Queen*—perhaps, in doing so,
gathering materials for his representation of *Gloriana*.
Christopher Marlowe's lawless life was drawing to a
close; but he had anticipated his compeers by bringing
out his *Tamburlaine* in 1587. His *Edward II., Jew of
Malta*, and *Life and Death of Dr. Faustus*, followed.
Critics see in *Edward II.* the precursor of Shakespeare's
historical plays; and in *The Jew of Malta* hints for
Shylock in *The Merchant of Venice;* [1] while on the same
lines on which the rough, wild production known as *Dr.
Faustus* was built, Goethe founded his *Faust*.

Shakespeare had come on the scene. In the absence
of all written data it is nearly impossible to determine
the order of his plays, or to discover the beginning and
end of the court patronage which he enjoyed. The fine
passage in which he paints the

"Fair virgin thronéd in the West"

was very likely homage paid to the Queen in her lifetime;
though the parallel passage at the end of the play of
Henry VIII., in which there is a magnificent foreshadow-

[1] Green.

ing of the infant Princess Elizabeth's high destiny, did not see the light till after her death. An integral sign of this exists in the prominence given to the wrongs and sorrows of Catherine of Arragon, a choice which could hardly have been made in the reign of the daughter of Anne Boleyn. *Winter's Tale*, in which Catherine is supposed to appear again as *Hermione*, was written when James was king.

It does not admit of much reasonable doubt that Shakespeare's plays—with the dramatist in the *rôle* of a player—were acted before Elizabeth. Beyond this assurance there is great uncertainty. There is no convincing evidence of the pretty story that *Twelfth Night* was a commission from the gentlemen of the Temple for the delectation of their Queen on one of her visits to them; or the other story, that Elizabeth was so diverted by the character of Falstaff in *Henry V.*, that she requested the author to make the fat knight in love for her further amusement, and that the broad and boisterous humour of *The Merry Wives of Windsor* was the result. But however much or little of Shakespeare's plays Elizabeth saw or heard, it is certain that it was in her reign he inaugurated his grand creations and began his noble gallery of men and women of all types and times, for which the work of every other writer seems but to serve as a foil.

Even "rare Ben Jonson," with his *Every Man to his Humour*, his *Alchemist*, and *Catiline*, though he was Shakespeare's rival in the flesh, cannot be mentioned in the same breath, now that posterity has set its seal on their work.

But the bubbling up of fresh and vigorous ideas was not confined to literature. The spirit of invention and adventure was everywhere. William Lee, a Cambridge scholar, hit on the stocking loom, a humble but useful conception—not so romantic, but as beneficial in its way

as that search for a north-west passage to the Indies
through Polar regions, which fascinated Frobisher, and in
which Sir Hugh Willoughby, the "captain tall," perished.

Drake's plundering expeditions to the Spanish Main
were diversified by the search for undiscovered lands, in
which Raleigh was a marked figure. He found for his
pains at different times, and claimed for England, in
North America, the State of Virginia, named in honour
of the Virgin Queen ; and in South America the province
of Guinea, which he attempted to colonise. But first he
brought back with him among his trophies the potato
plant, and the accomplishment of smoking tobacco, which
was so detestable to King James.

Elizabeth could enter into all these interests. Mr.
Green writes of her : " She could talk poetry with Spenser,
and philosophy with Bruno. She could discuss euphemism
(superfine language) with Lyly, and enjoy the chivalry of
Essex. She could turn from talk of the last fashion to
pore with Cecil over despatches and treasury books. She
could pass from tracking traitors with Walsingham, to
settle points of doctrine with Parker, or to calculate with
Frobisher the chances of a north-west passage."

Miss Strickland has collected a few particulars of Elizabeth's tastes and habits, in what was still the mellow
afternoon of her life, before the dark shadows of evening
descended. She transacted business, and saw the members of her Privy Council in the morning. If the sun
shone later in the day, she would walk in the garden
(when in town) ; and if the weather were unfavourable
for out-of-door exercise, she would walk in the galleries
of her palaces, attended by the best company, in the
shape of the most intellectual members of her court.
She devoted part of every day to study ; she was regular
in the religious exercises, which had her sanction and
approval. When she dined in public, it was with much
ceremony, and a great display of gorgeous plate. Supper

was her merriest meal, and her time for enjoyment. She disliked dwarfs; she had her mother's fondness for little dogs, and her sister's love of children. When she retired for the night, she was accompanied by the married ladies of her household—one of the ladies always slept in the Queen's bedchamber. In addition to her guards, several gentlemen of quality took turns in waiting up in one of the palace rooms, that the Queen might be roused on any emergency.

Though Elizabeth would storm in her Council, and on provocation slap her maids of honour, she had endless patience and good-humour for her people at large. She allowed them easy access to her presence, took and read their petitions, and had a friendly word for the meanest. Her taste for hunting and dancing did not pall till the end was near. She had a passion for the open air, and would hold a court seated under a tree. Her predilections in this respect are in support of the popular belief that she was sitting under a tree at Hatfield, though it was in the month of November, when she was told of her sister's death. She never wearied of the superb royal progresses from one great house and one town to another, which were such features of her reign, and were long a great delight to the populace.

In this halcyon interval Elizabeth's domestic relations were less troubled and stormy than at any other period of her life. She had always something to fear from her father's kindred, and their schemes in connection with the succession to the throne. Her harshness to the Greys, Brandons, &c., has been severely condemned; but it was not entirely without cause. There is a significant passage in Camden which throws some light on the subject. In noting the death, in 1596, of Margaret Clifford, Countess of Derby, only daughter of Henry Clifford, Earl of Cumberland, by Eleanor Brandon, niece to Henry VIII., the historian remarks: "Through an idle mixture of curiosity and ambition . . . she much used the conversation of necromancers and finger-flingers, so losing latterly the Queen's favour."

In the case of another younger cousin several times removed, Elizabeth had grave reason for offence. It was by the crafty plot of the Countess of Shrewsbury ("Building Bess," in turn Madam Barlow, Lady Cavendish, Madam St. Loe, and Lady Shrewsbury), one of the most energetic and unscrupulous women of her time, that a marriage was effected between Charles Stewart, younger son of the Countess of Lennox, and younger brother of Henry Lord Darnley, and a daughter of the Earl of Shrewsbury. The young couple followed each other speedily to the grave, but they left an unfortunate bone of contention in the shape of Arabella Stewart— "the little Lady Arbel, or Arbell," whom the grandmother at least, destined for the future Queen of England. The involuntary claimant paid the penalty, but she was still little more than a child in Elizabeth's day. To her mother's kindred — the Howards, Careys, and Knollyses—Elizabeth was uniformly kind apart from some fault of theirs, and they tried her more than once. It was to her credit that she did not enrich them out of the public money.

The greater the favour in which the Queen had formerly held any gentleman or lady of her court, the more she took to heart his or her marriage. Thus Elizabeth's gallant and accomplished courtier Raleigh, whose first passport to her notice had been the grace and presence of mind with which he flung his velvet mantle on the muddy spot in her path, was sent to the Tower for the misconduct which ended in his marriage with Elizabeth Throckmorton. It was while he was still under a cloud for this escapade that he made his voyage to Guinea. Essex fell into similar, if less pronounced, disgrace by a private marriage with Frances Lady Sidney, who had been

Sir Philip's wife, and had paid him the unusual mark of respect in that generation of remaining a widow for four years. But as a rule the Queen was appeased ere long, and presently both the offenders were restored to their former privileges.

Elizabeth was now upwards of threescore, and it is well that her later biographers have recognised the stupid blunder by which earlier historians persisted in dealing with her affection for Essex and the handsome Mountjoy —young enough to be her sons—as a foolish old woman's doting, hankering after lovers to the very verge of the grave. Elizabeth was no fool at any stage of her life, though traces of her vanity and coquetry lingered to the last. The sole excuse for the monstrous supposition is the superabundance of laudation and the extravagant devotion with which the young, no less than the old, courtiers continued to address her. But it was the court language of the period. Not a foreign sovereign who desired to recommend himself to her addressed her in any other terms. She was always the bright western star, the glorious sun, whose effulgence dazzled the petitioner. He was either scorched by the splendour of her beams, or pining in darkness for lack of them. Judged by our standards, the royal correspondents might each and all have been enamoured to the last degree.

No candid person can view in Elizabeth's treatment of Robert Devereux, Earl of Essex, any other sentiment than that of the mingled admiration, apprehension, and indulgence of a woman advanced in life for an eager, enthusiastic young man, possessed of many attractive qualities and of considerable promise, while beset with temptations and difficulties which threaten to mar that promise. On Essex's side, his wilful turbulent behaviour towards the Queen was exactly that which might have been adopted by her spoilt godson Harington.

Robert Devereux was the son of that second cousin,

Lettice Knollys, whom Elizabeth had no reason to like or
esteem.   Indeed, Camden mentions expressly, " 'twas
with some difficulty he was raised to the condition of a
favourite, the Queen happening to have no respect for his
mother."   Doubtless neither was his sister Penelope Lady
Rich anything save an obstacle to his winning Elizabeth's
regard.   However, he was her distant relation through his
mother, and he was also Leicester's stepson.   It was on
the death of Leicester, and in succession to him, that
Essex was named Master of the Horse, a post which
ought to have kept him near the Queen's person ; she also
made him a Knight of the Garter and a Privy Councillor
when he was only twenty-three years of age.   He was
handsome, impulsive, distinguished by all the romantic
graces of a knight-errant rather than by the prosaically
useful aims of a sober soldier and statesman.   He was too
wild and free a bird to submit willingly to what were to
him the galling restrictions and the enervating influence
of a court.   What he desired was to win his spurs and do
great deeds, to make a name at which all the world should
wonder.   Twice he escaped from bondage, being on one of
the two occasions recaptured and brought back, full of reluctance, by a special messenger from the Queen.   Everywhere—in the Low Countries, in Portugal, on board ship
with Raleigh, in Ireland—that dear conquest of earlier
English sovereigns, which Elizabeth's statesmen were
struggling desperately to bring into submission and keep
in order—he sought to carve a career; always he was
baulked by his own impatience, insubordination, jealousy,
and recklessness.   Camden has an amusing account of
one of Essex's fiery disputes with the Queen, when in
the heat of his argument he turned his back upon her—
a slight she was not likely to overlook.   She boxed his
ears on the spot, in presence of the Lord Admiral, Sir
Robert Cecil, and Windebank, Clerk of the Seal ; she
further bade the culprit " go and be hanged."   He clapped

his hand upon his sword, so that the Lord Admiral was forced to come between the disputants. Essex swore with a great oath that he neither could nor would put up with such an affront, nor would he "have took it from the hands of Henry VIII. himself," and left the court "in a great passion."

The quarrel did not last; but it was a different England in which such scenes could take place; a different London, when in a great drought, not long before, the Thames was so low that a man could ride over it at London Bridge; a different world altogether, when Elizabeth and the "old young man," James IV. of Scotland, remained on such amicable terms that she not only condescended to approve of his marriage with Anne of Denmark, but stood sponsor for his son Henry, Prince of Wales, in the manner in which she had stood sponsor for James himself, as if no Mary Queen of Scots had lived, and died by the headsman's axe at Fotheringay.

It is as hard for us as it was for Elizabeth not to deal forbearingly with Essex. He was so boyish in his worst scrapes, so frank and manly in his greatest errors. It is said he wished to model himself on the *preux chevalier* Sir Philip Sidney; if so, he fell far short of his model, though it might have been part of the modelling to woo and wed Sir Philip's widow. Certainly Essex was unfit for any grave charge. He was so arrogant that it could be said of him he disparaged all whose actions were not of " his own square." He would not brook contradiction, he was utterly regardless of consequences. It was also reported of him that the goodwill he inspired in Roman Catholic and Protestant alike was merely the fruits of the pains he had taken " to gain the caresses of the vulgar." He was accused of "having a way of screwing favours from the Queen, joined to a coldness and disrespect for her," and of " carrying his passions on his forehead." But the last charges may be suffered to drop; two of them at least showed that he was not a practised courtier, far less an accomplished hypocrite.   It was an ill-omened distinction that he had claims to royal blood, though it had run through various and tortuous channels before it reached his veins.   He was descended distantly from Thomas of Woodstock, son of Edward III., and from a sister of Edward IV.   It was a more tangible and creditable honour that he was the friend of Spenser, the friend of Shakespeare's friend the Earl of Southampton, and of the Earl of Pembroke, who was Sidney's nephew, being the son of Mary Sidney, the lady addicted to "pleasant studies," and the grandson of Catherine Parr's sister Ann.

Elizabeth was at Nonsuch when Essex defied alike duty and propriety.   He had been sent to occupy the highest post in Ireland, which had never ceased to be rent asunder by the machinations and open rebellion of disaffected nobles like Desmond, and wild chiefs claiming to represent native kings like Bryan Barough.   As a matter of course Essex would not co-operate with his subordinates in command.   Believing himself thwarted, he took the mad undisciplined course of suddenly abandoning his post, without leave asked or granted, and quitting Ireland. Arrived in England, he went straight to the Queen, but showed so little sense of what was due to her that he entered her private apartments early in the morning unsummoned and unannounced, still wearing the muddy boots in which he had travelled.   Justly indignant, the Queen ordered him to his apartments.   The Council which met on the serious offence of his unceremoniously throwing up his command in Ireland removed him from the Council, suspended him from his office of Earl Marshal and Master of the Ordnance, and sentenced him to be kept in confinement during the Queen's pleasure.   Essex passionately petitioned Elizabeth that she would let him depart in peace, and she, softened by what she understood to be his submission, bade him be set at liberty.

But the worst side of Essex's haughty, rash nature was in the ascendant. He complained that the Queen had degraded him to the state of a private man, and that he could not "fawn himself" into a higher post. There were also malicious tongues which told her he had said of her that "she was now grown an old woman, and was as crooked within as without." He did not stop there; regardless of the warning which she had given him that she might forgive a slight to her person, but if he touched her sceptre he must take the consequences, he commenced to traffic with treason. He was found to be in correspondence with King James, urging him to support his claims by force of arms. Essex was also suspected of seeking to suborn his successor in Ireland, Mountjoy, so that he might transfer his forces from Ireland to Scotland. Noblemen and citizens whose loyalty was of a doubtful character were known to frequent Essex House.

Essex was once more called on to appear before the Council, an order with which he refused to comply, alleging illness. At last he took guilt to himself, and committed the most heinous of his acts. He flew to arms, and in company with Lord Southampton, four other nobles, and three hundred gentlemen, attempted to raise London against the Government. He rode at the head of his band into the City, shouting "For the Queen! For the Queen! My life is in danger!" But there was no response to his appeal. Baffled, he sought to return, but found "a chain drawn across the street near the west gate of St. Paul's, with pikemen and musketeers placed there by the Bishop of London." Essex had his hat shot through, and drew his sword in his own defence. He got by boat to his house, in which were his wife and his sister, Lady Rich, with their gentlewomen. (It is a strange association of "Stella" and "Pastorella," Sydney's first love and his wife, united by their common interest in another man, the brother of the one and the

husband of the other!) It would seem too as if their own
safety occupied them largely, for the place was filled with
the cries of the women, while the Lord Admiral was calling
on Essex to surrender. The privilege of a safe conduct
was granted to the clamorous women, Essex and the
noblemen with him yielding at ten o'clock at night.
They were conducted first to Lambeth and then to the
Tower.

The insurrection was quelled in its birth; but Essex
was doomed. It was impossible to spare the ringleader
in so criminal an attempt. He was arraigned before his
peers in Westminster Hall. He did not defend himself
beyond a solemn protest that he was guiltless of any
design against the Queen personally. He interceded not
ineffectually for his friend Southampton. He impeached
some of the other conspirators, including his stepfather,
Sir Christopher Blount, and Essex's successor in Ireland,
Mountjoy, whose rule was so acceptable that Elizabeth
settled "not to know of the accusation."

Essex is said also to have requested to see and seek
forgiveness from some of his opponents whom he might
have wronged. He thanked the Queen for allowing him
to have a private execution, so that his mind might not
be discomposed; and his expression of penitence was
certainly not for the purpose of saving his life. He died
with firmness and fortitude. He was beheaded in the
courtyard of the Tower on Ash Wednesday, 1601. He
had not completed his thirty-fourth year.

Essex's sometime shipmate and later enemy, with whom
he had quarrelled violently, Sir Walter Raleigh, is said to
have been present on the occasion. For this apparently
cold heartlessness in the brilliant soldier, sailor, and adventurer, which caused a common friend to remonstrate,
to advise the interested spectator not to press on the
dying man at such a time, and to induce Raleigh to withdraw to the armoury, from which he could witness the

execution, the excuse is made that he dreaded Essex would denounce him on the scaffold, and was there to hear the denunciation, and declare his innocence.

Within the month, Lettice Knollys, the "Helen" of Elizabeth's reign, suffered a terrible retribution for her sins. Her only son had already perished, and her third husband, Sir Christopher Blount (he is said to have plundered and ill-treated the woman who had befooled the elder Essex and Leicester), followed by the same dark road. He died confessing his profligacy, but denying his treason.

The widow of Robert Earl of Essex and of Sir Philip Sidney married for the third time the Earl of Clanricarde, who was supposed to bear a striking personal resemblance to Essex.

The often retailed story of the ring given by Elizabeth to Essex, which he sent back to her as a last entreaty for pardon, is somewhat as follows. The ring was put into the hand of a boy, who in mistake delivered the jewel—not to Lady Scrope, as he had been directed, but to her sister, Lady Nottingham. A whole chapter of misfortune followed, in popular belief. Nottingham (the Lord Admiral Howard, married to one of the Careys, Elizabeth's cousins), was Essex's deadly enemy. His wife confided to him the commission entrusted to her, when he intercepted and withheld the ring. Lady Nottingham, on her death-bed ere long, was full of remorse for the trust she had betrayed. She sent and begged to see Elizabeth, that she might disclose her treachery. The remorse was transferred to the Queen, who thus went mourning to her grave.

The tradition is entirely discredited by modern authorities. Green and Beesley dismiss it with contempt. Brewer holds up the main points of the story to ridicule, remarking on the improbability of Essex's being so slightly guarded as to enable him to dispose of the ring in the manner stated, and dwelling mischievously on the detail of the boy "with the pleasing countenance," who was so opportunely on the spot beneath Essex's window, together with the more than doubtfulness of such a boy's having access to either Lady Scrope or Lady Nottingham.

Another long-cherished general persuasion is also dismissed with scant ceremony. It was that Elizabeth's health gave way, and her death was hastened as the result of her inconsolable sorrow for Essex's fate. That she regretted it, like any other humane woman given to lively attachments, goes without saying; but the regret was not immoderate. He admitted the justice of his sentence, and she had done no more than her duty to her people in condemning him; a fact so queenly a woman was not likely to forget. So far from being overwhelmed by more than the natural sadness with which the old see the fortunes of the young, in whom they have taken a warm interest, fatally overcast, she threw off the incubus, and was unusually well and cheerful, in spite of the idle speculations of some of her companions, during the spring and summer which followed Essex's death. She certainly survived him nearly two years. She went on "maying" as of old in the neighbourhood of her palace at Greenwich, entertained company at her palace at Richmond, and once, more with the malicious intention that the gentleman might report to his impatient master her undiminished health and agility, permitted the Scotch Ambassador to spy on her as she danced for her private diversion to the music of "a small fiddle."

But the long bright day was nearly done, and dark night was coming down on Elizabeth Tudor. One after another of her old friends and favourites had fallen around her. Leicester was gone; Hatton was gone—even Essex's youth had not saved him. Bacon had died years before; her kinsman Hunsdon was dead; her faithful servant Burleigh, who had been her right hand through her troubled youth and glorious middle age, had laid down the burden of his duties and honours in his seventy-eighth year, and was sincerely lamented by his grateful mistress. He left a son, Sir Robert Cecil, well-nigh as famous as his father, yet a smaller man in every respect. He was notably small in stature, with a pale handsome face and great dark eyes. Elizabeth used to call him—to his smothered mortification—her "pigmy." He was less disinterested and more moved by personal enmities than his father had been. There was an impression that he did not act as a true friend to Essex, and that Cecil was largely instrumental in the well-nigh wanton condemnation of Raleigh in James's reign. Elizabeth's greatest enemy, Philip of Spain, had passed from the world five years before her.

Her lot, always lonely, grew lonelier and lonelier. Her kinsman and Admiral, Lord Nottingham, was almost the sole survivor of her earlier trusted servants.

Elizabeth's temperate habits, and her fondness for out-of-door exercise, had caused her to enjoy, for the most part, robust health. A comical story is told [1] of the Queen's lack of submission under a violent attack of toothache, and at the same time of her great demur to the use of the primitive instruments of the dentist or barber-surgeon of the period. In the strait, Aylmer, the old Bishop of London, came gallantly to the rescue, according to his biographer, Strype. The Bishop, with the deprecatory statement that he had not many grinders to lose, magnanimously underwent the extraction of a tooth in the Queen's presence, that she might be encouraged to follow his example, and permit the operation.

In a description given of Elizabeth by a German traveller who visited England and saw the Queen going to prayers in her sixty-sixth year, he tells of her majestic carriage, fair but wrinkled skin, dark, pleasant eyes, hook nose, false red hair, narrow lips, and black (discoloured)

[1] Agnes Strickland.

teeth. He appends a naïve explanation that it was a
defect the English were subject to from their too great
eating of sugar.

Elizabeth kept up her indoor and out-of-door recreations with tenacious determination. She danced no longer
for pleasure, but for exercise, preferring the high dancing
exhibited by her father and her aunt Margaret Tudor,
when they were a merry boy and girl, celebrating the
marriage of their brother Arthur with Catherine of Arragon. Elizabeth rode and hunted when she could scarcely
sit her horse, and had to be lifted to and from her saddle.
She tarried in her gardens till it was feared she would die
there. But when three score and ten years have well-
nigh come and gone, the accredited means for the preservation of health and vigour are apt to fail, or to act in a
manner the reverse of what was intended.

The greatest blow to the Queen, if she was conscious of
it, would be any decrease in that love of her people which
was beyond all things precious to her. As Green has it,
they were colder to her than they had been formerly.
They had changed, while she was essentially the same.
The nation had grown thoughtful and serious, and their
Queen had not kept pace with them. They began to be
repelled by her impartial indifference to spiritual questions, her rampant worldliness, her love of gaudiness and
glare.[1]

If Elizabeth recognised the slightest decline in her
popularity, it must have stung her as the very serpent's
tooth of ingratitude, since it was for her people she had
schemed and striven, and stood aloof from family ties.

Of one thing the Queen could hardly fail to be aware—
she had steadily refused to appoint a successor throughout
the whole course of her reign. She was influenced by
motives of policy, in the first place. In the second, she
had not forgotten the scenes on the occasion of her sister

---

[1] Beesley denies that Elizabeth's popularity suffered any eclipse.

Mary's death, when the dying woman was forsaken, while the courtiers flocked to hail the rising sun at Hatfield.

In spite of Elizabeth's precaution, a like experience befell her; and she was too astute, too entirely in possession of her senses, not to suspect that many of those around her were in communication with James of Scotland. Sir Robert Cecil had propitiated James by a much-needed loan of money from Cecil's private resources. The dashing, versatile Raleigh was in correspondence with the King of Scots. Even the Queen's petted godson, Harington, had sent the King a jewel, bearing a significant inscription. Her cousins, Robert Carey and his sister, were planning the surest arrangements by which Carey should know the precise moment at which the Queen's breath went out, and ride straightway with the tidings to the heir.

Towards the close of the year 1602 Elizabeth's body and mind were alike failing, though she had still flashes of her old spirit. "Her face became haggard, her frame shrunken almost to a skeleton." At last she had grown indifferent to her toilet, and "would not change her dress for weeks at a time." The Queen was at her pleasant palace of Richmond, but nature had lost its charm for her. Camden says her illness was increased by the circumstance that the last day of January, on which she removed from Westminster to Richmond (her last journey in life), was a very stormy day. He adds that she went "to enjoy the remains of life with more freedom," while the courtiers, who were watching each sign, remarked that "the Queen was never more constant to the services of the chapel." The superstition of the watchers was worked upon by the accident of the Queen's having ordered "the ring, in which she had been espoused in form to her kingdom at her coronation, which had never been took off before, to be filed from her finger, because it was so grown into the flesh that it could not be got off any other way."

Her fiery temper rendered her doubly difficult to deal with. Like her sister Mary in her evil day, Elizabeth's courage— the dauntless courage of the daughters of Henry VIII.— broke down in keeping with the shattered nerves. She would have a sword beside her, "and thrust it from time to time in the arras, as if she heard murderers stirring there." She had an ailment in her throat which incapacitated her to a great extent from speaking and swallowing. Her godson Harington describes her, as he saw her holding a gold cup which she often put to her lips; "but in truth her heart seemed too full to need more filling." He sought to amuse her by reading some of his verses, whereat she smiled once, but said, "When thou dost feel creeping time at thy gate, these fooleries will please thee less. I am past relish for such matters. Thou seest my bodily meat doth not suit me well. I have eaten but one ill-tasted cake since yesterday night."

She would take neither physic nor nourishment, and at last refused to go to bed, because her fevered fancy brought to her pillow ghastly dreams and weird fancies; while she scouted with her old, strong common-sense, so far in advance of her day, the idea suggested by Sir Robert Cecil (one can see his melancholy black eyes opening wide as he spoke), that she was beset with spirits. She sat for four days among cushions on the floor, mostly silent, with her fingers to her mouth; an attitude which seems rather an instinctive indication of her suffering from her throat, and of the impediment it presented to speech, than, as has been conjectured, a sign of deep dejection. Her Council and attendants, in their perplexity, sent at last for the old Admiral Lord Nottingham. He was her nearest surviving relation, as well as the oldest of her friends. He had married another of her cousins, the heroine of the apocryphal ring story, and it was on account of his mourning for her death that he was absent from court.

He came, and induced Elizabeth to swallow some broth, feeding her from a spoon. Sir Robert Cecil told her that to content her people she must go to bed. She turned upon him with the high spirit of former days; she reminded him that "must" was not a word to be used to princes, finishing indignantly, "Little man, little man, if your father had lived, ye durst not have said so much; but thou knowest I must die, and that maketh thee so presumptuous."

By mingled entreaty and compulsion her aged kinsman got her laid on her bed. Her Council made a final effort to ascertain her wishes with regard to her successor. The members assembled round her bed, and begged her by word or sign to convey her will to them. They mentioned the King of France (to try if she was in her right reason, it is alleged), and she did not stir. They suggested Lady Catherine Grey's son, Lord Beauchamp. Her dislike to the Greys caused her to rally for a moment. "I will have the son of no rascal (or low-born man) in my seat," she said scornfully. They named the King of Scots, and here accounts differ. Camden, writing from hearsay, declares that the Queen, when pressed by her Council, said faintly, "that as she had held a regal sceptre she desired no other than a royal successor." When urged further by the secretary, she explained, "I would have a king succeed me, and who should that be but my kinsman the King of Scots?" If we accept the testimony of some of those said to have been present, she did no more than bow her head at the name of King James; other eye-witnesses maintained she made no sign.

The Archbishop of Canterbury and one or two of his colleagues had been summoned to pray with the dying woman. Once more the evidence is very conflicting. Professor Beesley quotes a report that she rated the priests with what breath was left her, bade them be packing, said she was no atheist, and took it for an indignity that they should speak to her. He also mentions that she finally received their ministrations. Camden, perhaps fain to believe that his Queen died in an edifying manner, represents her as full of attention and reverence, winding up his narrative with the assertion that she "lifted up her hands and eyes to her Maker when she could do no more." The Careys confirm this statement, and add that the Queen kept the Archbishop praying for an unusual time by her bed.

The chief details of Elizabeth's death are supplied by Robert Carey and Mistress Southwell, one of the Queen's maids of honour. But there is a certain truthful unexaggerated ring in Camden's simple account of what might very well have come to his ears. He attributes the Queen's depression to various causes: the great expenditure, with no result, in Ireland; the reports from France of letters between her courtiers and James of Scotland, with a mere incidental reference to Essex's death as a source of regret. Camden states distinctly that "some of the nobility (not to mention the ladies)" forsook her either because her Majesty was "ancient," or that they, tired with the length of her reign, longed for a change. The Queen, looking upon herself as helpless and forsaken, would cry, "They have now got me in a took (?). I have nobody left me that I can trust." These servants did not hesitate to embitter her sorrows by hinting to her that she had lost much of her sway over the hearts of her people. The rest of his narrative is lifelike and pathetic. "In the beginning of March the Queen was seized with a kind of stupor and heaviness, with a pettishness common enough to old persons. She would sit in one posture and not eat, and would confine her discourse to the Archbishop of Canterbury."

Elizabeth died at three o'clock in the morning of the 24th of March, the day before Lady-Day, 1603. She was several months from the completion of her seventieth year, and had reigned forty-four years and four months. Robert Carey was hovering close at hand, waiting for confirmation of the end. There is another ring story brought in here, but at least it has the support of considerable probability. The tradition is, that the concerted signal between Carey and his sister, Lady Scrope, was a ring known as "the blue ring" (sapphires), to be flung by her from a particular window. A different account, furnished by Carey himself, is that he heard by a sentinel the Queen was dead, and hurrying to the sufferer's chamber, found all her ladies assembled there, weeping bitterly. In whatever manner the information was received, Carey started post-haste on his long ride, day and night, to Scotland, that he might be the first to carry the news to King James, who afterwards created the messenger Earl of Monmouth.

Elizabeth's body was embalmed and conveyed by water to Whitehall. When her funeral passed through the streets to Westminster, a vast concourse of people witnessing the procession, a reaction in feeling had already taken place. As men and women beheld her wax effigy lying, according to the custom of the time, on the coffin in royal robes, a crown on the head, a ball and a sceptre in each hand, they broke into loud wailing and weeping for their best friend, the wisest, greatest sovereign England had seen.

Very many of the readers of these papers must have looked on the stately monument in white marble which King James erected in Westminster Abbey, over the tomb in which Elizabeth's coffin lies by the side of her sister Mary's. Before long a similar monument was raised in the northern aisle of the same chapel (Henry VII.'s) to Mary Queen of Scots, whose body was brought by her son's command from Peterborough, taken through London by torchlight, and deposited in Westminster Abbey. Thus the famous Queens rest in death within a stone's-throw of each other.

The monument in the Abbey was not the only one designed to commemorate Queen Elizabeth's virtues. In the fresh glow of love and gratitude in the hearts of her subjects, the Londoners alone reared tokens of their admiration and reverence in all the chief London churches—St. Saviour's, Southwark ; St. Mary Woolnoth ; St. Lawrence Jewry ; St. Mildred's, Poultry ; St. Andrew Undershaft.[1]

[1] Hare's " Walks in London.'

THE VENERABLE MARGARET[1]

BY MARRIAGE A TUDOR

FIRST in point of time, and by far the first in order of merit, comes "The Lady Margaret," Countess of Richmond, the "venerable Margaret" of Gray's verse, the mother of a race of kings, of whom her biographer could write with truth, "She was the friend of the friendless, the comforter of the afflicted, the munificent patroness of learning, and the meek but strenuous supporter of religion."

She was the great-granddaughter of John of Gaunt, Duke of Lancaster, her father having been John of Gaunt's eldest grandson, John Duke of Somerset, while her mother was the heiress to the Lords Beauchamp. Old Fuller declared of her that "she was fair field and fair fort, fair body and fair soul. . . . Taxed for no personal fault, but the errors of the age she lived in." She was born in her mother's house of Bletsoe, in Bedfordshire, in 1441. She was left fatherless, the heiress of her father's great estates, at the age of four years. To be born and left a child-heiress in those days was generally to become an object of fierce strife, in which the future peace and happiness of the coveted child were scarcely thought of, and in this sense the little creature ran the heaviest risks. Accordingly, the first distinct glimpse we have of the future woman, is from a statement she herself made in after years. We find the little girl kneeling, on the eve

---

[1] Miss Halsted Cooper, volume of the Antiquarian Society, Cambridge, Fuller.

of the day when she was called on to give her decision,
as to which of two powerfully supported candidates for
her hand she should choose to be her betrothed husband.
Henry VI. said his half-brother, Edmund ap Tudor; her
guardian, the Duke of Suffolk, said his son, John de la
Pole; and Margaret, at the tender age of nine years,
was to choose between the rival suitors.   The innocent
umpire sought, in her perplexity, the counsel of an old
gentlewoman whom she loved; she, in her turn, bade
the small maiden pray to St. Nicholas, the patron and
helper of maidens.   As the tiny white figure fell pros-
trate in prayer, a vision seemed to pass before the child's
reverently shut eyes—"whether sleeping or waking," the
truthful woman who told the story in later days, humbly
owned she could not be assured; but she knew it was
about four of the clock in the morning when a man,
arrayed like a bishop, appeared to stand before her, and
put into her mouth the name "Edmund."   So to Edmund
ap Tudor, whom the King created Earl of Richmond,
she was betrothed, and to him she was married in 1455,
when she was in her fourteenth, and he in his twenty-
sixth year.

We feel as if the world went with fearful rapidity then,
and events, whether of joy or sorrow, followed in each
other's train in hurried succession.   In the course of two
more years, when Margaret was sixteen, we see her a
youthful widow, the mother of a child not yet six months
old.   She was fain to find refuge in the Castle of Pembroke (where her baby was born), because it was regarded
as an almost impregnable fortress, built as it was on
a steep rock, and nearly surrounded by water.   In this
isolated castle, which belonged to her late husband's
brother, she stayed some five years, during which she married, at the age of nineteen, her second husband, a kinsman, Sir Henry Stafford, son of the Duke of Buckingham.
Never were the stout arm and trusty championship

of a good husband needed more.   The Wars of the
Roses were raging beyond the castle walls, and in these
wars Margaret lost many relations and friends, amongst
them her stepfather, Lord Wells, who fell at Towton; her
uncle, the Duke of Somerset, killed at St. Albans; and her
father-in-law, the Duke of Buckingham, slain at Northampton.   We have a glimpse of the young châtelaine and
her doings in the Welsh stronghold.   She rose at five
o'clock every morning, and passed several hours in prayer
and devotion.   Having been instructed in medicine and
chirurgery, she spent a portion of each day in dressing
the wounds and ministering to the ailments of the sick
and poor, the castle's dependents.   "Right studious she
in bokes, which she had in grete number, both in English
and French."   For she had been unusually educated for
the period.   She could not only read and write English
well—which was more than most noble ladies could accomplish—she was familiar with French, and had some
acquaintance with Latin.   Her skill in embroidery was
so great that the products of her needle were the wonder
of succeeding generations.   One of them, still cherished
by her descendants, is a carpet, bearing a representation
of the arms and alliances of her family.

But she did still more.   In these troubled years, when
visiting, except in the immediate neighbourhood, was
impossible, and when such public and private news as
came was touched with alarm and sorrow, she diverted
her active mind and occupied what was left of her well-
filled time, by honourable authorship, and this at an era
when printing had only just been introduced into England
by Caxton, and when vocabularies and lexicons were not
in existence!   We may see the young, high-born authoress
—the first English authoress—seated at her escritoire,
translating with infinite toil and patience, for the good
of her soul and of fellow-souls, a French work, itself
a translation from the Latin, which she named the

"Mirror of Gold for the Sinful Soule." Oh, admirable
Margaret!

When her little son was five years of age, and Margaret
but twenty-one, an end came to this comparatively peaceful period of her life. In one of the successes of the York
faction the earldom and castle of Pembroke were taken
from Jasper ap Tudor, Margaret's brother-in-law, a pronounced Lancastrian, and given to William Herbert, a
zealous Yorkist. It would seem that the child was given
with the castle, for he was ten years in the keeping of the
new earl, a man of honour, and of his motherly countess,
until a turn of fortune restored Pembroke Castle to Jasper
ap Tudor, and the lad of fifteen to his mother. Their
reunion was of brief duration. Again the Lancastrian
fortunes fell. There was a siege of Pembroke Castle, by
a partisan of the House of York, in which Margaret was
involved, and when the siege was raised by an adherent of
the Tudors, she saw herself under the necessity of urging
her brother-in-law to flee with her son, who had become a
dangerously prominent representative of the losing side.
She accompanied the fugitives to Tenby, where she bade
them a long farewell. She had to be content with the
sorry tidings that they had been cast ashore on the coast
of Brittany, and though they had escaped with their lives,
and were beyond the reach of their worst enemies, they
were, in fact, captives. In the meantime, young Richmond's lands were attainted, though those of his mother
were spared.

Margaret's second husband, of whom little is known,
died nine or ten years afterwards, in 1482, when she was
forty-one years of age; and in the precipitancy with
which, in those days, even such widows as she was,
resigned their peculiarly forlorn and perilous state of
widowhood, and accepted fresh defenders of their persons
and property, she married soon afterwards a kinsman of
her own again, a near enough cousin to require a Papal

dispensation to be sought for their marriage. He was Thomas, Lord Stanley. He was, like herself, in middle life, and he was a widower with a large family. It may seem strange that he was a Yorkist; but he was also a gallant, high-spirited gentleman, certainly not unwilling to be influenced by Margaret in his political opinions. While he was still in favour with Richard III., not only he, but also his wife, had to fill prominent places at Richard's coronation. We read of the stately and learned Margaret appearing in sumptuous attire, bearing the train of the unhappy Queen Anne, Warwick's daughter, who, by the way, was also the widow of the murdered Prince Edward of Lancaster, nephew of Margaret's first husband, Edmund, Earl of Richmond. But the great countess's heart must have ached sorely behind the " purfled " crimson velvet and cloth of gold, not only because of old, painful memories, which would not be silent, but for want of her son, her only child. The boy of fifteen was now a man of seven-and-twenty, and in the interval the poor mother's yearning eyes had never once rested on the face which his contemporaries said was so manly and handsome. What wonder that when Margaret was journeying, soon afterwards, to the shrine of our Lady of Worcester, to offer up her prayers and vows, chancing to encounter on the road her second husband's nephew, the Duke of Buckingham, on his way to Shrewsbury, the countess begged the duke to intercede with King Richard that her son might return to England. She would promise that he should marry one of the daughters of Edward IV., without anything to be taken or demanded for the said espousals, but only the King's favour. Tradition will have it, that though such a marriage had been bruited more than once before, it was these words of Margaret's which first drew the attention of the chief of the Lancastrian party to the double claim to the throne that young Richmond, wedded to Elizabeth of York, would possess, which would thus render him the most formidable opponent to Richard.

However, the first rising of the Lancastrians was premature, and Margaret had the misery of seeing it collapse and Buckingham perish, while only her husband's favour with Richard saved her own life. As it was, her eldest stepson was detained a hostage at court. But better days were at hand. Henry of Richmond landed at last at Milford Haven. Richard, whose unscrupulous crimes had disgusted not England alone, but his most faithful followers, met his enemy at Bosworth; the Stanleys, in spite of the deadly peril of their heir, deserting from the King's standard on the eve of the battle. Bosworth Field was lost and won. Richard was slain, and his crown, found not far off, near a hawthorn bush, was placed on the head of Margaret's son by Margaret's husband.

On Henry VII.'s coronation in Westminster it is recorded that the Lady Margaret "wept marvellously," for the greater her prosperity the more she dreaded adversity, with reason enough, poor tried soul! But her worldly trials were over; thenceforth she was the honoured mother of my lord the king, appearing with the royal family in great state at all family ceremonies, the festivals of Yuletide and Easter, and dispensing princely hospitality on her own account. We cannot help pausing to ask whether Margaret, great-hearted as we know her, was not disappointed in the son who had returned to her, the silent reserved man of nine-and-twenty, with the long, pale face, which so soon grew singularly haggard, and the foreign accent which clung to him? There is this to be said in excuse for his defects, that from childhood he had been a prisoner, a fugitive, and an exile, but he was woefully unlike his mother. He was, according to an excellent authority, "thoroughly commonplace." He was jealous, grasping, both of money and of power, and hostile to the new dawn of learning which Margaret was

striving, with womanly enthusiasm, to foster. He himself
was not an unlearned man, for he had availed himself of
the lagging hours of his captivity to master Latin, as well as
to study the old legends of his ancestor, Arthur Pendragon.

The only point in which mother and son resembled each
other, was that while he was undoubtedly a brave soldier,
he was also a lover and promoter of peace. At the same
time he was a dutiful and affectionate son, showing the
Lady Margaret great outward reverence, and yet, as Bacon
adds significantly, "not listening to her." But doubtless
the mother in her saw the best of him whom she styled
"my own swete and most dear kyng, and all my worldly
joye," "my good herte," signing herself his "faithful, true
bedeswoman and humble modyr." And she was on the
friendliest terms with her meek and generous daughter-
in-law, Elizabeth of York.

We must consider Margaret once more, in her noble
public services, her enterprising attempts to drain Bedford
Level; her great grants to numerous churches; her liberal
benefits both to Oxford and Cambridge; and, above all,
her magnificent endowments of St. John's and Christ
Church, Cambridge. In the building and establishing of
the last she took great interest, reserving apartments for
herself in the college, when she should come to inspect
its progress. It was on such an occasion, that looking
from a window, and seeing the dean call up a faulty scholar
for correction, she chimed in with her "*Lentè, lentè*" (gently,
gently), "as accounting it better to mitigate his punishment than to procure his pardon. Mercy and justice
making the best medley to offenders," ends Fuller, with
his quaint sententiousness. Her zeal for the deliverance
of the Holy Land from the infidel was so great that she
was known to say in her age, "If the Cristen princes
wold have warred upon the enemmyes of his fayth, she
wold be glad yet to go follow the hoste, and help to wash
theyre clothes, for the love of Jhesu."

Margaret survived her promising grandson Prince
Arthur, her good daughter-in-law, the queen, and Margaret's own worthy husband, created Earl of Derby, who
died in 1504. The couple are said to have been like-
minded in this, that while living in the world they "entered
on religion;" that is, took the vows of a religious life.
This is given as the reason why Margaret, who in the lifetime of her husband could not have been a nun, is nevertheless frequently represented in a nun's habit and veil.
In the portraits and medallions which survive of her, she
appears with fine strong features, which might have been
beautiful in youth, and must have been full of dignity and
benignity in age. She was sixty-three when Thomas Earl
of Derby died, and it was in the same year that the last
specimen of her authorship appeared in a translation of the
fourth book of an "Imitation of Christ," from a treatise
similar in design to that of Thomas à Kempis. She had
yet to sustain another severe loss in the death of her beloved son, King Henry, in his fifty-third year, when she
was sixty-eight years of age. She lived a few months
longer, during which she acted, in some respects, as
guardian to her young grandson Henry VIII. Then, in
1509, we have the last piteous pathetic scene as described
by Bishop Fisher in her funeral sermon. He laments over
"these merciful and liberal hands that had to endure the
most painful cramps—so grievously vexing her, and compelling her to cry, 'Oh, blessed Jesu! succour me.' It
was a matter of great pity. Like a spear, it pierced the
hearts of all true servants that were about her, and made
them cry also of Jesu, for help and succour, with great
abundance of tears. . . . But specially when they saw
death so haste upon her, and that she must needs depart
from them, and they should lose so gentle a mistress and
so tender a lady. Then they wept marvellously; wept
her ladies and kinswomen, to whom she was full kind;
wept her poor gentlewomen, whom she had loved so

tenderly before; wept her chamberers, to whom she was full dear; wept her chaplains and other faithful servants."

Thus passed away, fitly bemoaned, the noblest life we know of in that generation. All that was mortal of her lies buried under a costly monument in her son's splendid chapel in Westminster Abbey.

ELIZABETH OF YORK [1]

BY MARRIAGE A TUDOR

ELIZABETH OF YORK, eldest daughter of Edward IV. and
Elizabeth Woodville, his Queen, was born at Westminster
in 1466. In the varying fortunes of the house of York,
during the Wars of the Roses, Princess Elizabeth, with
her mother and sisters, was repeatedly driven to flee from
the Palace of Shene, the royal children's usual home, and
to take sanctuary within the shadow of the Abbey of
Westminster. At one time it was in fear of the victorious
Lancastrians, at another in dread of Richard Duke of
Gloster—the ambitious uncle, whom posterity has been
accustomed to look back upon as a monster in human
form, whom more authentic records bring before us as a
great deal more crooked in mind than in body. He was
merely a man of low stature, with possibly an inequality
of shoulder so slight as to be imperceptible to most
people's eyes, and a rather handsome, intellectual face;
for he was a keen-witted, cultured man for his day, while
he was bent on the attainment of his ends, and, in order
to secure his object, capable of criminal violence and the
most cold-blooded cruelty.

In the meantime Elizabeth's father, Edward, when his
cause was in the ascendant, attempted to further it by
means of a royal alliance. Having lost his own chance
of achieving a powerful connection, and alienated the
king-maker Warwick by marrying a subject to please his
eye, rather than a princess to promote his interest, he

---

[1] Agnes Strickland.

tried to make use of his little daughter's hand by offering or promising it in marriage to a variety of eligible
suitors. Perhaps never had a small damsel so many
offers of matrimony—the Dauphin of France; the King
of Scots; the hereditary foe, poor Prince Edward of Lancaster; the most powerful representative of the great
barons; a young member of the mighty house of Neville;
and the man who afterwards married her, Henry Earl of
Richmond, were all at some time in the lists. Yet Elizabeth was still unwedded, a girl of seventeen, at the date
of her father's death, 1483. She was tall and fair to see,
with the blonde complexion, brilliant colour, and bright
golden or reddish hair, which were the personal attributes
of nearly all the Tudor race in their young days. It is a
popular type of beauty, and Elizabeth was styled, in the
doggerel verses of the time, "The Fair Lady Bessy." The
family characteristics, in her case, were rendered still more
attractive by delicate regularity of feature, and the sweet
expression which belonged to a mild temper and a kind
heart. It is quite possible to conceive, even four hundred
years afterwards, what a shock the affectionate, girlish
nature must have received, from the melancholy fate of
the two little lads, her brothers, in their uncle the Duke
of Gloster's keeping, and from her mother's despair at
the catastrophe. It is necessary to remember that the
reality must have been a great deal worse to the relations
of the innocent victims than if the princely boys of
thirteen and eleven years had been openly slain. They
simply disappeared, and the mode of their disappearance,
however strongly suspected, was kept a dark secret, and
has never been clearly brought to light; their very bodies
—or the skeletons supposed to represent them—were not
found under the steps of the Tower Chapel till a century
after the princes' death. At the time their poor mother,
sisters, and remoter kindred were tried and tortured
by the most terrible doubt and uncertainty. One can

understand that the health of the young girl Elizabeth, apparently never robust, may have been permanently undermined by the horrors of the tragedy in the family; but what is simply incredible is, that a timid, tender creature, such as she showed herself to be, could have given any encouragement, in the lifetime of the invalid Queen Anne, to the gruesome idea that King Richard, on his wife's death, should pay his addresses to his eldest niece, Princess Elizabeth. Her mother, Elizabeth Woodville, whom we might expect to be the less sensitive and the more hardened in the world's ways of the two, is said to have shrunk with unconquerable repugnance from the suggestion. It is still less likely that her young daughter would feel inclined to overlook the ghastly obstacle to the match. Yet it is just possible that, taken from her mother's custody and detained at Richard's court, she may, in mortal terror of her suitor, have dissembled her loathing of him, so long as Richard himself entertained a scheme which, he had soon to see, was too unnatural in his people's eyes to be tenable.

Richard's defeat and death at Bosworth must have been a blessed release to Princess Elizabeth, and her transference to the wise guidance of Lady Margaret a fortunate event in her history. Elizabeth was then a charming young woman of nineteen, a fit mate in every respect for Henry VII., the bridegroom who awaited her. The marriage was celebrated at Westminster in January 1485, with great rejoicing on the part of the nation, because of the union of the rival houses of York and Lancaster, and with no end of banquets, bonfires, and pageants, in which white and red roses figured prominently.

It is said that Henry's jealous temper took umbrage at his Queen's independent claim to the throne. If so, it was from no provocation on her part. Never was there princess or woman who asserted herself less, or who in all wifely deference appears to have been more willing to

render her pretentions entirely subservient to those of her
husband. The income settled on her was too small for
her wants, though she was personally economical, well
nigh to parsimony, and was only generous to relations
and dependents. Henry helped her at intervals from his
private purse; but there is no mention of any attempt on
his part to get her inadequate allowance increased, or to
prevent the humiliating anomaly of the Queen having
sums doled out to her by the keeper of her purse, which,
even when the difference in the value of money is taken
into account, sound ludicrously small for her rank and
needs. "The Queen was supplied with ten shillings," is
sufficiently comical, but where the sum falls so low as
"four and fourpence," the contradiction is still more
mirth-provoking. Henry was a cold-mannered undemon-
strative man, over whom the Queen possessed not the
slightest influence; while it had been currently reported,
at the time of their marriage, that if he had got his
choice he would have wedded one of the daughters of the
Countess of Pembroke, with whom he had spent ten years
of his early youth. But he was a loyal husband; he gave his
wife all the respect and affection which he had to bestow;
he was "companionable" to her, in Bacon's phrase; and
she was happy in their kindred—both his and hers—his
noble mother, her own mother, her lovely young sisters, to
whom she was warmly attached; three of them became
the wives of English noblemen, while one, Princess Bridget,
was a nun. Above all, Elizabeth was destined to be the
happy mother of several fine children. The heir, Arthur,
was born at Winchester in September 1486, and was
hailed with as much gladness and triumph as had attended
on his father and mother's marriage.

The attempted rebellions on the part of Lambert Simnel
and Perkin Warbeck, who claimed to be, respectively,
Clarence's son Warwick, and Richard Duke of York, the
younger of Elizabeth's brothers murdered in the Tower,

disturbed the peace of the reign. In the case of the last the pretension must have been peculiarly trying to the Queen, though there is not the slightest evidence that she ever wavered with regard to the claimant's identity, far less passed over to his side, like his supporters, her aunt the Duchess-Dowager of Burgundy and James IV. of Scotland. The compassion which Elizabeth displayed towards Perkin Warbeck's young widow, Lady Catherine Gordon, who bore his cognomen, "The White Rose," to whom the Queen gave a place at court, till Lady Catherine's second marriage to a Welsh knight, was due solely to an instinct of humanity, with which even the phlegmatic King sympathised, and to Elizabeth's gentle character.

The poor Queen was sorely tormented with ague, which passed into consumption, and must have rendered the burden of her royal rank, with all its ceremonious obligations, often a dire distress to her. She played her part in the arrangement of the marriages of three out of four of her princes and princesses. She welcomed Catherine of Arragon as the bride of Arthur, Prince of Wales, and five months afterwards she had to lament his untimely death in his nineteenth year in 1502. There is much simple pathos in the scene (the details of which Miss Strickland industriously sought out) when the news was broken to the King and Queen. The King's confessor brought the grievous tidings to the King, prefacing his communication with the solemn words, "If we receive good at the hands of God, shall we not sustain the ill He sends us?" When the King knew the worst he sent for the Queen, saying that he and his wife would take their painful sorrow together. On her arrival she forgot her own grief in striving to sustain and comfort him. Among other words she spoke, with loving tact, were these:—"And remember that my lady, your mother, had never no more children but you only. Yet God, by His grace, has ever preserved you, and brought you where you are; now, over and above, God has left you yet a fair prince and two fair princesses, and God is still where He was, and we are both young enough. As your Grace's wisdom is renowned all over Christendom, you must now give proof of it by the manner of taking this misfortune." The brave, ailing woman retired to her chamber, where her own sorrow, restrained till then, broke forth with such violence that her attendants, alarmed, sent for the King to console her in turn. He reminded her "what wise counsel she had given him," and that "if she would thank God for her dead son, he would do likewise."

Elizabeth's days were numbered; she lived to see the marriage, by proxy, of her elder daughter Margaret, a girl of twelve years, and then withdrew to the Tower, an ill-omened retreat, where Elizabeth's eighth child (she had lost a baby prince and princess in addition to Prince Arthur) was born, and in the course of a week the royal mother died on her thirty-seventh birthday, February 11, 1502. Her death was bitterly lamented by all connected with her, who doubtless saw then, if they had not seen before, the full beauty of her unselfishness, modesty, and meekness, and by the people at large, who had learned in their homely sagacity to call her "the good Queen Elizabeth." She was laid, with all honour, in the goodly chapel which Henry VII. destined for his own resting-place, where he now lies by her side, under the joint monument designed by the Italian sculptor Torrigiano. Perhaps it is one of the highest compliments which he paid to her memory, that though her King was not more than forty-nine when his Queen died, and although he survived her five years, he gave her no successor. This does not mean that fresh alliances were not thought of for Henry. It was said that he himself contemplated the perpetuating of the much-valued connection with Spain, by obtaining a Papal dispensation which would

enable him to marry the nominal widow of his son
Arthur; and when she and all others who were consulted
protested against the unnatural project, he transferred his
proposals to her widowed sister Joanna, who was then as
mad a princess as was ever placed in durance. There was
also an overture made for his marriage with a third
widow, the Austrian Princess Margaret of Savoy. But
after all, these more or less languid suggestions began
and ended in talk.

MARGARET TUDOR[1]

QUEEN OF JAMES IV. OF SCOTLAND

NEVER was grand-daughter more unlike her grandmother, godmother, and name-mother than Margaret Tudor was unlike the Lady Margaret, who, on the infant's christening, on St. Andrew's Day (in the church of St. Margaret's, Westminster, in token of her future destination, already settled), bestowed on the unconscious object of her favour a silver and gilt coffer full of gold pieces. Young Margaret was equally unlike her gentle mother and her silent, cautious father, for if she had a great desire to acquire money, like Henry VII., she had an equal talent for spending it, which he certainly never exhibited. Even the luxuriant fair hair and bright bloom, which were the attributes of the Tudors in youth, took in Margaret Tudor the style of a barn-door beauty, if one may apply such a description to a princess. The eldest daughter of Henry VII. and Elizabeth of York was born at Westminster, in November 1489. After a brief and not very well-spent girlhood, considering that she managed to make as little use as she possibly could of every advantage of education offered to her, she was married by proxy at the age of twelve years, a few days before the death of her mother, to James IV. of Scotland, a man of thirty, one of the most gallant and accomplished princes of his day.

A deputation of men of the highest rank in Scotland

---

[1] Bohn's edition of Agnes Strickland for 1888, with the latest additions —"Pinkerton," "Lindesay of Pitscottie," "William Dunbar."

had come south to claim their King's bride. Among
them was a gentleman who was paid an allowance for his
services, under the curious title of "The Rhymer of Scotland." This was not an older rhymer—"Wise Thomas" of
Ercildoune, already long lost in fairyland—but one of the
gently-born Scotch poets of the generation. Two of them
celebrated the King's marriage and the budding charms of
Margaret : Gavin Douglas, the priest, afterwards Bishop
of Dunkeld, son of the all-powerful Angus, in his " Palace
of Honour ; " and William Dunbar, the aforesaid rhymer,
by profession as well as by taste.

Three months before the King's marriage Dunbar wrote
his poem of " The Thrissel (thistle) and the Rois " (rose) ;
so much satisfaction did it give in high quarters, that he
is understood to have been appointed, in his literary
capacity, to accompany the royal commission which went
to accomplish the King's marriage and bring home the
Queen.

"The Thistle and the Rose" is a quaintly beautiful
allegory, in which a nymph, the spirit of the May, intro-
duces the poet to a wonderfully fair and mystic world.
The lion, king of beasts, figures in it; so does the eagle,
king of fowls; but fair flowers and singing birds are
its most significant symbols. The nymph takes Dunbar
into "a lusty garden," where among other herbs he
sees—

"The aweful thistle,[1]
. . . kept with a bush of spears,
Considering him so able for the warrs,
A radius crown of rubies she him gave,
And said he should go forth to find the lave " (rest).

The thistle, of course, represents King James, and soon
the poet and his guide encounter the rose, the emblem of
Margaret.

---

[1] The spelling is for the most part modernised to render the words
intelligible to Southern readers.

> "None other flower in such dainty
> As the fresh rose, in colours red and white,
> . . . no flower is so perfyte (perfect),
> So full of virtue, pleasure, and delight,
> So full of blissful angels' beauty,
> Imperial birth, honour, and dignity."

To identify the rose still more closely with the Princess Margaret, we have the lines—

> "A costly crown, with clarified stones bright,
> This comely queen did on her head enclose;
> While all the land illumined of the light,
> Wherefore methought the flowers did rejoice,
> Crying . . . Hail to the richest rose!
> Hail herbs' empress! Hail freshest queen of flowers!
> To thee be glory and honour at all hours."

The mavis (thrush) hails her; the merle (blackbird) hails her, and all the other birds follow suit, singing her welcome.

In the end Margaret was a rose full of thorns to Scotland. But there was little expectation of such misadventure, when, very little subdued by the sad death of her best friend, which had darkened the marriage rejoicings, the girl princess set out with "a noble and magnificent retinue," under the charge of the Earl of Surrey. She was to make the long journey on her two white palfreys, and in her litter, through the northern counties and over the borders.

In truth, it was a triumphal progress, the strong willed, giddy brained heroine of which was received with acclamation at every stage of her route, lodged sumptuously each night in manor house, castle, and abbey; greeted as she passed through the larger towns with gifts and largesses.

James came to Dalkeith to meet his young Queen, standing before her bonnet in hand. It is quite in character that the girl of twelve, far from her family, in a strange country, received, without embarrassment or emotion, the grown man, who was already her husband, on whom so much of her future welfare depended. She was perfectly able to exhibit her chief accomplishments of playing on the lute and dancing with Lady Surrey a *basse* dance, whatever that might have been.[1] He in his turn played on the clavichord (a miniature piano) for her gratification. Lord Surrey delivered over his charge, who was to be a pledge of peace between the sister countries, but as the old historian, Pinkerton, was tempted to add, in striking antithesis, the earl gave " a blooming bride to James, whom he afterwards defeated and slew."

One would have had more faith in the chivalrous homage paid by " the Squire of Dames," if it were easier to forget the fact that he had passed, with small delay, to his wooing of an empty-headed, self-confident child, from his mourning for Margaret Drummond, the fair, unhappy woman whom he had privately married in his romantic youth, who, with her sisters Sybella and Euphemia, had been foully murdered by an unknown murderer to prevent the King's open acknowledgment of her as his wife.

There is a touch of nature and of girlish feeling on the part of Margaret, in the account of the fire which broke out at Dalkeith on the night of Margaret's arrival. The young girl's cherished white palfreys perished in the flames, and she was so inconsolable for their loss, that the King paid her a second visit to divert her thoughts and entertain her, before her public entrance into Edinburgh, which she made with much magnificence and in a picturesque Darby and Joan fashion; the King, superbly attired, riding on a palfrey, with Margaret in an equally rich and gay dress on a pillion behind him. So the royal couple passed through the narrow crowded streets of tall houses, every window full of noble company, the castle on its rock frowning down on them, and Arthur's Seat keeping stern guard over the whole stirring scene.

In the early years of Margaret's married life she lost three infant children, and was " sore vexed with sickness,"

[1] *Basses* dances were slow and stately measures in the style of minuets.

like her mother; but she was not prevented from entering into hot contention with her husband, from allying herself with the Douglas faction against his wishes and interests, and from starting the grumbling begging letters—about the payment of her legacy from her late brother, Prince Arthur, in the first place—for which she was conspicuous. Not even a play in which "Davie Lindesay" played before her taught her sense and contentment. Margaret's fourth child—the first which lived beyond a few months—was "ane fair prince," born in Linlithgow Palace in 1512, and immediately committed, by day and night, to the same stout, sagacious Davie Lindesay, whose loving tales of the royal boy's childhood are still preserved in the tutor's verses.

Our next view of Margaret is when she was passionately opposing James's reckless invasion of England and march on Flodden. In reality Queen Margaret had right and reason on her side in this dispute, though the argument which she used that he had but one son, "which was but a weak warrant to the realm of Scotland," was not a particularly lofty one. She so won the gratitude of her adopted countrymen, by her excellent advice on this occasion, that they at once gave her credit for an amount of prudence and good judgment which her subsequent conduct did not by any means justify. Margaret was not supposed to confine her urgent remonstrances to words. She was believed to have been concerned in the dreams and visions and midnight proclamation at the Market Cross of Edinburgh—womanly enough devices, all intended to turn James from his resolution, and scare him from his headlong course.

In fair Linlithgow Palace, by its peaceful lake, there was long shown a turret-chamber called "Queen Margaret's Bower," in which she is said to have spent, in tears of bitter mortification, the day of her husband's departure to invade her brother Henry VIII.'s kingdom; and where she awaited, through a long and terrible night, the news of how James lay, stiff and stark, the centre of a knightly ring, on the fatal battle-field by the Till. Lamentable as the tidings were, Margaret was not overwhelmed or even deeply depressed by them. At the same time, there is not the slightest evidence that she then, if ever, shared in the doubt with regard to the lifeless body of her husband, which caused some of his subjects to cling fondly to the belief that he was not slain with so many of his faithful nobles, but would one day return. It is not difficult to imagine such a woman as Margaret rising up hastily from her passing dismay at Scotland's desolation, and her baby prince's ruin, wiping away her few fleeting tears for the death, in his manly prime, of the husband whom she had never greatly loved, who had not loved her much, and taking refuge in elation at finding herself mistress of the situation, with the Regency of Scotland within her grasp.

She retreated at once with her son to the strong northern town of Perth, wrote to her victorious brother, begging him to spare her "little king, very small and tender, being then only one year and five months old." She presided over "the mourning coronation," 1513, when the crown was held by strong hands, amid sighs and sobs, above the soft brows, too feeble to bear its weight.

The Lords in Council confirmed James IV.'s will, by which he left Margaret Regent of the country during James V.'s minority. She was then in her twenty-fourth year. A description of her by Pinkerton, when she was supposed to have "merited and possessed the admiration of all ranks," is life-like and in keeping with much which we know of her. "Her youthful beauty and graces rather proclaimed the bride than the widow. Her circular countenance displaying gaiety, her vivacious eyes, her person rather rustic than delicate, were accompanied with a corresponding vigour of health." Her "vigour of health," like what the historian says further of "the talents which threw her faults into the shade," existed mainly in the writer's imagination, for Margaret was frequently seriously ailing, and though she acted, as might have been expected, with dauntless audacity, there is little other indication of her showing any capacity to rule. She had spirit enough at this time to refuse the asylum which her brother Henry speciously offered to her and her little king, making the refusal on the plausible ground that she was surrounded by guards and spies. But she added, "An I were such a woman that I might go with my bairn on my arm, I trow I should not be long from you."

Yet one of her first acts was to conceal and appropriate, for her own use, the sum of money found in her late husband's treasury, and one of her next, four months after she had given birth to a posthumous son, named Alexander, and created Duke of Ross, was to marry the grandson of the great Earl of Angus (Bell-the-Cat). No doubt the path which Margaret would have to tread was rough and full of pitfalls. She was a young, defenceless woman among Scotchmen, whom, with certain exceptions, she persisted in regarding to the end of her days as her natural enemies, while to marry the Scotchman of foremost rank of his time was to take the bull by the horns. Still, young Angus was one of those haughty Douglases whose overweening pretensions threatened the throne. He was a mere lad of nineteen, though he was already a widower and troth-plighted for the second time to a girl he loved, Lady Janet Stewart, of the house of Traquhair, and he was simple and weak, totally unfitted for the post to which he was elevated. His principal recommendations were openly said to be his lofty stature and handsome face.

On the announcement of Margaret's marriage, the Lords in Council deposed her from the Regency, and invited the little king's kinsman, the Duke of Albany, to come over from France and assume the guidance of affairs. Then began the tug of war between Margaret, to retain possession of her children, and the well-bred man of the world, Albany, to foil her in her purpose. It was a case of diamond cut diamond, for the pair met each other with the most disarming courtesy, while neither was inclined to yield a jot. However, Margaret succumbed so far as to weep and beseech grace from Albany for her husband's grandfather, Lord Drummond, and his uncle Gavin Douglas, who had both been cast into prison, the first for striking a blow at Lord Lyon King-at-Arms, when he was delivering a message from the Council to the Queen; and the second because Margaret had appointed him, without proper authority, to the Archbishopric of St. Andrews. As for Albany, he granted the prayer with courtly grace.

Four peers were sent from the Parliament House to Edinburgh Castle, where Margaret and her children were established, that she might select three out of the four to whom she would confide her sons. The peers proceeded with great state, amidst a concourse of people, to accomplish their delicate mission. When they reached their destination, they discovered that a fine spectacle had been provided for them and the public, since Margaret had a decided eye for dramatic effect.

"The gates were thrown open, and the people beheld with sympathy and admiration the young and beautiful Queen standing at the entrance, with the infant king by her side, his hand locked in hers; behind was the nurse, with the other royal babe in her arms; around appeared Angus and a few attendants."

Margaret then challenged her visitors, "Stand and declare the cause of your coming."

The peers, answering that they were sent by the Parliament to demand their king and his brother, were struck with awe and confusion when the Queen's command resounded through the hum of voices, "Drop the portcullis," the massy grate of iron being immediately let down.

Behind the barrier, Margaret, in a short, dignified harangue, told her assailants that the castle was part of her enfeoffment of which the king, her late husband, had made her sole governess. She would give up the command to no mortal, but she respected the Parliament and the nation, so she requested six days to consider their mandate, for her charge was of infinite consequence, and her counsellors were now, alas! few. Having spoken her mind, she retired, and the baffled peers withdrew, doubtless comparing notes on a woman's wit and *dourness*.

Margaret maintained the same defiant attitude after her young husband had deserted her in her strait, and retreated to the Douglas fastnesses, when Albany followed her and her children to Stirling, to which town she had fled. The Regent required her to give up the fortress in which, as being the strongest castle on its rock in Scotland, the princes were to be lodged, for their greater safety, with the Forth winding its links at their feet, the green Ochils helping to fence them in, and the blue Grampians forming a solid rampart in the background. Again Margaret met the foe at the gate, and saved her pride by putting the huge keys of the keep into the little king's hand, and bidding him resign them to Albany, who received them kneeling, and treated both mother and child with the utmost forbearance and kindness.

But the Queen was not to be baulked in her intention of keeping the power in her own hand, if an unscrupulous woman's determination to carry her point would win the day. She engaged in a scheme to carry off her sons to her brother's court, and conducted it with a singular mixture of courage and craft, in spite of the very halting support afforded her by Lord Angus, and of her own delicate state of health. She went with her ladies to the palace of Linlithgow, in preparation for the birth of her sixth child, and professed to practise the utmost seclusion. Under the plea of illness she summoned " My Lord of

Anguish," as she and her country people generally, persisted in calling the lukewarm young peer. Under cover of night she stole out with him, attended only by a handful of servants, met by appointment an escort of horse under Lord Home, and succeeded in gaining the Douglas's strong square castle of Tantallon, on the Firth of Forth, not very far from Berwick and the English border.

This was but half of the bold plot. It included further unhesitating details. Home was to "fire a town" in order to attract Albany's attention from Stirling, when Home, who as Lord Chamberlain could command access to the little princes, was to carry them off in the confusion, and take them to their mother at Blackadder Castle, a step nearer to England. The unprincipled enterprise failed in consequence of Albany's declining to be decoyed away from his charge. In fear of the vengeance of the Regent, and of the whole Scotch nation, wife and husband fled in different directions, Margaret withdrawing in such haste to the sanctuary of Coldstream Nunnery, that she left her jewels and plate behind—spoil politely sent after her by her lordly enemy.

The Queen was in dire distress. She could not venture to enter England without her brother's permission, and under the circumstances of her defeat it was doubtful whether Henry and his minister Wolsey would come to her aid. Henry did at last send her an invitation to Morpeth Castle, but she became so ill on the road that she was taken "in a fainting state" to the rude border Tower of Harbottle. Its master, Lord Dacre, one of the Wardens of the Marches, admitted his sovereign's sister in her extremity, but flatly refused to allow "any Scot, man or woman, to follow her." There, not very far from the tragic field of Flodden, in connection with which Margaret must surely have had some mournful memories, her daughter "Lady Margaret Douglas" was born, while the Queen lay in peril of her life. It was not till after several weeks that she was able to quit her uncomfortable quarters and resume her journey to Morpeth. In the meanwhile the Scotch Lords of the Council besought Margaret to return to Scotland, even promising her the guardianship of her children, provided she would pledge herself not to remove them from the kingdom.

But such limited privileges did not suit her imperious ideas. She doggedly declined to come to terms with her son's subjects. She professed to see in the position which James V. and the Duke of Ross held with regard to their kinsman Albany a remarkable resemblance to the situation of her maternal uncles Edward V. and the Duke of York when they were in the keeping of her grand-uncle Richard Duke of Gloster. Unfortunately for Margaret's recovering a more rational and charitable frame of mind, as she still lay ill in Morpeth Castle, the poor little Duke of Ross was attacked with some childish ailment, and died at Stirling, when his mother, in her wretchedness, did not refrain from saying in plain terms that he had been poisoned by Albany. She was seized with typhus fever, and while she lay at death's door was the unseemly occasion which "my Lord of Anguish" took to make terms with Albany, and forsake the Queen's cause.

At last Margaret was able to travel to London, under very different circumstances from those under which she had journeyed north, about thirteen years before, a much-thought-of thoughtless bride, not yet in her teens. She was now in her twenty-sixth year, a woman who had been buffeted by fortune, who had suffered many trials, who had also made, to a great extent, her own by no means enviable reputation.

The Queen was received with apparent sympathy and cordiality by Henry and his Queen, Catherine of Arragon, and saw again her beautiful sister Mary, still in the flower of her youth, from whom Margaret had been parted when the younger princess was a little child. In the interval

she also had married, been widowed, and had married for
the second time.

Margaret has been accused of deliberate treachery in
furnishing the King and Wolsey with information in
reference to the state of Scotch affairs, and in pledging
herself to support the English interest in Scotland.   Her
payment is believed to have been the powerful support
and the grants of money she received from Henry VIII.
But, though it may well have been that she stood more in
awe of her redoubtable brother than of her other relations,
she does not seem to have taken much pains to keep on
good terms with him ; and as to her devotion to English
interests, it was not found incompatible with her subsequent wish to marry Albany, who held a French peerage
and great possessions in France, and was French in all his
proclivities.

Margaret returned to Scotland the following year, and
encountered at Berwick the recreant Angus, of whom she
was, not without reason, heartily tired, and from whom
she sought a divorce.   The evil facility with which royal
and noble marriages were dissolved in that generation
recommended itself to Margaret.   She tried to show, on
tenable grounds, that Angus had been not merely troth-
plighted but married to Lady Janet Stewart, his early
love.   When the Queen was at a loss for any other plea,
she had the audacity to bring forward the extraordinary
argument that there had been no satisfactory evidence
of the death of her first husband James IV. at Flodden,
and that he had been seen alive three years after the battle.
Her efforts to free herself from her second husband were
violently opposed by Henry VIII., who sent a Roman
Catholic priest, high in the favour of the court in
England, down to Scotland to remonstrate with the in-
subordinate wife, in vain.

Margaret was fain to welcome the return of Albany,
who had been absent in France, to defend her from the

claims of Angus. Perhaps the most detested of these was that she had settled upon him at the time of their marriage some of the dower lands, which she had no mind that he should continue to enjoy. It was with regard to this matter that the lamentable grammar and orthography which Margaret displayed in her letters reached their climax. She declared that there should be "no peace till I is done justice."

The Queen had never been personally hostile to Albany, the handsome, gracious Regent. Her foolish vanity had been persuaded that had it not been for her hasty marriage to Angus, he, Albany, would have been a suitor for her hand, in spite of the fact that one of the richest heiresses in France was already his wife. Margaret owed to him the respite afforded to her by his sending "my Lord of Anguish" to France to act as Scotch Ambassador there. When he returned from France he went to the English court, where it was Henry VIII.'s cue to receive him cordially. There Angus and Margaret's little daughter was reared, as standing in near relation to the English throne, her mother having given her up, apparently without the smallest difficulty.

In 1522, when Margaret was thirty-three years of age, she was attacked with small-pox, and lost what beauty remained to her. Her features and skin were thenceforth blurred and roughened. In addition she had the growth which is called "a pearl" on one eye.

Still her incorrigible levity kept her from being satisfied with the sincere affection of her son, a boy of fourteen, and caused her to project another alliance for herself, should she succeed in divorcing Angus. She hankered still after an ambitious marriage with the mature Albany, whose French wife had just died. When he did not avail himself of his freedom, she reverted to her old discreditable preference for very young men. She fixed on a gay, swaggering lad named Harry Stewart, a younger son of Lord

Avondale, and the captain of her son's guards, for her future husband. In every way—in age, rank, and character—he was an utterly unsuitable husband for the Queen, even more unsuitable than Angus had been, and her choice aroused a tempest of opposition.

Henry VIII., of all men, was most indignant, and threatened to send back Angus to capture his wife. Strange to say, Margaret was not altogether unwilling to take a reunion with Angus into consideration, when so far talked over by the specious tongue of the prelate sent down to remonstrate with her. He enlarged cunningly on the improvement in Angus's manners effected by his stay in France, and on the sensation which his magnificent stature and fine looks created in the English court. Margaret wavered. When Angus arrived in Edinburgh, though she professed to be under the necessity of taking refuge in the castle, she consented to see her second husband, and to talk with him in a familiar, friendly way over their separation. But probably she did not find the improvement in his manners which had been promised, or still more possibly the whole proceeding was a deceitful farce, for the impression prevailed that she was by this time privately married to Harry Stewart.

The Queen was doing her utmost to alienate her son. However, she shared with the boy the glory of his first Parliament, while she so impressed him by her "*haught*" words, that the poor, perplexed young King would "gloom and *glower*" at his lieges.

Hostile as he was, with a kind of hereditary antagonism, to the whole Douglas race, James V. made common cause with Angus, when the King summoned his mother to surrender the Castle of Edinburgh, where she and Harry Stewart, at last openly acknowledged as her husband, were residing. Here Margaret availed herself of another chance for scenic effect by flinging herself at her son's feet, in order to implore pardon for her third husband and his brother, who were nevertheless kept in durance for a season.

Eventually King James showed himself merciful and generous. He gave his mother the barony of Methven in Perthshire, in order that she might bestow it on her land-less husband, and created him Lord Methven—a title which fared no better on English lips than that of Angus. Henry VIII., who refused to acknowledge his third Scotch brother-in-law, and treated him with great disdain, set the example of styling him contemptuously "Lord Muffin." [1]

Margaret's residence was thenceforth Methven Castle, but she still retained apartments in Stirling Castle and Holyrood, which she sometimes occupied. She continued to appear occasionally in public, in great state, with her son, as when they went together on a grand Highland hunt, given in their honour by the Earl of Athole, and when there was a royal shooting-match at St. Andrews, described with much relish by Lindesay of Pitscottie. Lord William Howard had come on an embassy from England, accompanied by a bishop and other gentlemen, whom Pitscottie is careful to say were able men and "waled" (picked) men for all kinds of games, shooting, running, "louping" (leaping), &c. ; but even they "tint" (lost.) The King's mother favoured the Englishmen, and wagered on their side against her son in a trial of archery between six of these English gentlemen and six Scotch archers. The wager on either side was a hundred crowns and a tun of wine. The place of contest was the wind-swept sea-braes of St. Andrews, part of them known to this day as "The Scores," the bow-butts having been erected there, where soon, in grim contrast, was to blaze the funeral pile of noble Patrick Hamilton, the first martyr of the Scotch Reformation. The Scotch archers—the sur-names of three of them are still familiar sounds in the neighbourhood of the old University town—"shot very

[1] The Scotch pronunciation of Methven is "Meffen."

near and warred (defeated) the Englishmen," as their historian puts it with innocent triumph, "which made the King very merry that his men should have the victory." He spent his winnings on a grand banquet, in which both victors and vanquished shared.

Margaret lived nearly twenty years after her declared marriage with Harry Stewart, Lord Methven, and bore him a son and a daughter, who are understood to have died in childhood. She tired of her last husband—who appears to have been a better husband than she deserved—as she had tired of his predecessors, her first quarrel with him having arisen from his transfer of the estate or barony of Doune, which she had got for him from the King, to his penniless brother. She was as greedy and untrustworthy as ever. She actually proposed, in one of her quarrels with Lord Methven, to repair to England and there be re-married to Lord Angus. "Though I be forgotten in England, never shall I forget England," she wrote effusively, while she was almost as great a thorn in the side of England as in that of Scotland.

Margaret was still living when Magdalene of Lorraine came, a dying bride, to Scotland, but by that time the Queen-mother had fairly worn out the patience of her long-suffering son. She was struck with palsy at Methven Castle, during a temporary reconciliation with Lord Methven, and died in November, 1541, when she was fifty-two years of age, before King James, who had been summoned from Falkland Palace, could arrive in time to see her alive. Her chief concern during her last hours was for her conduct to Lord Angus, to whom she begged her son, through the priests in attendance on her death-bed, to be gracious. She requested her goods to be given to her daughter "Lady Margaret Douglas," as she "had never done anything for her." (In fact, beyond an expression of lively indignation that a daughter of hers should be sent to the Tower, as Lady Margaret had been sent, for receiving the suit of Lord Thomas Howard, the Queen had largely ignored this child's existence.) In spite of her avarice Margaret seems to have died comparatively poor.

Thus Queen Margaret ended, with little honour, a life which had begun so fairly. She had spent it in a persistent determination to gratify her own inclinations, however mean and low, in utter disregard of the claims of others. She was rapacious, passionate, faithless, and one of those brawling women of whom the wise man gave it as his verdict that it were better to live on the housetop than to dwell in her company. The grand funeral at Perth which Margaret's son decreed to her did not include much lamentation for the princess of high estate, with magnificent opportunities for good, who had squandered all on the basest forms of selfishness.

MARY TUDOR[1]

QUEEN-DOWAGER OF FRANCE, AND WIFE OF CHARLES
BRANDON, DUKE OF SUFFOLK

MARY TUDOR, youngest daughter of Henry VII. and
Elizabeth of York, was born at Richmond in 1498, nine
years after the birth of her sister Margaret, to whom she
bore little resemblance.   Mary was not more than three
years of age when she lost her mother, and when her
sister was married to James IV. and set out for Scotland.
Naturally enough the little princess clung to her governess, Lady Guildford, who had been Margaret's governess
also, and had accompanied her to Scotland, but was not
permitted to remain there.   Mary was so lovely a child
that the probability of her growing up the most beautiful
princess in Europe was taken into account in the disposal
of her hand, as such considerations rarely are in State
alliances.   Mary's budding beauty was an additional item
in her value as a princess.

As with her mother and sister, she was very soon an
object of treaty.   In this case the future bride was not
more than nine years of age, when, chaperoned by her
sister-in-law Katharine, the young widow of Prince
Arthur, Mary received Katharine's royal kinswoman,
Joanna, Queen of Castile, who when in England supported the proposals of marriage of her son, Charles of
Austria, afterwards the Emperor Charles V., to the young
English princess.   With the sweetness and docility derived

---

[1] Agnes Strickland—Bohn's edition for 1888, with many additional particulars.   Mary Robinson's " Life of Marguerite d'Angoulême, Queen of
Navarre."

from her mother, which were afterwards marked features in Mary's character, she played her juvenile part to the admiration of all. It is half comical, half pathetic, to read how she danced her basse dances, played at tables (chess or draughts), and did her best to entertain the lady who was at Windsor in the *rôle* of the small maiden's future mother-in-law.

With the same child-like earnestness and good faith, Mary bore herself with such simple dignity at her betrothal, and at the accompanying tournaments and banquets, that her wonderful " modesty and gravity," quite as much as her rare beauty, enchanted all beholders. The *fiançailles* went so far that the child Mary received the ring of espousal, wearing it " on the first joint of the ring finger," and took the title of Princess of Castile. But when she was left fatherless by the death of Henry VII., in 1509, the marriage went no farther, ostensibly because Henry VIII. appropriated and refused to relinquish the superb cluster of diamonds that the Emperor Maximilian, the grandfather of the bridegroom, had given in pledge for Mary's dowry, which had been paid into his hands.

There was a suspension and again a renewal of the overtures of alliance, where Austria was concerned, while Henry, on State occasions, ostentatiously wore in his hat the diamonds which were the bone of contention.

In the meantime the Princess Mary was rapidly passing from childhood to youth, an orphan in a court which was not a school of manners or morals. Probably her best friend was her sister-in-law, the Queen, Catherine of Arragon, the widow of Prince Arthur, who, in the year of Henry VII.'s death, became the wife of Arthur's brother, Henry. Catherine was a good and honourable woman, but she was considerably older than Mary, and as queen had sufficient cares and anxieties of her own to occupy her attention. One of the most admired figures at the

court, after that of the handsome, high-spirited young
king, was Henry's chosen comrade from boyhood, Charles
Brandon, whom the King created Duke of Suffolk.   Brandon was not of royal or even of noble birth.   He was
the son of Henry VII.'s standard-bearer at the battle of
Bosworth, who had saved the King's life at the expense
of his own.   In gratitude for the service, Henry VII.
made the dead man's son a ward of the Crown, and
Henry VIII.'s favour did the rest.   Brandon was older
than Henry, and therefore a good deal older than Mary.
He was frank and brave and handsome, which included
the advantage so much thought of in those days, of
being taller by the head and shoulders than his fellows.
This was the very attraction which in " my Lord of Anguish" had been so irresistible to Mary's sister.   It remained
to be seen whether my Lord of Suffolk was another Lord
of Anguish.   He had certainly found favour in women's
eyes already, and had availed himself more than once of
the strange and disgraceful license, in breach of contract,
and of the most solemn vows, which was so common at
the time.   Some will have it that this was because of a
mistaken conception of these reformed doctrines, rapidly
gaining ground, which denied that marriage was one
of the Church's sacraments, so that men's minds were
shaken for a time as to the sanctity of the marriage tie ;
but the pretext of dissolving marriage contracts on any
or on no grounds began earlier than the Reformation,
and was as prevalent in countries which were, and have
continued, Roman Catholic, as in those pervaded by
Protestant teaching.

Charles Brandon is said to have been twice married,
and to have twice repudiated his wives in his first youth,
while Mary was still a child ; he was also troth-plighted
once at least.   But that neither his friend, King Henry,
nor anybody else, recognised there was any obstacle to his
forming a third marriage is clear from the fact that his

name was coupled with that of the Duchess of Savoy, the aunt of the Prince of Castile, who came on her own account to England to advance her nephew's suit. It is believed not to have been the fault either of Henry or of Brandon that there was no truth in this rumour; while the mere circumstance that the favoured courtier raised his eyes so high was a sign that a faint heart would not spoil his fortunes. It could hardly be expected that Mary, an inexperienced girl of fifteen, should have a higher standard than that held by the older and wiser people around her, neither do we find among her lovable qualities keen discrimination in the choice of friends. It may be that the worst fault of that "Moder Guildford," who was sent back both from Scotland and France, to which she conducted two royal brides, was over-indulgence to her charges, or else a dangerous amount of patriotism at a foreign court. But "Jane Popincourt," another of Mary's best beloved ladies, has been accused of graver offences. It is extremely likely that this Jane acted as *confidante* in the idle and foolish love-passage which passed between the fair, simple, fifteen-years-old princess and the *beau chevalier* Suffolk, who was certainly ten years his young mistress's senior.

While the marriage of Mary and the Prince of Castile was still pending, and Suffolk and Mary were secretly exchanging tokens, Louis XII. of France lost a good wife, whom he had loved, in Anne of Brittany. Though he was sixty years of age and infirm for his years, he sought, in the supposed exigencies of the State, the beautiful English girl-princess for his third wife. The story goes that the busybody, Jane Popincourt, had her finger in this pie also. In spite of what she knew of Suffolk's audacious pretensions and Mary's inclination to respond to them, Jane's good offices with Mary were secured for the French King by the Duc de Longueville, then a prisoner in England.

Easily led and submissive as Mary was by nature, she made a stand against the unequal marriage, and that to no less a person than her brother, who, if he was generous in those days, was also notoriously despotic. His reply to her terrified remonstrances was the coaxing assurance that if she submitted quietly to be the pledge of peace between England and France, she should please herself in her choice of a spouse the next time she bestowed her hand—a compromise from which we can only hope that Mary at the time recoiled.

Mary was wedded to the elderly French king by proxy, the Duc de Longueville acting as his sovereign's representative, in August, 1514, at the Grey Friars' Church, Greenwich, where so many gay doings took place in that reign. In great good-humour with the poor little bride of sixteen, King Henry, with Queen Catherine, accompanied her to Dover, where they had to stay a month before the stormy weather abated sufficiently for the crossing, dangerous even then, to be accomplished. From the castle on the white cliffs Mary, petted and flattered, had still plenty of time to look down with a sinking heart on the rough waves which were so soon to roll between her and all she had held dear. Henry saw his sister and her imposing train of ladies and gentlemen embark for France. In the train were Anne Boleyn, or Bullen, and almost certainly Jane Seymour. The nobleman who had the honour and responsibility of escorting Mary to her king was the same Surrey, at this date Duke of Norfolk, who had accompanied Margaret as the bride of James IV. to Scotland. What is more difficult to understand is that Charles Brandon, Duke of Suffolk, was also in the train ; it need not be said with the knowledge of the King. Henry, who had taken upon him to encourage Brandon's daring aspirations to the hand of an Austrian princess, might never have dreamt that his favourite's presumption could reach the height of seeking a mate in his sovereign's sister, or the King might disdain and treat with contempt such sentimental coquetting between princess and subject as had been practised at his court. But it is hardly to be questioned that Brandon's presence in her suite must have inflicted many a sorrowful pang on Mary's tender, childish heart which might have been spared her, all the more because she had resigned herself to her fate, and decreed that the duke was to be nothing to her. The circumstance reads like a gratuitous piece of cruelty, a refinement of injury.

However, Louis—a patriarch for those days—welcomed his young wife when she arrived in France, in that stormy October, with a fatherly kindness to which the gentle fatherless and motherless girl responded without fail.

It would appear as if jewels—the glittering playthings of grown-up children—were to play a great part in Mary Tudor's history. Her marriage with Charles of Castile was broken off, on the surface, by the non-restoration of a cluster of diamonds; her wooing by Louis of France was conducted chiefly by means of the diamonds, rubies, and pearls of a fairy tale. He lavished them upon her, he said himself, not all at once, but with deliberate pauses between, that the wise donor might earn many and repeated thanks.

The first shock dealt to Mary, in the middle of this truly Oriental courtship, was the announcement of the honourable dismissal—which meant that they should be forthwith sent back to England—of the greater number of the ladies, among them the two most cherished by her, "Moder Guildford" and Jane Popincourt. Mary had been so apprehensive of this disaster, that she had written the prettiest of letters to Louis, to ward it off, even before she quitted England. Later, in the middle of the sparkling shower supposed to dazzle her youthful eyes, she overcame her timidity to beseech the gallant, grey-bearded gentleman to reconsider the resolution which was so hard to her. "My Moder Guildford was also discharged," she also wrote piteously to Wolsey, "by whom, as you know, the King and you willed me in any wise to be counselled."

But Louis was inexorable, and who shall say he was wrong in the light of the qualities which "Moder Guildford" had been so unfortunate as to instil into Queen Margaret, and of Jane Popincourt's tricks? But one part of the argument for his conduct sounds comical in his mouth. "My wife and I," he said to the English Ambassador, "be in as good and perfect love as any two creatures can be; we are both of an age to rule ourselves, not to have servants that should look to rule her or me. If my wife hath need of counsel or to be ruled, I am able to do it."

It is a little difficult to identify in this gay, politic old Louis the sullen, reckless Duke of Orleans, whom his terrible uncle Louis XI. so detested and thwarted, as represented to us by the master-hand of Sir Walter Scott, in the pages of "Quentin Durward." Louis had been in the interval husband of the lame Princess Joan, and then, since it was he who set the bad fashion of annulling marriages on small grounds, of his first love Anne of Brittany, the great heiress and the widow of his cousin Charles VIII., so that she was twice Queen of France in right of her two husbands. Oddly enough, she also was a lame woman, but she was able and influential, while Joan was weak and powerless, though she was a king's daughter. Above all he loved Anne and hated Joan, according to the old preference for the petulant Rachel before the patient Leah.

An inopportune fit of the gout, during which Mary waited dutifully on her king, delayed for a little her coronation. Louis's old courtiers grumbled that his young queen had impaired his health, by inducing him to change his habits late in life. He had been accustomed to dine at eight in the morning, and to go to bed at six in the

evening. To please her, he took to dining at noon and
sitting up till midnight.

Mary was crowned at St. Denis with the crown of Jane
of Navarre, so heavy a weight for the slender girlish neck
to bear, that her husband's cousin, son-in-law and heir,
Francis of Valois, stood behind her, and held it over her
head—as her nephew the baby-king of Scotland had his
crown held at his coronation.

On Mary's entrance into Paris, she sat alone in a chaise,
or chair, drawn by two white horses. Her pale golden
hair was crowned by a circlet of large pearls. Her neck
and bosom sparkled with diamonds. She was surrounded
by the Royal Scotch Archer Guard, commanded by the
Duke of Albany, the future Regent of Scotland. Francis
of Valois, and other representatives of the princely houses
of France, Bourbons, Vendômes, Guises, &c., &c., rode before her. Verses have been preserved of one of the songs
sung on the occasion which may be contrasted with Dunbar's poem of "The Thistle and the Rose," of which Queen
Margaret was the heroine. The homage to Mary ran
thus :—

> " The fence of gold, the purple towers,
> The eagles and the lily-flowers,
> Rejoice in Dame Maria,
> *Réveillez-vous,*
> Joy to Lady Maria."

At Mary's coronation, at her entrance into Paris, and on
the three days' tilting, in which he bore his part, while
Mary stood the whole time in order to see and be seen,
Brandon was present a witness to her honours, which she
bore meekly enough, seeking not so much to be admired as
to please King Louis. So far as we can judge, she was trying
her utmost to be one with him and with France. Among
other gracious acts, she at once exerted herself to do a service to her new countrymen by interceding with her brother,
King Henry, for the French prisoners in England.

Mary's reign as Queen Consort of France was of the briefest duration. It began in the month of October, and it ended with the death of King Louis on the last day of the same year, 1514. Three days before he had written a letter full of his affection for his queen. She was now, while still only in her seventeenth year, *une Reine Blanche* —a royal French widow in her white weeds. There is an avenue running off the Champs Elysées which is still pointed out as having been set apart for the airings of royal widows. But that was when their white were exchanged for black weeds. There were no airings during the first month of widowhood, which Mary elected to spend in the little palace of the Hôtel de Cluny, adjoining the Convent de Cluny, where she could have the consolations of religion close at hand, and where she was under the capable guardianship of Louise of Savoy,[1] mother of Francis of Valois, who by the death of Louis had become Francis I.

We may take it for granted that Mary's soft, affectionate nature found some tears to shed for the kind old king who had been more like a father than a husband to her. But, indeed, the young girl was full of perturbation where her own fate was concerned. She might not mind so much as a more ambitious worldly woman would have cared, that she had suddenly fallen from her height of earthly grandeur; it might in some respects be a deliverance to her; nevertheless, she had many troubles pressing upon her. She was frightened by the extravagant admiration expressed for her by the newly-made king. She was indignant at the bare idea of being handed back to her first suitor, Charles of Castile, who, in the persons of his envoys, had shown no eagerness for the fulfilment of her promise.

---

[1] Louise of Savoy had been herself left a widow at eighteen, by the death of a husband greatly her senior, but she had lived long enough with him to be much attached to him, and she was the mother of a son and daughter to whose interests she was devoted.

Her maidenly pride was piqued, or else she revolted at the notion of being again, after so short a space of time, a mere pawn used as a pledge between two governments.

Mary begged her brother, King Henry, to fetch her back, and he increased the disturbance in her mind by despatching the Duke of Suffolk, of all men, to escort her home to England. Certainly, before the duke started, his master required from him a promise not to abuse his trust, but this was a common form gone through with every emissary. As it has never been alleged that Henry had any intention of bringing about a union between his sister and his courtier, his choice looks as if he possessed no knowledge of any former attachment between the young Queen-Dowager and her escort, or had no faith in it. It is difficult to imagine that he voluntarily exposed the pair to the risk of incurring his displeasure. There is much more plausibility in the impression which survives in French minds that the shrewd, imperious Louise of Savoy laid a snare for the English princess and the Duke of Suffolk, with the intention of removing her out of King Francis's way, that he might not be too much tempted to follow a course which had precedents, but would be highly offensive to the French nation. His subjects would hardly forgive him if he set aside his young Queen Claude, their old King's daughter, whose simple virtues they respected, for her equally youthful stepmother, till recently a stranger and foreigner amongst them.

When Mary's white widowhood ended, a month after Louis's death, and she was at liberty to wear black, go abroad, and receive visitors, she was waited upon by certain friars, who brought her, it is not said from whence, the tale that Suffolk had been privately instructed by King Henry to land her not in England but in Flanders, where she was to be joined by Charles of Castile.

Cut to the quick, Mary summoned Suffolk to her presence, and appealed to him. The account of the interview is drawn from his defence of his conduct to Henry, but there is no reason to doubt his word, granted that he was afterwards shown to be vainglorious and every inch a courtier.   To believe him we have only to take all the circumstances into consideration—Mary's extreme youth and guilelessness, her rank, which gave her the initiative in addressing the duke, what seemed to her the extremity of the situation, together with her girlish partiality for the man to whom she was speaking, and his earlier attempts at making love to her.

She must be short with him, and show him her pleasure and mind, she said, in desperate agitation.

She reminded him how good a lady she had been to him, "an" added that, in fine, if he would be ordered by her, she would verily have none but he.

An ever she came to England she never would have him; and he married her not then, she would never have him, nor come to England.

Suffolk, according to his own tale, answered her soothingly and discreetly.   She said that but to prove him withal, he told her.

An she went to England, the Princess insisted in her distress, then would she be sent to Flanders, and she would be torn in pieces sooner than come there.

"And with that," continued Suffolk, "she weeped as never saw I a woman so weep."

He tried to comfort her.   He said, in allusion to the report that he was to carry her to Flanders, there was never such a thing, by his faith, and bade her write and get King Henry's consent, without which he dared do nothing, because of his promise.

Her angry reply was that of a poor girl standing at bay. She would have the time to her own desire, else she would think he had come to "tice" (beguile) her.   He should never have such a proffer again . . .

"And so," the narrator, in the character of a humble

penitent, ends his narrative abruptly, " she and I were married."

Another version of the romantic story is that Louis of Savoy, having plotted to bring about the meeting, surprised the couple while Mary was still weeping bitterly, professed to reproach them with the indecorousness of the scene, and to advise that they should at once resort to the adjoining chapel, where they were at her instigation wedded or troth-plighted, the ceremony taking place appropriately enough on St. Valentine's Eve, the 12th of February, 1515.

Of all hasty royal marriages poor young Mary's was the hastiest, for her old King had died so recently as on the last night of the previous December. It is doubtful whether Charles Brandon was worth the immense trust she put in him; but at least she found no fault with him, then or ever. She freely offered her brother Henry all the jewels (those jewels which were fated to figure prominently in her history) and all the plate given her by the late King of France, to earn his forgiveness for having taken her fortune into her own hands, and to protect Suffolk from the King's vengeance. She made herself the sole person to blame for the love match, and used all her tender eloquence to those who were in authority, that they should not be " miscontented with my Lord Suffolk."

We have again to remind ourselves of the rough old times in which Mary lived, that we may make allowance for the unshrinking eagerness with which she reminded Henry of his promise, that if she submitted to marry in order to please him in her first espousals, she should be allowed to please herself in her second; and for the perfect frankness with which she styled the jewels and plate —the bribe she offered,—her " winnings in France," as if she had speculated with her youth, beauty, and sweetness for the price which Louis was willing to pay for them.

As a further security for Brandon, Mary ventured to

appeal to Francis I., and to confide in him. He was vir-
tually her sovereign so long as she remained in France,
and if he chose to intercede for the delinquents his pleading was not likely to be in vain. She told Francis of the
love passages between her and Suffolk before she came to
France or ever saw the King's face, repeating to him "the
pass or by-words" by which the lovers had secured for
themselves a few minutes' private conversation in the
middle of the publicity of a court.

Francis behaved with the magnanimity which has been
attributed to him more than once in other circumstances.
He became the friend of the young couple, and exerted
himself to propitiate Henry. Those must have been happy
honeymoon weeks which Mary spent at the French court,
with Suffolk received as her husband, while she was waiting for Henry's consent to return to England. In her
happiness the bride of seventeen did not forget to show
kind concern and care for her former household, the members of which had of necessity lost their posts when she
ceased to be Queen Consort of France. Among these
retainers out of place were young Anne Boleyn and Jane
Seymour, who were taken into the service of Queen
Claude.

After all, Mary's exile did not last six months. She
sailed in the sober autumn to make the acquaintance of
her elderly husband; she returned in the sweet spring-
time wedded to the lover of her choice. By May she was
in England again. Henry met her and his former comrade with a bluff amnesty, and with such a princely
endowment for Suffolk in the forfeited estates of the
unfortunate De la Poles, the former Dukes of Suffolk,
that the broad lands might well have been held by Henry
as an ample equivalent for the costly baubles which Mary
transferred to him, to the value of two hundred thousand
pounds. These were her modest "winnings" in France.
On one of them, a special ruby, Francis I. had set great

store, but he could not, in spite of his good offices, recover
it, either from Mary or Henry.

Mary was publicly remarried to Suffolk at Greenwich,
where her marriage with Louis XII. had been celebrated
half a year before. At one of the gay tournaments which
celebrated the event, Suffolk bore on his banner, in
allusion to his humble origin, the pithy motto which has
survived to the present day—

> " Cloth of gold, do not despise,
> Though thou hast wedded cloth of frieze ;
> Cloth of frieze, be not too bold,
> Though thou hast wedded cloth of gold."

It was about this time that poor Queen Margaret paid
her solitary visit to England, a disappointed, discontented
woman, and had to share in the public rejoicing, sitting
under the same canopy with Mary, in her flush of youth
and happiness—their emblems, the daisy and the mari-
gold intertwined, their fates so like and yet so unlike.

Mary's first child, a boy, was born in 1516, when his
mother was eighteen years of age. He was named for
King Henry, who stood sponsor for him, and created
him Earl of Lincoln. Her later born children were two
daughters, Lady Frances and Lady Eleanor Brandon.
Mary showed a decided preference for country life, especially at Westthorpe Hall, Suffolk; but there was
another reason besides her inclination for the preference ; Suffolk had spent large sums of money both in
France and England at the time of his marriage, which
Wolsey refused to defray from the treasury. The lowly-
born duke was a man of lavish, extravagant habits, and
in spite of his great estates, continued in permanent difficulties. Mary tried to relieve them by spending many
of her days in comparative retirement, while he abode
at the court in which he had been reared from boyhood,
in which he held high office, made a fine figure in every

gala and pageant, and was Henry's fast ally in all the
King's changes of mood and creed. But though Mary
sought to diminish her expenses, she always maintained
—whether from her own sense of the fitness of things,
whether from the desire of her ostentatious husband—
great state in her privacy, never losing sight of the fact
that she was Queen-Dowager of France.

Mary was a happy woman, still surrounded by husband
and children, when, at the age of twenty-two, she met for
the first time the suitor to whom she had been troth-
plighted as a child, from whom she had recoiled in the
first days of her widowhood, Charles of Castile, by this
time the great Emperor Charles V., on a visit to his aunt,
Queen Catherine of Arragon. Curious eyes watched the
encounter with the woman who had been destined for his
wife. It was Lord Herbert of Cherbury's impression that
the mighty ruler before whom so much of Europe trem-
bled, was so struck by Mary's "dazzling loveliness" (or
was it by the touch of what is best in human nature, in
her matronly peace and bounty?) that he was rendered
pensive, and declined to dance for the rest of the evening.
It is an unpremeditated testimony to Mary's domestic tastes
and contentment with her lot, that nobody seems to have
dreamt she experienced regret because she was not the
sharer of an Imperial crown. Another brilliant interlude
in Mary's quiet life and a brief return to the splendours
and triumphs of former days, was when she accompanied
King Henry and Queen Catherine to France to meet her
former champion, King Francis, on the Field of the Cloth of
Gold. Mary is said to have been the acknowledged beauty
alike of the English and French courts, and we must not
grudge her an innocent gratification in the consciousness, when, in the temporary withdrawal of the respective
Queens of France and England, she rode through the gorgeous encampment between two such magnificent squires
as Henry and Francis.

But such galas were not in the general tenor of Mary's later life. She had withdrawn more and more from the gay world, and given herself up to the care of her children, when she received a severe blow in the death of her only son, a boy of eleven years of age, in 1527. He fell a victim to "the sweating sickness" then devastating the country. Modern inquirers have conjectured with regard to this dreaded epidemic that it may have been neither more nor less than the worst type of influenza. For the remaining six years of her life Mary retired almost entirely from court, which in all probability had less attractions for her than ever, when the friend of her youth, Catherine of Arragon, had to give place to the Maid of Honour, who had formerly served Mary in the same capacity, Anne Boleyn.

Agnes Strickland, who was herself an East-country woman, familiar with Norfolk and Suffolk traditions, refers to Mary's popularity in Suffolk, to the patronage which she accorded to native goods and manufactures, and to the punctuality with which she graced year by year, the Bishop of Bury's great fair at Bury St. Edmund's, holding receptions and attending balls in its honour, or in the honour of the bishop. Like her grandmother, "the venerable Margaret," Mary was a faithful friend to all the monasteries within her husband's jurisdiction. As it happened, she reared in her household her successor, the Duke of Suffolk's last wife, Katharine Willoughby, daughter of Lord Willoughby and his Spanish wife, who came to England as Maid of Honour to Catherine of Arragon.

The elder of Mary's daughters, Lady Frances Brandon, was like her beautiful mother, and her ambitious father early arranged her marriage with Henry Grey, Marquis of Dorset; the young bride and her husband living with the Duchess of Suffolk at Westthorpe Hall. The second daughter of the house was married in her turn, while barely

in her teens, to Henry Lord Clifford, eldest son of the
Earl of Cumberland, and remained also with her mother.
Mary was long in declining health, and took several journeys from Westthorpe Hall to London to seek the counsel
of physicians. She had not long returned from one of
these fruitless journeys, when the end came, on the 25th
of June 1533, eight years before the death of her sister,
Queen Margaret, at Methven. At the time of Mary's
death she was, like her mother, Elizabeth of York, only
in her thirty-seventh year. The Duke of Suffolk and his
sons-in-law, Lord Dorset and Lord Clifford, were all three
absent in London, in attendance on the coronation of
Anne Boleyn, but Lady Dorset and Lady Clifford were
with their mother.

A singular incident occurred at Mary's funeral, which
points to one of the greatest troubles in her life—the revival of claims made by the Duke of Suffolk's repudiated
wives. Mary's daughters—the eldest just sixteen, at the
date of her mother's death—acted as her chief mourners,
following the coffin on black horses to its place of inter-
ment in the Abbey of Bury. In the course of the ceremonial, each daughter advanced and placed in turn on the
coffin a pall of cloth of gold, a costly mark of honour to
the dead. "To the surprise of everybody, their half-
sisters, Lord Suffolk's daughters by a previous marriage,
did the same," when the young Ladies Dorset and Clifford,
outraged by the act which claimed Mary as the stepmother of the intruders, left the church without waiting
for the end of the funeral service. Thus the haunting
shadow of shame, bred of the unrighteous facility with
which betrothals and marriages were made and unmade,
that had harassed poor Mary in the interests of her children throughout her life, followed her to the very grave's
mouth, and disturbed her obsequies.

When Bury Abbey was put down, with so many other
religious houses, by Henry, the townspeople removed

Mary's coffin from the monument under which it rested to the Church of St. Mary's, Bury St. Edmunds. The same coffin was again exhumed on account of alterations in the church in 1734. On the second occasion the coffin was opened, when the embalmed body was not only found in perfect preservation, but the beautiful golden hair which Mary had inherited through her mother from her grandmother, Elizabeth Woodville, fell in glittering profusion about the shoulders. The present writer remembers reading in the catalogue of the treasures of the noble house of Stowe, which were brought to the hammer, the ticketing of one lot as a lock of the hair of this princess, thus offered for sale by one of her descendants. It is said other locks, abstracted from the coffin when it was opened in 1734, found their way into the hands of local antiquaries.

Mary Tudor's intellectual attainments, though decidedly superior to those of her sister, do not appear to be of a very high order. She signed herself on at least one occasion Henry's " suster." In moral character, if thoughtless and impulsive in her early youth, her worst faults are but spots on the sun compared to her sister Margaret's offences. Mary was in her girlhood easily led, and impressionable. In her maturity she was, amidst the distractions of a court and the temptations of her rank and beauty, a loving wife, an attached mother, a kind mistress, and a liberal bestower of such benefits as she had it in her power to dispense. Whether in youth or in age, hers was a sweet, tender, essentially womanly nature.

CATHERINE OF ARRAGON[1]

BY MARRIAGE A TUDOR

ALL the romance and glory of Spanish history were at their height when Catherine of Arragon was born. For the princess whose mother was the high-spirited, generous Isabella of Castile, the friend of Columbus, whose father was Ferdinand of Arragon, the conqueror of the Moors; for the child who was cradled among the orange groves of Castile and the pomegranates of Granada, a nature as full of the sunshine as of the storms of the South, a fate grand, if chequered with adversity, might have been predicted. But sunshine was not a prominent characteristic either of Catherine's temper or her career, while her entire history had in it more of humiliation than triumph, culminating in the piteousness of undeserved downfall. Happily for herself and all under her influence, she was upright and good, but her greatness belonged to her adversity. Her misfortunes were her chief abiding crown.

Catherine was born at the town of Alcala de Henares, 15th December 1485, and her marriage with Arthur, Prince of Wales, elder son of Henry VII., was proposed at so early a date, that the intended bridegroom was but a baby of twenty months, and the bride a child of three years. The Spanish ambassador and his suite were allowed to inspect the baby prince, so that they could certify he was all such a princeling should be; but it is said that Isabella demurred at the ordeal for her daughter, child though she was, and that the English commissioner

<hr />

[1] Agnes Strickland, Froude, Du Boys (edited by Charlotte Yonge).

QUEEN CATHERINE OF ARRAGON.

had to be content with seeing the little Catherine in her
mother's arms at the national spectacle of a bull-fight.
This was a somewhat barbarous entertainment for a small
princess, who was to be brought up in all the learning in
which her ardent and enthusiastic mother—as brilliant and
accomplished on one side as she was domesticated and
homely on another—delighted.

From Catherine's fourth year she was styled, in right
of her betrothal, "Princess of Wales," and before she
was in her teens she corresponded in Latin with her boy-
bridegroom, he replying in the same stately language, the
manner and matter of the letters being naturally equally
stilted.

Catherine did not arrive in England till October 1501,
when she was about sixteen years of age, and the Prince
of Wales was approaching his fifteenth year. She travelled attended by an imposing Spanish suite, which
included three bishops as well as four young ladies. She
had a dolefully bad passage to begin with, and the poor
girl suffered severely from sea-sickness, to little purpose,
as it seemed, since the ship was driven back and the
party had to embark a second time, landing finally at
Plymouth.

Henry VII. and his young son travelled in the dull,
dark days of November to meet the Spanish princess,
but the weather was so rainy and the roads so nearly
impassable, that they made only slow progress. They
were anticipated by the Spanish party riding in advance
of the main body, and coming to warn the bridegroom
and his father that, according to Spanish etiquette, they
could only meet the bride at the steps of the altar in the
church where the marriage was to be celebrated.

But this was a punctilio which no Englishman, be he
king or commoner, could consent to, therefore Henry left
his son behind him; and riding forward to the town of
Dogmersfield, at which Catherine had arrived, announced

that he was there to see and welcome his daughter-in-law.

There was still some demurring, an archbishop, a bishop, and a count barring the King's way, and declaring that the Lady Infanta had retired to her chamber. In the end, common-sense and discretion prevailed, and the Infanta consented to grant the King an audience. Neither could speak to the other unless in Latin, for Henry knew no Spanish; and it does not seem to have occurred to Catherine's guardians and preceptors, as one might have expected in the circumstances, to give her an acquaintance with English. The high contracting parties had to content themselves with exchanging dignified compliments through an interpreter.

In the meantime the Prince arrived, and Henry presented him to his betrothed wife. In order to make things doubly sure, the King caused the betrothal, which had before been performed by proxy, to be gone over again in person, the medium being that Latin tongue, which was "understanded" by all the royal personages, as well as by the prelates in attendance.

In deference to the ideas of decorum at the time, the King and the Prince supped in private, returning afterwards to the company of the ladies, when, as usual, music and dancing—those universal heralds of good-fellowship—were started. Catherine danced with the Spanish ladies some of the basses dances. The Prince was unacquainted with them; but not to be outdone, he took out Lady Guildford, who was governess to his two sisters in succession (the "Moder Guildford," to part from whom cost young Princess Mary the first tears she shed in France), and danced right pleasantly and honourably." The couple probably accomplished one of those voltas or high dances which appear to have been indigenous to the soil of England, and were more remarkable for agility than for grace.

We do not know much of how the Prince and Princess, thus formally introduced and united, looked and felt on this occasion ; but we can judge a little from future descriptions.   Arthur was a fair lad, puny contrasted with his big young brother Henry, and he had the hectic poison already working in his veins and painting his cheeks.   We know that though he was considered a youth of admirable promise, he was not favourably struck by the innocent bride, with whom the great advantage of an alliance between England and Spain had thus prematurely endowed him.   It may be that, though he was a scholarly lad, the Latin love-letters which he had been made to address to her in his boyhood, that had served for school-exercises with their accompanying censures and impositions, still rankled in his immature mind as a grievance against her.

As for Catherine, we hear later that the girl of sixteen had large, regular, rather heavy features, so high a forehead that half of her face was forehead, and, for a wonder, considering her extraction, a fair complexion, and a profusion of auburn hair—prized distinctions which would in themselves constitute her a beauty at the Spanish court. She was not tall, while her figure, like her features, was inclined to be large and full, no disadvantage on the whole to a girl of sixteen.   She was staid, far beyond her years, probably a little prim, pleasing the elderly formal King far more than she pleased his young son by her decorum and dignity.

Catherine, with her suite, made the rest of the progress alone, by a succession of stages, and was welcomed with great demonstrations of respect and regard at every point, till she reached Lambeth Palace.

Henry repaired to his Queen, Elizabeth of York, at Richmond, and the Prince of Wales eventually took up his quarters at Blackfriars.   The good Queen came by water to greet her daughter-in-law, whose firm friend she remained.

Catherine's public entrance into London was of course carried through with much splendour and ceremony, and had some peculiar details. She rode on a Spanish mule, having on one side of her Henry Duke of York, a fine boy of eleven years of age, and on the other the Pope's legate. She wore a broad hat like a cardinal's, and the younger ladies in her suite wore the same. The Princess had a coif of carnation colour under the hat, beneath which her auburn hair fell on her shoulders. Her saddle was a small, richly ornamented arm-chair, fastened on the mule. Her *dame d'honneur*, riding near her, was in black, after the Spanish fashion, or as the English chronicler expressed it, "like a religious woman." The four young Spanish ladies rode on mules also. It had been proposed that four English ladies on palfreys should ride, each by the side of one of the Spanish damsels, and should courteously lead her mule. But by a queer and comical *contretemps*, which was no laughing matter to the Master of the Ceremonies, and appeared a little ominous to the superstitious, the fact that different national customs in riding made the English and Spanish equestrians sit on different sides of their horses and mules, had the undesirable effect of the riders seeming to sit back to back, as the result of a quarrel.

On November 14, 1501, Catherine was married to Arthur in old St. Paul's, King Henry, Queen Elizabeth, and the King's mother, the Lady Margaret, witnessing the marriage from their latticed box. The Archbishop of Canterbury, assisted by no less than nineteen bishops and abbots, tied the knot.

The bride's magnificent dress of white satin, very long in bodice and sleeves, had certain foreign touches. It had an arrangement of little hoops below the waist, which was the introduction of the farthingale into England.

Another innovation was the coif of white silk on the bride's head, from which fell "a scarf bordered with gold, pearls, and precious stones, five inches and a half broad," which, as the old historian said, "veiled great part of her visage and person." This was no doubt an adaptation of the Spanish mantilla, but it may also have been the inauguration of the wedding veil. Blushing brides of succeeding generations little dream that they owe the picturesque mark of their state, and shelter for their blushes, to the hapless Catherine of Arragon. Whether or not the typical orange-blossoms are derived from the same source, we are not in circumstances to verify.

Certainly poor Arthur has set no fashion in bridal costume to modern bridegrooms, since, according to the taste of the time, his doublet and hose were of white satin, like the gown of his bride. At the great door of the cathedral, with the people for his witnesses, he endowed her with a third of his estate, a pledge which he did not fulfil.

The Prince and Princess of Wales stayed for one night at the Bishop of London's palace, and proceeded by water next day, escorted by the King, to the home prepared for them—Baynard's Castle, on the Thames. Later, there were great rejoicings of tilting and feasting at Westminster, when Arthur had the place of honour on the King's right hand, and Catherine the same place by the Queen.

In the dancing, which was a prominent feature in the scene, Arthur showed that he had mastered the mysteries of the *base* or *basse* dance by dancing one with his beautiful Aunt Cicely, while Catherine came down from the Queen's side to dance twice—still with her Spanish ladies, wearing the Spanish costume, her persistent adherence to which was hardly likely to recommend itself to English spectators. The dancing of the lively voltas, or high dances, was confined on this occasion to the young Prince Henry and his sister Margaret, already entitled "Queen of the Scots." One cannot help thinking that the style of the performance was in keeping with the character and future careers of the rosy-cheeked, riotous pair. They gave unmingled satisfaction in this instance, especially when Henry, finding himself encumbered by his court suit, suddenly threw it off to his jacket, and thus displayed his nimbleness in company with the gay skipping of his buxom sister.

In the last pageant before the return of Catherine's Spanish escort, a detail of the entertainment was the letting loose in the crowded hall at Westminster of a number of white doves and rabbits, a primitive diversion in itself, which was supposed to be a complimentary adoption of a Spanish custom in similar circumstances. When Catherine mourned sympathetically over the parting with the friends of her youth, King Henry's mode of comforting her was a piece of homage to her own and her mother's acknowledged learning, and a decided improvement on other modes of solacing the grief of royal brides. He first took her into his library, and showed her "many goodly, pleasant books . . . both in English and Latin," before he brought forward a jeweller with a collection of rings and gauds, and bade her choose from them, while he would divide what remained among those Spanish ladies she was allowed to retain in her service, and her newly appointed English ladies.

Early in spring, the Prince and Princess of Wales set out for Ludlow Castle, in Shropshire, where they were to maintain their Court, and from which Arthur was to govern the adjoining principality of Wales. Catherine rode the whole way from London to Ludlow on a pillion, behind her Master of the Horse, her ladies riding also, the state of the roads not admitting of wheeled carriages. The only respite from the long ride, renewed day after day, was the resting in the litter swung between a couple of horses or mules. Catherine's stay at Ludlow was destined to be short. Arthur died in April, 1502, according to some accounts, from the mere development of his consumptive malady; according to others, from a sudden

outbreak of the plague. It was just three months from his
arrival in Shropshire, and six from his marriage. He was
buried with sufficient pomp on "the foulest, cold, windy
and rainy day," the procession meeting with such obstacles
from the rutted mire it had to pass through, that the
car with the Prince's body stuck fast in the mud, and at
one place yokes of oxen had to be employed to drag it
forward.

There had been but little dawning regard between the
youthful couple so lately strangers to each other, and still
unable to converse unless in ponderous Latin, or by the
help of an interpreter. In addition to the shock of the
death—so sudden in the end—of her husband of eighteen,
all Catherine's girlish ambition was blighted, and her
pride, if not her affections, received a severe blow from
the open and marked slight put upon her by the will,
in which Arthur, in breach of his marriage contract,
bequeathed his entire personal property to his sister
Margaret.

Queen Elizabeth, in the middle of her grief for her son,
remembered the forlorn girl left behind him. She sent
immediately for Catherine, and had her brought to
London in a litter composed of black velvet and cloth, for
which the Queen gave express directions to her tailor.

The next nine years which Catherine spent in England,
while she passed from girlhood to womanhood, were particularly trying. She soon lost the friendly protection of
her mother-in-law by the Queen's death, and two years
afterwards the young widow sustained a still greater
misfortune in the death of her own mother, Isabella of
Castile. Isabella had counselled her daughter's return to
Spain: and Catherine's continued stay in England is only
to be accounted for by the fact that her large dowry had
been half paid, and only half paid, and by the characters
of the two princes concerned in the transaction. No ele-
ments of the prudence and wisdom which were attributed

to Henry and Ferdinand were more conspicuous than their
rooted inclination to keep, and their equally rooted disinclination to disimburse, whatever sums of money came into
their hands. However, it is now tolerably well understood that it was to the urgent endeavours of Ferdinand
to maintain, at any cost, the Anglo-Spanish alliance, that
Catherine became a victim, with a train of evils to
follow.

While the two kings disputed over the arrears of dowry,
including the very plate and jewels which poor Catherine
had brought, her income, as the Prince of Wales's widow,
was so persistently detained and curtailed that the letters
she wrote to her father are full of complaints and remonstrances. She not only urges the non-payment of her
ladies' salaries as a serious grievance to a high-spirited
honourable mistress, she represents her own wants as
having reached a climax. She had been forced to sell
"some of her bracelets" to buy a black velvet gown, as
mourning for her mother, and it was only the third gown
she had got since her arrival in England; she had not where-
withal to supply herself with linen for chemises.

Catherine's worries were increased by the trial of a
foreign climate, and of a way of living which did not
agree with her constitution. She suffered from the chill
shivers and fever flushes of the tertian ague. She pined
for the fresh salads and the juicy fruits of the South,
which were not to be obtained to replace the grosser flesh
diet of the North.

As the last touch to her troubles, there was a suspicion
that Henry was willing to wed her himself rather than
imperil the Spanish alliance. If this extremity was ever
seriously thought of, another resource was found. Two
years after the death of Arthur, Catherine, in spite of the
reluctance which she then expressed, was betrothed to
Henry Tudor, a boy of twelve, while she was a young
woman of eighteen.

But a year afterwards, though the incident was not known for some time, Henry VII. caused his son to sign a protest against the betrothal. The only conceivable reason for this act on the part of the King is that given by Mr. Froude, whose attitude in defending Henry VIII. is well known. Mr. Froude's explanation is that the betrothal had been pressed for by Ferdinand of Arragon, whose wishes the King was not in a position to set at nought. However, as soon as the boy Henry was thirteen, the earliest age at which he could legally act for himself, he was made to take upon himself the responsibility of disowning the betrothal, which might indeed be contrary, eventually, to his conscience and his feelings. There can be little doubt that the act of disowning the engagement, though there was a report current that the lad did not know the contents of the paper he signed, must have left a distinct impression on his mind.

In those years of uncertainty and repression which helped to mould Catherine's character, she could not even have derived much comfort from the short visit of her sister, Joanna of Castile, who, with her husband, Philip the Fair of Austria, had been on their way to take possession of her inheritance on the death of her mother, when the vessel in which they sailed was driven ashore on the coast of England, and the royal pair came to Windsor. Their thus coming out of their way, and the length of their detention in England, were believed to be pieces of statecraft on the part of Henry VII. Joanna had already given indication of the jealous frenzies of temper which rapidly developed into insanity. Her attack, in the presence of her husband and several members of her household, on an offending maid-of-honour, whose hair she tore and cheeks she buffeted in the most uncourtly manner, had caused a violent quarrel between the Princess and Philip. The mortifying news was said to have hastened the death of her poor mother, Queen Isabella. The quarrel was patched up, but Joanna was not a woman to trust to, or to resort to for counsel. The main use of the visit was that it afforded opportunity for the proposal of the never-fulfilled alliance between the pretty, bright nine-year-old Mary Tudor, younger daughter of Henry VII., and the Prince of Castile, the son of Joanna and Philip. Joanna's husband died soon after he left England, and, in spite of her blind devotion to his memory, which became a mad mania, concentrating itself upon his ashes which she carried about with her, the insult was inflicted on her misery of a talk of her marriage with Henry VII., just as there was also a talk of his marriage with a third widowed daughter of Ferdinand and Isabella, the Queen-Dowager of Naples. Hard as Catherine's circumstances were at this time, it is clear enough that they were rendered still harder by a certain rigidity and obstinacy of disposition, which existed along with the possibilities of noble steadfastness. For the greater part of her youth in England, she had failed to acquire the English language, apparently setting herself against the acquisition in a manner not altogether unknown among young queen-consorts,[1] but not the less repugnant to common-sense and right feeling. The consequence was that she spoke and wrote English badly to the end of her days. She clung to her Spanish mode of dress, which would have been natural and pardonable enough in a private person, but was unwise in a queen as an index of the direction in which her sympathies turned. Her devotion was early marked by asceticism. She was more stately than gracious. She had an unhappy faculty, noteworthy in so young a woman, of differing from, and complaining bitterly of her advisers, the two Spanish ambassadors in succession. Probably they had recommended to their too honest and decidedly querulous

[1] Henrietta Maria vexed and mortified Charles I., during the first months of her reign, by perversely declining to make use of English in her speech.

"Dona Catalina" a more diplomatic, if not a more accommodating and ingratiating style of behaviour.

With Henry VII.'s death in 1507 a great change came over Catherine's fortunes. Henry VIII., then a manly lad of eighteen, while Catherine was twenty-four, in place of appearing desirous to avail himself of the protest which he had signed, showed himself eager to confirm and complete the betrothal, to which Catherine no longer professed herself averse. Whether actuated by pity and generosity, as some of his chroniclers think, whether influenced by the tendency of very young men to be enamoured of women older than themselves, he gave every evidence of being sincerely and heartily attached to Catherine, whom, by his own solemn declarations, he never ceased to respect and esteem. In place of being plain, she was then a fine-looking young woman in her own peculiar style, and the harshness afterwards attributed to her manners certainly did not display itself in the first place to the young King.

Several of Henry's Council—notably Wareham, Archbishop of Canterbury—opposed the match, in spite of the Pope's dispensation, because of the relationship existing between Henry and Catherine;[1] but he had his way, as he continued to have it in later life. He and Catherine were married in the Friar's Church, in Greenwich Palace, on the 11th of June 1509, some six weeks after the death of the late King. The marriage was solemnised precipitately and privately, almost secretly. Not so the entrance of the royal couple into London on St. John's Day, twelve days later. Prominent among the midsummer galas was the pretty sight of maidens in white, bearing white wax palms, lining the way from Cornhill to Old Change. Catherine herself was in bridal white, her

---

[1] Miss Yonge has pointed out how immaterial the relationship must have appeared to Catherine, since one of her sisters, Mary of Naples, married the widower of her deceased sister Isabella, and reigned in her stead.

fine hair hanging down her back; on her head a jewelled coronet. She was in a litter of white cloth of gold, supported between two white horses. But the ladies in attendance on her, who, at the coronation banquet in Westminster Hall, sat under the table at the Queen's feet, holding her "pocket-handkerchief, table-napkins fan, and purse," were driven in "whirlecotes," the expressive name given to the first variety of coaches. In the middle of the festivities, bringing them to a summary conclusion, the tidings arrived of the death of the King's grandmother, the much-honoured Margaret of Richmond and Derby.

The beginning of Henry's reign was a period of unclouded sunshine. "Bluff King Hal" was personally very popular in his younger days; and, as a help to the general harmony, the late King had left an overflowing exchequer. The last of Catherine's dowry was at length paid. She was Queen of England, and her King was one of the most hopeful and handsome of European princes. A relic of his affection which had awakened hers, survives in a gorgeous missal that had belonged to his mother, and was given by Henry to Catherine at this time. In it he wrote a sentence in old French, which, translated into modern English, reads thus: "If your remembrance is according to my affection, I shall not be forgotten in your daily prayers, for I am yours—Henry R. for ever." Alas, for the "for ever," Henry's love was like summer lightning, swift and brief in its brilliancy. Catherine's was slow but sure. She wrote beneath the portrait of St. Margaret of Scotland, in the missal—

"By dayly probe, you shall me fynde
To be to you both loving and kynde."

Catherine's serious, reserved nature certainly opened up and blossomed in her passing prosperity. She did her best to enter into the noisy whirl of splendid gaiety in

tiltings, masqueings, and mayings, in which the young
King delighted, with which her graver character and
maturer years could hardly sympathise.   She feigned to
be charmed by the boisterous surprises which he was constantly providing for her, when he appeared in strange
disguises, and after he had outshone all competitors in
mimic war or sport or the dance, threw aside the unknown
armour, or the mask which had hid his face, and revealed
the gay and gallant chief of the revels.   She endured the
merry riot when the faithful Commons, permitted to watch
the grand doings, took the liberty of bursting into the
royal circle and helping themselves freely to their share of
the finery.

The one point in which Queen Catherine ran counter
to her husband's wishes, and offended him by her contumaciousness, was by refusing to go into the fields, as English ladies went, hawking and hunting.   There might be
some show of reason in the objection when, with the strain
of doggedness in her nature, she maintained that the ladies
of her country were not accustomed to ride on horseback
and indulge in such exercises.   But for a biographer of
Catherine's to urge that the woman, who as child and girl
had been accustomed to share in the brutal national entertainment of the bull-fight, refrained from having anything
to do with English field-sports, because of the superior
womanly kindness and delicacy which rendered their
coarseness and cruelty offensive to her, carries a broad
contradiction on the face of the argument.

Catherine made an honourable effort to follow her
mother's good example in inducing the King to welcome
learned men to the court.   She herself particularly
favoured Sir Thomas More.   Erasmus, too, has borne testimony to her intelligence and courtesy.   Though she had
been so long in learning English, she expressed a wish
that he should increase her acquaintance with Latin.   But
the name of the daughter of the generous patroness of

Christopher Columbus is not once mentioned in connection with the very slight encouragement which Henry gave to the Bristol adventurer, Sebastian Cabot, and his enterprise.

Catherine employed herself and her ladies in busily manufacturing flags and banners for Henry when he went to the French wars. At a later and less happy period of her life, she came out to receive the commissioners sent to treat with her, with a skein of red silk hanging round her neck, and proceeded to explain how innocently and humbly she and her women had been engaged. But her housewifely attainments did not reach the supreme height of her mother Isabella's, since she is said, in the middle of the cares of Government and the distraction of the struggle with the Moors, to have made, with her own royal hands, a shirt for her Ferdinand.

Doubtless, Catherine was at the summit of her prosperity and happiness when she acted as regent of the kingdom in her husband's absence in France, and had the satisfaction of telling him of the English victory at Flodden. In the letter which gives him the news, though she inquires, by the way, what is to be done with the body (or the supposed body) of the King of Scots, the aggressor in the war with his brother-in-law, which she seems to have wished to reserve for funeral honours beseeming his relationship to the majesty of England, there is not a word of pity for the slain man's widow; yet this was Henry's sister Margaret, who had been Prince Arthur's favourite among all his kindred, who had not so very long ago danced that lively high dance with young Henry, before their late Majesties at Westminster, in the course of the festivities on Catherine's first marriage.

Other periods of dignified enjoyment and natural triumph on Catherine's part, were those in which she entertained her nephew, the Emperor Charles V., and when with Henry she received his proposals for her little

daughter Mary, to whose aunt Mary he had been betrothed
without anything coming of it.   At the same time she is
said to have been aroused to the danger of being "too
Spanish," and either did not feel, or did not express, much
affection for her nephew on his first arrival in England.
According to the Spanish ambassador, as quoted by Du
Boys, she hardly answered when Charles spoke to her.

Catherine accompanied Henry to Calais in order to assist
in the splendours of the Field of the Cloth of Gold, while
she was content to let Mary, Duchess of Suffolk, be the
reigning beauty of the magnificent assembly.   Catherine
was satisfied so long as she and Queen Claude (poor young
Queen Claude! slowly dying of consumption) were the two
queens, who exchanged visits of gracious ceremony every
day, and even took the Holy Communion together, in token
of the amity they sought to establish between England
and France.   One does not like to think that there was a
conscious absence of sincerity in the solemn pledge, and
there is no ground for supposing that Queen Claude acted
with any reservation, but Catherine, under her apparent
indifference to Charles, was devoted to the interests of her
nephew, which were not exactly those of France.   The
beginning of the enmity between her and the great Cardinal, Wolsey, did not proceed from her indignation at his
arrogance, or her displeasure because of the rôle he had
played in the death of Buckingham.   It was on account
of his wrath at finding all his well-thought-out plans for
building up the monarchy, bringing about peace and not
war between England and France, thwarted by Catherine's
standing on the side of her kinsman, and by the influence
she exercised over Henry to induce him to adopt the cause
of Spain and Austria, in reality to become the tool of the
infinitely more astute Charles.   For Henry was still a
young man, and his early popularity with his people,
which was so great that it is said his death then would
have been regarded as a terrible national misfortune,

though it had some foundation in what was generous and lovable in him in those days, was due much more to his fine person, his manly addiction to all martial exercises and field sports, and superiority in them, and to his frank, jovial humour, than to any aptitude for business or sound discretion in European politics. Even a foreigner who chanced to see Henry playing bowls, breaks out into an enthusiastic panegyric on his zeal and prowess in the game, on his stately height, breadth of shoulder, white skin, and golden beard.

In the middle of Catherine's temperate mingling in the amusements of the court, and even on her own account playing tables (chess or draughts), tric-trac (backgammon), and cards, she heard mass celebrated several times every ordinary day, and many times on church festivals. She had books of devotion read to her for two hours in the middle of the day. She rose in the course of each night and repaired to her oratory, spending a considerable portion of the time praying on her knees, on the cold stones of the pavement. She wore a penitential robe belonging to one of the orders of St. Francis—open to women—of which she was a member, beneath her sumptuous apparel. She revived the devout practices of the King's grandmother Margaret, though Catherine was certainly behind her model in breadth of judgment, genuine studiousness, and enlightened benevolence. Besides, the fashions of the times were changing, and it was now openly said that Catherine's behaviour would have better suited the abbess of a convent than a queen in her court. Her conduct so affected Henry's for the moment, that the light-hearted, headstrong young man not only attempted to confute the tenets of Luther, and obtained from the Pope the title of "Defender of the Faith," of which Catherine was very proud, he grew nearly as great a professor of religion as his wife was. Perhaps no king ever combined so much hunting with the hearing of so many masses, unless it were the unfortunate, blamelessly respectable Louis XVI.

Catherine's tragic fate was foreshadowed betimes by the death of her eldest child, a son, born on the 1st of January, 1511, whose auspicious birth was hailed with much rejoicing, but who died in less than two months, deeply lamented by his mother. Of three more children—two of them boys, only one child survived, a girl, Princess Mary, born in February, 1516. The King ardently desired a male heir, as the greatest security for the continuance of his race on the throne of England, and for the stability of the kingdom itself. The repeated disappointment of his hopes in the deaths of his infant sons certainly awoke in him a superstitious dread that heaven was punishing him, his house, and his realm, for the illegality, in spite of the Papal dispensation, of his marriage with his brother Arthur's widow. Along with the dread, the fickle, evil, tyrannical possibilities in the temper of the man began to show themselves.

A lingering and severe illness, which Catherine suffered about 1524, when she was in her fortieth year, aged her to a great extent. It tended to confirm in King Henry's mind the persuasion that the Divine vengeance was pursuing him and his wife. In addition, a sickly, despondent woman, with a tendency to moroseness, was little likely to be an agreeable companion to a pampered autocrat, a self-indulgent, frivolous man, who was six years her junior.

According to Mr. Froude, there had long been differences between them, and so far as the contrast in their characters went, this was nearly inevitable. They were only alike on one point, and unfortunately it was that of an imperious temper common to both; while Henry was "hot and impulsive," and Catherine "cold and self-contained." Her Castilian austerity, her "harsh and haughty manners," were alike against her. Yet even her critic

admits that if she had renounced her rights, and withdrawn from the contest early in the struggle, she would
have carried with her the good wishes and affectionate
remembrances of Henry's subjects. It is remarkable,
when one considers her foreign extraction, which was
made unnecessarily obtrusive to begin with, that the sympathies of the country went with her to the extent they
did. For she was never called "the Spanish woman," as
Marie Antoinette was styled "the Austrian woman." A
large proportion of the people clung to her cause, as that
of their good "Queen Catherine." The obtrusive hootings
and jeerings were for "Nan Bullen," her successor—not
for Catherine.

The notion of getting a divorce from Catherine on
account of the illegality of her second marriage, and of
Henry's thus being enabled to contract another, and, as it
appeared to him, more suitable match, took by degrees
entire possession of the King's mind. At first he was
covertly encouraged in the idea by Wolsey, partly because
he was not a servant who would contradict his master,
partly because he desired to be rid of the hostile influence
which overthrew his schemes.

But the difficulties to Henry's attaining a divorce were
very great. The Pope had given a dispensation, and to
withdraw it was not merely to deal a blow to the Papal
infallibility, it was to draw down on the Holy See the
indignation and vengeance of the greatest sovereign in
Europe, the Emperor Charles V., who owned Austria,
Spain, and the Low Countries as his personal possessions,
while he had the additional authority of the imperial rank
to which he had been elected. Catherine was universally
respected, if not universally beloved, in England; and she
had the accidental advantage on her side that, if her
powerful kindred were set at naught, England, which had
been recovering from the ruinous Wars of the Roses,
and was beginning to reassert itself as likely to grow

into a rich and powerful trading community, would find her commerce, chiefly with the Low Countries, fatally hampered.

For seven long trying years the painful controversy lasted, and included the appeals to the Pope, the arrival of the legates sent to decide the matter, and the summoning of councils of bishops and learned doctors of law and divinity, to overrule the halting indecision of the legates. The contest ended with the great conclusions that the Church of England was a Christian Church apart from the Roman hierarchy and independent of it, and that what the King and the foremost of the English prelates decreed, was ecclesiastical law.

Catherine must have suffered agonies of humiliation and wounded affection—affection in her so tenacious, from her first apprehension of the King's purpose, to its final enforcement.

Much shedding of blood and many a crushing downfall marked the strife. Very different victims—Sir Thomas More, who was an honour to the name of Englishman; good Bishop Fisher, who had been the King's tutor; the peasant girl, Elizabeth Barton, who, as the "Holy Maid of Kent," threatened to be an English Jeanne d'Arc—all perished. Great Wolsey, who had latterly refrained from urging on the divorce, seeing that the King's will was not to contract a great foreign alliance, but to wed with a subject, was degraded from his dignities, and died broken-hearted.

Occasionally it seemed utterly impossible that the divorce could be carried out; occasionally, also, the King appeared to waver and to return to his old allegiance. Shallow, coarse-natured, and despotic as Henry was, there was something in him that never ceased to esteem and respect Catherine. All that was true and gentle in a nature once full of promise suffered from the course he pursued, and the very suffering blinded him to his mixed and baser motives. It was not hypocrisy, it was the composite nature of the man which caused him to pause in his vehement maintenance of his measure, to seek Catherine's company at times, to go upon more than one royal progress with her, and, in the friendliness and kindness of his behaviour, raise fresh hopes in her aching heart. Poor Catherine, on her part, sought with unwonted patience to promote this happier turn of affairs, and with painful anxiety laboured to increase her personal popularity by smiling and bowing to the people, "as she had not done before." Though aged far beyond her years, and inclined to embonpoint, she was not without claims to being a handsome woman still. Indeed, her style of good looks was better suited to extreme youth and to middle life than to the days of her prime.

But her autumnal attractions, such as they were, had small chance against the summer charms of the gifted and fascinating rival whom the King had elected to put in Catherine's place. Towards this rival, Anne Boleyn, who was then, and for years, one of the Queen's maids-of-honour, she never deigned to show either jealousy or rancour.

Catherine behaved with the greatest dignity and intrepidity when summoned before the Ecclesiastical Court at which Henry was present. Shakespeare's noble figure of Queen Catherine, so long identified with the grand acting of Sarah Siddons, was not nobler than the real woman at this stage of her adversity. Catherine refused, like herself, to submit "proudly, resolutely, gallantly, not without the scorn she was entitled to feel," admits Mr. Froude. She rose from her chair of state, and answered, protested against the legality of the tribunal, on the ground that her judges held benefices under the King, and appealed to Rome. When her name was called a second time, she rose, followed by her ladies, and passing the legates without a word, went round the Court till she reached the chair in which the King sat, and kneeling before him, pled to him "in her broken English," with infinite spirit and pathos. She appealed to him in the name of all the love which had been between them, and of the love of God. She reminded him that she was "a poor stranger born out of his dominions," without counsellor or friend save him. She called him to witness that she had been his true, obedient, loving wife, and that for a period of twenty years. She was the mother of his children, though it had pleased God to call divers of them out of the world, which was no fault of hers. She urged other powerful arguments, ending with the prayer that in the name of charity, and for the love of God, who was the just Judge of all, he would defer the sentence of the Court till she could hear from her friends in Spain. Rising in tears, she bowed low to the silent, agitated King, and walked out of Court.

"Madam," said Griffiths, her receiver-general, on whose arm she leant, "you are called back," for the crier made the hall ring again with the summons, "Catherine, Queen of England, come again into Court."

"I hear it well enough," answered the dauntless Catherine, "but on, on, go you on, for this is no Court wherein I can have justice." It is said she added, with proud humility, "I never before disputed the will of my husband, and I shall take the first opportunity to ask pardon for my disobedience."

In June 1529, after Cranmer had advised the King to take the advice of the universities of Europe and the prelates of England with regard to the legality of his marriage, irrespective of the verdict of the Pope of Rome, Catherine was required to quit Windsor Castle, and to leave behind her daughter, Princess Mary, then a girl of thirteen years of age.

From Ampthill, where Catherine resided for some time, she wrote motherly letters to and about her daughter.

Catherine had been Mary's teacher in Latin, but the
Queen magnanimously declared she was glad that the
Princess should change her mother for a better tutor, and
charged the young girl to profit by his instructions. A
touching letter was addressed by Catherine to the Minister,
Cromwell, on hearing that her daughter (always delicate)
was ill. The poor mother begs to see her child again,
urging " the little comfort and mirth she would take with
me would be half health to her." It is difficult to asso-
ciate the idea of easy intercourse and merriment with
Queen Catherine at the best of times. Although she is
said to have relished lively discourse on occasions, we have
always seen her a little heavy and solemn in her seriousness, even at the height of her prosperity ; and not much
cheer could be expected from her in those dreary days of
banishment and adversity ; but what will not a mother's
love attempt and achieve where the welfare of a child is
concerned ?

The Queen's entreaty was not granted. There was a
rumour of her having been offered, at an earlier date, the
guardianship of Princess Mary, with an allowance in
proportion to the position, on condition that she submitted
to the King's will, and united with him in seeking to procure a divorce. It was further said, that having refused to
submit, she was denied the boon of her daughter's company. But there was ample reason for the refusal on
other grounds, even though King Henry never ceased to
profess his perfect confidence in Catherine's many virtues,
and his reverence for them. There can be no doubt that
Catherine and Mary were the centre of a great political
party in England, apart from the supporters of their
claims abroad. In the eyes of the stricter Catholic nobility
and gentry (the Poles, the Nevilles, the Courtneys, &c.,
&c.), who remained firm to their creed, Mary would be
still the King's heir, let him marry whom he would in
Catherine's lifetime ; a great part of the Church, profess-

ing themselves impressed by the prophecies of Elizabeth
Barton, who predicted the King's death if he did not
repent and return to Queen Catherine, held the same
view. It was asserted that they had gone so far in their
schemes as to plot the King's removal from the throne, on
the plea that he had disqualified himself for reigning, and
the proclamation of Mary as sovereign in his stead. In
these circumstances the safe custody of Mary became a
question of the utmost importance, and to commit her to
the keeping of her mother was a political impossibility.

In May 1533, the sentence declaring Henry's marriage
with Catherine null, and giving liberty to the contracting
parties to marry elsewhere, was given in the Archepiscopal
Court held at Dunstable, and was read publicly in the
Lady Chapel of Dunstable Priory. Thenceforth Catherine
was addressed in all court communications as Princess-
Dowager of Wales, in right of her widowhood to Arthur,
Prince of Wales. The first time she saw herself thus
addressed, she took up a pen and drew it through the
offending words with such force that her erasure stands
in a bold, black line on the State paper to this day. When
bidden to give up her title of Queen, she rejected the proposal with great indignation from the bed on which she
was lying, lame and sick: "I would rather be a poor
beggar's wife, and sure of heaven," she protested, "than
Queen of the world, and stand in doubt thereof by my
own consent. I stick not so for vain-glory; but because
I know myself to be the King's true wife, and you call me
the King's subject; I was his subject while his wife." A
good deal more she said with much point and plainness,
utterly regardless of the fact that the sentence of contumaciousness had already been pronounced against her, and
that to be accused of contumacious resistance to the
King's will was no light matter in the England of those
days.

It would not be fair to refuse to acknowledge that,

seeing things as he and his counsellors did, Henry acted towards Catherine in her attitude of defiance to his will with some amount of respectful forbearance ; compared to his later treatment of those who opposed him, his conduct was tolerance itself. His character was by no means destitute of magnanimity, till self-indulgence in every form —in a violent temper, among other undesirable defects —association with unprincipled and vicious companions, and health and strength fearfully squandered and ruined —had destroyed the balance of his nature. He could not let Catherine continue his queen ; he could not suffer her to stay where she liked ; he was forced to deprive her of the company of her daughter ; but whether actuated by a sense of justice, by lingering regard, or by dread of her kindred, he stopped short of persecuting her in any form, or of driving her from England. He allowed her to have her household and friends around her. He interfered very little with her visitors, native or foreign, though there was strong reason to believe that they were hostile to him. If her income of five thousand pounds a year, as Princess-Dowager of Wales, was not paid regularly or fully from an exchequer no longer overflowing as when Henry succeeded to his father's hoards, it is quite possible that he was not aware of the remissness, or altogether accountable for it ; and that it was the fault of the Minister Cromwell or of his subordinates.

From Ampthill, Catherine was removed to Mote, and then to the bishop's palace of Bugden, in Lincolnshire— localities which were all displeasing to her. She considered them damp and cold, while her wishes pointed to the neighbourhood of London, which on other grounds was not admissible as her place of residence. Her pecuniary affairs were in the uncomfortable condition in which they had been during the earlier years of her stay in England, without any fault of hers. Her ladies' salaries and servants' wages were in arrears, and she and her household were but scantily supplied with what was requisite for them.

To speed the lagging hours the deposed Queen and her ladies worked diligently on the rich embroidery used in altar cloths and ecclesiastical vestments. At the window of a chamber looking into the chapel, Catherine would pray for hours, both by day and night, on the bare stones, from which the cushions had been removed. Some of her servants reported that they found the stones against which her head had rested, " wet as though a shower had rained upon them," from the tears which had poured from her eyes.

On Catherine's praying that she might be removed from Bugden, as the air was prejudicial to her health, Fotheringay, which had been settled on her as Princess of Wales, was appointed for her residence. But the ex-Queen regarded the choice as an attempt to entrap her into an appearance of consenting to her deposition, and doggedly declined the change, saying that though his Grace had the power, "yet ne may she, ne will she go, unless drawn with ropes."

Finally Kimbolton Castle was fixed upon for her dwelling, though she objected to this arrangement also, because there the air blew from the fen countries, and was likely to be chilly and noxious to a foreigner and a native of the South. To Kimbolton Castle, however, she was sent, in despair of contenting her or of finding a more suitable home for her.

There is a pleasant description of Kimbolton, as it was then, given by one of its owners, and quoted by Miss Strickland. It had 'a "tower and gateway and double ditch." It was " a house buried in wood," with open uplands to the east and west, each knoll of which was crowned by either abbey tower or village spire—a green, bright country, full of deer and birds and fen wildfowl, free to the March winds, asking of its dwellers who would keep in health a good deal of exercise on horse and foot. But, alas! the Spanish-bred Catherine could neither walk nor ride.

She did not live more than two years at Kimbolton. Her health grew worse, till a report of her death reached King Henry from the Spanish ambassador, and startled and shocked him. On inquiry, her physician asserted that he had asked his patient to get more medical advice, and she had answered that she would in no wise have any other physician, but would wholly commit herself to the pleasure of God. It is said that Catherine again petitioned to see her daughter, from whom she had been separated for six years, who was by this time a young woman of nineteen years of age. But there is no evidence that this petition was ever made, though there is still extant a letter which Catherine wrote to Henry, assuring him of her love and forgiveness, which moved him to tears. It caused him to despatch immediately to Kimbolton her nephew, the Emperor Charles' ambassador. He was to greet kindly from Henry his "dear sister," as he had styled Catherine from the time of their separation, and to act as the representative of her kindred and her countrymen in hearing the dying princess's last wishes, and in giving her the ambassador's counsel and support. There is every presumption that the same impulse of regret and pity induced Henry to grant leave to one of Catherine's earliest friends to repair to her side. This friend was one of the maids-of-honour who had accompanied the princess in her girlhood from Spain to England. Her Spanish name was Dona Maria de Salazar. She was the daughter of Don Salazar, a captain of Ferdinand of Arragon's guard, and was a relation of Catherine's. She had married Lord Willoughby d'Eresby, and settled in England. She had been left a widow at twenty-eight years of age, and so was in one sense mistress of her actions; but according to her own statement, she had the King's authority for the step she took. This faithful lady accomplished a long journey on horseback, in the depth of winter, and sustained in addition a heavy fall from her horse, before she arrived, on New Year's Day, 1536, at the gate of Kimbolton Castle. There was some demur at admitting her, but she pleaded cold and exhaustion, begged to go to a fire, and declared she had letters on her which would exonerate everybody from the responsibility of giving her entrance. She at last succeeded in reaching the sick woman, the much honoured Dona Catalina of former days. What a meeting for the friends!

Catherine was happy in seeing and being able to speak in her mother tongue to both Lady Willoughby and the Imperial Ambassador, and in dying calmly in their presence. She was fifty years of age at the time of her death. Catherine's will was full of her natural thoughtfulness and conscientiousness. She chose her place of burial, and named the masses she wished to be said for her soul. She bequeathed the gold collar which she had brought with her from Spain, to her daughter. She referred to gowns of hers, apparently robes of state in the King's possession, and asked that they might be given to the convent in which she wished to be buried, with the exception of the fur on them, which she desired her daughter to have. She earnestly requested that small bounties, in proportion to their rank and length of service, might be bestowed on her ladies and servants, including "ten pounds to the little maidens, every one of them." She carefully recorded her few debts, among them her year's wage to her apothecary, the charge for making a gown which was due, and her laundress's bill.

It has been said that Catherine's wishes with regard to her place of burial ("in a convent of Observant Friars") were neglected; that there is no proof of her legacies and debts having been paid, and that Henry seized her effects by means of an unworthy subterfuge. But the fact is

that the King destined for her a noble memorial; that
the sole legacy she left, of which anything is known, is
shown to have been paid; and that the course which
Henry pursued with regard to Catherine's property
was the only one legally open to him in the peculiar circumstances.

Catherine was buried with fitting honour in Peterborough Abbey, which was afterwards spared, it was
believed for her sake, in the destruction of so many
ecclesiastical edifices. Henry is reported to have said
that "he would have to her memory one of the goodliest
monuments in Christendom."

At Greenwich the King and his court kept the funeral
day of Catherine in mourning, with religious observances,
while Anne Boleyn and her partisans were so self-engrossed
and ill-advised as to rejoice openly.

Catherine's daughter Mary proposed to have her mother's
body removed and placed in the tomb which should hold
her own remains, but the intention was unfulfilled. A
small brass plate has alone, from the first, marked the spot
where Catherine lies. Local superstition has sought to
raise other monuments to the pious, upright, hardly used
princess and woman. When Catherine's successor suffered
a still more terrible doom, the church officials of Peterborough would have it that the tapers surrounding the
hearse which had brought Catherine to her last resting-
place a few months before, and still stood over her grave,
were lit, and afterwards extinguished of themselves. The
legend of a royal ghost is one of the precious possessions
of the present lords of Kimbolton. The vision of a stately
lady in flowing white, wearing the regal crown of which
she was deprived in life, glides in fancy through the
old rooms, descends the turret stair, and kneels in the
chapel.

ANNE BOLEYN[1]

BY MARRIAGE A TUDOR

In the room of the grave Spanish lady we have Anne
Boleyn, whose singular attraction for her contemporaries
seems to have lain rather more in her lively wit than in her
piquante but by no means flawless beauty.

Anne, who was long declared to have been the elder, is
now believed to have been the younger daughter of Sir
Thomas Boleyn, or Bullen, of Blickling, Norfolk. Her
mother, Lady Elizabeth Howard, was a daughter of the
Duke of Norfolk's, and figured as a court beauty amidst
the many festivals during the early years of the marriage
of Henry VIII. and Catherine of Arragon. There is considerable uncertainty about the date of Anne's birth, some
authorities giving it as 1507, but there is far greater probability in the statement which makes it 1501, the year
in which Catherine came to England. Lady Elizabeth
Boleyn, Anne's mother, died in 1512, when her younger
daughter was in all likelihood eleven years of age. Anne,
her sister Mary, and their brother spent their childhood
and their youth between Blickling, with its grand avenues
of oaks and chestnuts, and Hever Castle, in Kent. In
both places the Boleyns had for near neighbours the
family of Sir Henry Wyatt, who, in company with
Sir Thomas Boleyn, was joint-governor of Norwich
Castle. The future Queen, Anne Boleyn, the future
poet, Thomas Wyatt, and his sister Mary were early
playfellows.

[1] Agnes Strickland, Froude, Du Boys. Mary Robinson's "Life cf
Marguerite d'Angoulême, Queen of Navarre."

Anne was carefully educated in French as well as in English, and in music and needlework. Her attainments in French, for which she had a French governess, were sufficiently marked for the time to cause her to be chosen, at the age of seventeen (according to the more probable estimate of the date of her birth), as one of the young English ladies who were to accompany sixteen years old Mary Tudor to France, to join King Louis, to whom she had already been married by proxy at Greenwich.

As a necessary step to Anne's promotion (her eager, grateful anticipation of which is preserved in a girlish letter to her father, wherein she apologises for the faults in the composition, and tells him the French spelling is entirely "from her own head"), she had to go to court and be presented to Queen Catherine. In connection with this ceremony, the girl remarks enthusiastically that it will render her still more desirous of speaking and writing French if she is permitted to converse with "so sensible and elegant a princess."

One word of description of the eager young girl, who went with so much goodwill in the royal cavalcade to Dover, and waited in the Castle there till the stormy sea would suffer the King of France's bride to cross the Channel, who, a little later, figured in the splendours of Mary's wedding, at Aberville, and triumphal entrance into Paris. For if Anne did appear at court, and reside in the Castle of Dover, her first meeting with Henry must surely have occurred long before the various periods at which the event is said to have taken place. She was a tall, slender, well-shaped girl, with black hair, dark eyes, and a brunette complexion. She had two curious defects in addition to the fact that one of her upper teeth projected slightly; on the little finger of her left hand there was a double nail, together with an indication of a sixth finger, while on her throat was a small wen or raised mole, called "a strawberry," which she commonly covered by a collar band. Her

voice was marvellously sweet, both in speaking and singing. Her vivacity and skill in repartee were from the first
remarkable.

According to Du Boys, Sir Thomas Boleyn, Anne's
father, was in the Princess's suite. If so, he may have
received permission to take with him his daughter Mary,
though she was not in the regular retinue, since she
finished her education in France while her sister Anne
was there. Among the English girls of rank in Princess
Mary's immediate suite, recent investigations have discovered sufficient proof to reckon Jane Seymour, as well
as Anne Boleyn, the two being about the same age.
Neither returned with Lady Guildford and the ladies sent
back to England by King Louis, nor did they go home
with Mary Tudor after she was Duchess of Suffolk. They
had left her service on the death of the French king,
when certainly Anne Boleyn, and it is believed Jane
Seymour, were admitted by favour into the household of
Queen Claude, the young wife of Francis I. The notion
that Anne Boleyn retired for a time from court service,
and entered, by her father's wish, a convent school at
Brie, in order to render her French education more complete, doubtless arises from some confusion in which the
sisters Mary and Anne Boleyn were mixed up together.
To later students of their histories, Mary, not Anne, must
have been the convent pupil.

If the young lives of Anne Boleyn and Jane Seymour,
which were destined to cross each other tragically in later
years, ran already in parallel lines, there is no evidence of
such friendship between them as might have been expected to unite contemporaries and countrywomen in a
foreign country. It is certain that Anne's popularity at
the French court far surpassed that of Jane, though the
latter is said to have been the more regularly beautiful of
the two. Anne's fascinations excited unbounded admiration among the gallant courtiers of Francis I. Even the

court ladies were fain to copy her style of dress, so quick,
and without limit was her invention, so exquisite her taste.
Next to this art, in the estimation of the gay throng, was
the degree to which Anne excelled in singing, and in
playing on the lute, harp, and rebec.   Further, she was a
proficient in dancing; so graceful and lightfooted was
she, that she not only reconciled the fastidious French to
the skipping and bounding of the English voltas or
high dances, she appears to have set the fashion in introducing them at a foreign court, adapting and varying
their figures, so as to lend to them the charm of constant
novelty.   Never was there a gay, brilliant, thoughtless
girl better qualified to be the star of a pleasure-loving
court.

The household of Queen Claude was no suitable field for
such accomplishments and graces; but then the Queen's
household was a gentle, modest contradiction in the middle
of unbounded luxury and licence.   Poor Claude is a sweet
and peaceful figure, relieved against a splendid, restless,
vicious background.   She was younger even than her
young English maids-of-honour, or her beautiful English
stepmother, who had reigned for so brief a space, been so
short a time a "white widow," and then had wedded and
sailed away with the lover of her youth.   Claude, one of
the two daughters of King Louis and Anne of Brittany,
was not more than fifteen years of age when her husband
Francis succeeded her father on the throne.   She was
meek and devout, "a quiet, narrow-chested girl. . . .
gentle, pious, and awkward, with neat, pure features,
and smooth-braided hair, that had no special charm or
grace."   "She sat in her chamber reading her missal,
submitting to her mother-in-law, and embroidering red
silken counterpanes."   She left Francis's devoted mother
and sister, Louise of Savoy, and Marguerite d'Angoulême,
Duchess d'Alençon, to help him to rule his kingdom;
the one with an imperious, ambitious woman's strong will,

the other with a tender-natured, intellectual woman's kindly graciousness, and dreamy far-reaching speculations. To both, the girl-wife Claude, neglected by her dashing knight-errant of a husband, was but a child to be protected and petted, and left to the retirement she preferred. Her simple history had a pathetic ending. All along consumption had marked her for its victim, and she died at the age of twenty-five, leaving behind her a family of six little children, to whom her sister-in-law Margaret, the fanciful poet and story-teller, the ardent reformer and the charming woman of society, was a loving mother.

In Claude's lifetime her strenuous, honourable aim was to keep her ladies pious and virtuous amidst the surrounding levity and wickedness. Her patient practice was to lead them in procession to mass, as well as to have them to form her train in public, and to sit with them at their embroidery frames in private. So far from encouraging the idle dalliance and bold coquetry between the ladies and gentlemen of her suite, on which the Duchess Marguerite smiled, Claude banished the gentlemen from her circle.

There was little field for a girl like Anne Boleyn in that convent-like household. One cannot help thinking that tranquil, docile Jane Seymour must have been much more to innocent young Claude's mind. But Anne was not fated to continue long in Claude's service. She passed from the Queen's household into the much more congenial establishment of the Duchess d'Alençon, in which the newcomer was better calculated to shine. To Duchess Marguerite, with her love of art and beauty, her utter lack of personal jealousy, her passion for high-flown romance, and her impressionable, generous temper, the lovely, accomplished, witty maid-of-honour must have been a delight.

But what is to be said of the blue-eyed, fair-haired Marguerite as a guide and example for youth? Her own conduct was free from reproach; she was good; she was

even noble, in many respects.   She was the foster-mother
of the Renaissance—the new dawn of learning in France.
She was the friend and protectress of the French Reformers.   Not one of them desired more earnestly than she
did the purification of the Church from its errors; not
one was more sincere than she was in her mystical devotion.   Yet withal she was an amiable, sentimental enthusiast, living in high-flown fantastic dreams.   She was
humane and compassionate; but she was also unpractical
to her finger-tips.   She tried in vain to recall the picturesque unsubstantial visions of the vanishing Middle Ages.
She could not realise what the world was to commonplace people of more worldly natures; worst of all, she
had lived in a capital and court notoriously the most
corrupt in Europe, till her moral sense was thoroughly
blunted; she entirely dissociated religion and morals.
Good herself, she was absolutely tolerant, well-nigh
quiescent, where evil in others was concerned.   She even
suffered herself to be entertained and amused by it, of
which there is ample proof in the stories she wrote and
left behind her.

Under Marguerite's care, Anne Boleyn, with her far
harder and lower nature, was, to say the least, unshel-
tered from temptation.   In the lively, adventure-loving,
defiant company she learnt a freedom of speech and manner which was no gain to her in after-life; and while still
in France, before she was twenty, accusations of folly—
not likely to be softened by censorious rivals—marred her
fair reputation.   There is a description of the beautiful,
giddy girl preserved by an old French historian.   She is
described as wearing blue velvet with gold bells hanging
from the points of the short mantle—the vest and surcoat
starred with silver and lined with minever.   She has the
great hanging sleeves which she had herself introduced at
court to hide the defect in one hand.   Her feet are in
blue velvet brodequins, with diamond stars.   On her head

is a cap—half cap, half veil—of gold-coloured gauze, beneath which her dark curls fall.

The brilliant and learned biographer of Marguerite states authoritatively that Anne Boleyn attended her mistress to the Field of the Cloth of Gold, and that there she first met Henry VIII., which could hardly have been : nor can we discover elsewhere more than a presumption of her presence, in an entirely subordinate character, on the occasion.

In 1521 or 1522 Anne returned to England, in her twenty-first year, according to Lord Herbert of Cherbury, after an absence of three or four years. She was recalled either by the threatening of war between England and France, or to further an arrangement of her father's. He had projected an alliance between one of his daughters and the heir of Sir Piers Butler, a kinsman of his own, by which a disputed inheritance might be amicably settled on the couple. Sir Thomas's elder daughter Mary had already entered into the first of the imprudent love-matches which excited the wrath of her family, and was, of course, *hors de combat;* therefore Anne, the younger daughter, was in request. If the suggestion had been carried out, history might have heard nothing more of poor, merry, reckless Anne Boleyn. She might still have redeemed the thoughtlessness of her exposed youth, by settling down into a noble English lady, content to be the fair and gentle châtelaine of her husband's castle. But that scheme, if seriously proposed, came to nothing, and instead Anne was appointed one of the maids-of-honour to Queen Catherine. There was the less chance of her continuing under her father's guardianship, since he had some time before taken as his second wife a lady of comparatively humble extraction, who, at the first glance, was not likely to be an acceptable stepmother to the grand-daughter of the Duke of Norfolk and to the rest of her mother's kindred. Eventually Lady Boleyn and her

daughter became great allies, and a warm attachment
subsisted between them.

A very popular tradition assigns the garden at Hever
as the scene of King Henry's first accidental encounter
with Anne, when he is said to have been struck by her
peculiar style of beauty, and still more pleased by the
frank charm of her manner and conversation. She was
calculated to adorn and enliven the court, whose royal
gaieties flagged a little as years went by.

A third inference is that Henry's introduction to Anne
occurred at court, after she was Catherine's maid-of-
honour. Be that as it may, without question she was the
most admired of the beauties in Henry's palaces, as she
had been in those of Francis; and her love of admiration
grew on what it fed upon; so did her careless, scornful
volatility, under which there was a certain sparkling
hardness. It was a nature not incompatible with strong
affections, and with possibilities of profound melancholy.

Another opening presented itself, by which Anne might
have escaped her doom. In the ante-rooms of Sheen,
Windsor, and Greenwich, in which jesting, laughing
maids-of-honour congregated, a young nobleman in Wolsey's suite tarried till his heart was lost. The loser of
the heart was Lord Percy, eldest son of the powerful
Earl of Northumberland, and the winner was Mistress
Anne Boleyn. She listened to the suit paid to her with
gracious favour; for both love and ambition would have
been satisfied if she had wedded Lord Percy.

But all the great powers of State interfered—Henry,
Wolsey, and the Earl of Northumberland—and dared the
young man to carry out his purpose. It is doubtful
whether it had gone so far, as one of the evil, ambiguous
troth-plights of the day, secretly entered into by the pair.
For although Anne was made to confirm the suspicion just
before her death, Lord Percy had already denied it on
oath. To plead such a contract would have served them

little at the time, since a similar contract, which might
be made to mean anything or nothing, had already been
formed by the Earl of Northumberland, between his son
and a daughter of the Earl of Shrewsbury's, and this the
two fathers insisted on completing. The young peer
offered some resistance, but assailed as he was on all sides,
gave way and married Lady Mary Talbot, so that Anne
lost both her lover and the opportunity of sharing a great
earl's coronet.

Deeply mortified and bitterly resentful against her
opponents, especially Wolsey, it is said Anne withdrew
in some measure from court, retiring to Hever, even returning to France, and there or at Hever she spent three
more years. But in 1527 she was again, by her father's
will, in waiting on Catherine of Arragon. Anne was now
five-and-twenty years of age—in the meridian of her
bright beauty and of the lightning play of her wit.
What was called in solemnly mysterious language "the
King's secret matter"—his intention of getting a divorce
from Queen Catherine—was more and more bruited
abroad, while to discerning eyes it was plain that Henry
had fixed on Anne Boleyn as the Queen's successor.

Wolsey, striving for Henry's honour and authority, and
through the King for his own and the Church's supremacy
in England, could not believe in the infatuation which
would place a subject in the room of the daughter of
kings. But Henry's absolute subjection to the fancy of
the hour, and his violent anger against all who attempted
to cross his will, were gaining on him, and Anne's ambition was keeping pace with them. For she saw in the
King's determination the means of indemnifying herself
for her wrongs. She would solace her wounded pride.
She would fill her starved and disappointed heart, empty
of purer, sweeter aims, with the dreams of power which
should replace the old craving for personal homage. She
would overwhelm her rivals and enemies; she would pro-

mote to eminence and affluence her kindred and friends
in the remotest degree. Before these great and terrible
temptations, all loyalty and gratitude to her grave, sad
mistress, whose majesty alone survived the wreck wrought
in her by care and sorrow, paled and died—nay, was sup-
planted by insolent self-assertion and exultation in her
own rising fortunes.

In adopting the King's views with regard to the rank
she was to fill, Anne stooped to dissemble, to pretend to
bow down before the great Cardinal, to seek to win him
over by flattery, while she never wavered in her implacable hatred to his person, and war against his claims.

At the same time it is not necessary to think that Anne
Boleyn was solely influenced by self-seeking in her inclination to rank herself on the side of the reforming party
in the Church, which was beginning to be headed by
Cranmer. She had heard the most advanced doctrines of
the Reformation freely discussed and eagerly favoured in
the salon of Marguerite d'Angoulême, while Anne herself
was a woman of a quick wit and an independent, fearless
spirit. Du Boys, who is not her friend, states—while
making a grossly unfounded assertion against the manner
of living of the Reformers—that she brought her reformed
doctrines from France with her.

Students of the time and of the man have remarked on
the fearful deterioration in Henry's character under the influence of Anne, under the rack of suspense, and under the
evil of his association with her friends and kindred. With
hardly any exceptions, and among the last her worldly old
father could not be reckoned, her natural allies were unprincipled, frivolous, and dissipated. Less attention, and
that more indirect, has been bestowed on the deterioration in Anne, which was yet true and sad enough. Her
habits of dainty self-indulgence increased; her passion for
coquetry waxed stronger; an element of untruthfulness,
hitherto absent from her nature, began to show itself.

The naïveté in her fine eyes gave place to craft; her mouth, never the best feature in her face, showed symptoms of repellent coarseness.

Still a third loophole and warning offered itself to Anne before her destiny was sealed. When the "sweating sickness," which cost Mary Tudor her only son, came to England, Anne Boleyn was the first person at the court attacked by the malady. She withdrew to Hever, where she was brought to the point of death. She recovered to meet another fate.

Henry had already created Anne's father Lord Rochefort, and in 1532 he created her Marchioness of Pembroke, with an income suited to the title. In October of the same year, Anne, as Marchioness of Pembroke, went in the train of Henry to Boulogne, where he had a second meeting with King Francis; but to her sore affront, her former acquaintance failed to bring with him the ladies of his family. Not even Anne's old easy-minded mistress would, by countenancing her, acknowledge her title to the position she was already assuming.

At last the lagging course of Henry's divorce from Queen Catherine approached its completion, and the public proclamation at Dunstable in May was anticipated by the private marriage at Whitehall, in January 1533, of the King and Anne Boleyn. In April the marriage was more publicly solemnised, and in May the legality of the union was confirmed at Lambeth. Anne was then thirty-two years of age, still a beautiful and stately woman, in the portrait which represents her in a gown of tawny velvet, "studded with emeralds," matching in colour her green velvet mantle. She has a double row of pearls round her neck, partly hiding the mole on her throat; her coif is composed of rows of stringed pearls meeting a green velvet hood.

Anne was crowned with great ceremony and magnificence at Westminster, on Whit Sunday, the 1st of June.

She went a few days before in a gala-barge—one of a fleet of fifty similar barges, "blazing with gold and streaming with banners," on her progress to the Tower. Before her was the Lord Mayor's barge, the stage of a gorgeously grotesque pageant, in which a dragon, with the usual attendant monsters, spirted wildfire into the Thames. At the Tower the King met and welcomed Anne with every mark of love and respect. She made a public entrance into London, like so many of her predecessors; she sat in a litter of white and gold, and she herself wore silver tissue lined with ermine; on her flowing hair she had the matron's coif and a circlet of rubies. A canopy of cloth of gold was borne over her head by four knights. Ladies of the highest rank in the country rode behind her, on palfreys and in chariots. The City outdid itself in pageants and decorations. On that day and the next, which was the day of her coronation, every fountain and conduit ran all day with wine, and the bells of every steeple rang lustily.

She was then the wonan whom the King delighted to honour; but it was a significant fact that only the State of Venice and the Kingdom of France, among all the European powers, sent their ambassadors to represent them on the occasion.

Anne's child, a daughter, was born in Greenwich Palace, and christened Elizabeth, in honour of the King's mother. The child's sex was a severe disappointment to the King, who desired, above all things, male heirs; and to Anne, who, as mother of a Prince of Wales, might have hoped to see her prosperity indefinitely prolonged. The succession to the Crown was settled, in the first place, on the baby Elizabeth, to the exclusion of Catherine's grown-up daughter Mary; the title of Princess was taken from her, and she was styled simply "The Lady Mary."

For refusing to ratify the deed of settlement by their oath of allegiance, Sir Thomas More and Bishop Fisher,

old and fast friends of Catherine's, were committed to
the Tower, not without a shrewd suspicion that Anne
instigated Henry to the tyrannous act. Then was spoken
the famous prediction which has descended to posterity.
When More's devoted daughter, Margaret Roper, visited
him, he inquired how Queen Anne did.

"In faith, father, never better," Margaret answered.
"There is nothing else in the court but dancing and
sport."

"Never better!" repeated Sir Thomas. "Alas! Meg,
alas! it pitieth me to think into what misery, poor soul,
she will shortly come. These dances of hers will prove such
dances that she will spurn our heads off like footballs;
but it will not be long ere her head will dance the like
dance."

But history retains proofs that poor Anne, in the middle
of her desperate, incurable, mocking levity, and that biting
wit of hers, which kept telling her of the insecurity of her
position, now that she had gained the prize she had coveted,
was not without some visions of reigning worthily, like her
former mistress, Marguerite, now Queen of Navarre, and as
became a Queen of England. She might dream of thus
atoning for the betrayal of her late mistress Catherine,
with whom Anne had been proud to converse when she
came a country girl to court, for the betrayal of that
mistress's daughter, and the sins against Anne's conscience, which had paid dearly for a doubtful and pre-
carious boon. It was partly due to her influence that
the Bible was translated into English. She interposed
to protect those who were exposed to danger in this service. She exerted herself to befriend Latimer; she won
the praise of Cranmer. During her brief period of power
she sent donations (also like Marguerite) from her privy
purse, to relieve distress in the country villages. She had
schemes for introducing remunerative manufactures into
the country. She wished that capable youths should

receive college education at her expense. She hoped that
their talents and learning might profit the Church and the
country. She made an effort to be more decorous and
sedate in her demeanour, and more domestic in her ways,
reviving the example of Queen Claude, even of Queen
Catherine, in sitting at work among her ladies. Anne
and her women are said to have executed some of the
tapestry still extant at Hampton Court—more ambitious
and creditable work than the red silk counterpanes which
had exercised the needles of the ladies of France. Queen
Marguerite was likewise skilled in embroidery; but she
possessed resources which, unfortunately, Anne, with all
her gifts of music and dancing, did not own in nearly the
same degree. Marguerite kept a couple of secretaries, a
man to the right and a man to the left of her, as she
worked. To the one she dictated her large correspondence; to the other she recited the pastorals, songs, and
hymns which she improvised on the moment. Marguerite
was to the manner born; with all her anxieties and
troubles, she could be tranquil and disengaged. But how
the feverish pulses of Anne's restless heart throbbed!
And how the very tenacity with which she clutched power,
signified the absence of confidence in its stability, when
she cried out—she might have grown deceitful, but she
was never reserved—with open joy on hearing the news
that Catherine's sufferings and sorrows were ended!
"Now I am indeed a queen!" said Anne. She was
washing her hands in a costly basin when the tidings
were brought to her, and she immediately bestowed the
basin on the messenger. With the same audacious, nay,
indecent exhibition of delight, she congratulated her
parents and friends on the removal of her enemy, whom
she was to follow by a dark and blood-stained way in the
course of four short months. On the day of Catherine's
funeral, instead of the black which the King enjoined for
the court, Queen Anne and her ladies appeared in all the

ostentatious gaiety of yellow. It was a mistake to suppose that yellow served as mourning in any court in Europe, according to an explanation which some historians have attempted to give.

In January 1536, Anne gave birth to a dead son—a misfortune which dealt another blow to her prospects. It was clear that her influence over Henry was on the wane, and not without some provocation on her side; apart from King Henry's shameful fickleness and recklessness, apparently Anne could not overcome her inveterate vanity and levity. She had been free of speech to indiscretion always. After she was queen she continued, except on rare occasions, impulsive and heedless, encouraging idle compliments and foolish pretensions, laying herself open to unwarrantable liberties from her attendants, because she would not take the trouble to keep them at a due distance, or to preserve her royal place, in half despising the precautions required by her station, while she was yet resolute to retain that station. She had fits of hauteur succeeding her hours of unbridled relaxation[1]; but the hauteur would not repair the mischief which was done by the relaxation. Her conduct was particularly trying to a man of Henry's exacting, jealous temper, and with a single exception he had known nothing like it in the women of his family. His much-reverenced grandmother, Margaret of Richmond and Derby; his gentle mother, Elizabeth of York; his first wife, Catherine, were all models of high-bred dignity and propriety—absolutely beyond reproach. Mary Tudor had been betrayed into a little pardonable folly in her early girlhood; but her character in after-life had been that of a noble and stainless wife and mother; only his sister Margaret, whom Henry neither respected nor loved, had been as wilful

---

[1] Chapuys, the Emperor's Ambassador, wrote to his master of Anne's insolence to the old nobility, and of her treating her uncle, the Duke of Norfolk, as no dog ought to have been treated.

and regardless a woman as he was a man. To increase his irritability, though he was little more than forty, his health was seriously failing. His great bulk was becoming heavy and unwieldy. He was lame from a painful ailment in one of his legs. The premature infirmity and suffering, which in the end maddened him almost to frenzy, were beginning to do their work.

Anne seemed to have a dim foreboding of what was coming upon her. Her health was not good, and her spirits were often depressed. She frequently shunned society, in which her place was no longer by the King's side. There was no more gay shooting at the butts, in which the two competed together. No more sweet singing and playing for one privileged listener, by an accomplished musician, whose gifts and skill had formerly entranced the best trained audiences. No more of the two-handed games of cards or dice, in which Anne, always fond of excitement on her own account, had sympathised with Henry's inordinate love of indoor sport, when he could not command out-of-door exercise : thus the pair had been accustomed to play together, winning and losing large sums of money in the process.

Anne had a great liking for dogs, while she abhorred the monkeys which Catherine had patronised. Anne's affection ranged over the whole canine race, from the spaniel which each maid-of-honour was allowed to keep, to the great boar or wolf-hound (her particular property) which accomplished the feat of killing a cow, down to the little dog called "Little Purboy," to which she was so much attached that, when it was accidentally killed, no one dared to tell her, till the King undertook the task. In those days of despondency and foreboding, she would wander with "Little Purboy's" former comrades in the remotest recesses of Greenwich Park, or she would sit for hours in the quadrangle of the palace, surrounded by the four-footed friends whom she found more faithful than many human satellites, listlessly playing with them or watching their gambols.

At last the blow fell; she was accused of high treason and infidelity to her marriage vows. It is quite impossible at this date to establish the truth or the falsehood of the outrageous and horrible accusations. A singular witness in Anne's favour has been found within the present generation. Chapuys's correspondence with his injured master has been discovered in the State archives in Vienna. Chapuys was Anne's deadly enemy. He hardly ever mentions her name without making use of an opprobrious epithet. He entertained the conviction, held by Catherine of Arragon and Princess Mary, that Anne was trying everything in her power to compass their deaths; yet not only was he evidently incredulous of her guilt, though he was satisfied that the King believed in it, he supplied proofs of the terrible atmosphere of hatred and malice which surrounded her. The principal nobility detested her. The Imperial party were hostile to her because she notoriously and uniformly took the part of France in the political complications of the day. The Roman Catholics abhorred her for the double reason that she favoured the Reformers, and that she had taken the place of their rightful queen. The moment Henry's passionate regard for Anne appeared on the wane, and he had hardly spoken to her for months before she was accused, her innumerable enemies assailed her with every infamous charge which could be devised. The evidence laid before the members of the Council, and the peers (already aware of the King's verdict) has long ago been destroyed, and the cautiously whispered contemporary opinions on her innocence or her guilt vary as widely as the contending religious and political factions of the period differed. The particular behaviour which brought her affairs to a crisis is thus described. With her natural love of talking and foolish jesting, she had betrayed a lamentable lack of delicacy and of good feeling, even at a time when manners were coarser than they are to-day, by referring lightly, in speaking to one of the members of her household, as to what might happen and whom she might marry if the King died, winding up the flighty tirade by declaring it should not be her hearer, in spite of his professions of regard for her. Anne's second conspicuous offence was, that when present at a tilting-match at Greenwich, she threw down her handkerchief to one of the combatants, who, after wiping his heated brow with it, or kissing it—according to different views of his action—took it upon him to return the handkerchief to the Queen on the point of his lance, when Henry immediately quitted the tilting-yard in a towering passion. Yet, silly and unbecoming as the proceeding was, it would have been simply looked upon as a piece of poetic licence, from queen or lady, prince or gentleman, in the household of Marguerite d'Angoulême, in which Anne spent the most impressionable days of her youth. When one thinks of it, was not what is known of Anne's objectionable bearing, and of the bearing of her courtiers, which reflected hers, but a transplanting to an uncongenial soil, a vulgar, matter-of-fact, misunderstood rendering of the gay and gallant doings in what was called Marguerite's " Court of Love " ? There high-flown homage and platonic devotion were bandied on all sides, and addressed to Marguerite herself, without a thought of blame. But the high-born lady of the revels was merely playing at a fanciful game, the dream of a poet. She was far removed from any ordinary interpretation of the situation. She knew how, when, and where to make her courtiers stop by her very faculty of pure idealisation and imaginativeness.

This we do know of Anne in her adversity, that in her native land she was more forlorn than the foreigner Catherine was in her evil day. The accusations brought against Anne were infinitely more crushing and disgraceful. So far from having many friends among her countrymen, some of her kindred were among her accusers. These included her sister-in-law, Lady Rochefort, with whom Anne had always been on bad terms, and her uncle the Duke of Norfolk. He was a distinguished soldier, while he is also described as "a small, spare, dark man, with cruel lips, and a more cruel temper." He is said to have treated Anne with marked rudeness while she was under examination at Greenwich. "Tut, tut!" he cried, in answer to her protestations of innocence. It was he who conducted her to the Tower on the 2nd of May 1536. Just three years after she had entered the gloomy precincts, in the triumph of her approaching coronation, she returned by the Traitors' Gate a hapless prisoner.

When taken to her former lodging, she protested "it is too good for me;" whether with the satire which rose so readily to her lips, whether from a sense of retribution because of the mistress at whose downfall and death Anne had rejoiced when the spring was still young. Probably both feelings, however opposed, were at work in her mind, for she added, "Jesu, have mercy on me!" and burst into tears; and the next instant broke into laughter; and this inclination to bitter laughter continued with her at intervals during the short and doleful time that was left to her.

But Anne did not fail in serious realisation of what was likely to be her end, and in preparing for it. While protesting her innocence, she desired to have the sacrament in her closet, that she might pray for mercy. She cried, "Oh, my mother, thou wilt die for sorrow!" referring to the homely stepmother whom Anne had learned to love better than the worldly father, who had become by a fresh creation Earl of Wiltshire.

Anne had already left directions for the care of her little daughter Elizabeth, nearly three years of age, with her chaplain. If she begged to see her child, there is no record of the petition. But it was remembered that she

sorely regretted her conduct to "the Lady Mary," Catherine's daughter, whom Anne had helped to part, not only
from her mother, but also from her father.

She wrote to the King [1] asserting her loyalty, beseeching
him to do her justice, and praying God to pardon him if
he condemned her. If her fate was sealed, she implored
him to consider favourably the case of the innocent gentlemen who were in the same strait with her, accused of complicity in her guilt, and likewise lying in the Tower.

To the Council of Peers which tried and condemned
Anne, her former lover, Lord Percy, who had succeeded
his father in the Earldom of Northumberland, was summoned. He obeyed the summons, but was seized with
sudden illness, and left the hall of the Tower before the trial
began. He did not long survive the woman he had loved.

The Queen defended herself wisely and well, as it was
acknowledged; but while the rumour without was that
she had cleared herself, her condemnation was a foregone
conclusion. She heard with composure the terrible sentence, which even Norfolk pronounced with tears—" To be
burnt or beheaded, at the King's pleasure." When her
stern uncle finished the words, she appealed to Heaven
with clasped hands and raised eyes. "O Father! O
Creator! Thou, who art the Way, the Life, and the
Truth, knowest whether I have deserved this death."
She again addressed the Court, declaring that she had ever
been a faithful wife to the King, though she did not say
that she had shown him that humility which his goodness
to her and the honour to which he had raised her merited.

Anne then left the Court quietly and with dignity. The
King signed the Queen's death-warrant, and afterwards
sent Cranmer to her. Cranmer advised her to submit, and
it was believed at the time that she took the advice in
the sense, that if she submitted her sentence might be
commuted to banishment.

---

[1] The authenticity of the letter is disputed.

On the 18th of May, Anne, as part of her submission, consented to be taken to the Archbishop's palace of Lambeth, and to go through the form of appointing proctors, who admitted in her name that she had entered into a previous contract of marriage before she was wedded to Henry, on which Cranmer declared her marriage with the King null and void.

On Anne's return to the Tower, the tolling of the bell announced to her that her brother, and the other gentlemen sentenced with him, had passed to execution, and any hope she might have entertained of the remission of her sentence was dashed to the ground. The Queen herself was to be beheaded on the following day, on Tower Green, before St. Peter's Church. On the eve of her death she is said to have written some pathetic verses; but it is more likely that they are due to a compassionate contemporary. The verses begin thus—

> " Oh, death, rock me asleep !
> Bring on my quiet rest :
> Let pass my very guiltless ghost
> Out of my careful breast.
> Ring out the doleful knell,
> Let it sound my death-toll ;
> For I must die,
> There is no remedy—
> For now I die."

Anne was the first Queen of England or noble English lady who was sentenced to die on the scaffold. For this reason a French headsman was brought to England to do the deed. Anne had loved France and French fashions, but she could little have anticipated the last with which she had to do.

The Queen spent a long morning in devotion, in the course of which she summoned the Lieutenant of the Tower, Sir William Kingston, to hear her last protestation of innocence before she partook of the sacrament. There was a little unexpected delay in the execution, which did not take place till noon. The delay was the result of an attempt to keep the hour unfixed and unknown to the last, in order to avoid any public demonstration. For, however ill the people had taken a subject's promotion, and however free they had made with the name of "Nan Bullen" in the days of her prosperity, her melancholy fate awoke indignation and pity. Anne sent for the Lieutenant and said she was very sorry for the delay, because she had thought to be dead by that time and past her pain.

She was answered, the pain would be little; it was so subtle.

On which she replied—"I have heard say the executioner is very good, and I have a little neck," putting her hands about it laughing.

This was the last of poor Anne's repartees, and the utterance of it, at such a moment, caused the listener to protest and wonder—"I have seen men and women also executed, and they have been in great sorrow; but to my knowledge this lady hath much joy and pleasure in her death." But Anne's laughter was not for joy when it was all the answer she gave to the assertion made to her, that she would receive justice at the King's hands. She had sometimes spoken wildly and wanderingly to the elder ladies placed around her (selected from the set which had been adverse to her), as if the enormity of her injuries were turning her brain. She had declared there would be no rain till she was out of the Tower. She had threatened that if she died, there would be the greatest punishment for her that had ever fallen on England. The next moment she had talked lightly again, and laughed idly.

According to Lord Bacon, who believed Anne innocent, she sent one more message to the King, which the messenger dared not deliver. It was full of her ready wit, if not of her quick mirth. "Commend me to his Majesty," she said, "and tell him he hath ever been constant in his career of advancing me. From a private gentlewoman he made me a marchioness and a queen, and now he hath left no higher degree of honour, he gives my innocency the crown of martyrdom."

The Queen is said to have bestowed on the officer on guard, named Gwyn, in token of her gratitude for his respectful "conduct to her," a small golden *étui*, richly chased, in the form of a pistol, the barrel serving for a whistle, and enclosing a set of toothpicks. There is a further tradition that she told him it was the King's first gift to her.

When the hour for the execution arrived, Anne was led out by the Lieutenant of the Tower. She wore a black damask gown, with a deep white cape. In the opinion of an eye-witness, she had never looked so beautiful. She was still not more than thirty-six years of age. She was attended by the maids of honour who, with the elder ladies, had been with her in the Tower.

Among the maids was her early playfellow, Mary Wyatt; for Anne had always remained faithful to the Wyatts, and the Wyatts were faithful to her. Thomas Wyatt, the poet brother, admired her, narrowly escaped perishing with her, and though restored to the favour of Henry, continued to defend Anne's memory to the last of his life.

Around was a circle, in which were the Lord Mayor —with the other civic authorities — Charles Brandon, Duke of Suffolk, the Secretary of State, Thomas Cromwell, &c.

Anne asked leave to speak to the authorities, but said little. One report of her speech is lifelike : "Masters, I here humbly submit me to the law, as the law hath judged me ; and as for my offences (I here accuse no man), God knoweth them ; I remit them to God, beseeching Him to have mercy on my soul, and I beseech Jesu to save my sovereign and master, the King, the most godliest, noblest, and gentlest prince that is, and make him long to reign over you." It should be remembered that exaggerated praise of the King and honour to him in all circumstances, at all hazards, was the rule in that generation. It was a curious strained example of lip-loyalty. If Anne made any vague reference to her cause, it was to say that she was not there to accuse her enemies or defend herself, and if any man would meddle with her matter, she required him to judge the best. She thus took leave of the world and her audience. She is said to have spoken with a smile on her lips.

With her own hands she removed her little hat and collar, and put on a linen cap. She took a kind farewell of her ladies, and gave to Mary Wyatt a little book of devotion which the Queen had carried in her hand.[1] According to one account, she refused to let her eyes be covered, and as her gaze disturbed the executioner, he signed to an assistant to advance, as if to deal the blow, on one side, while the principal headsman came forward, without his shoes, on the other. The Queen turned her eyes to the side from which she heard approaching foot-steps, and at that moment the sword fell.

On that summer day, away in the oak and chestnut shades of Blickling, and in the gardens of Hever Castle, the birds sang as merrily as ever. In the ante-chambers and corridors of the Louvre, brilliant courtiers and gay ladies thronged, and chattered and laughed, while she, who had been a bright child under those trees and in those walks; a merry, beautiful girl, the admired of all admirers among the great and noble, perished by a violent, shameful death, and slept in a bloody grave. Where her dust rests is uncertain; most probably she was buried, like so many victims of that and of succeeding

---

[1] The *étui* presented to Gwyn and the little book given to Mary Wyatt were both exhibited in the Tudor Exhibition.

reigns, within the Church of St. Peter, on Tower Green. Just possibly, as her Norfolk kinsfolk liked to believe, permission was granted for her body to be removed in silence and secrecy to her native county, and laid with her ancestors in their vault in the old church of Salle.

JANE SEYMOUR[1]

BY MARRIAGE A TUDOR

HENRY VIII. showed a strange incapacity to avail himself of previous experience, and an equally strange indifference to old associations, by marrying for his third wife a second maid-of-honour, who, like Anne Boleyn, had spent a portion of her youth in France, where Anne was supposed to have learnt her freedom of speech and manner. But, at least, the King indicated something of the alarm and repulsion with which his late wife's foolish conduct had inspired him, by choosing for the next sharer of his throne a woman who, though she had passed through the same hurtful ordeal which had helped to mould Anne, was from the first as quiet and staid as her former companion was sprightly and giddy. Except in the detail of receiving and accepting a royal lover's suit, a worse than doubtful honour, which in those days seemed utterly to dazzle and blind the recipient where higher considerations and finer feelings were concerned, Jane Seymour went through a not very long life with the modest reserve and wise abstention from meddling with questions out of her province, characteristic of those happiest of private women who have no history. Hers was not the distinction (which compelled precedence) of surpassing excellence in the much-prized accomplishments of singing and dancing, or of a reckless, witty tongue. She had the gift of beauty, certainly ; but it was beauty of a tranquil, it might be

---

[1] Agnes Strickland. Froude.

248

JANE SEYMOUR.

slightly inanimate type.[1] Her other gifts were comprised in her common sense and prudence—excellent qualities in women and queens—and in that good nature which caused her to weigh more calmly, and deal more fairly, with conflicting claims than ever Anne Boleyn or Catherine of Arragon had done. If Jane Seymour had not the grandiose dignity of the cruelly used daughter of kings, she had the ordinary respect-inspiring merit of a woman who had tried, for the most part, throughout her life, to do her best according to her light.

It is no grave disparagement to either Jane Seymour or Anne Boleyn to say that, differing widely as they did in dispositions and standards, they could never, however intimately associated at different periods of their lives, have been friends; indeed, no historian pretends they were. Judging from human nature in the abstract, it is much more likely that both as girls and women they misunderstood and misjudged each other, and were more or less opposed from the first. Therefore no bond of friendship was necessarily outraged by the marriage which rendered Jane, Anne's successor; and when one considers that the two had served as equals in the courts of Mary Tudor, when Queen of France, and of Claude, who succeeded Mary, it is rather idle to speak of Jane's disloyalty to a mistress who had formerly been her fellow-servant, and had not been her mistress for more than three years at the utmost.

The great stain on Jane's name and memory is her prompt acceptance of Henry's suit—unseemly in time if not in place—and her consent to marry him with indecent haste. How much a royal tyrant's despotic will, as well as the dread of losing his fleeting favour, or how much the urgent recommendation of his council and peers, that Henry should marry immediately, had to do with this

---

[1] According to Chapuys (the Imperial ambassador), Jane was short, fair, rather pale, " of no great beauty ;" but tastes differ.

error, is no longer within a chronicler's power to decipher.

As part of the wholesome obscurity which surrounded Jane Seymour's early days, little or nothing is remembered of them—even the date of her birth has not been preserved. It is known that she was one of the daughters of Sir John Seymour, of Wolf Hall, Wiltshire, and of Margaret Wentworth, daughter of Sir John Wentworth of Nettlestead, Suffolk. She is understood to have been one of eight children. There is proof sufficient to show that she went along with Anne Boleyn to France, in the suite of Mary Tudor, and, like Anne, passed into the service of Queen Claude.

A portrait of Jane as a maid-of-honour has been discovered in the Louvre, and serves to prove how fair of face the young Englishwoman was at this date. If no other record survives of her attractions, such as was retained of Anne Boleyn's manifold charms, Jane escaped the poignant shafts of envy and detraction — no evil tongues were busy with her name.

More than ten years afterwards Sir John Seymour made interest to have his daughter appointed one of the maids-of-honour to Queen Anne, doubtless putting more weight on their former connection than it was worth; anyhow he gained his suit.

At the time of Anne's death, Jane Seymour was at her father's house in Wiltshire, where preparations were going on with such haste for her marriage with the King, that they were actually wedded on the 20th of May 1536, the day after Anne's execution.[1]

Anne's melancholy fate had produced no softening of Henry's wrath against her, a result which reads as if he had persuaded himself of her guilt. He may also have

---

[1] Chapuys wrote that Jane was in London, and went the day after Anne's execution to the palace where the marriage contract was signed. He was greatly surprised and a good deal disgusted by the marriage, but acknowledged that it gave general satisfaction.

persuaded Jane Seymour of Anne's worthlessness, so that the two came to regard, with a perverted logic, their immediate marriage as "a tragic necessity," a righteous protest against the dead woman's crimes, and an emphatic assertion that they had a right to behave as if she had never been.

It would appear that when Henry arrived at this frame of mind with regard to any of his queens, he was of opinion that a fresh marriage blotted out the previous one, alike in his own eyes and in those of his subjects, and that therefore the sooner it was accomplished the better for all parties.

In looking back on the dim past, there are two ideas little short of manias of the men of the time, the paramount effect of which strikes and startles us. There was a divinity which hedged a king, so that unless it came to the point of his being deposed and slain, he was rendered absolutely exempt from censure, and from well-nigh all responsibility in public judgment and speech. There was a haunting dread of the King's dying without direct heirs, and so plunging the country into the miseries of civil war, such as happened on the accession of Mary. With Mary set aside, and Elizabeth also dispossessed of her inheritance, the King's successor could only be looked for amidst a company of contending claimants.

There is a grim and grisly legend that Henry waited, either in Richmond Park or in Epping Forest, surrounded by his huntsmen and hounds, under the pretence of being engaged in the chase, for the signal gun from the Tower which should announce that he was free from the last link that bound him to Anne Boleyn. Then the King and his train turned in the direction of Sir John Seymour's seat, where they arrived the same night, on the eve of the royal bridal. But there was no call for so dramatically unnatural a situation. There were decorous messengers in abundance to carry the news, to the person principally concerned. with more certainty and privacy.

The fact that the bridegroom as well as the bride wore white—a custom then dying out for men of Henry's age and size—at the ill-omened marriage, may have been significant of the asserted integrity of the motives of the pair. The same day the newly married couple dined at Marwell. They proceeded next to Winchester, and arrived at last in London about the season of Whitsuntide, the time of the year which figured so conspicuously and so often in Henry's nuptial rejoicings. On St. Peter's Eve the King took the new Queen to Mercers' Hall, where she stood by one of the windows to witness the annual ceremony of setting the City Watch.

In the first Parliament after the King's third marriage a bill was passed, excluding Henry's two children by his former marriages from the succession to the crown which was settled on the heirs of King Henry and Queen Jane.

Miss Strickland quotes a singular instance in which the new Queen was favoured by a compliment intended for her predecessor. Coverdale's English Bible, published at Zürich in 1535, was dedicated to King Henry and Queen Anne, and an attempt was made to cause the dedication to suit the change in the Royal Family by printing the letter " J " over the name Anne.

As on a former occasion, the whole kindred and connections of Jane Seymour profited by her elevation to the throne. They filled the places formerly occupied by the displaced and superseded Boleyns, the whole unblushing system being a strong argument against the marriage of a king with a subject. But so far as Queen Jane's personal influence went, she exerted herself to enlist the King's interest in "the Lady Mary." Even before her marriage, Jane had advocated the cause of Mary, for whom she had displayed a kindly regard.[1]   Mary, in her turn, always

---

[1] Chapuys referred to Jane Seymour's "great affection for Princess Mary." Elsewhere he reported that it was said Queen Jane was proud and haughty, an impression given probably by the difference between her manner and Anne's.

viewed her stepmother Queen Jane as her good friend.
By Jane's instrumentality, Henry was partially reconciled
to his daughter, at this time in her twenty-third year,
and Mary came several times on visits to the court during
Jane's reign. The concession was gracious and honourable in the woman, who was herself walking on a slippery
path, and that so blamelessly that it could be said of her,
"her name was mentioned both by Protestants and
Catholics with unreserved respect." The writer whose
verdict is least favourable to Jane Seymour, while the
Queen reaped golden opinions from other historians,
including her contemporaries, remarks, as the worst judgment that could be passed on her behaviour after she was
Queen: "She purposely steered her course of royalty so
that her manners appeared diametrically opposed to those
of Queen Anne, while her actions were utterly passive and
dependent on those of the King."

As to the first count, to say Queen Jane had royal
manners totally unlike those of Queen Anne, was a considerable meed of praise to Queen Jane. With regard to
the second indictment, how her actions could have been
active and independent of those of such a lord and
sovereign as King Hal—rapidly waxing brutal in his
bluffness—it would be hard to say. Jane Seymour's
motto was "Bound to obey and serve;" Anne Boleyn's
had been "Me and mine."

In the January following Jane Seymour's marriage, that
of 1537, the rare event occurred of the freezing of the
Thames; so that she crossed it on horseback, in the
company of the King, on their way to Greenwich Palace.
In the following summer she was with the King in a
progress to Canterbury.

Her coronation, for which she does not seem to have
pressed, was deferred on account of the ravages of a
pestilence then raging in the country. Therefore, in lieu
of the gorgeous accounts of state dress and princely

pageant, which none gives better or with greater zest than Miss Strickland, she furnishes us with two personal descriptions of the Queen, taken from a drawing and a picture of Hans Holbein's, in which the writer hardly leaves Queen Jane the claim to a vestige of the beauty for which she was celebrated in her day. "Coarse and apathetic-looking;" "a large face, with small features;" "the expression sinister;" "the mouth very small;" "the lips thin, and coarsely compressed;" "the eyebrows very faintly marked;" "high cheek-bones, and a thickness at the point of the nose." To crown the condemnation, the comment is added that Holbein "generally gave a faithful representation of his subjects." The more finished portrait is admitted to be less unfavourable; the complexion is allowed to be fine, and the features regular. Still, even here, the expression is reckoned "cold and hard," while the figure is pronounced "stiff," and the elbows "very square." Nay, though no fault is found with the flowing scarlet robe, the representation of a little poodle curled up on it comes in for its share in the detraction: "A queer little white poodle; and which looks the sourest, the mistress or dog, it would be difficult to describe." Blue-eyed, fair-skinned Jane Seymour, serene and discreet, the aspersions of your beauty and temper will not trouble you now—they were praised enough in their generation.

Jane's child was born at Hampton Palace on October 12, 1537, with great danger to the mother, during which she is said to have begged those around her "to take care of her infant in preference to herself." The child was a boy, and his entrance into the world was hailed with almost mad rejoicing. His christening was conducted with the greatest pomp. The procession went by torchlight from the Queen's chamber to the chapel in Wolsey's palace. We may take it for granted it was by the motherly Queen's wish that the two princesses, Mary and

Elizabeth, figured prominently in the ceremony. Mary presented the child at the font to Archbishop Cranmer. Elizabeth, a little girl of four, carried the chrism while herself borne in the arms of the Queen's brother. The inveterate old courtier, the Earl of Wiltshire, father of Anne Boleyn, was not conspicuous by his absence; he appeared bearing a white wax taper, and having a towel hung round his neck. As the boy had been born on the eve of St. Edward's Day, he was named Edward, and was carried back to his proud mother's apartment to receive her blessing.

But sorrow succeeds joy, as night follows day. The Queen had caught a chill, had eaten some unsuitable food, and was seized with violent illness. After one or two alternations in her condition, she died in the night of the 24th of October, to the great grief of the King and the universal lamentation of the nation. Calculating her age as near that of Mary Tudor, Queen of France, and Anne Boleyn, she must have been thirty-six or thirty-seven years of age when she died.[1] The Queen's body was embalmed, and lay in state for several days. It was removed from Hampton Court to Windsor, and buried in St. George's Chapel with every honour. The old custom of having a waxen image of the deceased exposed in the funeral-car was in full force. The image which represented Jane Seymour was clothed in her robes of state, wore a crown, beneath which the long hair fell on the shoulders, a gold sceptre was in the right hand, the fingers were covered with rings, and the neck with jewels. The shoes and hose were of gold cloth; the head rested on a pillow of gold cloth and gems. Throughout the funeral rites "the Lady Mary" acted as chief mourner.

Henry spent the first part of his widowerhood in strict retirement. He and the whole court remained in deep

---

[1] Chappuys made her only twenty-five at the time of her marriage, which must have been an error.

mourning for three months. It was the solitary instance in which Henry put on mourning for a wife ; that which he wore for one day, in recognition of the funeral day of Catherine of Arragon, was ostensibly mourning for a sister-in-law. As a further proof of his tender friendship for Jane, the King desired that "the bones and body of his true and loving wife Jane were to be placed in his tomb." In 1813 Jane Seymour's coffin was discovered and left close to the gigantic skeleton of Henry VIII., which had been previously exposed. The vault which contains both is now sealed up.

ANNE OF CLEVES[1]

BY MARRIAGE A TUDOR

THREE years passed after the death of Jane Seymour, in 1537, before Henry VIII. wedded a fourth wife. According to his enemies, the cause of his delay was the unwillingness on the part of suitable princesses to run the risk of sharing the fate of two of their predecessors. According to his partisan, Henry was in no haste to replace the queen whom he had loved and honoured to the last—who had borne him the fair son on whom the King set such store. But it is certain that in the interval he looked for a wife in more than one direction.

The princesses whom he would have preferred as royal partners appear to have been a French princess, the widowed Duchess of Longueville, better known as Mary of Guise, mother of Mary Queen of Scots, and another young widow, Christina, daughter of Christian of Denmark and of Elizabeth of Austria, and widow of the Duke of Milan. However, Mary was already promised in marriage to James V. of Scotland, as the successor of his poor, consumptive girl-bride, Magdalen of France, daughter of Francis I. and the good Queen Claude. As for Christina of Milan, the beautiful girl-widow of sixteen, of whom Henry had two portraits done expressly for him by Holbein, the larger being the very marvel of the painter's art, and the glory of the recent Tudor Exhibition, she was destined to take for her second husband Mary of Guise's brother, the Duke of Lorraine. According to tradition Christina dismissed Henry's proposal with the saucy speech

[1] Agnes Strickland. Froude. L. Aikin.

that she had but one head; if she had two, one should be at his Highness's service. The fact that she sat for the portraits which were to be sent to this formidable suitor is an implied contradiction to the story. Besides, the more accurate report of her speech is said to have been no more than "that the ambassadors would lose their labours, for she minded not to fix her heart that way." Even with regard to this modified version, when asked by Wriothesley if she had ever used such words, she solemnly denied them, bade him say so, and declared herself "at the Emperor's commandment."

The whole cluster of royal and political alliances, of which this was to have been one, broke down, not because of the reluctance of the lady, but because of Charles V.'s dissimulation, and his failing to keep his engagements with Henry.

The King's, or rather his minister Cromwell's, choice at last fell on Anne of Cleves. She was the second daughter of John, Duke of Cleves, a leader in the Reformation. A still stronger connection with German Reformers lay in the fact that her beautiful and high-spirited elder sister, Sybilla, was the wife of the great Elector of Saxony. The marriage so eagerly promoted by Cromwell was considered highly politic, as, by uniting Henry with the Northern German princes, it would counterbalance the alliance recently entered into by the Emperor and Francis I.

Anne was born in 1515, and had therefore reached what was viewed as the mature age of twenty-four years when she was proposed as a wife for the colossal but infirm Henry, then in his forty-eighth year. Her sister Sybilla was reputed to be a woman of many attractions, both mental and personal; but in the case of Anne, Cromwell was warned by his correspondent, the English ambassador, Wotton, "I hear no great praise either of her personage or beauty." It was perhaps significant that her father evaded the request to have her picture taken by his own painter, in addition to that painted for the King by Hans Holbein. This artist is believed to have greatly flattered the lady whom it was intended to represent. It may be that stout Hans had a soft spot in his heart for his country-woman ; it may be that he had an eye to his own interests in wishing to see a German queen on the English throne, or it may be, as was suspected, that Holbein was instructed by the minister, or his agents, to make the best of his subject, for "an agreeable portrait was expected from him." If either of the latter influences was at work, the result showed that honesty would have been the best policy. Such miniatures as that which was furnished for Henry were encased in ivory, carved to look like a white rose, and, by a pretty fashion of the day, were worn over the heart, as a token of love and homage to the original of the miniature.

It would be comical, if it were not pitiful, to recognise the wary devices by which the ambassador limited the list of Anne's attainments, and at the same time exalted her virtues. She could read and write, as well as speak her German or Flemish tongue ; she sewed very well. As for music, especially vocal music, which Henry prized greatly —against which he had not been set by the lamentable sequel to poor Anne Boleyn's sweet songs—Wotton admitted that Anne of Cleves knew nothing of it; but he excused her ignorance on the plea that "it was not the manner of her country to learn it"—strange reflection on the musical Germany of modern days ! He sought to impress on his master that Anne was of "very lowly and gentle conditions," which so recommended her to her mother that the duchess was loath to let the princess go. He stated that Anne and her younger sister Amelia had never been "from the elbow of their mother, who had brought them up straitly (strictly)." Again, Anne occupied herself much with her needle. She would no doubt learn the English tongue "so soon as she put her mind to it."

"She had no taste for the heavy-headed revels of her countrymen." So far as we can find, neither Wotton nor Cromwell ventured on any particular personal praise of Anne, unless it were of "her princely proportions," which, for that matter, nearly rivalled those of Henry. Indeed, when first spoken of to the King she was referred to as "plain."

Of this poor Anne, who was thus weighed in the balance, we have tried hard to form a correct judgment. The King's great defender (Mr. Froude) honestly admits that "she was simple, quiet, modest, sensible, and conscientious. In presence lady-like . . ." We in our turn, in striving to hold the scales evenly, are forced to the conclusion that Anne, notwithstanding these excellent qualities, was a dull-witted as well as a hard-favoured young woman, possessed of a stolid sluggishness of temper. She does not appear to have shown the least shrinking from the dubious honour offered to her. She does not seem to have expressed any strong regret at parting from her kindred and country for ever, or any lively interest in the new country for which she was bound. Reading between the lines of her history, it is difficult to see her otherwise than as a woman of entirely negative characteristics. She looks and acts, thrown up against her sixteenth century background, as if she were as deficient in wistful tenderness and generous devotion as she certainly was in keen self-assertion.

By an odd coincidence, there had been an approach to an earlier contract of marriage on Anne's behalf, entered into by her father, with the very Duke of Lorraine whom her rival in Henry's favour, Christina Duchess of Milan, ultimately married.

The death of the Duke of Cleves while his daughter's treaty of marriage with Henry VIII. was still pending, delayed its fulfilment for a time; but the brother, who succeeded the father, gave ample assurance to the suitor that there was no legal obstacle in the former unfulfilled contract.

The marriage contract between Anne and Henry was signed in September 1539, at Düsseldorf, which the bride left in the beginning of the following month, setting out with a large and splendid train for England, by Antwerp and Calais—the latter, of course, an English possession then.

No faint foreboding of what was to come hindered the great homage with which Anne was received at Calais by the Earl of Southampton, the Lord High Admiral, whose own state and sumptuousness were so magnificent that the very mariners in his ship were clad in Bruges satin. The noise of the guns fired in the Queen's honour well-nigh took away her retinue's breath. The smoke from the cannon rendered the central object of attraction invisible. Yet the very ships — the *Lion* and the *Sweepstake* — waiting to convey Anne across the Channel, had fought her countrymen the Flemings in the Downs but two years before. Lord Southampton was secretly aghast at her lack of all womanly charms, and hit on the device of teaching her to play cards. He had time to spare for the task, since the Queen, who had already been more than two months on her journey, was detained by stress of weather at Calais fifteen days, according to some accounts; twenty, according to others. Even the less critical observers were struck by the number of foreigners in attendance on the silent Queen, and by the absence of tact which had caused her to fill every post about her person—except the few reserved for the King to dispose of—with her own countrymen and countrywomen. However, banners waved, trumpets blared, and offerings of purses of gold abounded. Plain and stupid as Anne was, she gave no active offence by her manner and bearing. Nay, her new subjects seem to have regarded her with some satisfaction, as a solid piece of royal goods that would wear well.

In spite of the King's impatience, Christmas Day passed before the Queen could set sail. She went on board on the 27th of December, and was fortunate in crossing the Channel with her convoy of fifty ships the same day. "The wintry twilight was closing in when she first set foot on English soil, under Deal Castle." She was received by the Warden, and afterwards conducted by the ubiquitous Charles Brandon, Duke of Suffolk, and his last duchess, accompanied by the principal nobility and gentry of Kent, to Dover Castle, to rest there for a couple of nights.

On the following Monday, a stormy winter day, Anne set out for Canterbury. She travelled in her own chariot. "The whirlicotes" which figured first in England at Henry's marriage with Catherine of Arragon, had made considerable progress in the coachbuilder's hands in the intervening thirty years. Anne's equipage was of gilt, as beseemed the state equipage of a Queen or a Lord Mayor, and was elaborately carved.

Near Canterbury the Queen was met by the Archbishop, three bishops, and a great company of gentlemen, who attended her to her lodgings. On the last day of the year the Duke of Norfolk and another great company conducted her as far as Rochester, where she spent New Year's Day in the Bishop's palace. There Henry came *incognito* with eight gentlemen of his chamber, all dressed alike in marble colour, to make the acquaintance of his Queen, and, in his own words, "to nourish love."

The King sent in advance Sir Anthony Browne, the Master of his Horse, to tell Anne that Henry had brought her a New Year's gift, if she would choose to receive it. According to Sir Anthony's statement, "he was never so dismayed in his life as to see a lady so far unlike what had been represented." But he was wise enough to allow the King to form his own opinion, which he was not long of doing. Henry did not conceal his surprise and disappointment; in the words of an eye-witness, he had never seen his Highness so marvellously astonished and abashed as on this occasion.

In the meantime Anne, whose woman's heart, however slowly it beat, must have been smitten with a pang of humiliation, sank with due deference on her knees, from which the King had the grace to raise her. His chroniclers differ greatly as to his subsequent behaviour. Hall says the King gently took her up and kissed her; further, that he remained with her all the afternoon, communing and devising with her, and that he afterwards supped with her.

But if we are to believe Strype and Stowe, the interview lasted but a few minutes. In addition to her other demerits in Henry's eyes, his fastidious ear was unreasonably offended by the sound of her German, and he would not continue to speak with her, even by means of the interpreter ready to play his part in the conversation.

The angry bridegroom had no sooner left the unlucky bride's presence than he assailed her escort the Admiral and his other companions for their opinion of the lady's charms, and swore roundly that he had been deceived, and that "he loved her not."

Now what were the looks of the scorned woman which called forth such a strong sense of repulsion in the man who had certainly heard of her as "plain," while she had not been represented by Holbein's flattering pencil as more than comely? So far as can be drawn from contemporary evidence, and from such likenesses as survive of her, Anne of Cleves was a tall, stout young woman, "her figure large, loose, and corpulent."[1] Her nose was too large, and her mouth had a certain coarseness in the lines, in spite of her temperate living. Her complexion was brown or swarthy ("thick and dark"). According

[1] Contrasting her with Henry's other five wives, two of them—Catherine of Arragon and Jane Seymour—were "short;" two more—Catherine Howard and Catherine Parr—were very little women, while Anne Boleyn, in her youth, was remarkable for her slender shape and "little neck."

to the French ambassador, she was pitted with small-pox. Her eyes and hair were coal-black; the latter she wore in long, flat bands, coming down low on each side of the face—a style of hair-dressing hitherto unknown in England. In connection with her meaningless expanse of forehead—for though the Queen's graces might be moral, they were no more intellectual than they were personal— the bands of hair at the side of the large face had a tendency to increase the effect of its length, and of the heaviness of the lower portion. After the fashion of the day, the Queen substituted, on special occasions, the long tresses of a yellow wig for her own black hair, an exchange which was peculiarly trying to her dark complexion.

A considerable amount of *mauvaise honte* might have been pardonable, even promising, under the circumstances; but Anne's clumsy awkwardness partook of the nature of uncouthness. Her armorial bearings, which happened to be a couple of white swans, were singularly inappropriate. Shall we be forgiven for saying that a couple of grey geese would have been more in keeping with their owner, for never was royal goose less swan-like?

Surely on the principle that bonnie feathers make bonnie birds, Anne had brought with her the costliest wardrobe that ever queen-consort displayed in England. But, as might have been expected of the uneducated, un-refined woman, she was destitute of taste in dress, while like Catherine of Arragon in the matter of the Spanish mantilla, Anne showed an invincible inclination to intro-duce and perpetuate the stiff Dutch modes of which she was such a poor illustration. She appears to have had a preference for the colour red, since in two of the portraits which we have of her, red is freely used in her dress. In one she holds a red carnation. Anne Boleyn's dainty devices, the exquisitely picturesque touches in her toilet, were as entirely wanting in the toilet of her namesake as

were the first Anne's charm of manner and ready wit.
Their absence might have been supplied by far more valuable qualities; but all that the self-willed, spoiled suitor
saw was the dearth of every outward grace. This Anne
must have struck her appalled Henry as a very Gorgon;
for had he not been accustomed to the stately dignity and
learning (by comparison) of Catherine of Arragon, the
beauty and brilliance of Anne Boleyn, the fair comeliness
—not without its French polish also—of Jane Seymour?
Here was a crushing downfall to the King who had aspired
to the hands of the accomplished, high-bred, far-famed
beauties of two courts—Mary of Guise and Christina of
Milan—and had to be content with the robust, rustic,
practically dumb, German Anne.

Henry is said to have testified his wrath and disgust at
the partner provided for him in a manner which savoured
of the sulky school-boy, as well as of the incensed volup-
tuary. The New Year's gift which he had brought for
Anne was a costly muff, tippet, and partlet, or boa, of
sables. He had intended to deliver the gift with his own
hand; but when he found how unattractive was the recipient, he contented himself with despatching the furs,
and a cold greeting, by a messenger.

The ladies of the court were no less shocked than the
gentlemen on their presentation to Anne. She might
have been the "Loathlie Ladye" of ballad renown.
There is an element of the ludicrous in their exaggerated
consternation. Lady Browne told Sir Anthony that it
was not only the Queen's "unsightliness" which was
objected to; it was her "displeasant airs." She had
"such fashions," and betrayed "a manner of bringing-up
so gross, that the King never would love her." One is
tempted to think of the primitive use of a knife and fork,
a constant neglect of soap and water, and such habits at
table, and in her chamber, as would strike even uncere-
monious ladies of pre-Elizabethan times.

The King complained loudly, with a total want of delicacy and good feeling, to those around him of his chagrin, and the moment he reached his palace of Greenwich, to which he retired, he attacked the alarmed Cromwell, as he had already attacked the Lord High Admiral, Lord Southampton, with furious reproaches for misleading him, and not undeceiving him, even at the last moment. It was in the course of these reproaches that Henry is said to have used the coarse comparison of Anne to "a great Flemish mare," which stuck to her, and has descended to later generations.

"I have been ill-handled; if it were not that she has come so far into England, and for fear of making a ruffle in the world, and driving her brother into the Emperor and French King's hands, now being together, I would never have her. But now it is too far gone, wherefore I am sorry," declared Henry, with a solemn candour that is well-nigh pathetic. And again, "I would not do what I have to do for none earthly thing save my realm," he protested ruefully.

But far gone as the matter was, he made a desperate effort to postpone the marriage for two days, in order to try if in that time he might not find a way out of the strait. He called a council, and laid before it the old shadowy obstacle of the alleged pre-contract of Anne with the Duke of Lorraine as a fact which might invalidate the marriage. In the meanwhile Anne had calmly advanced as far as Dartford, where she was delayed till the two ambassadors from Cleves in her suite, should proceed to Greenwich and produce documents to prove that the Queen's pre-contract had been certainly set aside. In other circumstances the investigation might have been a wise, if dilatory precaution; but it was, on the face of it, a mere subterfuge, as the question to which it referred had been satisfactorily disposed of before the contract between Henry and Anne was signed at Düsseldorf.

It is impossible to say how far Anne was acquainted with the King's dissatisfaction and unwillingness to fulfil his pledge; but even the densest of women must have had some suspicion of his reluctance—in fact, he took care to give her a hint of what was passing which no lack of acquaintance with the English language could prevent her from understanding. After the two ambassadors had behaved like true men, had acknowledged that they had not the necessary documents in their possession, but had readily sworn to their existence, and volunteered to remain in prison in England till the papers were forthcoming, an emissary was sent to Anne herself, to require from her a declaration that she was free. But the hint was not taken. The lady signed the declaration without an instant's hesitation. There was no help for it, the marriage must go on. "The King durst not scandalise Europe and affront the Germans. Subservient as Henry's Council often showed itself, it did not support him now; notably Cromwell, who had made the marriage, and Archbishop Cranmer warned the King that by drawing back at the last moment he would mortally offend the Protestant princes, with whom he was seeking to be in league."

As if to stifle his vehement distaste to his bride, and to render it still harder for him to change his mind at the eleventh hour, the King, when he had come to the decision that the affair must proceed, did not stint the ostentatious splendour of the accompanying ceremonial, or the hollow clamour of the public rejoicings. He summoned all his loving subjects in London, by the public crier, to come down to Greenwich and "pay their devoirs to my Lady Anne of Cleves, who would shortly be their Queen." The grandest, the gayest, certainly by far the most picturesque reception which Henry accorded to any of his six wives, was that given, as if with sardonic mockery, of which after all he was incapable, to the homely, stolid Anne.

The scene was Blackheath. It was a winter's day,

certainly; the trees on Shooter's Hill and in Greenwich
Park were bare, and the sky was bleak, whether in its
lowering grey or frosty blue, so that fires had to be lit in
the tents provided for the first stoppage of Anne of Cleves
and her ladies, to warm them in preparing for the remaining rites. There was no tender green in the woods and
the fields; no flush of sweet wild-flowers; no quaintly
fantastic masqueing, as when the King had gone a-may-
ing in former years to that very Shooter's Hill with
Catherine of Arragon. There was no dusky summer
seclusion in the bosky glades of the park, as when Anne
Boleyn, in the pensiveness of apprehended adversity,
wandered alone there with her dogs. But the glories of
spring and summer, of young life and love, seemed hardly
missed. If ever a living multitude, pranked out in silk
and velvet of all the colours of the rainbow, hung with
gold chains and glittering with precious stones, furnished
unmingled gratification to a still mightier crowd, for
whose accommodation all the furze and gorse on the heath
had been cut down, it was done on that day. The high-
waymen and cut-throats, whose field was the heath, must
have left off their occupation for the time being.

At twelve noon "the Lady Anne" came in sight,
attended by her English escort and her hundred German
knights. As for her fifteen German ladies, they were
coolly pronounced by the spectators to be even less fair
than her Grace. The cavalcade wound round Shooter's
Hill, and approached the tents at the foot, where the
Queen was received by the Earl of Rutland, her chamberlain, and other gentlemen, and by Lady Margaret
Douglas, daughter of the Queen of Scots, and her cousin
the Marchioness of Dorset, daughter of the Queen-Dowager
of France, &c. &c.

After Anne was rested and refreshed in her tent, and
had received information of the approach of the King, she
mounted on horseback and advanced with her train across

the heath to meet him at the cross in the middle of the heath, the site of which is still marked by a group of fir-trees.[1] Her dress was singularly unsuited for riding in. She wore a gown of cloth-of-gold, without a train, which might have served for a riding-skirt; but the German fashion, which was more sensible where walking was concerned, required that all gowns should be cut short. As for her head, what with its "caul," its round bonnet set with pearls, and its coronet of black velvet, it had enough to bear. But the most conspicuous feature of her attire appears to have been the "partlet" or flat ruff round the neck, which was a mass of precious stones.

In the meantime the King had set out from his palace-gate, riding in the centre of a party of noble horsemen. Not to be outdone in splendour, his bulky person was clad in a coat of purple velvet, covered with a network of gold. His slashed sleeves were clasped together with buttons of rubies and pearls. His girdle and sword-hilt were rich in emeralds. His "bonnet" blazed with the jewels on which he set such store.

The gorgeous pair met in front of the cross. What the King's feelings were it would be difficult to describe. As for Anne, her slowness of feeling and self-absorption amounted to apathetic indifference. Had it been otherwise, she would have protested and remonstrated ere now, and so might have altered her inglorious destiny.

The outward dumb-show was irreproachable. The King took off his bonnet and saluted the lady; she assumed her place at his right hand, and the bride and bridegroom rode on together, "like a wedded couple," followed by their respective households, through the ranks of their huzzaing supporters (including the chief magnates of London town), into the Park, up to the court gate, where the riders came in full view of the Thames—leaden, not silver in hue, on the winter afternoon—but thronged with gala barges.

[1] Under these trees George Whitfield preached in later days.

When Henry and Anne alighted, he again embraced her, bade her welcome "to her own," and led her through the hall.   All this display of courtesy did not prevent a few last frantic struggles on the King's part to break off the marriage, although he had admitted that the despised bride's person was "well and seemly (that is, neither crooked nor hump-backed), but nothing else."   His Council was again summoned, and he had various interviews with Cromwell before he gave his grudging consent to "go through with it"—the ceremony of the following day.

It was Twelfth-day, the 6th of January, 1540, and the early hour of eight o'clock in the morning was fixed for the marriage.   Henry appeared in the Presence-Chamber before that hour, in a crimson satin coat, and a "gown" of cloth-of-gold, flowered with silver and trimmed with fine fur.

It is almost a relief to find that Anne kept him waiting. It was one of the very few occasions on which she resisted his will.   As might have been expected from the woman, the act was not in itself either a very wise or graceful proceeding.   It was probably the result of an obstinate standing-out on her prerogative as a bride.   When she did join the displeased bridegroom in the gallery to which he had come to seek her, she was in all the glory of cloth-of-gold flowered with pearls.   The tresses of one of her yellow wigs flowed over her shoulders.   Instead of a velvet coronet, she wore a gold crown set with gems, and, of all things, sprigs of bristling, sombre rosemary!   According to Miss Strickland, rosemary, as an herb of grace, could be worn by maidens alike at weddings and funerals.   But surely it must have been unimaginative maidens who consented to the melancholy association.   To counterbalance the rosemary, Anne wore, round her massive neck and portly waist, jewels of surpassing value.   In her manner she was entirely cool and composed, as she greeted her grumbling lord with three low curtseys.

The Archbishop of Canterbury performed the ceremony, while one of the Flemish gentlemen in Anne's suite gave her away. Round her wedding-ring was inscribed the motto, "God send me well to keep."

Henry behaved for the rest of the day as if he had returned to the devout practices of his youth. In company with his Lutheran bride, he was present at two masses, and vespers before supper, after which were masques and sports. The usual tiltings and festivals followed on succeeding days.

In the month of February, Henry accompanied Anne by water to Westminster—the Mayor and Aldermen with the City Companies gracing the procession, and the Tower guns firing an appropriate salute. How many processions of the kind Henry must have recalled, with what conflicts of lingering doubt and regret envenomed by his bodily and mental misery! For surely bully and despot as bluff King Hal—the gay and gallant prince of other years—had gradually grown, he could not take everything as a matter of course, like his consort. In the middle of his grudge against her and her people, whom he accused of deceiving him, Henry showed faint sparkles still of his former generosity. He not only entertained the foreigners right royally, he permitted a considerable number of them to tarry behind the others, till their mistress should become better acquainted with England and the English.

It has been said that Henry laughed at the Queen, and encouraged his courtiers to do the same. If so, she was as impervious to ridicule as to other forms of injury. But the charge is not proven, nor is its truth likely. The King was in no laughing mood when he announced himself weary of life because of his ill-assorted marriage. Besides, the accusation does not fit in with his character, which was simple and downright in its very savageness. He might be brutal, he could hardly be malicious. On the other hand, there is sufficient testimony to show that he treated Anne with personal kindness. How could he act otherwise to the great, heavy, harmless creature, whose want of knowledge of English left her as defenceless as a child? The absence of all private resentment on Anne's part, for her manifold wrongs, goes far to maintain the latter view of their relations.

It was Anne's fortune to dwell for sixteen years on alien soil, but not for one little year as Henry's queen. His dislike to her person and manners was no doubt accentuated by the irksomeness of all necessary speech between them being carried on by means of an interpreter. For Anne made no more rapid progress in acquiring English than Catherine of Arragon had done, with far less compelling cause to be a diligent student.

As the very worm will turn, the King complained at last that she waxed wilful and stubborn. The poor woman was in a strait; she could not, with her simple wiles, please a man who declined to be pleased. She sought interviews with Cromwell, who had advocated her cause in vain. Cromwell had need to look to himself. Bloody executions for treasonable correspondence were the order of the day. The violent deaths of two near kinsmen of the royal house—those of the King's cousin, the Marquis of Exeter, and of another descendant of the Plantagenets, Henry Pole—filled men's minds with anxiety and alarm. Yet still stately tourneys and pageants, which their majesties graced by their presence, were held in honour of the marriage—not six months old, even after the stale device of a divorce had been suggested, or had occurred to Henry, to free him from a hated bond. He persuaded himself that her Lutheranism distressed his conscience, though Anne had been as complacent with regard to her form of the Christian religion as she had been in most other differences between the couple. He declared that he had done his best to get "the consent of his heart and mind" to the marriage, but could not—he

was superstitious about his aversion to Anne. He asserted
that their union was a mere form. The old story of Anne's
pre-contract with the Duke of Lorraine was raked up
again, and it was said that "the papers relating to its
dissolution had never been forthcoming." And here,
though she must have been quite aware that divorces on
the ground of pre-contracts were common enough in Germany, her folly came to Henry's aid. She is reported to
have been sufficiently provoked to make the idle boast that
"if she had not been compelled to marry him, she might
have fulfilled her engagement to another, to whom she
had promised her hand."

At this crisis Anne's countrywomen, "The strange
maidens," as they were quaintly called, who had been
suffered to stay behind with her, were sent back to Cleves,
and the Queen was left doubly forlorn among the English
ladies—one of them Catherine Howard, her mistress's
successor— with whom Henry replaced them at court.
This is not to say that Anne awoke enmity among her
English subjects, any more than she aroused depths of
compassion or heights of enthusiasm. The prudence and
patience with which, as a rule, she minded her own business, and certainly meddled with nobody, served her in
good stead in a negative light.

Warned by Cromwell, she is said to have made a final
effort to propitiate Henry by assuming for him the regard
which she had not hitherto pretended to feel ; but so trans-
parently unreal was the profession, that Henry had enough
wit at once to attribute it to its prompter, and was far
from being softened either to the prompted or the prompter
by the attempt to coax and flatter him.

Cromwell's downfall followed, and his death on Tower
Hill. Henry had bestowed on him the Earldom of Essex
in the interval which had passed since the King's marriage,
but had never forgiven the part which the minister had
played in it. Thus Anne lost her first champion, while a

mortal enemy had started up in her path. This was the
Catholic, Gardiner, Bishop of Winchester, who began to
exercise a prominent influence in the King's council. He
was eager to provide Henry with a fifth, and, if possible,
a Catholic wife. As it was in the struggle to set aside
Catherine of Arragon and promote Anne Boleyn, the
contest again became political, and assumed a religious
motive; the Protestants standing by Anne, as at that
date, a Protestant princess; the Catholics showing themselves ready to be ranged on the side of Catherine Howard,
of an old noble Catholic family, herself a Catholic by
creed, and the new candidate for the dangerous post of
Queen.

Catherine of Arragon's divorce took six years to bring
about. Anne's was accomplished in as many days. A
convocation of clergy was once more summoned, Parliament requesting it, the King consenting to it, and the
assembly unanimously declared the recent marriage null
and void, Cranmer announcing the decision to the Houses
of Parliament. Anne, as a foreigner, ignorant of the
language of the country, was not required to appear before the convocation. It was fortunate where her credit,
courage, and sense were concerned, for she would certainly
have conducted herself in a very different fashion from
that in which Catherine of Arragon had behaved in similar
circumstances. No doubt Anne had no child to be affected
by the decision of the court. The contract between her
and Henry had been of the most arbitrary and worldly description, while its date was of the latest. She was married
in January, and the marriage was dissolved in the following July. Nevertheless, she had her own woman's rights
and matronly character and position to assert. She had
to maintain the credit of her family, and to justify their
hopes and expectations for her. She had the King's
dignity and honour to shield and preserve. All were so
far in her keeping to defend, or to yield without a

struggle. Catherine of Arragon would have died sooner than give in. Anne of Cleves acted in every respect differently. She had been sent down to Richmond, and was staying in the palace there when the commissioners, the Duke of Suffolk, the Earl of Southampton, and the King's secretary, Sir Thomas Wriothesley, arrived to announce the verdict of convocation, with the King's determination to carry it out, and to ask her consent to the divorce.

Anne was so thoroughly panic-stricken that she fainted before the gentlemen could deliver their message. After she recovered consciousness, and found that she was not to be carried off to the Tower and beheaded straightway without further ceremony, the collapse was still more complete. She was ready to consent to anything and everything—the old farce of being styled the King's sister (by adoption in this case) instead of his wife, to resign her title of Queen, and resume her old designation of the "Lady Anne," on condition that she took precedence of all the ladies at court, with the exception of Henry's future wife and his daughters. She willingly, and with apparent gratitude, accepted the award of lands to the value of three thousand pounds a year for her support; she wrote whatever Henry wished, in giving up her claims. These letters were not only to him but to her relatives in Germany, to deprecate their indignation and interference on her behalf.

Her complacence was so great that Henry himself could hardly believe it, and rewarded it by sending her at once five hundred gold marks, as the first instalment of her jointure, by lavishing on her palaces and jewels, and by paying her a visit, when she received him with the utmost politeness. On this as on other occasions, when he supped with her after their separation, Anne's place was no longer by the King's side, as it had been when she was Queen. She sat at a separate table, placed at the corner of the table where the King sat, and at a little distance from him.

Nothing moved Anne; she returned Henry his wedding-ring, with an obliging letter in German. She consented cheerfully to the manner in which he reduced and re-modelled her household. She might have figured to all time as a perfect Griselda, had she shown the least token of being crushed or broken-hearted by her undeserved degradation. On the contrary, she was in excellent spirits, "never so lively before," exhibiting a fresh gown from her superb wardrobe, with a child's unsophisticated inexhaustible satisfaction, on every fresh day. She entered into such amusements as she cared for, and settled down with evident appreciation of the solid comfort to be derived from her own house and household, and the liberty to go her own way—that is, to live a peaceful, uneventful life, busy with her sewing and her attempts at cooking—according to some evidence, at Chelsea Palace, and in the other houses appointed for her. She did not betray the slightest sense either of humiliation or of self-sacrifice in the change in her lot. Pity would have been wasted upon her. She might have returned to her native Germany, from which she had not been absent many months. She might have married again—such a prospect is natural enough to most young women of twenty-five years. With regard to the latter alternative, her single experience of matrimony probably sufficed for her. It is more difficult to dispose of the former question. There might have been some lingering element of womanly pride and sensitiveness even in her phlegmatic disposition, that hindered her from going back to Cleves, which she had quitted with such distinction, a slighted and rejected wife. But the great likelihood is that her prudence was alive to the reservation by which she only held the estates settled on her in England so long as she resided in the country, and she would not risk them by so much as a visit to Germany. It is a shrewd guess that " she preferred a splendid independence in England to poverty at a petty court in Germany."

It must be taken into consideration also that what might have been the chief inducement for Anne to repair to Cleves was withdrawn by the death of her mother, the Duchess, not long after the daughter's separation from Henry. As for her brother, the Duke of Cleves, in spite of his sister's representations, he deeply resented her being set aside as Queen of England, and to the last refused to give in his adherence to the deed. Neither he nor his brother-in-law, the Elector of Saxony, could be expected to show themselves further reconciled to her unqualified submission to Henry, by the fact of her subsequent profession of the Roman Catholic religion in opposition to her own interest, to her whole training, to their strong convictions, and to what had rapidly become the traditions of her house. The origin of this, perhaps the only independent step which Anne took in the course of her life, has not been discovered. No strain of eccentricity was visible in her nature, such as in the unhappy history of her two brothers ended in madness. Anne's wits were not of the kind allied to madness; nothing shook her inflexible, shallow philosophy, her good-humour, well-nigh grim in its imperturbability. She received further visits from Henry, as if these were the most welcome and seemly incidents in the world. She was even so lost to common feeling as to return the visits, by going to see the King and his new wife, and spending some days with them at Hampton Court. Henry's immediate marriage to the beautiful and wretched young Catherine Howard had not affected Anne, neither did her successor's miserable, shameful fate affect her, nor Henry's sixth marriage, nor his death, worn out by stormy passions and frightful disease, long before he could have been counted an old man.

The light in which Anne was regarded by the English people, to whom she was the next thing to dead for eighteen years, was a peculiar one. During her brief reign it was openly said that she was laughed at by the courtiers; but after her deposition she had the sense to retire from the unequal contest, for which she was unsupplied with weapons. She lived for the most part in complete seclusion. At the same time there was something so anomalous, alike in her personality and her position, that it was difficult for them altogether to escape jeers and sneers. Even the most benevolent and kindly were tempted to laugh at the fiasco of "the Lady Anne."

On the other hand, though her virtues were largely negative qualities, these are by no means without their value in a striving, selfish world. She was the author of no turmoil, no bloodshed; she interfered with nobody. Her home life was blameless in its simplicity and restfulness.

She was not quite so thrifty and successful in the management of her household as might have been expected from a Royal German *Hausfrau*, unless indeed her rents were sometimes withheld from her, a misadventure not without precedent. She got, at one period, into some little debt and difficulty, and her servants' wages fell into arrears. She had to apply for help to her brother, the Duke of Cleves, who in his turn appealed to the English Government, when a modest grant of money was made to relieve Anne. In every other respect her life recommended itself to the respectable English public. Beyond cavil, there was a certain peaceful, if plethoric, magnanimity in her abstention from all reprisals, her freedom from such manœuvring and plotting as might have kept the King and the nation by the ears.

Anne's relations with her stepchildren had always been amicable; indeed, there is something touching in the placid, childless woman's fondness for the lively young

Princess Elizabeth, who had been still a little girl of only seven years when Anne was married. It is said that, with the determination which was characteristic of Queen Bess's maturer years, the child sought to be presented to her new Queen and mother, in spite of the King's refusal. The reason which he gave is quoted as the solitary instance which even tradition has preserved of any mention he made of the once dearly loved Anne Boleyn after her death. He spoke gruff, gloomy words to the child, to the effect that this woman was so unlike Elizabeth's own mother that she should not wish to see her.

Notwithstanding this check, an affection sprung up between the dissimilar pair; and one of Anne's petitions to Henry on their separation—a petition which was granted—was that Princess Elizabeth might be allowed to visit her.

Princess Mary, who was the same age as Anne of Cleves, was on such friendly terms with her as to spend several days with her, on at least one occasion. Latterly their common faith must have been a bond of union. Chelsea, Bletchington, the abbey at Dartford—for which Anne had a special liking—were among her dower-houses and ordinary residences.

The ex-Queen was seen occasionally at Edward's court. Her last public appearance was with Princess Elizabeth on Mary's coronation.

During the sixteen years which Anne passed in England she learnt to speak and write English; the last not very intelligibly, but, perhaps, not much less clearly than many of the English ladies of the time wrote their mother-tongue. In her letters she signed herself "Anne, the daughter of Cleves." In one instance there seems to have been a confusion between her recently acquired English and her native German, for the daughter became "doughter."

Anne died in her forty-first year, 1557, after a gradual

decline of health and strength. It might have been said
of her that nothing in her life became her better than her
manner of leaving it. Her serenity and patience came out
in fair colours. She bore her sickness with calm resignation, while she was carefully waited upon by her attached
servants. Her will showed her methodical cast of mind,
her honesty and single-heartedness. Like Catherine of
Arragon, Anne expressed anxiety for the discharge of her
debts, for the payment of a year's wages, and for sundry
legacies to her servants, for their future maintenance.
She made minute and special bequests of her jewels; the
best to Queen Mary (then also forty-one years of age),
coupled with a humble request that she would see the will
carried out, and that she would care for Anne's servants;
the second best jewel to "the Lady Elizabeth" (then
twenty-four years of age), with an earnest entreaty that
she would take into her service one of Anne's poor maids
named Dorothy Curzon. Rings, set with fair diamonds
and rock rubies minutely specified, &c. &c., to members
of her own family, and to her English ladies, the Duchess
of Suffolk, the Countess of Arundel; several pieces of her
gold and silver plate to various English gentlemen ; to
her chaplains a black gown and five pounds each ; to her
laundress (Elsa Turpin) four pounds, with a request to
pray for her. This request was made to the greater number
of legatees, whether priests or laymen, men or women.
She left the place and manner of her burial to be settled
according to Queen Mary's will and pleasure ; and ended
by an acknowledgment that she died in the Roman
Catholic faith.

Anne of Cleves was buried with every token of respect,
and no stint of magnificence, by Mary's directions, in
Westminster Abbey. Among the crosses and banners
borne before and after the body were four white banners,
as a sign that she died unmarried. A requiem was sung
for her, the Bishop of London said mass, her coffin was

"censed," and she was laid in a place of honour near the high altar. Her tomb was never finished, and is only distinguishable by the remains of her monogram, " A.C." The stately hearse, hung with cloth-of-gold, was rifled, and the banners placed near her resting-place were carried away within a fortnight of her funeral.

CATHERINE HOWARD[1]

BY MARRIAGE A TUDOR

THE most disastrous and degrading of Henry VIII.'s marriages was that contracted with Catherine Howard in August 1540, eight months after his marriage with Anne of Cleves. Henry was an unwieldy, ailing, irritable man (to put it mildly), in his forty-ninth year. Catherine Howard was an orphan girl of not more than eighteen or nineteen years of age, unformed, ignorant, erring, whose childhood and youth had been grossly uncared for. She was, however, of noble lineage, being the daughter of Lord Edmund Howard, and the granddaughter of the Duke of Norfolk, through whom she was full cousin to Anne Boleyn, the father of the one and the mother of the other being brother and sister.

Catherine was probably born in her father's house at Lambeth about 1521 or 1522. Lord Edmund was a brave but poverty-stricken soldier, with a numerous family. When his first wife, the daughter of Sir Richard Culpepper of Hollingbourne, died, he was reduced to consigning the child to the keeping of her mother's kindred, among whom she spent her earliest years. A little afterwards, when he was relieved from his extreme poverty by his appointment as Comptroller of Calais and the French marches, he married again. Settled as he was in France, he consented that his daughter Catherine should be adopted and reared by her step-grandmother, the Duchess of Norfolk.

The old Duchess is accused, with reason, of not only

[1] Agnes Strickland. Froude. L. Aitkin.

having wholly neglected the child under her charge, but of having kept a disorderly household of illiterate mischief-making corrupt gentlewomen and maids, in whose society the little girl was left both day and night. These evil companions, in their folly and viciousness, began with amusing themselves by promoting one of the secret marriage contracts which were the curse of the age, between the child Catherine and a grown man as bad as themselves, utterly out of her rank, a player on the virginals in the Duchess's household, and possibly Catherine's music-master, named Henry Maddock or Maddox. In those days Lambeth was largely made up of houses of the nobility and gentry, with gardens and orchards sloping down to the Thames. The Duchess had one of those houses, such as Catherine's father had possessed, and the poor, misguided, silly child was accustomed to walk with the unmanly, unprincipled scamp Maddox at the back of her grandmother's orchard.

Presently, in consequence of a squabble, and doubtless from some fear of detection and punishment among these unworthy gentlewomen, the game was broken off. But a little later Catherine, still a mere foolish girl in her early teens, engaged herself afresh, without the knowledge of the Duchess or the family, to a cousin of one of the gentlewomen, a gentleman pensioner in the service of her uncle the Duke of Norfolk. This not too honourable young man, called Francis Derham, was nearer Catherine in rank; he was, in fact, a distant kinsman of hers, as well as a favourite with the old Duchess. But though he aspired to marry the young girl, it was very doubtful, to say the least, whether the alliance would ever be acceptable to her family.

Catherine was kept either entirely without pocket-money, or with a very slender supply, while she had an empty-headed love of finery. Derham had a fuller purse, and the ill brought-up girl had so little honourable, maidenly pride and discretion as to borrow money from

him and to allow him to supply her with articles of dress
of silk and satin, on the vague promise that she would
repay him some day. How the circumstance escaped
the Duchess's notice is only to be accounted for by the
explanation that she was an old woman engrossed with
her own affairs, who paid little or no heed to her grand-
daughter's looks, words, or deeds. It is piteous, in anticipation of the tragic end of the story, to see for what trifles,
light as air, Catherine was ready to barter her independence, and make herself indebted to Derham. Miss
Strickland describes one of his gifts or loans as an artificial flower in silk, called "a French fennel;" all the
court ladies were wearing it, and Catherine was wild to
get it; yet after it was in her possession she was frightened to appear in it in the presence of the Duchess, till the
untruthful girl had persuaded an equally untruthful woman,
Lady Brerton, to say that she had given it to her. Such
malpractices can only end in more or less demoralisation.

Matters went so far between Catherine and Derham
that before she was sixteen years of age, what was vir-
tually a contract of marriage had been entered into
between them privately. He entrusted his money to her
when he was leaving London for a time, as he would have
entrusted it to his wife, and on one occasion consigned to
her keeping her own bond for as much as a hundred pounds,
which was due to him from her.

By the connivance of his cousin and the rest of the
Duchess's women, he brought fruit and wine, and entertained the whole party at what has a great resemblance to
a schoolboy's banquet.

He left the service of the Duke of Norfolk and entered
that of the old Duchess as her gentleman usher, in order
to have more frequent opportunities of being in company
with the young lady whom he presumed to call his wife.
The suspicion of Lady Norfolk was at last aroused; she
did no more, at first, than make contemptuous remarks,

and treat the pair like a couple of naughty children—from whom one of the two was not far removed. When Derham was missing, the old lady would bid him be sought in "the maid's chamber," where her gentlewomen and servants of a lower rank sat embroidering and spinning.

Once when she found Derham and Catherine Howard engaged in a romping play, she fell upon them and beat them both, finishing by giving one of the elder gentlewomen who was present a box on the ear for permitting such conduct in her company.

When the terms on which the couple stood were discovered there was great indignation, Derham fled "for his life" to Ireland, where, according to some other accounts, he was guilty of piracy on the high seas, in order to procure a living. A much called for reformation took place in the Duchess's household, and Catherine Howard was at last carefully looked after. In spite of this she managed, for a time, to correspond with Derham by means of a gentlewoman still in the house at Lambeth who eventually married and settled in Yorkshire. But when the confederate was gone, and Catherine attained her ardent desire of going to court, where her dawning beauty was at once recognised and made much of, her pride and ambition were aroused, she was quite prepared to turn against Derham, who seems to have been, after the fashion of a man who was neither high-minded nor scrupulous, honestly attached to her, and she was ready to deny that he had any claims upon her. She had soon the opportunity of giving the denial, for he returned secretly from Ireland, and, strange to say, was harboured again by the old Duchess. He found time and place to remonstrate bitterly with his plighted wife on her attendance at court, where he had always been opposed to her going, and on the rumour, which had reached him, that she was to marry her cousin—the heir of her maternal uncle, the Kent squire and knight, Culpepper. Young Culpepper was a

wild, handsome lad, with an appointment in the household
of Anne of Cleves.

To Derham's remonstrance the fickle and alienated girl
answered disdainfully—

" What should you trouble me therewith, for you know
I will not have *you* ? "

According to tradition, Catherine first met Henry in the
middle of his dire discontent with Anne of Cleves at a
banquet given to the King by Bishop Gardiner, who, ob-
serving the King's admiration of the young girl's rosy
beauty and sprightly mirth, conceived the idea of bringing
about another royal marriage by the aid of Catherine's
uncle, the Duke of Norfolk, one of the most powerful of
those old nobility whom Henry in the course of his reign
had systematically slighted.   But if a marriage with
Catherine should re-establish the shaken supremacy of the
Roman Catholic faith in England, it might also reinstall
the great families in their privileges.   If this combination
of bishop and duke existed, no remembrance of another
woman of Howard blood, far more highly gifted than
Catherine (granted that Anne Boleyn had been in their eyes
a heretic), deterred the schemers from their aim.

Catherine Howard was at this time about eighteen years
of age—six years younger than Anne of Cleves and Princess Mary—very small in size, brown-haired and blue-
eyed, with a tip-tilted nose and coral lips.   Her mental
abilities and her culture were of the most primitive kind ;
Anne of Cleves was a miracle of learning by comparison.
If Catherine Howard could read her mother-tongue correctly, there is a strong suspicion that she could not write
it ; and that the extent to which secretaries figured in her
troubles was caused by her being unable to pen a letter on
her own account.   Her very beauty was childish, with a
dash of vulgarity in it ; but, such as it was, it pleased the
discontented autocrat whose life was a burden to himself
and his neighbours.

The moment the heartless and worldly old Duchess of Norfolk awoke to the prospect opening before her young kinswoman, the woman used every effort to bring it about, loading the girl with fine clothes and jewels, instructing her how to behave, and flattering and caressing her. It is even said that the Duchess had the audacity to recommend Catherine Howard to the King as in all respects a fit wife for him.

The first step to the miserable promotion was, as before, the appointment of Catherine to be one of the maids-of-honour to the Queen, shortly before Anne's repudiation. On the eve of the girl's exaltation a great and ominous blow was dealt to her. She received a letter from the very gentlewoman in Yorkshire through whom Catherine Howard had kept up a secret correspondence with Derham two years before. This wily, treacherous ally having heard that the King was likely to marry the girl, now wrote to her, with impudent cunning, reminding her of what the writer, Mrs. Bulmer, had done for her, and boldly claiming a summons to London, and a place near the future Queen's person, ending the letter with the significant words—"for I know the Queen of Britain will not forget her secretary."

Silly and deluded by vanity as Catherine was, she could not have read the insolent application without a dim, horrified guess of the pitfall that was opening before her unwary feet. Even yet, if she could but have been true and confessed her contract to Derham, she might have escaped the bitter penalty that was waiting her. What present shame was equal to the disgrace of the future life of falsehood which would have to be lived by the victim, while she knew herself in the power of the tools who had become her masters? It was even possible, though by no means desirable for her real welfare, that Henry in his extravagant passion for Catherine, which was partly founded on what he believed to be her great modesty and

discretion, might have found means to break the contract
with Derham, as the King had brought himself to dissolve
other and more sacred ties, thus freeing her from the bond
which had grown detestable to her, and giving her the
rank and power she coveted.   But the low moral atmosphere, and the course of dissimulation with which Catherine had been familiar from childhood, were fatal to all
truth and rectitude.   She began her earthly ruin by the
coward's fallacious resource—she attempted to bribe to
silence Mrs. Bulmer and another gentlewoman who had
been formerly in the household of the old Duchess.   She
gave them, presently, posts in the royal household, thus
providing herself with daily scourges to be held over her
shrinking flesh.

The exact date of Henry's marriage with Catherine
Howard is not known, so privately was it carried out.   It
took place immediately after the King's divorce from Anne
of Cleves, in August 1540.   On the 8th of the month he
presented Catherine to his court as his Queen ; on the 15th
she was publicly prayed for as Queen throughout England.
Though there were no grand tournaments or festivals, no
talk of a public entrance into London, or other coronation
ceremonies—of which even Henry, with all his love of
show and increasing callousness, must have been heartily
sick—only a little country progress through Berkshire
and Buckinghamshire, his relations with Catherine were
very different from those he had maintained with her
predecessor Anne.   He was quite pleased with his new
plaything, and fond of her for the hour.   She served to
console him for the emptiness of his exchequer, which
chimed in with his humour in forbidding the public
display once so dear to him.   The last available contents
of his treasury had been squandered, first on the profuse
expenditure which attended on Anne's reception, and next
on the lavish jointure and gifts reckoned necessary to get
rid of her.

To what extent the wretched girl, over whose doomed head hung the sword of Damocles, was able to blind herself to the danger and misery of her situation none can tell. Very soon after the marriage rumours derogatory to her were whispered. The toils were fast closing in round her, when she saw herself forced to take into her household, not only the foolish, reckless old Duchess of Norfolk, her grandmother, but to receive into her service Mrs. Bulmer and Mrs. Tylney—the other gentlewoman referred to. That was not all: she had to provide a place for the rascally musician Maddox, who had insulted her hapless childhood. At last she was driven to appoint Derham her private secretary. This final act of madness is said by some authorities to have originated with the unprincipled old Duchess, who was at the bottom of so much wrongdoing and sorrow. From the time of Catherine's marriage to King Henry she seems to have cancelled all her grandmother's neglect and harshness, and to have clung to her for support and encouragement. In doing so Catherine was so short-sighted as to allow a breach to be made between her and her still all-powerful uncle, the Duke of Norfolk, who was on bad terms with his stepmother the Duchess. If he had been united with Bishop Gardiner in procuring his niece Catherine's promotion, he was in the end as alienated from her, as resolute not to imperil his own safety by becoming her champion, as he had been in the case of his other niece, Anne Boleyn. Derham's means of procuring his appointment was, it is easy to suppose, like those of Mrs. Bulmer and Mrs. Tylney —the mingled threats and importunities of persons mean and base enough to use for their own profit the power given them by the possession of a dangerous secret in connection with a person suddenly raised to high rank.

Catherine's compliance with the demands of her persecutors, whether suggested by the old Duchess or due solely to the girl's own terror of discovery, had no doubt also an element of childish cunning in its nature. She would strive to confine the knowledge of her pre-contract to Derham, as far as possible, within the circle originally cognisant of it. She was likely enough to receive letters, which, if they had passed into the hands of any other secretary, would at once have betrayed her secret.

Another professed friend, but deadly enemy, who dogged Catherine's tottering footsteps, was her kinsman, the playmate of her childhood, young Thomas Culpepper, now a gentleman of the King's Privy Council. He was a worthless, desperate man, who trusted to his cousin, the Queen, to shield him from the just consequences of his vices and crimes. Whether he, too, was acquainted with the unannulled pre-contract with Derham, which rendered Catherine's marriage with Henry illegal, or whether he merely pled that he was her cousin, and that his father's house had sheltered her infancy, and she was frightened to send away any of the friends whom she might soon need sorely, he certainly appealed to her in season and out of season, got money from her, and sought interviews with her in circumstances which were altogether out of keeping with her position as a matron and a Queen.

Catherine is not accused of having interfered in public affairs, unless she had something to do with the downfall and execution of Thomas Cromwell, occurring, as the last event did, in the early days of her favour with Henry. Some of her contemporaries were inclined to give her a share in it, but in her fear of discovery her sole aim seemed to be to please the King, and in this she fully succeeded. Henry's intellectual requirements in a companion had come to be of the smallest. Catherine's young, fresh beauty, together with her absolute submission to him, and her professions of regard for him, sufficed him. He showed his affection for her in every way, and openly expressed his preference for her over her four predecessors. Under all this honour, Catherine, in the quaintly expressive language of Scripture, "walked softly," and refrained from giving unnecessary offence by any attempt at regal state on her own account. At the same time we have glimpses of the original woman in such an implication as that of Chappuys, the Emperor's ambassador, when he wrote of her in her adversity, as being "as careful about her dress, as imperious and wilful, as at the time she was with the King."

A Catholic rising in Yorkshire had just been quelled, and had been followed, among other ghastly reprisals, by the execution of the old Marchioness of Salisbury, the last of the Plantagenets, and the mother of Cardinal Pole, who was believed to be the moving spirit in every trouble of the time. The poor old woman, whose chief fault was corresponding with her plotting son, had been under sentence of attainder in company with her daughter-in-law, Lady Exeter, and had lain in the Tower for many months. She was in her dotage, and when brought to the block refused to lay her head on it—" So should traitors do ; I am none," she said ; and, according to her son, the Cardinal, added, "Blessed are those who suffer persecution for righteousness' sake." She turned her head every way, telling the executioner that he might get it if he could, so that he had to seize her by the grey hair and hold her down by force while she was slain.

On the back of this brutal episode Henry departed for York in the autumn of 1541, with the double purpose of awing and appeasing his Northern subjects. He carried Catherine with him, and she was treated with special distinction during the journey, in the course of which she made the false and fatal move, already mentioned, of appointing Derham her secretary.

In the King's absence the government was largely in the hands of Archbishop Cranmer. It was when thus reinstated in his former supremacy, while in all likelihood he regarded it, and his very life, together with the final

establishment of the Reformed religion in England, as
endangered by the young Roman Catholic queen and her
growing ascendancy over Henry, that Cranmer was
formally informed, by one of the many persons acquainted
with the fact, of the previous contract of marriage which
had passed between Catherine and Derham. The in-
formant was a gentleman named Lascelles, who was
Derham's cousin, the brother of one of the gentlewomen
of the old Duchess of Norfolk. He was a zealous reformer,
as he proved by his life and death.

There was little room for doubt in the circumstantial
tale, but the Archbishop did not act on his own responsibility, or with undue precipitation. He laid the matter
before his colleagues in the government, and it was not
till they empowered him that he prepared to communicate
the information to the unfortunate King, in this instance
more sinned against than sinning.

There was nothing to warn Catherine that the hour of
retribution was at hand. The court had just returned to
Windsor, and then gone to Hampton Court, where the
festival of All Saints was to be kept. The King was so
entirely happy in his domestic relations that, on receiving
the sacrament along with Catherine on the 30th, he
thanked God aloud that after so many strange accidents
that had befallen his marriages—as by a marvellous moral
twist in his reasoning and a monstrous example of self-
delusion he described what had been his domestic relations
—a wife so entirely conformable to his inclinations had
been given him. Further, he desired the Bishop of Lincoln to prepare a prayer and thanksgiving to Almighty
God for his having provided the King with "so loving,
dutiful, and virtuous a queen."

The paper was to have been publicly read on All Saints'
Day. In order to prevent this most inopportune prelude
to his communication, Cranmer seized the opportunity of
Henry's attending early mass alone on All Saints' Day,

to present him with the paper containing the accusation lodged against Catherine, and to beseech him to consider it in privacy.

The King was wholly taken aback, and began by being utterly incredulous, but granted that the affair must be sifted, for the Queen's own sake. He summoned various members of his Council, and before them Lascelles and then Derham were examined and cross-examined. The former never wavered in his story; the latter at once admitted the pre-contract with Catherine, which in the eyes of the law constituted them man and wife, and rendered her subsequent marriage with Henry bigamy.

When the King could no longer refuse credence to the statement, he broke down and burst into tears. The floods of salt tears shed by Catherine of Arragon in her lonely vigils, the merciless prosecution of Anne Boleyn, the humiliation of Anne of Cleves were all avenged.

On the miserable girl-queen's learning that her perjury was laid bare, she called incessantly for the King, and made the most frantic efforts to reach him, in order to beg for his pardon and protection. She was bidden to remain in her rooms, but she was incapable of self-restraint. She made her escape twice, at one time getting as far as the door of the chapel where the King was hearing mass, and when she was taken back by force, her cries of anguish and despair rang through the chapel.

Henry left Hampton the next day without consenting to see the Queen. Instead, he sent Cranmer to her, as the King had sent the Archbishop to Anne Boleyn, to get her own version of the charge against her.

This was no easy task, for Catherine was not only nearly beside herself with distress and alarm, falling into what appears to have been fit after fit of violent hysterics, in addition she had so long departed from the path of truth that she was positively incapable of returning to it. If she had even in her last extremity been candid, she might have been believed when she solemnly asserted that she had been faithful to her marriage vows to the King; but in the teeth of the overwhelming testimony of her pre-contract to Derham, she persisted in denying it stubbornly, and in prevaricating about the merest trifles, till all lingering faith in her word was destroyed.

Cranmer certainly went to Catherine with the King's promise that her life would be spared if she confessed all, and she raised her trembling hands in token of gratitude for his clemency. But she did not confess, so that we may be spared the question if the King was perfectly sincere in his pledge, or if it was a mere ruse to calm the culprit and induce her to speak out, which her continued duplicity baffled. According to Chappuys, the King really wished to save Catherine from death, and sent some members of his council with a deputation from the Houses of Parliament, to propose to her to come to the Parliament Chamber and defend herself, as her cousin, Anne Boleyn, had done; but this proposal she declined, saying that she submitted herself to the King's mercy. Clearly she relied more on his pity than on her own eloquence, or on the justice of her cause.

The Commission of Inquiry sat at Hampton Court for a week. The Queen was placed under arrest, her keys taken from her, and her maids-of-honour dismissed. She was finally removed to Sion House, without indignity, and placed there in a kind of modified captivity, attended by four gentlewomen and two servants, and furnished with a wardrobe becoming her station. It was during her stay at Sion House that Chappuys told his master, as if from the mouth of an eye-witness, that she was "very cheerful, more plump, and prettier than ever," and further referred to her careful dress and imperious ways. Catherine was a practised dissembler; but it is also evident that though she professed herself in a general way deserving of death, just as she would have acknowledged herself a miserable sinner and declared that she expected the fulfilment of her sentence, she did not believe it would be put in force, but relied on Henry's former infatuation and on his relenting.

The house of the old Duchess of Norfolk was searched for evidence, and when it was shown that she and her servants had already destroyed the contents of Derham's trunks, which were in her keeping, the whole household with its mistress were put under arrest. The Duchess immediately feigned illness and retired to bed, a simple device which did not serve her, as she was lodged in the Tower, with the fate of the Marchioness of Salisbury before her eyes.

Derham and Culpepper were arraigned for high treason, questioned under torture, and sentenced to death. They were taken to Tyburn. Culpepper, as the better born man, was beheaded, Derham was hanged, and the heads of the two were placed over London Bridge.

Catherine remained two months at Sion House, till early in the following year, when Parliament met and she was attainted, along with her grandmother and various ladies and gentlemen of the Howard family, among them Lady Rochefort, the sister-in-law and bitter enemy of Anne Boleyn. The assent to the bill was taken by commission in order to spare Henry's feelings. The Duke of Suffolk and Lord Southampton declared in the House of Lords that Catherine had admitted her guilt to them, and had implored the royal mercy and charity for her kindred and servants. The Commons were summoned, the King's assent to the bill was read, and with the significant phrase, "*Le Roi le veut,*" the sentence of death was passed.

Catherine was brought on the 10th of February, 1542, from Sion House to the Tower in a barge, attended by several ladies and gentlemen. Another barge, containing the Lord Privy Seal and several members of the Council, preceded hers, while the rear was brought up by a third barge, in which were the Duke of Suffolk and part of his retinue.

The lords disembarked first. Then came Catherine, wearing a black velvet gown. There is no record of the manner in which she received her sentence of death, or of her conduct during the gloomy journey, except in a hint that there was some difficulty and resistance on her part at starting.

It has been conjectured, from the distance by water, that she could not have arrived at her destination till the darkness of a winter evening had set in. If so, she would be saved the cruel shock of seeing the heads of Derham and her cousin, Thomas Culpepper, exposed on the bridge which she must have passed under. Let us trust it was humanely contrived that she might miss the sight in the darkness. She was received with the respect accorded to her rank.

The following day was Saturday, and on Sunday she was told to prepare to die on Monday morning, along with Lady Rochefort, who, as Catherine's confidential friend and lady-in-waiting, was believed to be her accomplice. Weak, ignorant, and erring as the poor forlorn girl was, she seems to have made up her mind in the interval to her fate, and to have summoned all her courage to meet it, while still solemnly protesting to her confessor, the Bishop of Lincoln, her innocence of having broken her marriage vows to the King. She asked that the headsman's block might be brought into her room, that she might rehearse what she had to do, and the singular request was granted.

So, early as seven on the February morning the King's Council, including Lord Surrey, Catherine's cousin, assembled on the Tower Green, to which the melancholy little procession wended its way. Catherine died quickly and bravely, at last, saying very little beyond the general confession that her sins deserved the punishment they were about to receive, and that she committed her soul to God. So much was this the stereotyped speech on such an occasion, and so universally was it attributed to the sufferers, that one may have a reasonable doubt of its authenticity. Catherine Howard was only in her twentieth year, and had not been married more than eighteen months.

Lady Rochefort was much older, and is said by Chappuys to have been in a frenzy on the scaffold. Her state of mind could hardly have been allayed by the reflection that she was about to perish on the same scaffold as that on which Anne Boleyn—brought to the block chiefly by Lady Rochefort, her sister-in-law's evidence—had been beheaded. According to tradition Lady Rochefort declared, almost with her last breath, that she had been guilty of no other crime save her false accusation of Anne Boleyn and Anne's brother, Lord Rochefort, and she supposed it was for that wickedness she had to endure a shameful and violent death.

Catherine's lifeless body, hidden by a cloth, was removed by her ladies, to be buried at once in the Church of St. Peter's, most probably near the grave of her cousin queen.

The old Duchess of Norfolk, so much to blame in the lamentable story, was in the end allowed to live. The penalty she paid for her offences was the confiscation of such wealth as she had possessed.

CATHERINE PARR[1]

BY MARRIAGE A TUDOR

HENRY VIII.'s ill fortune, as he viewed it, in marriage, did not prevent him from seeking and getting a sixth wife. But instead of rushing again into wedlock with rash and unbecoming haste, more than a year elapsed between Catherine Howard's death and the King's marriage with Catherine Parr. His ultimate choice was, beyond measure, wiser and more honourable than that he had recently made. The single objection to it was that the lady, already twice a widow, had only lost her second husband three months before she became Queen.

Catherine Parr was of honourable though not noble birth. Her ancestors on both sides of the house—the Parrs of Kendal, and the Greens of Green Norton—were highly connected and wealthy squires and knights. In the case of the Parrs, they could trace a royal strain in their blood. Catherine's father, Sir Thomas Parr, of Kendal, died when she was only four years of age, leaving two little daughters and a son to the care of his young widow, Dame Maude Parr, a very marvel of discretion and worldly wisdom. She had been married at thirteen, and was but twenty-two when her husband died. Like Louise of Savoy, at even an earlier age, Dame Maude renounced every thought of a second marriage, and devoted herself to the rearing of her children. Like Louise, also, she signalised herself by planning betimes their advantageous settlements, and

[1] Agnes Strickland. Froude. L. Aikin. Strype.

by stoutly resisting any attempt to get the better of her in her schemes.

Catherine, the elder daughter, is believed to have been born in Kendal Castle, Westmoreland, about the year 1513. She was certainly brought up in the North of England, along with her brother and sister, and a young kinswoman in the neighbourhood, named Elizabeth Bellingham, daughter of Sir Robert Bellingham, of Burnside, to whom the child Catherine was greatly attached. Miss Strickland quotes a tradition of Catherine's youth. It is to the affect that an astrologer, having cast her nativity, foretold for her imperial majesty. The little girl was therefore wont to excuse herself from attending to domestic work by gravely or saucily asserting that her hands were ordained to touch crowns and sceptres, not spindles and needles. But probably any disinclination which little Catherine Parr showed for needlework was caused by her love of books, to which she was early introduced during the really extensive course of study which her mother decreed and secured for all her children. Catherine was not only taught the ordinary branches of an English education, she was well versed, for her years, in Latin, and had a little acquaintance with Greek. She was familiar with more than one modern language (doubtless French and Italian).

The first proposal of marriage which Dame Maude entertained for her small daughter was from the great North-country nobleman, Lord Dacre, on behalf of his grandson; but the project fell through on account of differences of opinion on money matters. Shortly afterwards Lady Parr accomplished a marriage between Catherine and a mature suitor, a distant relative, Lord Borough of Gainsborough, a widower with a grown-up family. He was, as may be supposed, a man of substance, possessing other fine seats besides that in Lincolnshire, to which he took young Catherine.

Death ended the marriage before long, and Catherine was left a beautiful and rich widow, while still no more than fifteen years of age. Her mother was already dead, and Lady Borough is supposed to have resided for a time with one of her stepdaughters, that is, the widow of one of her stepsons. This lady, herself remotely related to Catherine, had already been twice married. Her first husband was Sir Walter Strickland, of Sizergh, also akin to Catherine, whose castle his widow, though re-married and re-widowed, occupied during the minority of her eldest son. By one of the odd contradictions of the time, she is reported to have been fourteen years older than her husband's stepmother, whom she called duly "My good mother."

During Catherine's stay at Sizergh, she atoned, if family tradition can be depended upon, for her early dislike to needlework by employing her nimble fingers on a counterpane and a toilet-cover, in a device of wreaths of flowers on a foundation of white satin, which is still shown as a magnificent example of ancient art and industry.

A room in Sizergh, called "The Queen's room," panelled in carved black oak, and hung with tapestry, continues to be associated with Catherine, though she certainly never slept in it as Queen.

From her portraits in later years, Catherine stands before us a little woman, with delicate, rather *petite* features; very clear and sparkling hazel eyes; fair hair, and a blooming complexion. Her forehead was one of those expansive foreheads so conspicuous in the faces of Henry VIII.'s queens and of their contemporaries; one comes to the conclusion that, though in the case of Catherine Parr there was warrant enough for this sign of intellect, the effect was, as a rule, produced rather by the style of head-gear and mode of dressing the hair, than by a marvellous blossoming of intellect in the women of the generation.

In expression, Catherine Parr has been described as "full of intelligence and arch simplicity." Her taste in dress, after she was Queen, was as superior to that of Anne of Cleves and Catherine Howard as was her wit. She dressed magnificently, in accordance with her rank, but always with grace and simplicity in her hoods and kirtles, pearls and rubies.

Catherine Parr's second marriage, entered into apparently before she was twenty, was again with a far-away kinsman, an elderly widower, and the father of a family, whose third wife she became. The bridegroom was John, Lord Latimer, of the great house of Neville. Catherine resided with him at his house of Snape Hall in Yorkshire, where she superintended with care and kindness the education of her two stepchildren.

Lord Latimer was a staunch Catholic. Catherine may have sympathised with him to begin with, but she was destined ere long to show that her whole heart and soul were with the more liberal and intellectual Reformers. If she viewed with favour her husband's prominence on the opposite side, as a leader in what was called "the Pilgrimage of Grace," it was one of the errors of those days of darkness which she ultimately deplored. This Pilgrimage was a great gathering of the poorer Catholics of the North, supported by many powerful noblemen and gentlemen. They sent delegates, of whom Lord Latimer was one, to the King, to beg for the restoration of the Pope's authority and of the monasteries—a petition which Henry indignantly declined to grant. The peaceful pilgrimage ended in the Northern insurrection. Lord Latimer narrowly escaped being implicated in it. As he did escape, it is very likely he went with his wife to York, to pay homage to the King and Queen on their visit there, and then, if at no other time, Catherine Parr and Catherine Howard may have met in the characters of loyal subject and sovereign lady.

Lord Latimer did not long survive these troubles; he died about 1542 or 1543. Miss Strickland seems to argue that Catherine Parr was a Catholic till then; but as immediately after her husband's death she is found in constant association with the most prominent Reformers in London, it is almost certain that her Protestantism was of earlier date, though she might not have been able to profess it openly while Lord Latimer lived, and that there was no unity of religious opinion latterly, at least, between the two. The sole presumption against this is contained in the family records of Catherine's near relations, through her mother, the Throckmortons. These papers state that when Sir George Throckmorton, the husband of Catherine's aunt, was imprisoned, with his lands and life threatened by the covetousness and enmity of Cromwell, Catherine Lady Latimer interposed, and by her forcible representations to the King prevented the injustice, and procured the liberation of Throckmorton. But it is surely possible that Catherine, in the interests of her uncle, may have opposed the Protestant minister, though she was herself a Protestant, and that the said minister may not have felt himself warranted in granting a favour to the wife of the Catholic leader Lord Latimer, whatever her personal leanings were supposed to be.

It is certain that Coverdale, &c., frequented Catherine's house and preached in her State room within not very many weeks of Lord Latimer's death. It was ostensibly to attend these meetings as the member of a distinguished Protestant family, that a new actor, who was to play a prominent part in the later scenes of Catherine's eventful life, appeared in the foreground. He was the King's brother-in-law, the brother of Jane Seymour, Sir Thomas Seymour, afterwards Lord Seymour of Sudely, and Lord High Admiral. He could not have been young, but he was not much older than Catherine, and was still in the flower of his manhood. He was unmarried, handsome, gay, and gallant, a magnificent fop in that age of velvet, satin, gold embroidery, and precious stones without number. He had a singular attraction for women, not for frivolous women alone, but for those also who were his superiors in intellect and character. By the best of the Reformers he was viewed, in spite of his family and their tenets, with lively detestation.

Under whatever motive or pretext Seymour went first to the chosen haunt of the grave and learned Reformers, he began almost at once to pay court to the fair, learned widow, as well endowed with this world's goods as she was with beauty and sense. Catherine, who had made marriages of such exceptional worldly wisdom before, that her heart might have been supposed to be the most prudent of hearts, now forgot to be sage, and listened, as it would appear, to the voice of nature. She chose, like more foolish women, to lend a willing ear to the wooer who, though greatly her inferior in other respects, was a far more attractive and suitable match, in point of physique and years, than either of her former husbands had been. He was also, as one of the Reforming Seymours, in harmony with her on what was a matter of such moment as her religious creed, and she might trust that the power of a pure faith, together with her influence and example, would remedy what was inconsistent in the gentleman's practice. If she had already experienced discord in marriage on this ground, she would be still more inclined to cling to a man who could at least promise agreement with her on a cardinal question, which was at this date not only convulsing the country, but rending asunder many a private family within its bounds.

An insuperable impediment, not dreamt of to begin with, suddenly interposed to prevent the crowning culmination of Sir Thomas Seymour's bold aspirations, and the late shy dawning of Catherine Lady Latimer's love.

Le Roi le veut was as incontestable a saying as ever, though uttered in different circumstances. Catherine was fated to be the dutiful patient wife of elderly widowers, the thoughtful, affectionate stepmother of a succession of stepchildren. It entered the head of King Henry, or of some of his counsellors, that here at last was the proper wife for him. He was in his fifty-third and Catherine Parr in her thirty-first year. She would be his sixth wife, he would be her third husband. The priority in years and in the number of spouses was fitly on the gentleman's side. She had already been a good house-mistress and mother to two noble households and families. She would be a worthy queen-consort at the head of a court, and an excellent guardian for two of Henry's motherless children, the cherished Prince of Wales, a small boy between five and six, and "the Lady Elizabeth," an irrepressible little girl of ten years. As for "the Lady Mary," she was somewhat beyond tutelage, while her welfare was not very near her father's heart. He had been known to say that she was the worst enemy he had. She was a very resolute, strong-minded young woman of twenty-eight years of age, not quite three years younger than her last stepmother.

Poor Catherine Parr's solitary love-dream was rudely broken in upon. Ambitious as she was, without question, she is said to have shown some reluctance to accept the crown-matrimonial, till her suitor, Sir Thomas Seymour, quickly withdrew from a dangerous competition with his sovereign and brother-in-law. Then, moved a little by pique and mortification, perhaps, as well as by a desire for the power which she was so well qualified to administer, she consented to be a queen. The same necessity was present with her as that which had compelled gentle Jane Seymour to wed Henry the very day after her mistress and former companion had laid down her head on the block.

From the quiet shades of Chelsea, Anne of Cleves looked on with immovable philosophy at this fresh partner of her former lord.

There was no time lost in preliminaries. It was but three months from the date of Lord Latimer's death when, in July 1543, licence was granted for the marriage, without the proclamation of banns, of Henry VIII. and Catherine Lady Latimer. The wedding was not conducted secretly, like two of Henry's previous marriages. The Bishop of Winchester performed the ceremony at Hampton Court, and among the company present were the King's two daughters; his niece, Lady Margaret Douglas; Catherine's only sister, Mrs. Herbert, one of the learned ladies of the time; and many more of the bride's friends.

The Protestants at large, and their mouthpiece in particular, the University of Cambridge, rejoiced much over the auspicious event, the only one of Henry's six marriages which could be said both to begin and end happily. Catherine, a scholar in her own person, answered with much graciousness the University's congratulations.

Very soon the Queen's influence was exercised—not always successfully—in the protection of the propounders of the new learning. A little later she named Coverdale her almoner, and it was well known that she supported by all the means in her power his translation of the Bible. This was decidedly a more honourable use of her position than the promotion, however natural, of her relations and connections to posts in the royal household.

The Queen also showed a praiseworthy desire to promote the interests as well as to win the affection of the King's children. In the last aim she succeeded—especially where Princess Elizabeth was concerned; and, to the credit both of Catherine and Mary, who were so near in age and so divided in faith, they were on good terms.

Many womanly proofs of the fact are in existence to this
day in the record of kindly gifts from the Queen to her
stepdaughter, and of answering tokens, like the cushion
which the Princess worked with her own hand, from
Mary to Catherine.   In their unlikeness the two had
points of sympathy.   They both belonged to the group
of royal and noble ladies exceptionally educated for their
generation, who took genuine pleasure in serious studies
and intellectual pursuits.   With regard to her younger
stepchildren, Catherine seems to have enjoyed presiding
over their education and occupying herself with them.
When Elizabeth got into serious disgrace with the King
for some childish offence, and was forbidden his presence,
it was through Catherine's intercession that she was restored to favour.   A recent observer has remarked on the
close resemblance between Catherine's handwriting and
that of Edward VI.   "*Belle écriture*," the little boy called
his stepmother's penmanship, expressing his admiration
for it in writing to thank her for a letter to him, and he
must have made her characters his model.

The manuals of devotion which Mary and Elizabeth
compiled from Latin, French, and English sources are
supposed to have been made at the Queen's suggestion,
and she enlisted Mary's patronage and assistance on behalf of Udall's paraphrases on the Gospels.   Catherine
also stimulated and encouraged the princesses and their
cousins, the Ladies Grey, in their taste for classic authors.

The Queen, like the King's grandmother, the venerable
Margaret, was herself an author ; she too "collected out
of holy books" meditations and prayers in recommendation of suffering afflictions, setting at naught vain prosperity, and longing for everlasting felicity.   The collection
was printed in 1545, two years after Catherine's marriage.
A more original work was her "Lamentations of a Sinner,
Bewayling the Ignorance of her Blind Life" (while an
adherent to the Roman Catholic Church), "set forth and

put at the instant desire of the right gracious ladie, Catherine, Duchess of Suffolk, and the earnest request of the Right Honourable Lord William Parr, Marquis of North-Hampton " (Catherine's brother). This book, which contained too direct an attack on the doctrines of the Roman Catholic Church to be consistent with the attempts at a compromise between Protestantism and Roman Catholicism with which Henry ended his reign, was not published in his lifetime in spite of its laudation of him as a Protestant king. It was "imprinted at London, in Flete Strete, at the sign of the Sunne, over against the Conduyte, by Edward Whitchurche, the 5th day of November, in the year of our Lord 1547," ten months after Henry's death. It was reprinted " at the long shopp adjoining S. Wildred's Church, in the Poultrie, by John Aldis, in 1563," thirteen years after Catherine's death, during the reign of Queen Elizabeth.

The year after his marriage to Catherine, 1544, Henry induced his Parliament once more to set aside his daughters, Mary and Elizabeth, from the succession to the crown, by appointing that any children borne by Queen Catherine should succeed Edward, supposing the Prince of Wales died a minor. But his last marriage, like the two which preceded it, was childless. If Catherine did not protest against this new act of succession, it shows the extent to which ambition and political bias may blind an otherwise good woman to the plainest obligations of justice.

On Henry's last visit to France, to conduct the siege of Boulogne in 1544, Catherine was appointed Queen Regent, and ruled the kingdom, with the help of his ministers, in his absence. One of the visitations of the plague occurred while the King was abroad, when she carefully removed not only the precious prince, but the two slighted princesses, from Hampton Court to Oking, and dwelt with them there. Catherine's letters to Henry

are extravagant in their expressions of humility **and**
devotion, as such letters were in those days, but in other
respects are full of tact and good sense. In signing herself "Kateryn, the Queen," she always adds the initial
letters of her maiden name " K. P." Had this any reference to the circumstance that she was the third Catherine
who had signed herself the Queen in Henry's day? On
Henry's return, the same year, what is called "Holbein's
famous picture of the Royal Family" was painted. It is
usually, but not indisputuably, attributed to Holbein.
Agnes Strickland has an odd impression that Catherine
Parr was excluded from this picture, and that the portrait
of the lady seated by Henry's side, dressed in cloth-of-
gold, was not a likeness of the reigning Queen, but was
a representation of Jane Seymour, taken from the wax
effigy carried at her funeral, and was in consequence more
like a stiff, dim doll than a living woman. Miss Strickland deduces no authority for her belief, which seems to
have been founded, partly on the resemblance between
the portrait to other portraits of Jane Seymour, and to
the likeness of the little boy, her son, introduced into the
picture; partly, too, on an argument drawn from the
millinery of the period, because the painted lady figures
in a pointed hood, such as Jane Seymour had worn,
which had been superseded by the low, round French
hood introduced at court by Catherine Howard, and
ordinarily worn by Catherine Parr, as it is worn in
this very picture by the two princesses. But though a
plausible theory for the strange resuscitation of Jane
Seymour in this picture may be constructed from Henry's
special honour for the mother of his son, no satisfactory
reason can be given for the slight put upon Catherine
Parr, who was then in high favour with the King, by the
suppression of her existence. Reference has been already
made to the curious resemblance produced in Henry's
wives, and in other contemporary ladies, by the peculiar

fashions of the time. As to the difficulty in the matter of costume, the change in hoods was so recent that little can be drawn from it. Catherine Parr must have been accustomed to wear, a year or two previously, the pointed hood of Jane Seymour, and may have resumed it on this occasion, either from a caprice of taste, or, more probably, to distinguish her head-dress from those of her stepdaughters.

There is a preponderance of gorgeous red and gold throughout the picture. Henry's "gown" is of scarlet and gold, girded round the huge waist with a white satin sash, puffed at the breast with white satin, and surmounted by a collar of pearls, with ruby medallions. The Queen's gown is of cloth-of-gold; the little prince, leaning against his father, has a crimson velvet cap, and a dark red gown; the princesses, entering from different sides, are dressed alike in red brocade, with red trains. Besides the family, two figures can be seen through opposite doorways—both belong to the privileged class of fools or jesters. The one, a grotesque looking woman, is believed to be "Jane the fool;" the other, a man, is "Will Somers, the King's jester." He carries a monkey, or "jackanapes," on his shoulder.

Catherine's reign as queen-consort lasted three years, and her position at Henry's court is not without a resemblance to that of Madame Maintenon, after her private marriage to Louis XIV. at the court of France in a later generation. Catherine Parr was a legalised Madame Maintenon. She was much younger, much more attractive personally, and she was acknowledged queen, though she was never crowned—indeed, there was not so much as a proposal to that effect. She compelled the respect even of her enemies, and the breath of slander never touched her. Yet, somehow, it was never quite forgotten that she had been a simple gentlewoman. She was at the head of the King's household to manage it for him, to interest and amuse him, to nurse him in chronic illness, to help to rear his children. She was, for the most part, the Queen only in name. She had been found fit to act as queen-regent in his absence. She was rendered illustrious by her talents and acquirements. She was by far the most honourable and blameless of the four private subjects whom Henry raised to share his throne; still she somehow stood apart from the regal state to which she was elevated. It was better remembered of her than of those three predecessors— certainly far better than of Anne Boleyn in her arrogance and passion—that she had not been born in the purple, or grown up in daily familiarity with the dignity to which she had attained.

Undisturbed in her integrity and dutifulness by the presence at court of Sir Thomas Seymour, who was developing more and more into a reckless, restless lover of pleasure and amusement, and a notorious gambler, Catherine pursued the even tenor of her way.

In what was Henry's continually empty exchequer towards the close of his life, it was a great advantage to all concerned that Catherine held, independently of her allowance as queen, the liberal jointures settled upon her by her previous husbands, Lord Borough and Lord Latimer.

Henry's needs were so great that, after changing the value of the currency, and applying without response to Parliament, he was reduced to appropriate the revenues of the hospitals and colleges, placed at his disposal by the same Parliament, and it was only Queen Catherine's urgent representations which kept Cambridge from being impoverished. To Catherine's many engagements was added latterly that of sedulously nursing her formidable husband. He was immensely overgrown, dropsical, and in perpetual pain from an ulcerous leg. He was still but in his fifty-fifth year, while age—diseased and helpless, had descended on him. He was utterly incapable of taking any part in the splendid pageants over which he had loved to preside. The out-of-door sports and games in which he had delighted were far removed from him. His life-long rival and brother King, Francis I., who had long been dying by inches of a terrible malady, could yet lead the hunt, the fastest and fiercest rider in the company, on the last day of his life; but Henry had to sit in his arm-chair and be raised by machinery from one storey of his palace to another. His temper, always choleric, had grown chronically uncertain, with gusts of fury. It was to this poor man, once so full of life and strength and manly beauty, so splendid in his princely power and popularity, that Catherine had to minister.

She is said to have done it faithfully and tenderly; no doubt instructed by former experience in dealing with ailing, elderly men. According to the chroniclers of the period, she would remain hours on her knees fomenting and dressing the sores which he would allow no one else to touch, or he would rest his lame leg in her lap. When she could divert his mind in no other fashion, she would beguile the time by dwelling on the one subject of which he never wearied, the promise and prospects of his idolised son

A kind of mania with Henry, at the unhappy close of his life, was the mingled anger and vexation with which he viewed the religious distractions in his kingdom to which he had given the first impetus. It was as if he would have said to the waves of party strife, "Hitherto shalt thou come and no further." He ignored the fact that no great and vital change, whether in the individual or the nation, can take place without struggles and con-vulsions, relapses and fresh fights to regain lost ground.

It was in the humour of stamping out the causes of discord that Henry lent himself to support the more zeal-ous of the old Catholics—notably Bishop Gardiner—in restoring the landmarks in what came to be considered the fundamental principles of their religion. The result

was the persecutions and burnings, in one of which Anne
Ascue perished.

It is possible that when Queen Catherine lived in Lincolnshire, in her girlhood, she may have been acquainted
with the families of Ascue and Kyme—Anne's relations
by birth and marriage—among the country gentry. But
as for Anne herself, she was more than half a dozen years
younger than Catherine Parr, and so could only have been
a child of six when the latter dwelt, as Lady Borough,
near Gainsborough. But whether recommended by old
acquaintances, or introduced by the Queen's sister, Lady
Herbert, or the Queen's particular friend, Catherine Willoughby, Duchess of Suffolk—both of whom were known
to be very favourably affected to the Reformed faith—or
merely attracted to court by the report that the learned
and virtuous Queen held with the protesters against the
old corruptions and abuses in the Church, Anne came to
London and was received at Westminster. Young, beautiful, ardent, the very priests who were her opponents had
drawn back from the contest when they watched her reading the Bible in Lincoln Cathedral. Her husband had
turned her out of doors because of her adherence to the
new learning; but Catherine welcomed her, discussed with
her what was called heresy, and, along with Lady Herbert
and Lady Suffolk, read the heretical books which were in
Anne's possession. Very soon Anne was arrested and
thrown into prison. In her imprisonment she was reduced
to such poverty that her faithful maid, not daring to compromise the ladies with whom her mistress was acquainted
by asking aid from them, went out into the streets and
made "moan to the 'prentices, and they by her did send
in money." Not only the honest 'prentices' hearts were
touched; that of Bishop Bonner, not wont to be soft where
heretics were concerned, was moved by her.

It was commonly believed that the arrest and subsequent cruel torture on the rack of Anne Ascue had a

double motive. It was intended not only to punish a contumacious pretender to the right of private judgment, but to induce her so to implicate other women of rank—above all, the Queen—as to include them in the accusation of heresy, and procure a warrant for their arrest. The whisper went round that Gardiner "aimed at higher deer" than the Lincolnshire gentlewoman. But Anne was loyal and generous in her lofty courage. "They did put me on the rack because I confessed no ladies and gentlemen to be of my opinion." She wrote in the piteous fragments which survive of her account of the treatment she received, "and thereupon they kept me a long time, and because I lay still and did not cry, my Lord Chancellor (Wriothesley) and Master Rich (the Solicitor-General) took pains to rack me with their own hands till I was nigh dead."[1]

Neither screwings nor pinchings—which were certainly so severe that the Lieutenant of the Tower had to lift her up in his arms from the rack and lay her swooning on the floor, and that she had to be carried the following day in a chair to the stake before St. Bartholomew's Church—no, nor the blazing faggots amidst which she was chained, could make her give up the names of her friends, or betray their sympathy with her belief. It may be mentioned here that in the group of heretics who suffered along with Anne was a gentleman in the King's retinue named Lascelles. This gentleman is understood to have been the cousin of Francis Derham and brother of one of the old Duchess of Norfolk's gentlewomen, who gave the information to Archbishop Cranmer of the pre-contract between Derham and Catherine Howard.

It is easy to guess what grief it must have been to Catherine Parr to stand passive and witness these enor-

---

[1] The conduct of the great officers of State, Wriothesley and Rich, seems so barbarous that some people have believed they could not have been altogether in earnest, that their intention was rather to frighten than to hurt Anne Ascue, therefore they kept the rack in their own hands.

mities in the name of religion; but though she was both good and kind, she was not an Anne Ascue. Her inter-position at this crisis would probably have been useless, and her own life and liberty were in danger. If the mere possession of heretical books was dangerous, and a mes-senger had to ride post haste to warn the court ladies of their peril, still more condemnatory evidence existed in the fact that the Queen had written such a book as "The Lamentations of a Sinner, Bewayling the Ignorance of her Blind Life," which, though not printed till the follow-ing year, was almost certainly written at this date, 1546, and was no more likely to be an entire secret than the Queen's advocacy of the Reformation had been kept a secret.

The popular version of the risk Catherine ran, and her narrow escape, runs as follows :—Henry, always interested in theology, had not been unwilling to argue with Cathe-rine Parr on the great subject which had attracted him, even as a young man. He had been pleased by her intelligence and acumen, but she had gone too far. She had let him see that she could beat him in controversy, and there were two things which from boyhood he had not been able to bear—the one was, to be contradicted in an assertion; the other, to be defeated in any form. He was said to have especially resented her opposition to Bishop Gardiner, in the royal presence, for his hostility to the translation of the Bible into the vulgar tongue, and its free use. Possibly, the argument was ill-timed, for Henry was confined to his room and in great pain. Any-how, when Catherine quitted the King and the bishop, leaving them together, Henry relieved his ill-humour by saying, ironically, "A good hearing it is, when women become such clerks; and much to my comfort to come in my age to be taught by my wife!"

If Henry said nothing more than this, and had no ulterior meaning in the words provoked by weariness and suffering, the speech, though not complimentary, might pass. But Foxe, the enthusiastic and picturesque old chronicler of the martyrs, declares that Gardiner caught at Henry's words, and proceeded to insinuate accusations of the Queen as deeply tinged with heresy, and so naturally failing in duty and respect to her sovereign; farther, that the King let the bishop speak unrebuked, and was so worked upon by his words, and by Henry's own morose and jealous temper, as to consent that a commission should sit and articles be drawn up. These articles included charges of treasonable heresy against Catherine, her sister, and their particular friends, which placed their lives in danger.

The story goes on to say that the Queen was totally unaware of the plot against her, and might not have learned it till the storm burst, had not the Chancellor, Wriothesley, Gardiner's ally, accidentally dropped the paper containing the charge, to which the King's signature was given, in the gallery at Whitehall.

The paper was picked up by a friendly attendant, who carried it to Queen Catherine. She was struck with amazement, and overwhelmed with terror (in a manner totally unlike her usual quiet, composed demeanour). Retiring to her room, which was next that of the invalid King, she gave way to such sobs and lamentations that Henry sent to ascertain what was the matter. The answer given, by the authority of the physician, was that the Queen was dangerously ill, and that her illness was caused by mental agitation.

Prompted by repentance, returning affection, or suspicion, Henry had himself carried in his chair into the Queen's room, and showed so much pity for her condition, that Catherine declared herself " revived and rejoiced " by his visit. The next evening the Queen was sufficiently recovered to return the King's visit. She was accompanied by her sister, Lady Herbert, while Lady Jane Grey, a little girl of nine, already holding office in Catherine's household, bore the candles before the two ladies.

Henry was courteous and kind, but ominously turned the conversation to the old religious topics on which the couple had been accustomed to dispute. Catherine, taught by experience, and always more politic than heroic, fell back on her weakness as a woman, and deferred to his superior judgment as a man, as her husband, and, as by God's appointment, the head of the Church in England, so that, next to God, she would learn from him.

"Not so, by St. Mary," the King is represented as saying, with strong sarcasm, "Ye are become a doctor, Kate, to instruct us, and not to be instructed of us, as oftentime we have seen."

Then Catherine protested that her meaning had been mistaken; that it was preposterous for a woman to instruct her lord; that she had only wished to draw forth his opinion on nice points of doctrine and practice. She had believed that such discussions helped to pass the time in the confinement of his sick-room, while she profited by his discourse.

"And is it so, sweetheart?" inquired the appeased King. "Then are we perfect friends," and kissed her, in token of reconciliation.

Finally, when the King was able "to take the air," with the Queen and her ladies, in the garden, Lord Wriothesley appeared with forty of the Guard, prepared to make his arrests. But Henry hailed him furiously, with such abusive epithets as those of "beast, fool," &c., &c., forbidding him the royal presence.

Catherine, with her customary mildness, interceded for him, and said his fault might have proceeded from a mistake.

Henry, in his rage and contrition, exclaimed impetuously, "Ah, poor soul! thou little knowest; on my word, sweetheart, he hath been to thee a very knave."

These details are for the most part supplied by Foxe. But we are bound to remember that, however quaint, vivid, and vigorous the narratives of the old writer are, they cannot be quite relied upon as history. He was too much of a partisan—sincere as his partisanship was, and valuable and thrilling as his life-like pictures are—to permit his accounts to be taken as proven facts.

The objections to the tradition urged by Mr. Froude is that it is unvouched for, unalluded to by contemporary authorities as yet discovered,[1] and diluted through Protestant tradition for two generations, till it reached the ears of Foxe. But it is admitted that Gardiner might have brought complaints against the Queen, and that the King, after examining into them, might have eventually rebuked the complainer, and dismissed the complaints.

In Henry's last act of violence Catherine could have had no interest, save that of common humanity and a sympathy with intellectual culture. The victim was the gallant and gifted, but extravagant and profligate, Earl of Surrey. He died partly because he bore Howard blood in his veins, partly because his ambition and recklessness kept pace with the animosity of the Seymours. In vain " he proposed, according to custom, to fight his accuser in his shirt ; " in vain he made " a spirited, strong, and eloquent defence." He had quartered the royal arms with his own, as only the heir to the throne was at liberty to do.

He was supposed to aspire to the hand of the Princess Mary, though for that matter, at the age of twenty-seven, Surrey had already a wife and five children, whom he was prepared to repudiate. His " beautiful songs," his " Petrarchan sonnets," the totally different novelties which he introduced into England in the shape of the heroic blank verse of his translation of a book of the Æneid, and the curious training of dogs to " point " after game, were so many unavailing gifts to keep his memory

[1] Strype seems to infer some foundation for the story.

green.   When the King should have signed the death
warrant, his own end was so near and his hands were so
helpless that he could not write his name, so that a stamp
with the letters " H. R." had to stand for it.   The Duke
of Norfolk, Surrey's father, the hard and pitiless uncle of
Anne Boleyn and Catherine Howard, would have perished
also, but on the night before the morning of his execution
Henry himself was numbered with the dead.   His health
had long been wretched; he had been in a state of fever
for many weeks, but the end was sudden.   He is said to
have received the intimation that his death was to all appearance at hand with the characteristic fiery defiance of
the man; when Sir Anthony Denny courageously interrupted the King's impatient groans and cries of pain with
the verdict the doctors had given, Henry looked sternly
at Denny, and asked what judge had sent him to pass this
sentence upon him?   He directed Cranmer to be sent for,
but was speechless before the Archbishop's arrival, and
was only able to make a motion with his hand when asked
to give a sign of his trust in God and Christ.

There is some support given to the story that Catherine
had been or was in disfavour with the King, by the circumstance that there is no mention made of her towards
the end of his life, and she does not appear to have been
with him in his last moments.   But neither were his son
and daughters present when the King died, at Westminster, towards the close of January, 1547, in his fifty-
sixth year.   His body was taken to Windsor, resting by
the way at Sion House, where Catherine Howard was
imprisoned, and, as it happened, on the day following
that of the fifth anniversary of her execution.   The
King's coffin was deposited in the vault beneath St.
George's Chapel with Jane Seymour's coffin.   There is
nothing to be made out of Henry's will, in relation to the
terms on which he stood with Catherine Parr, at the time
of his death, for though she was greatly disappointed

when she found that she was not appointed regent during the young King's minority, there is a presumption that the main portion of the will was written some time before, on the eve of the King's going to France; in every other respect, save that of the guardianship of Edward, the provision for Catherine was liberal and kind. There is a high testimony paid to her virtues, and to the King's respect for them, and a handsome addition made to her jointure of three thousand pounds a year, [1] with the bequest of such plate, household stuffs, and jewels as she might choose.

Catherine was now a very wealthy widow, in possession of no less than three jointures. Her royal jointure-house was at Chelsea, on the site where Cheyne Pier was destined to stand. Chelsea was then a pleasant village on the Thames, with royal and aristocratic proclivities.

One cannot help wondering whether it was the same house which had been given, among others, to "the daughter of Cleves," and whether the imperturbable Anne, who survived Henry ten, and Catherine herself nine years, was at Chelsea in these eventful spring months—whether there were two queen-consorts of Henry VIII. in the same favoured village at one time; if Anne visited Catherine Parr as she had visited Catherine Howard—for that matter there was now no longer a burly, choleric obstacle between them—and did the renowned discretion of the little Queen Catherine vie with the unassailable philosophy of the large Princess Anne?

Catherine was not more than thirty-five years of age, a very comely and dainty, as well as a splendidly endowed little woman, in her third widowhood, when her former lover, Sir Thomas Seymour, about this time created Lord Seymour of Sudely, and Lord High Admiral, came hurrying to woo her once more.

By Henry's will sixteen executors were named who

---

[1] The value of money was much greater then than now.

were to manage the affairs of the kingdom; to these executors was added a council of twelve, as a council of regency, the old nobility being almost entirely excluded. A proposal was carried by the council that the Earl of Hertford—the head of the Seymours and the uncle of the young King—should be at their head, with the title and authority of Lord Protector. The executors then proceeded to fulfil what were declared to be previous arrangements of King Henry's, in conferring honours on various gentlemen, by which Hertford became Duke of Somerset, and Sir Thomas Seymour, Lord Seymour of Sudely; later he was created Lord Admiral.

Still in the prime of life, and as arrogant as his elder brother was amiable, he at once contemplated putting the finishing touch to his fortunes by making a splendid marriage. Quickly as he had reverted to his old love, she was not the first in his vagrant thoughts, if rumour did not lie. He aspired as high as the young Princess Elizabeth, but was forbidden to think of her by his brother and the rest of the council. Then Seymour cunningly sounded his nephew, the young King, whom he was always seeking to please by flattery and gifts in order to win his affections from his guardian—his elder and much more trustworthy uncle. Probably Seymour had depended on the boy's affection for himself, and on Edward's well-known preference for Elizabeth. He had counted on his youthful adviser's suggesting his favourite sister—the same little child whom Seymour had carried in his arms at Edward's baptism— as a fitting match for the soaring suitor. But the little lad of nine, in his innocence, first mentioned Anne of Cleves, as a proper recipient for his uncle's hand; and then, when the idea was not approved of, he made an amendment upon it, saying to the third person whom Seymour had employed to speak for him, "Nay, nay, I wot you what? I would he married my sister Mary, to change her opinions." Whether he would have changed

them for the better is more than doubtful, if Bishop
Latimer was right in describing the Lord Admiral as
"the farthest from the fear of God of any man he ever
knew." But Seymour himself was well aware that Mary
would have none of him.

It was after these interludes that Lord Seymour sought
the unsuspecting Catherine in her retreat at Chelsea; and
even yet it was so early in the days of her widowhood—
though these were still the times when men who coveted
such prizes had to strike hot and fast, or see them snatched
from them by more daring and unscrupulous assailants—
that a suit which would otherwise have been perfectly
admissible was rendered premature and indecorous, so that
secrecy had to be sought. The wooer came by a private
field-path across a footbridge, and was admitted by a side
postern to his mistress's presence, sometimes as early as
eight o'clock in the morning.

What was the attraction in this man which existed for
so many women? A contemporary praises his high spirit
and his courtliness, his stately person, his magnificent
voice; but, alas! the laudation is signally qualified, for
apropos of the voice, the narrator goes on to admit,
after praising the sound, "but somewhat empty of matter."
Who does not hear the glib sonorous voice of the handsome, hectoring Lord Admiral, "somewhat empty of
matter"?

Yet surely there was something else than a stately
carriage and a magnificent voice, which not only blinded
Catherine Parr to the man's radical defects, but so worked
on the royal young girl Elizabeth, that though she was
too proud ever to receive his suit, when he was free to
urge it—though she was shrewd enough, indeed, to have
a contempt for his blatant folly, still produced in her a
kind of "scornful liking" even for his memory.

Was it not a remnant of open-hearted frankness, a false
glamour of generous recklessness, though it was plainly

said of him that he loved only himself? There are traces of such a temper, however grievously marred, in his protest with regard to Catherine after she was his wife. Neither is there any evidence worth considering that he did not treat her with respect and affection, or that she was not in possession of such love as he had to give, though what he conceived his interest had stood in the way for a time. Certainly the love of a man like Lord Seymour of Sudely was not worth much, save, it might be, in the dazzled eyes of Catherine Parr, who, poor soul! was reported to have "adored him to the last." For the weak spot in her armour was that, with all her native sagacity and acquired culture—nay, with all her religious aspirations—she had a soft heart in her bosom for this strong, mature gallant, manly enough in his way, but no more her equal than was any one of her former mates.

Some of the letters which passed between the two at this date have been preserved, and are sufficiently curious. Hers have all the coyness of a maiden's first love-letters, and a pretty archness, "the arch simplicity" which has been noted in the expression of her face. They are also full of a pathetic devotion and humility in many a sentence besides that in which she signs herself—

"By her that is yours to serve and obey during her life,
"KATERYN, THE QUEEN, K.P."

His letters, while they profess ardent affection, are oppressively deferential in the manner in which he styles her, in every second sentence, "Your Highness."

The confidante of the wooing was Catherine's only sister, Lady Herbert. It is said that Catherine exchanged rings and a promise of marriage with Seymour within five weeks of Henry's death—a haste which was less called for than was haste in the case of the poor young Queen-Dowager of France and Charles Brandon, Duke of Suffolk. Whether the statement of the early promise of marriage is correct or not, it is certain, from Edward VI.'s diary, that the wedding of the couple took place in the month of May, 1547, though it was not publicly announced till the following month of June. Henry had died the previous January, so that about the same interval elapsed between his death and Catherine's fourth and last marriage, as had passed between Lord Latimer's death and his widow's marriage to the King. The feelings of the public were not very delicate in such matters in those days; but though Henry VIII.'s death could hardly be regarded as anything save a deliverance to Catherine Parr, there was just enough perception of outraged propriety to cause a reluctance to proclaim the fact of her precipitate marriage to the Lord Admiral.

But if Catherine could hardly be said to have done more than assume the "hood, and barb, and sweeping pall," which were the widow's weeds of a queen, her weeds for my Lord Latimer, with whom she had dwelt for ten years, were worn for no longer a period.

In broad contradiction to what she had been doing, yet in a frame of mind which is by no means without precedent, Catherine elected this time of all others as the season to write a letter in Latin to her stepson, King Edward, in which she not only enjoins him to continue his practice of religious duties and secular studies, and to answer her letter in the learned language in which she had written, but strives to impress on the boy her grateful love for the memory of his father, King Henry. Edward was a guileless lad, and might not be too much struck by the anomaly; and otherwise he was not ill-disposed to the marriage of his stepmother and his uncle.

The Lord Protector Somerset, on the contrary, highly disapproved of his brother's marriage, and showed his disapproval by depriving Catherine of the jewels bequeathed to her by the late king. The duke did this on

the plea that these were crown jewels, and one can
understand his difficulty, since he was all which his
brother was not—amiable, if weak, honestly religious,
and a lover of his country and his king, whom he
shrank from impoverishing in any part of his inheritance,
above all, when the duke's brother was to profit by the
impoverishment.

The wrangle for these jewels—maintained as fiercely
by Lord Seymour as if his wife had possessed no other
portion—which outlasted what remained of Catherine's
life, must have served to embitter it.   It was also fretted
by the strife between her and the Duchess of Somerset,
in which both brothers were embroiled.   The good duke
was unhappily mated with a haughty, violent-tempered
duchess, who boasted of Plantagenet blood in her veins,
as the descendant of Thomas of Woodstock.   Time had
been when it was this imperious lady's duty to carry
Catherine's train on state occasions; but she was not
slow in showing that she considered the Queen had forfeited her state, and must give place to the wife of the
Lord Protector.   Accordingly the Duchess of Somerset
refused to perform any service for the wife of her husband's younger brother, insisted on walking into a room
before her, and spoke of her slightingly as "Latimer's
widow."

One would think that Catherine was sufficiently wise to
have declined such petty rivalry, and to have held it
lightly.   Perhaps her husband's folly overbore her wisdom;
perhaps she had paid too dearly for her exaltation to give
it up easily; perhaps we all are small in our tenacity with
regard to some trifle.

The young King's faithful affection for his stepmother,
and his preference for his uncle, the Lord Admiral, not
only angered his naturally placable guardian still further,
it especially incensed his guardian's wife.   It also seemed
to awake in the scheming breast of Thomas, Lord Sudely,

the perilous fancy that he and the Queen might manage to supersede the Duke and Duchess of Somerset as Regents of the kingdom. As another hold over Edward, Lord Seymour planned to have the care of Lady Jane Grey, who was looked upon in the light of the destined wife of her cousin Edward, after the treaty for the marriage of the boy with Mary Queen of Scots, on which Henry had set his heart, had fallen through hopelessly.

An additional source of disturbance to Catherine, and to more than Catherine, during that sorely troubled last marriage of hers, was the arrangement by which the Princess Elizabeth, a lively girl of fifteen, had remained under her stepmother's charge, both at Chelsea and at Sudely Castle, Lord Seymour's chief seat, which was situated in one of the midland counties. In those days of greater freedom of manners, with greater laxity of morals, and of tumultuous changes both in political and family relations, the familiar terms on which the members of one household lived were apt to be regarded as dangerous where a man bold, insinuating, and irrepressible like the Lord Admiral, and a high-spirited youthful princess were concerned. Why might not Seymour pretend to the hand of Princess Elizabeth, if his wife should die, or by the method of dissolving marriages which many men found only too practicable? In that case he would be the brother-in-law as well as the uncle of Edward; nay, should Edward and Mary die, why might not the man whose success had already been so great, rise to the dazzling height of king-consort? In reality there is no proof that Lord Seymour, after he had married Catherine, cherished such an unprincipled project during her life. Whatever his faults—and they were many and grave—he seems to have been proud and fond in his way of his queen, who had sacrificed and hazarded much to be his wife. He was wont to say, "No one should speak ill of the Queen; or, if he knew it, he would take his fist to the ears of those who did, from the lowest to the highest." It was reported that she was vexed by his violent temper, as well as worried by his sister-in-law's rivalry; but Catherine had been well accustomed to deal with a passionate spirit. The foolish liberties which he took with the girl-princess were no more than what might have been expected from a man with little reverence and much presumption, and a carriage which in its gallantry was swaggering and rollicking. Catherine was quite cognisant of her husband's behaviour to young Elizabeth, whom her stepmother doubtless looked upon as little better than a child compared to Lord Seymour. For Catherine thoughtlessly encouraged him, as when she helped him to hold and tickle the girl, and on another occasion when the wife grasped the princess's hands till the husband had teasingly cut scores of holes in the princess's cloth gown. Rough play, but only play, though Catherine saw it had gone far enough, when she found the Lord Admiral rudely snatching a kiss from his royal ward. Catherine's discretion, which had slept, awoke, and she forthwith despatched her charge to be under the care of a more decorous and prudent host, receiving, in the room of Elizabeth, little Lady Jane Grey, who was as meek and modest as she was learned and high-minded, and was, besides, the destined bride of the King. That the stepmother and stepdaughter continued, though parted, on the most cordial and intimate terms, is clear from a letter which still survives. It was written by Elizabeth after she had left Sudely. She inquired in it, familiarly and affectionately, for information regarding the Queen's health, and wished she were back in Lady Jane's place.

As the last worry of Catherine's life at this time, she had in her keeping at Sudely the erring and insane wife of her only brother, William Parr, Marquis of Northampton.

It is pleasant to turn to the brighter side of the picture

to find Catherine, the former friend of Anne Ascue, having the Queen's book, which was a formal protest against the errors of the Roman Catholic religion, printed and circulated without fear of the consequences; to see her presiding over her stately and well-ordered household, in which, like Mary, Queen-Dowager of France, Catherine, the widowed queen of Henry VIII., still retaining much of the dignity of royal rank. She continued to have ladies-in-waiting, maids of honour, gentlemen of the chambers, and yeoman of the guard. She had chaplains chosen from the most learned and devout of the Reformers. With their help she instituted divine worship twice a day in the Castle, religious services which its careless, unruly master declined to attend.

At the close of August, 1548, Catherine's first and only child, a daughter, was born. Its birth had been anticipated with the greatest pride and delight both by Catherine and her husband. The nurseries and the staff of attendants provided for the infant were like those furnished for the heir of a kingdom. Some little disappointment was experienced when the child proved to be a girl and not a boy ; yet not even the big bouncing Lord Admiral confessed to any chagrin to speak of, as he wrote boastful, exulting letters, enlarging on the beauty of his little daughter.

In the middle of the rejoicing, Catherine was seized with fever, and died on the eighth day after the birth of her child. Nor was this all, from the testimony afterwards given by her close friend and companion for the greater part of her life—a daughter of Catherine's first husband, Lord Borough, and of course one of her earlier group of stepdaughters, whom on her marriage with Henry she had immediately nominated to the post of a lady-in-waiting. This Lady Tyrwhitt was induced to state that there was much that was sad and painful in the poor Queen's death. Her mind became distempered

and clouded by the nature of her illness, and in her
raving, which was not fully recognised as delirium, she
entertained the gloomiest fancies, and spoke mysterious
words of injuries she had suffered and wrongs she had
undergone.

In an apparently lucid interval, while insisting on the
nearness of her death, of which none of her attendants
saw any sign, she executed a short will.   In this will she
made no mention of the child on whom she had set such
store.   She left her whole worldly goods to her husband,
unconditionally, adding, as a last token of the tender regard in which she held him, that she " wished them to be
a thousand times more in value than they were."   But
even in this final effort of love and struggle for consciousness, the Queen's illness passed into another stage, common enough in such a malady, when the person best
beloved by the sick woman in health became the object of
vehement suspicion and violent dislike.   Catherine wildly
accused her husband of rejoicing at her death and mocking at her anguish, when, even according to the not very
sensible or unprejudicial evidence of Lady Tyrwhitt, given
on her examination before the Council, the doomed man
was standing in distress by his dying wife's bed, striving
in vain to soothe her.

The scene would have been but a piteous result of
illness in ordinary circumstances; it was otherwise where
the life of a queen was in question in troublous times.

In the meantime Catherine was honourably mourned
and buried.   She was not more than thirty-six years of
age—the age so fatal to many of the Tudor princesses
and their immediate descendants.   Elizabeth Woodville,
Mary, Queen-Dowager of France, her daughter, Frances
Brandon—in her turn Duchess of Suffolk—Catherine
Parr, Arabella Stewart — granddaughter of Margaret
Tudor—all died at about thirty-six.[1]   Catherine outlived

---

[1] Anne Boleyn was beheaded at the same age.

King Henry a year and seven months. Lady Jane Grey, still only in her eleventh year, was at Sudely when Catherine died, and led the procession of mourners, "with her train borne up by a gentlewoman." Six ladies walked two and two behind the chief mourner. Many ladies and gentlemen, yeoman of the guard, &c., followed the coffin to the chapel of Sudely Castle, where lessons were read and psalms sung, according to the form of the Reformed Church. Coverdale, the Queen's almoner, delivered an oration and read prayers, and each lady and gentleman, according to their rank, gave an alms to the poor.

Never were royal remains more desecrated than were those of poor Catherine Parr. It was a comparatively small matter for Cromwell and his Ironsides to dismantle the chapel and tomb. Idle curiosity and senseless outrage did their worst more than two hundred years after Catherine's death. A party of ladies, who happened to be in the ruined chapel of Sudely Castle in 1782, had their attention attracted by a block of alabaster. They had the ground opened, when they found the leaden covering of a body. This they had cut apart in two places, and then, frightened at the spectacle of the embalmed body within, had the earth thrown over it again. Fired by their example, the tenant of the land, for the time, also dug up the coffin, which was only two feet under ground, laying bare the inscription—

"K. P.

Here lyeth Queen Katherine,"

&c., &c.

and reopened the coffin, again exposing the body. Two years afterwards, a band of roughs in the neighbourhood, in what appears to have been wanton desecration, a third time invaded the grave, and cast the once dainty body—richly dressed, as in life, to the very shoes on the small feet—on a heap of rubbish. The vicar of the parish interposed, with much cause, and the body was reburied. But even then poor Catherine's dust was not suffered to rest in peace. In 1769 the coffin was again taken up, and its contents examined, this time with all care and respect, by leave of the owner of the castle. It was then, it was said, that the two members of the Antiquarian Society, who made the investigation, found a shoot of ivy had forced its way within the lead, and formed a wreath of living green for the uncrowned head of a good and gifted woman.

Even after that date rabbits burrowed in the chapel, scraped holes, and scudded round the grave. But at last castle and chapel have been fitly restored. All that was left of Catherine's mortal remains were installed with due honour in a vault beneath a tomb copied from the original monument, of which a rare woodcut is still in existence. Her effigy, in white marble, lies under a sculptured canopy.

Besides many locks of fair hair attributed to Queen Catherine Parr, in the late Tudor Exhibition, there was shown a ghastly relic which might have been procured on one of the occasions when her grave was despoiled; it was a discoloured tooth, set in silver, and labelled "a tooth of Queen Catherine Parr's."

Six months after Catherine's death, her husband, Lord Seymour of Sudely, was beheaded on Tower Green, partly on the ground of having poisoned his wife, of which nobody can now doubt his innocence. Even his severest critics acknowledge that, as he had nothing to gain and many solid advantages to lose by her loss, it is utterly improbable that he should have committed the crime. Another point which clears him is that Catherine's nearest relations—her brother, William Parr, Lord Northampton, and her brother-in-law, created Earl of Pembroke—continued, after her death, on excellent terms with the Lord Admiral. The truth was, that he had revived the old scheme of marrying Princess Elizabeth, and was suspected, with more warrant, of having bought over, to support his interests, her governess, Mrs. Ashley, and her cofferer, Parry. So Lord Seymour continued to bluster and intrigue against the most forgiving of brothers, until, on his second committal to the Tower, from which the Duke of Somerset had already saved him once, the very noblemen whom the accused man had trusted gave fatal evidence of his treasonable designs.

On the March morning when Lord Seymour was executed, two letters are said to have been found hidden in his velvet slippers. The writing was scratched with an agate, the addresses were to the Princesses Mary and Elizabeth, and the contents besought the sisters' interposition and protection for the writer.

The attainder and execution of Lord Seymour meant the ruin of the infant daughter whose birth had been hailed with so much triumph. For though the confiscation of the great property which she should have inherited was set aside, her estates were not restored, possibly because she did not live long enough to make the necessary claim for them. She had been named "Mary," probably after the elder princess, and she began life with the state of a princess; but on her father's disgrace she seems to have been handed about from kinsman to friend, and treated as a grudged encumbrance rather than a valued trust. There is a letter extant, written by Catherine Willoughby, Duchess of Suffolk, Catherine Parr's greatest friend, which reflects no credit on the duchess's loyalty and liberality; she complains bitterly of the burden imposed on her by the child and her train, and appeals to the little Mary's uncle, the Duke of Somerset, to grant his niece a pension, or at least to pay her servants' wages. The duchess represents the child's uncle on the mother's side, William Parr, Marquis of Northampton, as equally unable and unwilling to bear the little girl's maintenance. These were the people who sunned themselves in Catherine's

favour while she was Henry's Queen. Sorrow came to
soften the witty duchess's heart, and to teach her more
motherly compassion; for, just as her predecessor Mary's
boy had died of the sweating sickness, on its first appearance in the country, so, when it visited England for the
second time, Catherine Duchess of Suffolk's two sons,
lads of promise at Cambridge, were cut off by the
epidemic within an hour of each other.

Mary Seymour might have been more welcome to her
mother's sister, Anne Countess of Pembroke; but unfortunately Anne died when her niece was only three years
of age.

There are no details to be found of Mary Seymour's
death, beyond the fact that a contemporary writer refers
to her as dying young; while another chronicler states a
little more precisely that she died in her thirteenth year,
which is doubtless correct.

Miss Strickland had a different theory, founded on no
complete documentary evidence, but simply on a tradition
preserved in the family of a Sussex clergyman, supported
by a fragment of their genealogy and a few Tudor relics
in their possession. The written fragment, saved from
other papers which had been burnt, was entitled "A Good
Account of my Pedigree, given me by my Grandmother,"
and was dated 1749. It stated, among other particulars,
that a private gentleman named Silas Johnson, the son of
a Kent squire, married the daughter of Sir Edward Bushel
(supposed to be a gentleman in the household of Queen
Anne), who had married in his turn "the only daughter
of the Duke of Somerset's brother, Lord Seymour, which
daughter the Lord Seymour had by Queen Catherine Parr,
whom he married after the death of Harry the Eighth,
whose queen she was." The above Sir Edward Bushel's
daughter was "a great fortune" to Silas Johnson, and
their daughter, Mary Johnson, married the Rev. Francis
Drayton, of Little Chart, in Kent, where he and his wife

lie buried. The relics of the Tudors preserved in the family of the Sussex clergyman were a fine damask napkin—the pattern and motto corresponding with the arms of Catherine of Arragon, by whom the napkin is supposed to have been brought from Spain—a portrait, on panel, of Henry VIII., and a medallion in bronze of the royal arms of England and France, cut from the centre of a pewter plate." Agnes Strickland's conjecture is that the Duchess of Suffolk might have brought up the orphan, Mary Seymour. When the persecution of the Protestants broke out under Queen Mary, the duchess, knowing herself a marked woman in the Reformed Church, might have thought it well to marry her charge respectably, though not splendidly, before her protectress fled to the Low Countries, accompanied by her second husband, a gentleman of her household named Bertie. With him her adventures were strange and romantic, culminating in the birth of her son, "Peregrine Bertie," in the porch of a church where the distressed lady had taken shelter from a storm.

But though one would like to think that poor Catherine Parr's daughter lived happily and died peacefully in the safe retirement of private life, which her mother had quitted not altogether to her gain, the evidence is too slight and too destitute of corroboration for much dependence to be placed upon it.

MARY TUDOR[1]

A TUDOR BY BIRTH, AND QUEEN IN HER OWN RIGHT

FEW women have been so unhappy and unfortunate from
her girlhood till her death, in middle life, as Mary Tudor,
Queen of England; few have been more misunderstood.
Her kinswoman, Mary Queen of Scots, has been treated as
a royal heroine, whose errors have been largely condoned
for the sake of her beauty, her womanly fascinations, her
struggles against overwhelming odds, her violent death.
Her cousin Mary of England's history is little less mournful
and tragic. Yet for her harsh rule of five years, the result
of her blighted youth, her embittered womanhood, her
warped creed, her evil counsellors, little excuse is ever
made.

Mary Tudor, daughter of Henry VIII. and Catherine of
Arragon, was born in the palace at Greenwich in February,
1515. She is said to have been healthy as a baby, while
she was the only child of Henry and Catherine who outlived infancy. According to the custom of the time, she
was committed to the care of her relative, Margaret
Plantagenet, Countess of Salisbury, the same countess
whose aged head was held by force on the block till the
executioner's axe did its work. Three days after Mary's
birth she was baptized with great pomp, Cardinal Wolsey
being her godfather. She was named after her aunt
Mary, the Queen-Dowager of France, who gave to the child,
on the occasion, a gold pomander. A note to Agnes Strickland's "Queens of England" has supplied us with infor-

---

[1] Agnes Strickland, Froude, King Edward's Journal, Strype, Machin.

QUEEN MARY I.

mation as to the nature of this exploded ornament. A
pomander was a perforated ball, into which a ball of paste
composed of perfumes was introduced. The pomander
might either be worn at the girdle or carried in the hand.
Although the sex of the child was a disappointment to
both parents, there was no lack of fondness for her on the
part of her father, any more than of her mother, in her
babyhood. She was frequently visited by them, and she
was presented with apparent pride to magnates of the
court and to foreign ambassadors—a process which caused
some trouble when the little princess had a separate
establishment kept up for her, with Dame Margaret Bryan
as "lady mistress," under the control of the Countess of
Salisbury. This establishment was generally quartered
at Ditton Park, so that Princess Mary had to be rowed
across the Thames when her royal parents were at Windsor, and she was a feature in the day's pageants.

At the early age of four the small maiden held something like a court at Richmond, during the absence of the
King and Queen at the Field of the Cloth of Gold, was
visited by the Privy Council, and received foreign visitors
of distinction. It was on this occasion that she is said to
have accomplished the marvel of playing on the virginal
for the company's entertainment—a feat nearly equalling
that of another infant phenomenon, who " solved a problem
in Euclid, they tell me, before she could speak." The
gentleman who witnessed the performance might well
style it "a pleasant *pastime*."

There is other evidence, rather more convincing, as to
Mary's early taste for music, which was duly cultivated in
the course of her carefully conducted education. She played
on the harpsichord when a very little child, according to
the testimony of an Italian writer of the day, and she had
"a light touch, with much grace and velocity." At the age
of nine Mary is said to have been a very attractive child,
still rosy, having the dark eyes and hair which were not

found in her Spanish mother. She was, as yet, petted
and made much of. She was loaded with birthday
presents. She had a set of small actors brought down
from London to act a child's play for her gratification,
and the performance was conducted by the old English
dramatist, Heywood. That Mary should stand godmother,
at the age of five years, to the first of the crowd of her
god-children and name-children sounds less objectionable
than the fact—though that, too, had many illustrious precedents—that at the age of six the tiny princess should be
formally betrothed to a grave young man of twenty-three,
the great Emperor Charles V. of Germany, who came over
to England to visit his aunt, Queen Catherine, and to
secure the hand of this small cousin. Moreover, the same
young man had been betrothed in his youth to another
Mary Tudor, little Mary's aunt and namesake, and it was
during his stay in England at this time that he became
personally acquainted with the first Mary, in the noon of
her gracious beauty and sweetness, and of her happiness
as a wife and mother, when it was said he betrayed sundry
tokens of regret for what he had lost. Another and not
less striking picture in its way is Charles's introduction to
the second Mary, whom her stately mother led by the
hand to the hall-door of the palace to greet her royal suitor,
as he landed with King Henry from the barge at the
water-stairs. Mary, whose memory was tenacious, was
not likely to forget that meeting, or the signing of the
marriage treaty at Windsor. She knew that it was the
dearest wish of her mother's heart that she—the child—
should be Empress of Germany and Queen of Spain, and
young as the promised bride was, she never forgot the
claim to the proud title. Reserved, morose, self-absorbed,
Charles was not a man calculated to win a child's heart;
but he was her cousin the Emperor, and Mary was soon to
be as grave and self-absorbed, if less sagacious and subtle
than he.

It is hard to imagine how history would have unravelled itself if Charles had got his wish that his betrothed bride (whom he pledged himself to marry when she was in her twelfth year), should be sent to Spain and educated there. Mary and her mother were destined to rue sorely the refusal given to this proposal. We shall see how, in other circumstances, it was the dream of Mary's forlorn girlhood to escape from her father's jealous supervision, and flee from the England which she had come to regard as the land of her enemies and oppressors, in order to take refuge with her mother's kindred. In the meantime adversity was still unthought of when, as a child of eight, she was an intelligent, industrious pupil, reading Latin not only with her mother —who piqued herself on her classical attainments, even when she omitted to make herself mistress of the speech of the country of which she was queen—but also with her learned tutors, Linacre and Featherstone. From a Spanish authority on education Queen Catherine received hints for her daughter's training which she sedulously followed. These hints forbade all French and Spanish romances, and inculcated the study of the Old and New Testament, the works of the Fathers, selections from the classics, &c. The one fiction exempted from the general condemnation was the story of "Griselda." Rich dress was tabooed, as well as the recreations of cards, dice, &c.

When Mary was ten years of age, all hopes of her marriage to the Emperor were frustrated by his private betrothal and subsequent marriage to Isabel of Portugal. It is said that when the little Princess was made aware of the faithlessness of her mighty cousin, to whom she had sent, not long before, an emerald ring as a token, the small proud face was observed to grow pale with mortification.

Henry, who was already cherishing the intention of dissolving his marriage with Catherine—an intention which had reached the Emperor's ears—chose to make a

great parade of his recognition of Mary as heir-apparent
to his throne.   He sent her with a large establishment,
presided over by Lady Salisbury, to keep house at Ludlow
Castle.   One would have thought that this selection of a
residence for "the Princess of Wales," as Mary was sometimes called, was ill-omened, and that the associations with
Ludlow (still remote and inaccessible, not far from the
frontiers of the foreign principality of Wales) must have
been especially distasteful to Queen Catherine.   It was
there she had gone, with such difficulty in making the
journey into the wilds, a girl-bride accompanied by her
boy bridegroom, Arthur Prince of Wales.   There the boy
and girl lived together just long enough to discover how
ill-suited they were to each other; and there that other
sickly heir of England died.   But there is no sign that
Catherine made any remonstrance against her daughter's
destination; there is no trace of apprehension on the
mother's part, unless in her particular desire that Mary
should take regular exercise in gardens, and other "sweet
and wholesome places;" that she should occupy herself,
without too much fatigue, in practising her music, and
studying Latin and French; that she should dance when
dancing was in season, and that she should have proper
food, "served with comfortable, joyous, and merry communication, in all honourable and virtuous manner."

Mary resided at Ludlow Castle for eighteen months,
well away from the growing division between the King
and Queen.

Henry's preoccupation with his own affairs did not prevent him from making energetic efforts to settle Mary
in marriage.   For this purpose he employed the good
offices of the match-making widow, Louise of Savoy, to
induce her son Francis I. to give up the marriage, planned
when he was in captivity, to the generous and romantic
Leanora of Austria, Queen-Dowager of Portugal, and sister
of Charles V.   Failing the suggested alliance with Francis,

old enough to be Mary's father, which was a mere attempt to retaliate on the Emperor for his broken troth, there was some talk of a marriage between Mary and Francis's second son, Henry of Orleans, afterwards Henry II. of France, grandson of Louise of Savoy. But this proposal also came to nothing, partly in consequence of the progress which Henry was making in the divorce of Catherine, that must end in depriving Mary of her birthright.

Mary seems to have returned to court when she was in her twelfth year—the same year in which the Emperor's heir, Philip II. of Spain, was born. From this time, during the short remnant of her mother's reign, Mary took part in the court galas, not only dancing in the slow and fast dances, but playing in the masques. She appeared thus with five ladies and six gentlemen, all disguised in what was supposed to be Icelandic costume, and "danced lustily" before the French ambassadors.

As a dark side to these gaieties, Mary was now old enough to be acquainted with the proceedings for the disowning and setting aside of the mother whom she loved and honoured. In the girl's loyalty to her mother, and in the recognition that her own rights, which Mary's precocious womanliness would soon see, even without the assistance of others, were being tampered with, she took part with her mother, and made no concealment of her opposition to her father's designs—an innocent partisanship which Henry, with his hot, despotic temper, resented beyond measure. There were a few spasmodic intervals of relenting, and of brief revivals of their earlier relations, such as marked his last intercourse with Queen Catherine; but these soon passed away, and there remained hardly a vestige of Henry's pride in his child, and fondness for her. These honest affections were replaced only too speedily and surely by jealous suspicion and wrathful dislike.

One more prospect of marriage for the young Princess, whose fortunes were still trembling in the balance, is said to have been entertained, not by her father, but by her mother. The future bridegroom was no longer a great foreign emperor, but a simple English gentleman, albeit of princely descent, and a staunch supporter of the old Catholic Church. He was afterwards known as the plotting Cardinal Pole, who, from his palace in Rome, cost his English kindred dear. He was still neither priest nor cardinal. He was an able, accomplished, handsome young man of five and twenty years of age, a son of Mary's governess, the Countess of Salisbury, through her a descendant of the Plantagenets, and a cousin of the Tudors. Between her eleventh and her sixteenth years Mary saw a good deal of Reginald Pole—enough to grow warmly attached to him, as she was to the other members of Lord Salisbury's family.

But whatever might have been Catherine's wishes with the view of keeping her daughter in England, and contracting a marriage for her which would be popular with a large proportion of the people, Reginald Pole took no active step for the fulfilment of the scheme. Indeed, he announced that his destination was the Church, and withdrew from the court to a Carthusian monastery. Soon afterwards he gave Henry mortal offence by refusing to support him in his plea for a divorce from the Queen.

In 1531 Mary was separated entirely from her mother, and committed to the sole charge of Lady Salisbury, at Beaulieu, otherwise New Hall. Thenceforth Catherine was not permitted to set her longing eyes on her sole surviving child, who was just passing from girlhood to womanhood. The separation was a matter of State policy. The mother and daughter together would have been the rallying-point of all the Catholics in England; nevertheless, the act caused a cruel and unnatural breach of family relations.

When Elizabeth was born, Mary, as being nearly allied to the throne, was summoned to Greenwich. Her behaviour on the occasion was very much what might have been expected from a high-spirited girl indignant at her mother's wrongs. Her independent, disapproving bearing was not calculated to recommend her to Queen Anne—as high-spirited as her stepdaughter. Mary distinctly declined to comply with the order, even though it was issued by her father, to give the infant the style of princess. To have done so would have been to consent to the decree which declared that Queen Catherine's marriage was illegal. Mary said she would call the child "sister," but nothing more. Her determination may have accelerated the delivery of the sentence about to be pronounced. Henry had already declared the baby Elizabeth his heiress, and no sooner had Mary returned to Beaulieu than she received the decree of the Privy Council that she was to resign the dignity and state of a princess, and withdraw, in the character of a private gentlewoman, to Hunsdon. Hertford Castle had been the first place fixed upon, but in the end Hunsdon was preferred. There a royal establishment had been formed for the child Elizabeth, and Mary was to occupy an inferior place in the same house.

Mary replied to the message from the Council, delivered to her by her chamberlain, with great intrepidity for a princess not nearly out of her teens. She marvelled at his undertaking to "minish" her state and dignity without a commission signed by the King, or without letters from the King. She wrote both to the Lords in Council and to the King her father, bravely asserting her right, refusing to set it aside by her own act, and dauntlessly signing herself "Mary, Princess."

One is tempted to think that a loophole of escape from an awkward predicament presented itself to the blustering King at this time, when Mary's hand was sought in marriage by her cousin, James V. of Scotland, son of Margaret Tudor. But his suit was dismissed as untenable. Mary was compelled to repair to Hunsdon, and to submit to what was to her the humiliation of hearing herself addressed as "The Lady Mary." She saw her suite reduced to one or two domestics, while all the royal honours with which she had been surrounded from her birth were transferred to Elizabeth. By a kind of refinement of persecution, supposed to be due to the vindictive malice of Anne Boleyn, Mary's very ladies, among them her "lady mistress," Dame Margaret Bryan (a good woman, friendly to both sisters), after they had been dismissed by royal authority from Mary's service, were appointed to offices in the little Elizabeth's household. Such treatment was well calculated to arouse strong resentment, and awaken a rancorous grudge in the mind of the injured person; but there is no proof that Mary visited the deprivations she suffered on the unconscious infant to whom she was made to feel herself in all respects inferior and subservient. On the contrary, the girl is said to have been fond of the child whom she was willing to call sister. Mary, in her honesty and fearlessness, was still able to be magnanimous.

There is a curious and rather comical difference of opinion between two chroniclers of Mary's in order to account for a considerable item in her expenses at this date. No less than £25—a larger sum then than now— was claimed and granted annually in addition to the money already allowed for the maintenance of the household of Princess Elizabeth. This £25 was expressly stated to have been spent on meat breakfasts and suppers for the Lady Mary. On this assertion Mr. Froude appears to have founded his opinion that Mary, in spite, or probably because of, her ill-health, ate largely of meat—in fact, was "a voracious eater."

Miss Strickland, in standing up for the honour of her sex and of one of her princesses, took a different view, not without some ground also, of the cause of this undeniably large charge, and of the reason assigned for it. She reminded her readers of the chines of beef and the measures of ale dealt out for the breakfasts of the maids-of-honour in Henry's reign. She pointed to the circumstance that these substantial diets of food were to revert to the ladies' men and maid-servants, and to their dogs. Therefore she drew the deduction that Mary's meat breakfasts and dinners sufficed in turn for her waiting-women and serving-men—such domestics as she was not forbidden to keep, like any other gentlewoman, though she was deprived of the ladies and gentlemen-in-waiting of a princess. Nevertheless, Mr. Froude held to the conviction that Mary "ate like a man."

Miss Strickland might be right. Mary may have been unjustly accused of a gigantic, what may be classed as a truculent, appetite for a woman; at the same time it sounds strange that special meals of fresh meat instead of stock-fish should have been procured, largely for the ordinary domestics of a lady who was to be treated as a private gentlewoman. May not something have been implied as to the coarser practice of her predecessor, when Elizabeth's courtiers dwelt so emphatically on her delicate and dainty habits and her extreme moderation with regard to animal food?

Mary had few visitors at Hunsdon, and these were narrowly watched. She was not permitted to write letters or to receive them without supervision and reservation; but she was by no means without resources to cause the slowly dragging hours to pass more quickly. She was a good musician and a good embroideress. She could speak no less than four languages—English, Latin, French, and Spanish. She could read Italian, and had some acquaintance with Greek. Mary was not only one of the learned women of her generation, she was decidedly intellectual. In person she had not yet lost all the bloom and grace of youth. She was short, with a tendency to squareness both in figure and face, like her mother. She had one of

the large foreheads so plentiful among her contemporaries ;
in Mary's case it was beetle-browed. Her childish rosi-
ness had long ago faded, and the pale face, which was not
without a delicate colour at times, was rapidly growing
sallow, but it was not yet pinched or haggard. Her hair,
unlike her mother's, was dark, as one fancies the hair of a
girl of Spanish descent likely to be ; but it was frequently
superseded by a golden-red wig, representing the original
colour of Henry's hair, which was a fashionable colour,
and one worn by the courtiers in compliment to the King.
Those fine firm lips of Mary's had not become bloodless or
fallen into the straight hard lines which are considered
to betoken a bigoted and implacable temper. The eyes,
which have been described as " pale, cold, and relentless,"
were in reality beautiful dark-brown eyes, in keeping with
the dark hair. They went far to redeem the defects of
Mary's face while she was still young. These defects were
intensified by the flight of time, the ravages of disease,
fatal mistakes, and miserable failures, until Mary's personal attractions, like her virtues, have been wholly forgotten. The eyes, though short-sighted, were bright
and steady, and absolutely pathetic in their quick, keen
appeals.

Mary's voice was singularly deep for a woman's voice,
and what was deep in youth grew gruff in later years.

Queen Catherine and her daughter were parted for the
six years that the Queen survived the separation. During
these years Mary never wavered in her duty and devotion
to her mother, whom, in spite of the girl's eager entreaty,
she was not suffered to visit even at the last. But the
death of Queen Catherine in 1536, however great the grief
to Mary, wrought a beneficial change in her fortunes. The
bone of contention, if one may so speak, between father
and daughter was removed. The chief obstacle to her
submitting to be set aside, and to the renouncing of her
claims, no longer existed. For Mary, with all her des-

perate adherence to what she considered just and right, and her tenacity in not giving up a single point of conscience—as it seemed to her, never showed any great regard for her own interest and advantage, which she frequently imperilled by her rigid adherence to a principle, and her determination to take her own way in what she was persuaded was the path of duty and religion.

The downfall of Anne Boleyn was a still more powerful means of reinstating Mary to some extent in her father's favour, for Anne's child, Elizabeth, shared in her mother's disgrace. Catherine of Arragon seems always to have inculcated on Mary the obligation of deferring to her father and king, in every case except where her conscience and her religion forbade her. The Emperor, her chief friend and ally, gave her the same advice. The new Queen, Jane Seymour, had known Mary as a child and as a young girl, and had a great affection for her. Above all, there was no longer a rival queen to whom Mary was bound by every natural tie. She made overtures to mollifying her father and regaining his regard both through the minister Cromwell and through the Queen her stepmother. Finally, on receiving permission, she addressed Henry himself. Her appeals to him were couched in the humblest, most respectful language. She begged to be forgiven for her offences: she refrained from signing herself "Princess." She even put her hand to the resignation of her birthright, and accepted the designation and position of the Lady Mary, as if reckless of her rights, now that Queen Catherine was no longer alive to be injured and wounded by their repudiation; and as if weary of the vain altercation in which she was so ill-matched with the King and his Council, she signed herself, in addressing the king, his "humble and obedient servant, daughter, and bondswoman, Mary."

Henry was not easily propitiated. Mary had to copy letters dictated to her by Cromwell, conveying her im-

plicit submission to the King, her father. She was in no
cheerful mood when she went through the task because
of the pain in her head, and the teeth which troubled her
"so sore," that she had "but small rest day and night."
She had to receive a visit from Queen Jane's brother,
Edward, Lord Beauchamp, the Lord Chamberlain, to
accept from him a gift of a riding-horse, and to furnish
him with a list of the clothes she needed for her proper
appearance at court, as a substitute for the mourning
which she still wore for her mother.   Perhaps, in spite of
her submission, she hinted how much the suggestion went
against the grain with her, when she wrote in reply that
the King's highness's favour was such good clothing unto
her that she desired no more, and so she had written to
his Grace, resting wholly on him, and willing to wear
whatever his Grace should appoint her.

At the critical moment Mary demurred at signing away
her right to the throne; but an angry, well-nigh savage
letter from Cromwell, who had supported her hitherto,
overcame her reluctance.   Her household was then re-
established, still at Hunsdon, and still in the same house
with her young sister, who was now in her turn deprived
of the title of princess.   In the letters which Mary wrote
on the subject there is a great deal to her credit.   She
shows herself not only sensible and straightforward, but
well-nigh scornful, as far as she dared, of this bandying
about, and giving and withholding of the title of princess.
She is faithful in her wish to have her former servants
reinstated in their offices—above all, in her consideration
for her mother's old servants.   She is more than kind
in saying a word to the King in disinterested praise of
Anne Boleyn's motherless little daughter.   Long afterwards Mary persisted in still applying the term "her
Grace" to Elizabeth.

Mary kept house jointly with her sister for several
years.   The elder sister led a quiet, and what may have

been a pleasant life, according to the rules laid down for her. She read the Bible for herself, and she read the daily service with her chaplain, studied, worked at her embroidery, and cultivated her musical talent. Her playing on the lute, the harpsichord, and the virginal was highly praised by competent judges.

From the time she was twenty-one Mary was again permitted to appear at court. Henry treated her with courtesy, if with no great renewal of affection. Her friend Queen Jane supported her in all respects. The girl-princess's bearing was sufficient in itself to disarm censure. The one error which the record of her privy purse expenses shows is gambling. Wise and studious as she was, she did not escape the prevailing passion. Her losses at cards were considerable for her sex and years; so were the losses from the wagers she laid, chiefly in connection with the game of bowls, which she played with other ladies on the smooth sward of the bowling-greens. But the same trustworthy record also testifies to her generosity in the gifts she made, from her not too ample funds, to her relations and friends, and in her charity to the poor, especially to poor prisoners.

A singular item in Mary's expenses is charges incurred for "Jane the Fool," including food for her horse, a payment for the shaving of her head, a penny for needles for her. This female jester, a counterpart of "Will Somers," the male jester, seems to have been an appendage of Mary's.

Just as Catherine of Arragon was fond of monkeys, and Anne Boleyn of dogs, so Mary had a great liking for birds. She also took pleasure in importing and naturalising foreign plants, particularly plants from Spain, the country to which she always turned with wistful longing. Gentle tastes these, one would think.

Mary resided frequently at court, whether the King kept it at Richmond, Greenwich, or Hampton. At other times she stayed in the country, Beaulieu, or New Hall, in Essex, being her favourite among the manor houses assigned to her. Though her conduct was closely watched, for political reasons, in her domestic affairs she was practically her own mistress, and she behaved with such unaffected dignity and discretion that the voice of scandal was never raised against her. She was at Hampton Court when her brother Edward was born. She occupied the most prominent place along with Cranmer at his christening, and she had an equally prominent place at the sad ceremonies of Queen Jane's lying-in-state and funeral, which so soon followed the rejoicings at the birth of the son and heir. At the lying-in-state, Mary, as chief mourner, in deep black, with a white handkerchief tied like a hood over her head, knelt at the head of the coffin. At the funeral she followed on horseback the car with the body, in the procession from Hampton Court to Windsor. On either side of her rode Lord Montague and Lord Clifford. Behind them were her cousins of royal descent, and many noble ladies and gentlemen. On the melancholy journey Mary gave alms, and in St. George's Chapel the following day she commanded masses to be said, at her expense, for the soul of her dead stepmother, and distributed gifts like a right royal lady. Her health, always ailing, was affected by the great fatigue and exposure. She caught cold, and had to have a tooth drawn—a small homely touch, which brings near to us an irksome detail of the pomp of mourning.

Besides her constant association with her sister Elizabeth, Mary was very punctual and affectionate in her visits to the baby brother, the acknowledged successor to King Henry. She stayed over Christmas with her father, sharing his season of mourning. When he married Anne of Cleves, Mary was on good terms with the new stepmother, while she had nothing to do with her dismissal. But the learned and virtuous daughter of the

King made no protest against her fourth stepmother, the ignorant, vicious, young Catherine Howard.

Mary had affectionate intimacies with her cousins, especially with Lady Margaret Douglas, the daughter of Margaret of Scotland, and Lord Angus. Among the members of Mary's household, Miss Strickland tells us, was another kinswoman, Lady Elizabeth Fitzgerald— "The Fair Geraldine" of Surrey. Mary was present at Lady Elizabeth's second marriage, as the widowed Lady Clinton, to Sir Anthony Browne, when Ridley preached a sermon. A humbler *protégée* was the daughter of Margaret Roper, and grand-daughter of Sir Thomas More, with her husband.

In 1537 severe trials awaited the twenty-two years' old Mary. Her kindred, the Poles, were ruined. The eldest brother, Lord Montague, who had ridden with her at Queen Jane's funeral, and his cousin, Lord Exeter, were beheaded on a charge of high treason, while Lady Salisbury and Lady Exeter were thrown into the Tower, with their property under sentence of attainder. Mary was so far implicated in the charge that her income was only doled out to her in small sums, and she was allowed no separate establishment.

In 1538 occurred the outbreak of the Roman Catholics in the north of England, called the Pilgrimage of Grace. In all such *émeutes* Mary's name was freely made use of by the insurgents. The occasions were seasons of peril to her, when she was torn different ways, between the loyalty which she certainly cherished to her father, and her sympathy with the faith and aims of the rebels.

At intervals suitors for Mary's hand presented themselves, irrespective of creeds—Catholic and Reformed— with reference only to the pleasure of the King and the Council, though there was always a formal mention of Mary as having something to say in the matter. She displayed neither interest nor preference where the gentlemen were concerned, declared that she wished to lead a single life, but agreed to submit herself to the King's decision. In at least one case she had a personal interview with the wooer. This was in 1539, when Mary was twenty-four years of age, and Cromwell brought a stranger to Enfield, where she was staying, for the purpose of introducing him to her. This stranger was Philip, the Turk-fighting Duke of Bavaria, who was then in England to negotiate the marriage between Henry and Anne of Cleves, and apparently to take some steps towards bringing about his own marriage. The pair conversed together in German by means of an interpreter, and in Latin without assistance. The duke declared his satisfaction with the lady, but no great progress was made in the wooing; indeed, Mary was so dangerously ill at Blackfriars soon afterwards that she seemed nearer death than marriage. On the dissolution of Henry's marriage with Anne of Cleves, Mary was required by her father to send back to the duke the diamond cross which he had given to her in token of their engagement.

In spite of this summary dismissal, Duke Philip, who was a younger brother, but a gallant and renowned soldier, asked Mary's hand in marriage again, several years afterwards, and when his offer was a second time refused he remained a bachelor.

1540 was the date of another of Mary's violent illnesses. About the same time there was so much political strife throughout the country, that for greater precaution —because her name would be a tower of strength to the Roman Catholic party if they could get possession of her person—her establishment was broken up, and she was placed in the care of one or other of the great noblemen whom the King could trust. She had to endure the anguish—so great to one of her earnest, constant nature —of hearing of the violent deaths, under circumstances of peculiar horror, of her mother's old chaplain Abell, her own old tutor Featherstone, and her kinswoman and life-long friend, the venerable Countess of Salisbury. What could the effect of such cruel, barbarous tidings be, save to turn a wholesome heart to gall, and harden to stone an honest and affectionate, if never very soft or womanly nature?

There is no sign of Mary's attendance at court during the ill-fated reign of Catherine Howard. On her downfall, when she was taken to Sion, Mary, who had been staying there with her cousin, Lady Margaret Douglas, and the widowed Duchess of Richmond, left to make room for the prisoner.

In 1542 a matrimonial project, repeatedly broached for Mary, was once more brought forward. It was the alliance with Henry of Orleans, second son of Francis I. The preliminaries were entered upon, but were relinquished on the question of dowry, the French king asking a much larger sum than Henry and his Council were disposed to grant. No indefatigable historian has been able to make clear what were the feelings of the princes and princesses whose hands were thus bargained for, who were kept in intolerable suspense during the lengthened transactions.

Miss Strickland gives suggestive lists of Christmas and New Year's gifts made to Mary in various years. These lists supply a picture, in miniature, of the customs and fashions of the time. One will suffice.

"The Princess Elizabeth sent a little chain, and a pair of hose made of silk and gold."

"The Lady Margaret Douglas, a gown of carnation satin of the Venice fashion."

"Lady Calthorp, two pairs of gloves, whereof one pair was worked with silver and the other with gold and parchment lace."

"Three Venetians sent the princess a fair steel glass."

"My young lady of Norfolk, two pairs of worked sleeves, with a dozen handkerchiefs and a steel glass."

"Lady Anne Gray presented two artificial flowers. . ."

"Lady Kildare, . . . a comb-case set with pearls."

One of the presents Mary liked best to receive was a clock in some form. She had a hereditary taste for clocks.[1]

The Princess returned the gifts in kind. In the old February play of valentine-dealing the gentleman who drew the princess for his valentine had a special gift from her. Sir Anthony Browne, on an occasion of the kind, got from Mary "a brooch set with four rock rubies round an agate, enamelled black, with the story of Abraham."

Gloves, especially Spanish gloves, richly embroidered and perfumed, and partlets, or collars with ruffs, figured among the gifts the ladies exchanged; so did "worked smocks."

More interesting, as indicating Mary's tastes, are such entries as:—

"A little spanial," from Bexly, a yeoman of the King's chamber.

"A couple of little fair hounds," from Sir Bryan Tuke.

"A bird in a cage," from a woman in London.

Mary had also a white lark—the donor unknown. The bird was kept for her by the woodman of Hampton Court.

Henry's marriage, in 1544, to the cultured and kindly Catherine Parr—Mary's contemporary—was a happy event for the Princess. But when she was accompanying the King and his new queen on a summer progress, she was seized with one of the illnesses which so often attacked her, and had to be carried in a litter to Ampthill, one of her mother's temporary residences after her

[1] The presents sometimes consisted of eatables, such as orange or quince pies, even cockles and oysters.

downfall. Various members of the Princess's household were also sick, and she incurred so much expense on their account and her own that she had to sell "a pair of gilt silver pots and a jar of Budge" to pay her debts, while she was farther helped by a timely gift of forty pounds from her stepmother.

Perhaps Mary's happiest days at court, after her early youth was past, were spent under Catherine Parr's *régime*. In spite of the difference in their creeds, the two, nearly of an age, had many points in common. The relations between stepmother and stepdaughter were always friendly. In Catherine Parr's circle there were many intellectual women whose society must have been agreeable to Mary. Her cousins, the Greys, especially little Lady Jane, of whom her kinswoman was very fond, Jane Seymour (the niece of Queen Jane), and her sisters, the Countess of Bedford, Anne Lady Herbert (Catherine Parr's sister), Katherine Duchess of Suffolk (brought up by Mary's aunt, the Queen-Dowager of France), were all more or less scholarly or witty women.

Mary's weak health, her slenderly supplied purse, and her mental superiority, did not keep her from appearing in great splendour at a State ball given in honour of a Spanish grandee, on whom, as representing her mother's kindred, she was desirous of producing a good impression. She wore a kirtle of cloth-of-gold, an open robe of three-piled violet velvet, and a coronal or wreath of large precious stones. The stranger reported favourably of her person and manners to her cousin the Emperor, the betrothed lover of her childhood, and dwelt on her popularity, which at this date was great.

About the time of the King's last marriage he presented his elder daughter with a large gift of jewels (surmised to have been her mother's). With Mary's natural generosity she shared these jewels with her cousins. There is evidence of the transaction in their names in her handwriting, set familiarly before the articles in the inventory:—"Given to my cousin Jane Grey," "to my cousin Frances," or "Eleanor," or "Marget."

At the Queen's instigation Mary translated Erasmus's paraphrase of St. John from the Latin. It was published under the editorship of Udall, and the superintendence of Mallet.

We do not hear of Mary any more than of Catherine Parr at Henry's death-bed in 1546, when she was thirty-one years of age. His last will re-established his daughter in her position as princess, and devised to her £10,000 as a marriage portion if she married with the consent of the Council of Regency, and £3000 a year if she continued unmarried, the £3000 being the rents of the manors of Beaulieu, Hunsdon, and Kenning Hall already assigned to her.

With the Lord Protector Somerset and his duchess Mary began by being on excellent terms. There is still in existence a letter from the Princess to the imperious duchess, who claimed descent from Thomas of Woodstock, and thought little of vexing the soul of her sister-in-law, Catherine Parr. Mary addressed the duchess as "My good gossip," and "My good Nann," and signs herself "your loving friend, during my life, Mary."

The strong Protestantism of Somerset had not yet waxed aggressive. For that matter, he gave Mary liberty to "keep her sacrificing knaves about her."

The blustering Lord High Admiral, Somerset's brother, chose to ask Mary's sanction to his marriage with her stepmother after the marriage had taken place at least a couple of months. Mary, who was not hoodwinked, answered the request for her approval somewhat coldly, as any daughter would where the hasty nuptials of her father's widow were in question. But there was no quarrel or intermission of intercourse, since Lord Seymour of Sudeley was in communication with Mary, and even paid her a visit after his wife's death.

With her young sister Elizabeth, a half womanly girl of fourteen, and her little brother King Edward, not yet ten, low of stature, grey-eyed, with a pleasant delicate face, Princess Mary was at this time on quite happy terms. Edward had been in the habit of consulting her on his lessons, and of sending her his Latin exercises, as he sent them to Catherine Parr. But Mary was not present at his coronation, where only men figured. The boy King describes it with quaint detail in his journal; how he sat at the feast, with the crown on his head, and the Archbishop of Canterbury and the Lord Protector for his companions were at the King's table, while the lords sat at boards in the hall beneath; how the Lord Marshal's deputy had to ride about the hall to make room; and when Sir John Dymock, the King's champion, challenged all disputers of his claim, the little King drank to him, and Sir John had the cup.

Elizabeth, in writing to her sister at this date, when condoling with her on one of her many illnesses, and thanking her for her "oft sending," adds in pretty phrase : "Yet I have more occasion to thank you for your oft gentle writing, and you may well see by my writing so oft how pleasant it is to me."

Very soon Mary ceased to appear at her brother's court, in spite of the boy's vexation at her withdrawal. She had got into difficulties with the Protector and the Council on account of the celebration of mass in her chapels after it had been forbidden throughout the country by the Act of Uniformity. There is no doubt that Edward shared in the objections of his Government. Young as he was, he had as tender a conscience as Mary had in religious matters. And he was not only an extreme Protestant; he had, by anticipation, a dash of stern Puritanism in his faith.

In the middle of these disputes Mary's health was as unsatisfactory as ever; indeed, in the autumn of 1549 she was so ill as to prepare herself for death. The usual con-

valescence followed, and in the following year there were
more suitors seeking her hand, among them the Duke of
Brunswick and the Prince of Portugal.   To Don Louis,
Mary, warned by what had occurred with regard to her
religion, was distinctly favourable, but the prospect of the
marriage, after the fashion of so many similar prospects,
faded away like the mirage of the desert.

More than once it had been rumoured—not without
cause—that Mary would seek to make her escape to her
mother's powerful kindred. The project had been discussed
on Catherine of Arragon's death, when her daughter was
a very young woman, but had been relinquished from the
dread of Henry's vengeance. It was renewed now, fifteen
years later, by the help of the Regent of the Low
Countries. The Flemish Admiral Skipperus lay off the
coast of Essex, to which Mary was to ride, under cover
of darkness, from her house at New Hall. She was to
be taken on board the Admiral's ship, and conveyed to
Antwerp.

The whisper of this step filled the Council with consternation, since it was believed to be the signal of war at home
and abroad, when the Catholics in England would have
all the better chance because of the division of forces and
distraction of aims which would follow. It is impossible
to tell how the measure was viewed by Mary, weak in
health, yet dauntless in spirit—whether she welcomed it
as the promised realisation of her girlish dreams, the flight
from the relentless persecution of bitter foes to the warm
welcome of ardent friends and fellow-Catholics; the chance
of becoming acquainted at last with the sunny southern
land which was her mother's country, of which she had
heard the glories, after which she had always longed and
pined. Had she not sought wistfully, in a forlorn hope to
get to know it better, to introduce, and cultivate in the
gardens of her manor-houses, the fruits and plants which
Catherine of Arragon had missed most on her first

residence in England? Or did Mary shrink from kindling the blazing torch of domestic and foreign war? Did she cling to that England, which, however inhospitable at times, was her birthplace, her father's country, in which she had a multitude of friends, both small and great? She was English, not Spanish, after all; and she was capable of a proud and passionate patriotism.

There is reference made to Sir John Yates' having been sent into Essex "to stop the going away of the Lady Mary," in "King Edward's Journal." What a curious record *that* is of a marvellous boy—for marvellous he was in spite of the injury done to his memory by the extravagant, fulsome encomiums pronounced upon him by some of his contemporaries. He was a conscientious, precocious lad, a born student, an embryo philosopher, an earnest Christian, though his Christianity was of a somewhat narrow and harsh type. He bestowed an amount of intelligent thought on the condition of his country, and the remedies for its evils, almost incredible in a boy, even after he had entered the earlier teens which formed the limit of his short life. His journal, which was clearly intended as a brief abstract record of public events in England, the sister kingdom of Scotland, and the Continent, has not a scrap of private and personal feeling in it. The few references to "the Lady Mary" are all as to a political offender, who might have been an utter stranger to him. Yet apart from the breach between them on religious questions, they had always been on affectionate terms. Withal there is a dash of boyishness in the relish with which he gives the details of active warfare in Scotland, and the satisfaction with which he allows himself, tinged with austerity as he was, to pause and dwell a little on the tiltings and "pretty conceits" which were the accompaniments of certain court marriages and splendid banquets.

There is a *naïve* dignity in the manner in which he

writes of himself as "Me" with a capital M—"The ambassadors were at court, where they saw Me." . . . "Dined with Me," &c. The boyishness and the innocent self-importance are balanced by the grave, simple precision with which the writer states that the wool-winders were to take an oath to make good cloth, and records when and where the light horsemen and men-at-arms were to be paid their wages.

In 1551, Mary, who had for some time stayed away from court, and even absolutely declined to repair to it, was forced to alter her resolution ; circulars were sent out by the Council, accusing her of correspondence with the foreign powers then threatening to invade England, and calling upon her to present herself and answer to the charge. She obeyed the summons to appear before the King and Council. She was no longer a rash, inexperienced girl, but a tried women of thirty-five years of age. Her coming was regarded as an event of such importance by the citizens of London, that they believed it was foreshadowed and attended by supernatural signs and tokens. The earth shook, the gossips said ; armed men were seen in the air, three suns at once appeared in the sky. A friendly crowd thronged the streets to see Mary ride into London. She was the central figure in a great retinue of nobles and dames, the gentlemen and ladies alike wearing, along with the gold chains over their velvet mantles and robes, chains of black beads in token of their sympathy with Mary's opinions. Miss Strickland explains the display as black rosaries at the wearers' girdles. But Machin, the old London citizen, who must have been familiar enough with rosaries, makes the manifestation more conspicuous and peculiar.

Mary rested for two days at her house of St. John's—her town house, supposed to have been a house of the Knights Hospitallers, of which Henry had taken possession after their dispersion. She then went in state through

Fleet Street and the Strand to Whitehall, "amidst the blessings of tens of thousands of the people."

The Princess alighted at the palace and was conducted to the King her brother, the boy in his fourteenth year. The two—the worn, faded woman, and the delicate, prematurely thoughtful lad, walked side by side to the Council Chamber. Mary was bidden remember the Act of Uniformity in the practice of religion, and told that the celebration of mass in her chapels, which had been permitted so long in hope of her reconciliation to the Reformed religion, was to be suffered no longer.

Mary, "whose will had never yielded to that of man (unless of her father)" was fearless as ever before the august assembly. She said her soul was God's; she would not change her faith, nor would she dissemble her opinions with contrary doings.

She was further told that it was not her faith but her practice which was in question. She was not a king to rule, but a servant to obey the laws: her example might cause inconvenience.

But "consistent to her plea that laws made in a minority were no laws," she would neither admit their argument nor flinch from her resolution. It may well be said of her, that "what she believed and did, she believed and did thoroughly. She was an honest woman standing up for the right, as she saw it; determined, downright, fearless."

The very day after Mary's appearance before the Council, the Emperor's ambassador announced that if Mary were farther molested in the exercise of her religion he would quit the country, which would be equivalent to a declaration of war.

The Council, in perturbation, were forced to make a compromise, and "wink" at the celebration of the mass for Mary's benefit, a concession which is said to have brought tears to the eyes of the zealous, upright young King, though the culprit was his sister.

Mary was condemned to see the ultra-Protestant party in the Government use their power in retaliating on the Roman Catholics the injuries the Protestants had received. Bishop Gardiner and other churchmen lost their sees and benefices. Mary's chaplain, Dr. Hopton, was summoned to London, in stress of weather and in sickness, to answer for his contumaciousness.

The contention between the Princess and the Council, on the ground of her having mass said—not with closed doors—continued to smoulder, and to break out in alarming outbursts at intervals. Three gentlemen of her household were commissioned by the Council to carry a communication from them to Mary, then residing at Copt Hall, Essex. The messengers were enjoined to tell her that mass was forbidden, and their errand was neither an easy nor a pleasant one. The account of the interview is very graphic. The Lady Mary was "marvellously offended," and forbade the gentlemen to speak to her chaplains. She threatened to dismiss the unlucky gentlemen from her service, and remarked scornfully that she was not likely to obey those persons who were accustomed to obey her implicitly. She declared that she would leave the country. Her passion was so violent that the messengers feared the effects of it on "her heart complaint." They made one more attempt to discuss the matter with her, but her anger was worse than before.

After this indignity Mary wrote to her brother, and complained bitterly of the manner in which she had been treated. She implored Edward to suffer her to obey her conscience. "Rather than offend God and my conscience," she wrote, in her strong, terse way, when her spirit was roused, "I offer my body at your will, and death shall be more welcome than life."

Naturally, the members of Mary's household, who had

been selected by the Council for their purpose, respectfully refused to be employed on a like service a second time, and were detained in London in consequence of their refusal. When special commissioners from the Council, including the Lord Chancellor, became their own messengers to Mary, and delivered to her a letter from her brother as their credentials, she received the letter kneeling, and kissed it, because of the writer, she said, not because of the contents, which did not proceed from him. She warned her opponents that though she was sickly she would not die willingly; but if she did die, she would first protest openly that the Council had killed her. She knelt again, and gave to the Lord Chancellor a ring, which he was to carry to the King, with the words that she would die his true servant and sister, obeying him in everything, except in matters of religion.

When the commissioners left, Mary sent after them, asking them to speak a word to her at the window. They offered to return, but she would not allow it. They stood in the court while she spoke to them.

The circumstance and the figures are singularly characteristic; the great officers of State and courtiers, at a disadvantage, baffled by a woman, feeling awkward and embarrassed, knowing that they should doff their hats, but not knowing what else to do; the Princess, who always knew her mind, with her heavy brows and her sallow face, out of which the brown eyes looked straight and steadfast, and her man's voice telling what was in her mind, without ceremony or equivocation. She desired the return of the comptroller of her household, one of the messengers detained in London. She said that since his departure she had had to take the accounts of her expenses and "learn how many loaves of bread be made from a bushel of wheat; and, I wis," she continued, "my father and my mother never brought me up with baking and brewing." She was

weary of the office, and required the return of her officer.[1]
Mary ended her speech by praying God to send the commissioners well to do, in their souls and bodies too—for
some of them had but weak bodies—a pious and benevolent
wish, but not untinged with sarcasm.   The remark might
be "unaffected and straightforward," like the action of
speaking from the window, and like the woman herself,
but it was also blunt to harshness.   If there was a certain
womanly sympathy in the allusion to the weak bodies of
some of the company, it was a kindness which had a
caustic side.

In 1549–50 the downfall and execution of the Lord
Protector on the usual charges of seditious treason followed closely on the execution of his brother the Lord
High Admiral.   King Edward's special guardian was the
second of the uncles whom the royal lad knew to have
perished miserably.   He recorded the event with apparent
stoicism, just as he made similar entries in his journal.   But
evidence has been adduced from other sources to show
that he was kept in a constant whirl of occupation and
excitement to distract his mind from dwelling on the fate
of his kinsmen.   So far as Mary was concerned the position was not improved, for the place of the naturally
amiable and well-intentioned Somerset was taken by the
unscrupulous, unprincipled Dudley, Duke of Northumberland, already plotting madly for the aggrandisement of
his family.

In the spring of 1552 King Edward suffered from small-
pox and measles in succession — a fatal strain on his
always fragile constitution.   Symptoms of consumption
showed themselves, and already eager speculation and
wily schemes abounded in relation to his successor.

Mary, who seems to have been really attached to her

---

[1] In spite of Mary's remonstrance on this occasion it is plain, from what
are left of her household accounts, that she took a practical interest in
them, and was quite capable of managing them efficiently.

brother, visited him more than once. She came up to London from Essex in the month of June for the purpose. As was her wont, she broke the journey by staying a night at her house of St. John's. The next day she rode, with her suite—which was observed on this and subsequent occasions to be growing in size and splendour, and to be graced by the flower of the English nobility and gentry—to the Tower Wharf. There she embarked in her barge, and was rowed down to Greenwich, returning in the same style in the evening.

In the following month of July Lady Jane Grey, then sixteen years of age, visited her cousin, the Princess Mary, at her seat of New Hall. It was not the first visit that Lady Jane had paid to her cousin, but on former occasions she had been accompanied by her mother, the Duchess of Suffolk, or by other members of her family. This visit the sweetest and noblest of the Greys and Tudors paid alone, save for her retinue, and it was the last time she came. She had hitherto been a pet young kinswoman of Mary's, but, if Foxe's anecdote contains any foundation of truth, an incident took place during the girl's stay at New Hall which caused an estrangement between the former friends. Lady Wharton, a lady of Mary's household, in passing through the chapel at New Hall with Lady Jane Grey, curtsied to the Host on the altar.

Lady Jane asked innocently, or with intention, if the Lady Mary was present.

Lady Wharton said "No."

"Why then do you curtsey?" inquired Lady Jane.

"I curtsey to Him that made me," replied the Roman Catholic lady.

"Nay, but did not the baker make him?" retorted the Protestant Lady Jane, speaking with more girlish zeal and aptness in controversy than with either courtesy or discretion under the circumstances. The story goes on to tell that Lady Wharton repeated the conversation to the mistress of the house, who was seriously hurt and outraged.

In the autumn of 1552 Mary, when at Hunsdon, received a visit from the bishop of the diocese—Ridley. She had once before met him, and heard him preach at the marriage of the widowed Lady Clinton (Surrey's Geraldine). She received him courteously, and entertained him at dinner; but when he proposed to preach before her a second time, she told him roundly, with flushing cheeks, that the parish church was open to him, but that neither she nor any of her household would be present.

The young King, whose birth had been hailed with so much pride and joy, whom his formidable father had so loved, on whose fair head, wise before its time, so many hopes hung, was pining away beyond remedy. Mary visited him again at the New Year, 1553, and never had her *cortège* presented such a gathering of the highest in the land. Among them were such great ladies as Mary's cousin-germain, Frances Brandon, Duchess of Suffolk (Lady Jane Grey's mother), the Duchess of Northumberland, the Marchioness of Northampton (Catherine Parr's sister-in-law), &c.

In the month of May, Mary was living quietly at her country seat of New Hall, having been cunningly misinformed as to the state of her brother's health. She was assured that it had changed for the better. In the same month, through the audacious machinations of the Duke of Northumberland, and the weak folly of the Duke of Suffolk (formerly the Marquis of Dorset, who had married the daughter and obtained the title of his deceased father-in-law, Charles Brandon, Duke of Suffolk), the destined bride of the dying King, Lady Jane Grey, was wedded with great splendour to one of the Duke of Northumberland's sons, Lord Guildford Dudley. At the same time and place (Durham House, in the Strand), Lady Jane's younger sister, Lady Catherine Grey, a girl of fifteen, was wedded to the heir of an ally of the Duke of Northumberland, the Earl of Pembroke, the brother-in-law of Catherine Parr.

King Edward grew worse and worse. The doctors could do nothing for him, and as a forlorn hope he was entrusted to the care of a nameless woman, of whom all that was known was that she had undertaken the King's cure. Urged by Northumberland's craft, pitted against the earnest remonstrances of Cranmer, which were made in vain, Edward, weary in body and mind, and played upon through his passionate Protestantism, made a will breaking his father King Henry's settlement of the crown. He deprived, so far as he could, both of his sisters of their rights, and bequeathed the kingdom to his cousin, Lady Jane Grey.

Strange and unexpected symptoms not present in lung disease showed themselves in the King's illness. Edward's hair and nails fell off, and the joints of his fingers gave way. Sinister rumours arose and spread that he was being poisoned ; that Northumberland, having gained his object by the King's will, was tired of waiting for the end, and was hastening it by unlawful means. To appease the excited crowds collected round the palace of Greenwich, the poor lad was held up so that he could be seen through one of the windows; but so wan was his face that the spectators declared they had been mocked by the spectacle of a corpse.

Apprehensions were entertained that attempts would be made on the life of Mary. She was advised by her friends to keep away from the neighbourhood of London, and she followed their advice. Had Mary perished then by assassination, or had she died before her brother in one of the illnesses which so often prostrated her, she would have been widely and deeply lamented as a virtuous and learned lady, who might have been a noble queen, and left a glorious name behind her. Till the date of her accession, when she was in her thirty-eighth year, she had led, humanly speaking, a blameless and honourable life, "while her mother's misfortunes and her own sufferings had endeared her to the mass of the people of all ranks and creeds." Alas! for the stability of human favour, and still more for the stability of mortal merit!

Agnes Strickland quotes the private papers of the Throckmorton family in evidence that a plot was laid for the purpose of getting Mary into the hands of Northumberland. According to the Throckmorton papers, a letter was written to her, purporting to be at her brother's request, begging her to come to him at Greenwich. It was further said she had actually set out for Greenwich when she was intercepted by a messenger from the Throckmortons. One of the family was in the household of the Duke of Northumberland, and had become acquainted with his scheme. He informed his father, who warned Mary in time to retrace her steps. The tale is probable enough, but there is not sufficient extraneous testimony to bear it out.

On July 17, 1553, a violent storm broke over London, and to the panic-stricken eyes of the citizens it seemed that the hail which fell was as red as blood. At nine of the summer evening (the night being the anniversary of the death of Sir Thomas More—a coincidence well noted by the Roman Catholics), young Edward, who was not yet seventeen, breathed his last. The same night, through the dewy dusk, a courtier galloped to Hunsdon to bid Mary mount and fly, while the roads were still open, to Framlingham, in Suffolk, where she would be in the midst of her friends the Howards.

Mary fled first to her own seat of Kenning Hall, in Suffolk. She did not flee too soon or too fast, for Sir Robert Dudley, son of the Duke of Northumberland, whose name was destined to be so closely linked with that of Mary's sister, was on the track, and arrived at

Hunsdon for the purpose of detaining its mistress not many hours after she had left the house. She rode the first part of the night as far as Sawston Hall, in Cambridgeshire, the seat of a gentleman named Huddleston, and passed the remainder of the night there. According to tradition, she heard the following morning that the Protestants of Cambridge were in arms against her, so that she had to start afresh, in the guise of a market-woman, riding on a pillion behind her host, or a kinsman of her host, who was disguised as a serving-man. From the rising ground of the Gogmagog Hills Mary is said to have looked back and seen Sawston Hall in flames, kindled by the Cambridge insurgents. "Let it blaze," she said, as if it had been a bonfire lit to celebrate her accession. "I will build Huddleston a better"—and she kept her word.

From Kenning Hall, as unfit to stand a siege, she went on twenty miles farther to Framlingham. The town and stately castle were built on a wooded hillside, and the girdle of three moats rendered the place strong enough for Mary's purpose. On the road between Kenning Hall and Framlingham she was overtaken by the Dudleys—a critical moment in her history and theirs. But as the leaders dashed forwards to attack the Queen's little party the Dudleys' men turned upon them, declared themselves on Mary's side, and forced Sir Robert and his followers to "save themselves by the speed of their horses." Arrived at the castle, the royal standard was unfurled, and royal state was maintained.

Already Mary was showing that she had "a man's promptness in action"—that, as in the case of all the Tudors, "the time to see her at the best advantage was in the season of greatest danger." She did not wait to receive the counsel of her great kinsman and ally the Emperor; if she had waited we are told she would have been lost. For, unable as he was to render her, at the moment, any active assistance, his advice, when it came, was that she should tarry till the decision of the Council and the will of the people were made known. Mary and the few friends who were with her judged differently, and, as it turned out, more correctly. She at once claimed her right, addressing the Council as their Queen, commanding her proclamation; and without delaying till she had their reply, causing herself to be proclaimed where she was, and, through her friends, in all parts of the country.

At Framlingham the Howards, Mordaunts, Whartons, &c., immediately gathered round the Queen, coming in bands of horse and foot under their respective leaders, sons of noblemen, and representatives of the country gentry forming an ample means of defence. In the meantime, away in London was occurring the tragic little farce of the Twelfth-day Queen, in which Mary's cousin, little Lady Jane, acted a half unconscious, half heroic part. Northumberland had the girl of seventeen taken to Sion House, where she was told of the death of King Edward. While she was still thinking only of mourning tenderly for her young cousin and former playmate—who, if he had lived, and all things had gone well, might have been her husband instead of Guildford Dudley—she was informed that he had made her his heir, and bequeathed to her the crown. In incredulous amazement she sat and saw her father-in-law, Northumberland, and her sister's father-in-law Pembroke, with other mature men of mark in the Council, proceed to pay her homage, and hail her as their sovereign. She cried that she was unfit and unworthy, and then, in a revulsion of feeling, prayed to God to give her strength and wisdom to reign, if it were His will. She went in a State barge to the Tower, and was received there in silence. She was proclaimed at the Cross in Cheapside, and also at Paul's Cross, and in Fleet Street, still amidst the ominous silence of the mass of the London citizens.

On the other hand, all England was rallying round Mary. Lord Sussex declared for her, Lord Derby, with twenty thousand men at his back (it was said), did the same. Sir Peter Carew proclaimed her in Devonshire. The fraction of the nobility who had asserted the claim of "Queen Jane," in terror at the changed aspect of things, and at the overwhelming number of Mary's partisans, tried to make terms for themselves by hastily recanting, and giving in their adherence to their lawful sovereign. Pembroke, whose eldest son had married Lady Catherine Grey, as next in order of succession to the throne (a match which the imperious and wily nobleman would fain have unmade), was one of the first to turn his coat and proclaim Mary at the Cross in Cheap, where the whole air reverberated with shouts of "God save the Queen" from tens of thousands of throats.

Northumberland himself, the arch-conspirator in the plot for making his daughter-in-law queen, shared the panic, and proclaimed Mary in Cambridgeshire.

Suffolk, poor Lady Jane's father, rushed into her room in the Tower, tore down the canopy erected over her seat, and told her she was no longer queen. She said she was gladder to hear of her deposition than she had been to hear of her exaltation, and asked, in good faith, if she might not now go home!

The rapid renunciation of their pretensions saved some, but not all of the conspirators; Pembroke, amongst others, escaped the penalty; but Northumberland, Suffolk, and the most innocent traitor of all, Lady Jane, with her husband, Lord Guildford Dudley, were arrested, sent to the Tower, where they had recently played so different a part, and detained there as prisoners.

Mary was Queen of England, and without doubt her first thoughts were thoughts of mercy, and of sorrowful recollection of the young brother for whom she had never had time to mourn. She opened the prison doors within her reach. She would have announced a general amnesty had it not been for the remonstrances of her advisers—especially of Renard, the Emperor's ambassador. She dismissed with scorn the idea of making a child, like "her cousin Jane Grey," answerable for the deeds done in her name.

Mary insisted, against cautious warnings, that she would have a requiem and dirge said and sung for Edward, in order that her young brother might not "be buried like a dog"—that is, without the rites of the Roman Catholic Church, on which she set such store. It is agreed that in the first days of her reign her mind was more occupied with what she viewed as the last mark of regard and respect for the boy Edward than with her own brilliant prospects.

Mary's progress to London was a triumphal one, and as soon as she approached the capital she showed that she came in peace by dismissing the army which had accompanied her, with the exception of a bodyguard. At Wanstead, one of her seats, she was met by her cousin, Frances Brandon, imploring mercy for her husband, the Duke of Suffolk, sick in the Tower. She so worked on the Queen's pity that she granted his release after only three days' imprisonment. Probably the duchess did not dare to plead for the still more guiltless victim, her daughter, whose train the mother had borne during Lady Jane's brief experience of royalty.

At Wanstead Mary was joined by her sister, Princess Elizabeth, who came attended by two thousand horse and a suite of ladies. The Queen greeted the Princess and her ladies very graciously, raising each as she knelt, and kissing her. Elizabeth asked if the Queen desired her to wear mourning for their brother. The reply was, that Mary desired to see no mourning anywhere on so auspicious an occasion. It was a queenly and magnanimous speech.

Mary and Elizabeth rode into the City side by side.

They entered it by the port of Aldgate, hung with streamers in honour of the event. A thousand gentlemen in velvet doublets and mantles rode before the sisters; behind them came the City Guard, to which Mary entrusted herself. The streets were lined by the different trades with their banners. The Lord Mayor and his aldermen were in waiting to welcome the Queen. The whole scene was joyous and splendid, as if inaugurating a happy and prosperous reign. Mary was then in her thirty-ninth, Elizabeth in her twenty-first year. Elizabeth was a handsome young woman in full possession of the Tudors' fair, florid, stately style of beauty, and her majesty of feature and carriage were, even in youth, remarkable. Yet Mary, long past any delicate bloom which had ever been hers—short, thin, sallow, with symptoms of dropsy already perceptible—by sheer native dignity, and by dint of the frank, dauntless honesty which had hitherto distinguished her, was able to stand the comparison between the two. More than one spectator that day remarked on the Queen's attractions, even in such company, as more than mediocre. The flush of pride and satisfaction rounded and warmed her pinched brunette face, and lit up her brown eyes with a positive charm.

At the gate of the Tower, which was Mary's destination, a strange, pathetic spectacle was provided for her. Kneeling on the green were the State prisoners, old and young, men and women. Some of them she had known well in other circumstances in former days: all of them craved her mercy. The head of the Howards, the old Duke of Norfolk, the hard, pitiless uncle of the two miserable queens—Anne Boleyn and Catherine Howard—who had been under sentence of death when King Henry died in time to save him, was under sentence of death still. Another petitioner was the arrogant descendant of Thomas of Woodstock, the widow of the Lord Protector Somerset, who had squabbled for precedence with Catherine Parr,

whom Mary had addressed as her "gossip," her "good
Nan." A third was Edward Courtenay, Earl of Devon.
He had entered the Tower on the execution of his father,
the Marquis of Exeter, and the attainder of his mother,
Lady Exeter, when Courtenay was a wondering boy of
ten. He was now, after the lapse of fifteen years, an
exceedingly handsome, and of all things, considering his
gloomy surroundings, a frivolous, hare-brained young man
of five-and twenty. Two bishops were among the number
of petitioners—Durham and Winchester.

The tears ran down Mary's cheeks at the sight. "Ye
are my prisoners," she said, kissing each old friend, and
giving each liberty. She did more; she restored to them
such forfeited estates and dignities as she could reclaim
and bestow afresh. She made Gardiner her Chancellor,
and gave Lady Exeter the appointment of one of the
ladies of the Queen's bedchamber.

During Mary's stay at the Tower the funeral of Edward
VI. was celebrated in Westminster Abbey with Protestant
rites—in accordance with a compromise to which the
Queen consented reluctantly. Cranmer, Archbishop of
Canterbury, in one of his last official appearances, conducted the service. At the same time Mary, who had
persistently regarded her brother as a boy whose creed
was imposed upon him, had the requiem dirge and mass,
which she had promised herself she should procure for
him, sung and said in the Tower chapel. Mary, with her
household, was present at the service, but Princess Elizabeth was conspicuous by her absence.

The early days of Mary's reign began at once to be
troubled by the contending factions in Church and State.
A devoted daughter of her Church, she not only took steps
to assure the Pope's messenger of her unshaken allegiance; she followed these up by injudiciously bold and
illiberal efforts to bring back the country to the old faith.
She reinstated the deposed bishops, in the process igno-

miniously ousting their Protestant successors. She had mass restored at once, though some of the priests who celebrated it wore steel under their cassocks as a necessary precaution. She went on to forbid the Bible's being in the hands of the laity, to refuse to acknowledge married priests, and to prohibit preaching unless the preacher held a licence from her. At the same time she made no concealment of her rooted aversion to assuming the title and authority of the head of the English Church, a position which, in her eyes, could only belong to the Pope of Rome.

Yet in her private life Mary showed no disinclination to have Protestants about her person, neither did she begin by pursuing any means, save that of argument, to convince them that they were in error. When they remained unconvinced, she did not, at that date, withdraw from them her trust, or assail them with persecution. Among the ladies whom she appointed to be her maids of honour were her old friends the daughters of the Protector Somerset, brought up in ultra-Protestantism. Among the ladies of her bedchamber were two daughters of Sir Anthony Coke, the one the wife of Cecil, the other the wife of Nicholas Bacon, the father of Francis Bacon. These ladies were as distinguished for their intellectual attainments as for their Reformed principles. The only Roman Catholic lady, apart from Mary herself, who could compete with these learned maidens and dames was the bedchamber woman, Mrs. Basset, daughter of Margaret Roper, the translator of Eusebius. Lady Jane Seymour had been specially educated after the fashion of her cousin, the young king, with the hope that she, and not Lady Jane Grey, might become his queen. But the boy had preferred the cousin, who, through her grandmother, the Queen-Dowager of France, was, like himself, a Tudor.

One of Mary's gentleman pensioners was a Worcestershire squire of the name of Underhill, who, from his

fervent espousal of the Reformed cause, had received the
nickname of "the hot Gospeller." He was the author of
a satirical ballad against the Roman Catholics, which he
might have written to sing to the lute, on which he was an
expert. Underhill, who has left behind him a graphic
narrative of his times, was had up before the Council, and
was thrown into Newgate. But he was not only, with
Mary's consent, released presently, he was reinstated in
his office.

Mary was more vexed by her sister's attitude towards
the priests than by that of any meaner person. But even
here, where the discord between the sisters had its first
manifestation, Mary commenced by trying friendly remonstrances. In a formal interview which the sisters had
on the subject, in one of the galleries of Whitehall, with a
half-door closed between them—for Mary no longer refused, as at first, to sit down to a banquet which was not
graced by Elizabeth's presence, or insisted on leading her
by the hand to the seat of honour next herself—Elizabeth
temporised. She said that she simply worshipped as she
had been taught, and declared that she was willing to
receive instruction on the subject. Then Mary was quickly
appeased, and was eager to send her sister learned Roman
Catholic priests to be her instructors. With something of
the ordinary tendency of an elder woman to regard a girl
very much her junior as a child still in understanding and
wilfulness—(a tremendous fallacy in the case of Elizabeth,
who had a man's strength of mind combined with a
woman's subtlety of nature)—Mary sought to coax her
sister with timely gifts of jewelled rosaries, such as coquettish beauty might like to wear, as well as to convince her
by the disputations of masterly controversialists.

So little was there of natural cruelty in Mary's temper,
that though urged by her confidential advisers, especially
by the Emperor's ambassador, to show a necessary example
in punishing the recent conspirators, it was only with diffi-

culty that she could be brought to sign the warrant for the execution of Northumberland and two gentlemen of inferior rank, his aiders and abettors in treason; while his loud profession of Roman Catholicism on the scaffold did not procure for him a respite from the Roman Catholic Queen.

All the time Mary was seeking to spare her opponents, and was also, in defiance of the Emperor's advice, striving with a high hand to overturn the established religion of the country, her shrewdness and common-sense—of which she had no lack—told her how insecure was her hold of her kingdom; how alarming her danger; how strong the foes menacing her. Renard insinuated endless doubts and suspicions of Elizabeth above all, and pointed out that the Princess might at any moment, especially if she married Courtenay, the great-grandson of Edward IV., supersede her sister in the favour of the Protestant masses, and by them be elevated to the throne.

Mary was so conscious of the difficulties in which her religion involved her, that though she was loyal to it to the heart's core, and though she warmly welcomed the appointment of her old friend and kinsman, Reginald Pole, as the Pope's legate in England, she saw herself constrained to oppose the open announcement of the fact, and to urge that Pole might not be sent to England in this or in any other capacity, till the country was prepared for him. Mary was not happy in the trouble and perplexity which crowded upon her. With the restlessness of a harassed woman whose temperament was nervous and highly strung, she was eager to quit the Tower, where she felt herself controlled and overborne on all sides, and to repair to the palace at Richmond, where she might be more her own mistress. It is the greater credit to her, that she and her Chancellor, Gardiner, spent many hours at this time in projecting together what was the one redeeming feature of her administration. She agreed to discharge the debts of Edward's reign; she set about reforming many abuses; she prepared to practise many economies in order to fill a penniless exchequer; she determined to repeal many unrighteous and oppressive Acts of Parliament, and to see that justice was dispensed in a free and fair manner. In all this Mary acted like a true Queen; not Elizabeth herself ever showed greater concern for the welfare of her subjects. Would that this laudable spirit had been maintained throughout her reign.

In the uncertainty of her position Mary ardently desired her coronation. Money had been borrowed from the citizens of London for the purpose; but the Lords of the Council still delayed, on one plea and another, really with the intention of so altering the coronation oath that Mary, the most truthful of women, should be made to swear to an obligation to protect the freedom of conscience, and therefore the freedom in religious belief, of her subjects. When Mary could endure the delay no longer, at the last meeting of the Council to consider the necessary steps she appealed passionately to the members, and, flinging herself on her knees, besought them—Gardiner especially—to oppose her no farther by deferring the rite. The voluntary abasement of their high-spirited Queen extorted from the Council an unwilling consent to the measure.

Mary's coronation took place on the 1st of October 1553, not quite three months from the date of Edward VI.'s death. The ceremony, which was conducted with great splendour, was preceded by the almost equally dignified progress of the Queen and her court to the Tower. A procession of five hundred noblemen and gentlemen, including the foreign ambassadors, led the way. Mary came in a litter drawn by six white horses. She wore a blue velvet gown furred with ermine, and on her head a caul or skull-cap of gold network—so "beset" with pearls and precious stones, "that she was fain to bear up her head with her hand" because of the weight it carried. That weary, aching head, to be so gorgeously burdened! Princess Elizabeth, and worthy, phlegmatic Anne of Cleves, for a foil, were in an open chariot next the Queen, and wore robes and kirtles of cloth-of-silver. Mary's pony, led by her Master of the Horse, chariots with the maids of honour and the women of the household, seventy ladies in crimson velvet on horseback, made a fine sight for the City, which had furnished means for the show.

Not to be outdone, London supplied its own pageants to grace the occasion, and entertain its distinguished guests. Four great giants making speeches in Fenchurch Street; an angel blowing a trumpet in Gracechurch Street; conduits running wine on Cornhill and in Cheap; the Queen's old player, Heywood, who had marshalled his puppets to amuse her when she was a child, greeting her under a vine at St. Paul's School; Peter the Dutchman skipping on the weathercock of St. Paul's.

On the coronation morning, the Queen and her train went in barges to Westminster. She wore her crimson Parliament robes, and walked under a canopy borne by the barons of the Cinque Ports, the Bishop of Durham on her right hand, the Earl of Shrewsbury on her left, the Duchess of Norfolk bearing the Queen's train. Behind Mary walked Princess Elizabeth and Anne of Cleves, as the ladies next her in rank. Eleven bishops, headed by the Queen's friend, Stephen Gardiner, were ready to consecrate her, but no archbishop was forthcoming. Thomas Cranmer, Archbishop of Canterbury, and his fellow-Archbishop of York, were already prisoners under charges of treason and heresy.

Mary was the first queen in her own right crowned in England since Saxon times, and there was some difficulty, in the absence of precedent, so to arrange the ceremonial that it might suit a female sovereign. There was nothing specially Roman Catholic in the rites—when it comes to that, they had been framed for Roman Catholics. Mary took the precaution of having fresh "holy oil" brought from Arras, whose bishop blessed it, in case what was in use in England had been polluted by passing through the hands of heretical bishops and archbishops; but except in this instance, in having mass said, and in prostrating herself twice before the high altar, Mary's coronation did not differ greatly from other coronations. Her robes were twice changed, her final dress being purple velvet—surcoat, mantle, and train "furred with miniver and powdered ermine." As in the case of the boy king, her brother, she wore a crown at the coronation feast—the third or fourth crown with which she was crowned that day. The old Duke of Norfolk played the part of Earl Marshal, ushering in the first course of the banquet and clearing the centre of the hall on horseback; Sir Edward Dymock, the hereditary champion of the sovereigns of England, threw down the gauntlet as usual, in defiance of all the opponents to Mary's claim. Elizabeth and Anne of Cleves sat on the Queen's left hand, and had special services appointed for them.

Four days after the coronation Mary opened Parliament in person for the first time. The Queen and her lords rode, all dressed in scarlet, with trumpets sounding before them. Their first destination was Westminster Abbey, where mass was celebrated, and the harmony of. the assembly was disturbed by two of the bishops—the Bishop of Lincoln and the Bishop of Hereford—who refused to kneel at mass, being turned out of the Abbey.

One of the first acts of this Parliament was to annul the Act which in the reign of Henry VIII. had declared Henry's marriage with Catherine of Arragon illegal. Another act was the attainder of Lady Jane Grey and her husband; but though Lady Jane pleaded guilty, and was sentenced to death, there was no thought then that the sentence would ever be put into execution, and that the young girl would really suffer. Even when the offence was recent Mary had indignantly scorned the idea of making Lady Jane the scapegoat.

Almost simultaneously with Mary's accession the question of her marriage was started—that question which had been so often raised when she was a princess, and so often suffered to fall to the ground. It was much more vital now to herself and to her friends and foes. It became at once a source of heart-burning between them. Mary was not averse to marriage; as a younger woman she may have coquetted with such proposals, and professed herself either utterly indifferent, or inclined to lead a single life; but as a queen she did not propose, as Elizabeth did a few years later, to live and die a virgin queen. She did say on occasions, touching her coronation ring as she spoke, that her first marriage was to her people, and that she would never be unfaithful to that vow; but she did not profess to be determined against a second marriage. In the middle of the strife of faction, Mary, with all her self-reliance, was keenly conscious that she stood alone in her greatness; she wished the support which a husband could give her. The question was, whom should she marry? The desire of the nation was that she should marry an Englishman; but her pride rebelled at a union with a subject; and if a subject were chosen, only two recommended themselves strongly to the public. The one was Courtenay, Earl of Devon, whose misfortunes and romantic history appealed to the popular imagination. In addition he was the lineal descendant of the Plantagenets. But it is a mistake to hold that Mary ever hesitated in her rejection of Courtenay. He was an arrogant, dissipated, foolish, and fickle lad, without even the personal courage which distinguished Mary. His whole character was antipathetic to hers. His mother, Gertrude, Marchioness of Exeter, was one of

the ladies of the Queen's bed-chamber, whom Mary recognised as a kinswoman and friend; indeed, the Queen
admitted Lady Exeter to such a degree of intimacy that
she shared Mary's bed. But perhaps still more because
of the close intercourse with his mother, the Queen's
feelings towards Courtenay were more those of a second
mother than of a future wife. .She "treated him like a
child;" tried to restrain him, and to impress upon him
more regular and decorous habits. She put him under
the care of a nobleman on whom she could depend,
ordered at least one suit of clothes for him, and then
interdicted him from wearing it. But she never wavered
in her statement that she would not have Courtenay for
her husband. The fourteen years in which he was her
junior were the least of his faults. She greatly resented
his boastful self-conceit in proposing for himself such
high promotion. She would never marry him, she said—
never.

The other English subject—by birth—also of royal
descent, was much better suited to Mary, in years, moral
character, and mental attainments. He was Courtenay's
uncle, Reginald Pole, just appointed the Pope's legate.
True he was a priest, but the Pope could give him a
dispensation from his vows as easily as he could appoint
him legate. If old rumours had any truth in them, he
had been, after the Emperor of Germany, Catherine of
Arragon's choice as a husband for her daughter. Certainly he had been a firm and faithful friend to Catherine.
He was, in addition, the son of the slain Countess of
Salisbury, who had been Mary's early guardian. Pole
had been so long out of England, to which he longed to
return, that he might have been held in a sense a
foreigner. Still, he was an Englishman by birth, with
the blood of the Plantagenets in his veins, just as it
flowed in those of his nephew, Courtenay, and, with all
Reginald Pole's faults, he was a more princely type of

man. If he had not Edward Courtenay's blooming youth, he had what was more appropriate—the dignity of fifty years. He too had his share of the Plantagenet beauty of person—a refined cast of beauty in his case. His devout, fervid temperament was calculated to recommend him to Mary.

But for a second time Reginald Pole refrained from becoming a candidate for Mary's hand. He was a priest to the heart's core; no earthly temptation would induce him, even with the Pope's consent, to lay down his vows to the Church. Even if he had been less devoted, Mary's own conscientious scruples would have come in the way of the transformation.

The most desirable of her subjects being thus dismissed, Mary's attention was directed to a foreign alliance, and from the first this was her secret wish and dearest ambition. If a foreign alliance could be accomplished, why not the most splendid of all, with the royal house which at that time towered over every other European dynasty? Spain was in the possession not of Austria alone, but of the Low Country and the Indies—all that was just beginning to be reaped of the splendid fruits of Columbus's discovery of the New World, a discovery which he had made in the reign, and by the help of Mary's grandmother, Isabella of Castile.

With the tenacity of purpose which was so marked a feature in her character, Mary recalled the mighty prince to whom she had been betrothed as a child of six years, whose faithlessness to his troth-plight had cost her the first of the many mortifications she had to bear before entering on her high estate. He had, nevertheless, been her constant friend, protector, and counsellor in the days of her mother's degradation and her own, in her orphan condition up to the date of her ascending the throne. Charles was a widower between fifty and sixty years of age—why should he not at last fulfil his troth-plight and render Mary not merely a queen, but an empress? Here indeed would be support for her tottering throne and her woman's weakness.

But the Emperor when consulted was provided with a substitute. He had from the moment that his cousin Mary was Queen of England coveted the alliance for Spain, but not in his own person. He pleaded his years and his infirmities as a patent excuse for declining taking upon him new responsibility and a change of habits. He suggested his son and heir, Don Philip, to be Mary's bridegroom in the Emperor's stead.

Mary was dazzled but not at once satisfied. In fact, the years of Don Philip were little more than those of Courtenay. Don Philip was twenty-seven years of age—twelve years Mary's junior—therefore Mary pooh-poohed his juvenility, and doubted a little, with reason, whether she could inspire him with affection. She feared also what she had heard of the prince's wild youth. On the other hand, as a prince, the heir of a great inheritance, accustomed betimes to serious responsibilities and weighty duties, he had early attained a certain maturity. He was already a widower, the father of a son, the unhappy Don Carlos, a boy of eight or nine years of age ; for Philip had been married in his early teens to Mary of Portugal, a kinswoman of his mother, and had been at eighteen the father of a son. Surely such obligations must have sobered and steadied him, Mary was tempted to argue. Nay, she could easily ascertain that he had all his father's seriousness, with more than a shade of his sombreness, and that he was in all outward manifestations even austerely religious, according to the rites of the Roman Catholic faith, however widely his practice might differ from his profession. To such a young man, her kinsman, supposing him honest and kind—and the Emperor's ambassador, Renard, who was one of Mary's evil geniuses, was always ready to answer her anxious inquiries whether Philip were a good

man with solemn assurances of his many excellent qualities—would not the unbounded love of Mary, and her
unstinted duty, together with her queenly estate and the
kingdom she proposed to give him, make up for all other
deficiencies and disparities? The benefit to the country
of the alliance with the power and majesty of Catholic
Spain—though her wisest English counsellors distrusted
the measure, and the common people detested it—the
Queen was persuaded would be immense. She hesitated
a little, and was lost.

Thenceforth she was entangled in fresh warfare and
new difficulties with her Council and Parliament as to
the advisability of the Spanish marriage. She awoke the
wrath of the Protestant part of the community; she exposed herself to the insults of the scurrilous mob. These
she had let loose on her by annulling the Act which constituted libels against the Sovereign and the Government
high treason. But the fiercer grew the opposition, the
more doggedly Mary—supported by Renard of course,
though dissuaded by Bishop Gardiner—stuck to her resolution. The more her imagination dwelt on what she
believed were the advantages of the match, she exaggerated the supposed virtues and attractions of the bridegroom, till a woman's soaring ambition and a woman's
romantic love, so long trampled down in her lonely heart,
became concentrated with deadly power on the project,
and she was driven the length of saying that she would
give up her kingdom before she would give up Philip.
Ere the crisis was reached many stormy passages occurred
between Mary, her Council, and her Parliament.

In January, 1554, Count Egmont, one of the future
heroes in the wars of independence in the Netherlands,
arrived from Spain to arrange on the part of the Emperor
the treaty of marriage between Philip and Mary. So
great was the public hostility to the connection, that the
messenger did not pass through Kent without danger to

his life and liberty. The marriage settlements made under the direction of the Emperor were studiously framed to conciliate the English. All the advantages seemed with England. Among the most prominent provisions were, that the two kingdoms were to be governed separately ; that none but Englishmen were to hold office in the English Government and in the Queen's household. If Mary had a child, it was to succeed to her dominions in right of its mother, and to Holland and Flanders in right of its father ; while his elder son, Don Carlos, was to succeed to Spain and Austria. If Mary survived Philip she was, while she was to bring him no dowry, to receive an annuity of sixty thousand ducats. England was not to be involved in the Emperor's French wars. Fair words these, which Mary implicitly believed, but many of her Council doubted them. The marriage could not take place without a dispensation from the Pope, since the intending bride and bridegroom were cousins ; and while Philip in Spain was striving to escape the fate which involved exile in a country he hated, and marriage with a faded, haggard bride, altogether distasteful to him, Mary, in her unconsciousness, was hurrying the commissioners at Rome, and striving with feverish haste to get the marriage accomplished before Lent, because otherwise the religious season would delay the wedding till Easter.

But a period of terrible anxiety had to be undergone, and a path of blood and fire traversed, in which the lion-like qualities that Mary, as well as Elizabeth, had inherited from King Henry, again came into prominence, and served her well with her people, before the inauspicious event on which she had set her heart was accomplished.

The week after the public announcement of the Queen's marriage insurrections broke out all over the country— in Devonshire, under Sir Peter Carew ; in Kent, under Sir Thomas Wyatt; and in the Midlands, under the Duke of Suffolk and his brothers. The fact that Suffolk and

Carew were Protestant leaders, while Wyatt was a Catholic, is one of the proofs that the English Catholics and the English Protestants were alike violently hostile to the alliance with Spain. But the manner in which Protestants and Catholics were balanced against each other, and the fact that their mutual animosities did not even slumber while they were united in a common cause, are reasons cited by Mr Froude for the ultimate failure of their plans. It seems a matter of uncertainty to this day, whether Suffolk, in joining the rebellion, did so for the purpose of proclaiming his daughter, Lady Jane Grey, queen in all the towns he passed through—according to the testimony of one witness—or whether, as there seems some evidence to show, he joined Wyatt and Carew with the purpose of placing Princess Elizabeth on the throne, and of marrying her to Courtenay, thus combining their two claims, and ensuring an English husband to an English queen. Courtenay (professedly a Catholic) was undoubtedly in the plot, but there was no convincing evidence of Elizabeth's complicity. If she was a conspirator she took care that no clear sign of her share in the insurrection should survive, though her name of course formed the rallying cry; and there were not wanting rumours that she had a personal partiality for the handsome, feather-head Courtenay, to whom she was well suited in years.

The revolts in Devonshire, and in Warwick, Worcester, and other Midland counties, were speedily mastered; prematurely discovered, as they were by the cowardice and treachery of Courtenay, they vanished like morning dew before the sun's rays. Carew fled for his life; poor Suffolk, sick and sorry, hid himself in the hollow of a tree near Warwick Castle, was betrayed by a keeper to whom he had entrusted his secret, and, with one of his brothers, was carried prisoner to London. But Wyatt's rising was less easily quelled, and at one time assumed alarming proportions. The old Duke of Norfolk, sent to meet the rebels, incautiously exposed himself and his men to the enemy between Gravesend and Rochester, at the very moment that a Captain Brett, at the head of a detachment of trained bands from London, turned sides and went over to Wyatt. A general panic and confusion followed. The Duke was ignominiously routed, and Wyatt, with a large force, marched upon London, which was practically undefended, save by its citizens. Mary was at Whitehall when the news of Wyatt's approach reached her. In place of quailing and flying, she went straight to the Guildhall, and standing on the steps addressed the crowded assembly in her "deep man's voice," with her unshrinking courage. She made one of her vigorous, telling speeches; she said plainly that her subjects were in rebellion, and went on to declare as plainly that she believed her marriage with the Prince of Spain was the cause. She told her audience that she had sent to Wyatt, offering to hear and pay respect to the objections of him and his followers. She repeated his arrogant answer, that he could only treat with her when he had the Tower of London and her person in his possession. "She stood there," she said, "as lawful Queen of England, and she appealed to the loyalty of her great city to save her from a presumptuous rebel." She assured her hearers that Wyatt's object was "general havoc and spoil." As for her marriage, she said she had thought so magnificent an alliance could not have failed to be agreeable to her people. Marriage in itself was indifferent to her. She could continue happy in the virgin state in which she had hitherto spent her life. She would call a parliament, and the matter should be farther considered. If the Lords and the Commons disapproved of the Prince of Spain, "on the word of a queen she would think of him no more."

If Mary was not so entirely sincere in this as in most of her speeches, she was sufficiently in earnest to carry the hearts of her hearers with her. For a second time her prompt and brave action saved her cause. She "converted the Corporation." On the following day no less than five and twenty thousand men were enrolled for the defence of London.

Wyatt and his company arrived at Southwark. No one ventured to attack him, and a strange pause occurred, which lasted for four days. During these days the lawyers at Westminster Hall pleaded in harness. The judges wore armour under their robes. Dr. Weston sang mass in harness before the Queen. Tradesmen attended well armed behind their counters.

Wyatt, finding the other bridges either barricaded or destroyed, turned back and approached London by Kingston Bridge, after marching all night through mud and mire. One portion of his force, when it reached what is now Hyde Park Corner, divided and attacked St. James's Palace before and behind, while Wyatt himself advanced as far as Charing Cross, where several gentlemen, among them the recreant Courtenay, were stationed in command of a detachment of the Queen's Guards. In spite of the remonstrances of his companions Courtenay galloped off towards Whitehall, shouting " Lost, lost—all is lost ! " and spreading terror as he rode.

In the meantime Mary was at Whitehall unprotected, save by what remained of her guards and her gentlemen pensioners. So imminent did the danger appear, that she was roused at three o'clock in the morning, and her very ante-chamber was filled with such armed men as she could command, while her ladies went wringing their hands and bemoaning themselves. But Mary neither wept nor bewailed her hard fate. When more than one of her friends urged her, while there was yet time, to go in a barge to the Tower, she listened with a stout heart to Renard's sound opinion, that if she fled she was lost. She refused to stir, though her Chancellor Gardiner implored—it is said knelt—to her to go. When her cousin Courtenay dashed up, like a beaten hound, with his senseless clamour, she watched his arrival from a gallery unmoved. " If others durst not stand the trial against the traitors," she said, " she herself would go out into the field, and try the quarrel, and die with those who would serve her." There is a tradition that she even descended and stood in the gateway, where the *mêlée* was so complete, that some of Wyatt's followers, returning from St. James's, got mixed up with the Guards, and could only be distinguished by the mud with which their long night march had bespattered their hose. In other encounters between the Londoners and Brett's deserters in Wyatt's company, the uniform being the same, the mud still formed the distinguishing feature, and the cry of the Queen's men was " Down with the draggle-tails."

Frustrated on all hands by the unexpected resistance he encountered, and especially by finding Ludgate closed against him, Wyatt, who has been described as " the most gallant and accomplished gentleman of his time," surrendered, after fighting desperately at Temple Bar, to Sir Maurice Berkeley, who, in order to protect his prisoner from the violence of the rabble, took him up on his own horse and rode with him to Westminster. From Whitehall Stairs Wyatt and five of his followers were conveyed in a barge to the Tower, Mary looking down on them from a window in the palace.

Wyatt's insurrection was an era in Mary's history. It aroused in her the fiery, overbearing temper and reckless vindictiveness which her father had so often exhibited. On her accession she had been merciful to excess, and had been reluctant to punish even one notorious offender, Dudley, Duke of Northumberland. Now, goaded by Renard with representations—the truth of which seemed to have been proved already in her reign of six months— that clemency was a folly; plied with warnings that her throne would never be secure so long as she left her

enemies unpunished; tortured by repeated threats that
the Prince of Spain, the Emperor's heir, would not be
suffered to come to a country in so disturbed a state,
where his foes, and those of the true Church, received in
return for their crimes only a weak amnesty, Mary's
nobler, gentler instincts were warped, misled, and betrayed.
Within two days in that dreary February of 1554 she
signed the death-warrants, not merely of Suffolk, but of
her favourite cousin, little Lady Jane, and her husband,
Lord Guildford Dudley. Wyatt's rebellion had sealed
their doom : though lying, as the husband and wife were,
in the Tower when it took place, they were the merest
passive instruments in the strife. Yet, with that piteous
anxiety to do right, and to save the soul even though she
slew the body, Mary sent Abbot Feckenham to convert the
girl of seventeen, about to die, from the errors of her
creed, before the stroke fell. When the distressed and
kindly abbot pressed for greater time in which to do
his work, the Queen willingly granted three days' respite
to the condemned prisoner. This is not the place to tell
how heroically yet sweetly Lady Jane died, without a
murmur. Her chief concern, nay, her only trouble, was
lest her father should apostatise on the scaffold, as
Northumberland had done before him. But Suffolk, with
all his faults and weaknesses, was made of truer, manlier
mould, and died maintaining the Reformed doctrines in
which he had lived.

The Greys, and Wyatt himself, were by no means the
sole sufferers for the abortive insurrection. The victims
were of all ranks, and were executed wholesale. In order
to strike the deeper awe into their neighbours, those
citizens of London who had followed Wyatt's standard
were hung in all public places and thoroughfares, and
at the doors of the offenders' shops and houses, so that
the City, like the wayside trees of France in the reign of
Louis XI., was decorated thickly with the ghastly adorn-

ments of dangling corpses.   Some five hundred men, who
appeared before the Queen with halters round their necks,
were pardoned; but this was a grand exception to the
general rule.   The cruelty of the reprisals went far to
blot out of men's minds the guilt which had provoked
them.   Courtenay, in spite of his betrayal of his party, was
sent back for a time to the Tower, where his handsome,
soulless face had been familiar from boyhood to manhood.
But a greater than Courtenay was in danger.   Princess
Elizabeth, without any direct evidence against her, was
sufficiently implicated to be summoned to London to
answer for her conduct.   She was lying ill at one of
her country seats; but Mary believed her illness was
feigned, and when Elizabeth was at last able to come to
London, which she entered in an open litter, she was
dressed in white, and looked in her paleness, "lofty,
scornful, and magnificent."   She was taken to Whitehall, when the Queen refused to see her sister.   Alas!
alas! the family ties which bound together Henry VIII.'s
children were little likely to stand the test of time and
trial.   The daughters of different mothers, sinned against
and sinning, were only too liable to vindicate their descent.   The affection which the girl-Princess Mary had
shown for her baby-sister; the kindly passages between
them when, as simply the sisters of King Edward, there
was comparatively little rivalry where they were concerned; even the friendly intercourse which had existed
for a space on Mary's accession, were all things of the
past.   Possibly, in any circumstances, it would have been
a shock to Mary to realise that the child and young girl
accustomed to defer and look up to the sister older by so
many years, had developed into a haughty, beautiful
young woman, with a clear judgment of her own on all
things, and no lack of wit to support it.   Elizabeth was
far too sagacious openly to defy or disobey her sister, who
was also her queen.   She had also a suppler nature than

Mary, who, with her blunt honesty, had difficulty in dissembling her feelings. But however plausible and complacent Elizabeth might show herself, she made no disguise that she regarded herself as the next in the claim to the throne, nor did she make the least objection to be hailed as the hope of the Protestant party, whose tenets she held in a modified form. Add to these inevitable grounds of dissension the persistent, urgent representations of Renard, on the part of the Emperor, from the first day Mary was queen—to remove Elizabeth as a deadly danger from her path by fair means or foul. And now, to crown and give terrible point to the advice, was the suspicion of Elizabeth's complicity with Wyatt, though it rested only on the intercepted despatches of the French ambassador, and on the copy of a letter which the Princess had written to Henry II. of France, together with two letters from Wyatt to Elizabeth, which she solemnly declared she had never received.

It is hard to believe that Mary could have proceeded to the last extremity against her sister, or that, having gone so far, she would not have relented before it was too late. Yet the Queen had sacrificed her favourite cousin, the little girl of seventeen, to a mistaken sense of duty, and State policy ; and Mary's old wholesome heart was fast changing to gall. All the wrongs which Catherine of Arragon and Mary had sustained at the hands of Anne Boleyn—who, as Mary believed, had threatened their lives; all the devastation wrought by her and her party in the Catholic Church, were fresh again in the Queen's memory ; and Elizabeth was Anne Boleyn's daughter, a meet Jezebel to come between Catherine of Arragon's daughter and her people, to tempt them back into rebellion, and what was infinitely worse in rigidly Catholic eyes, into deadly heresy. The re-establishment by Act of Parliament of the marriage between Henry and Catherine of Arragon had necessarily invalidated his marriage with

Anne Boleyn, though care was taken neither to mention
her by name, nor that of the Princess her daughter, in
the Act. Still, the deposition of the Princess Elizabeth
from her rank and rights existed by implication if Mary
chose to act upon it, and Mary chose as far as even she
dared.

In the old days when goodwill was still possible between
the sisters, Mary had insisted, not without risk to herself,
on styling her little sister " her Grace ; " but, even before
Wyatt's rebellion was heard of, the Queen had made
Elizabeth walk in court ceremonies *behind* her cousins,
the Countess of Lennox (Lady Margaret Douglas) and
the Duchess of Suffolk (Frances Brandon). Altogether
it is idle to believe—even with the best opinion of poor
Mary's original character and earnest desire to do right,
beginning as they were to be fatally warped and distorted
—that any feeling save distrust and enmity, thinly veiled
by compulsory courtesy, existed latterly between Mary
and Elizabeth. The bad health and serious illnesses of
Mary, which did not cease with her accession, though
they were kept more in the background, had shattered her nervous system. The sudden exaltation to
the throne; the work, worry, and sharp warfare into
which she was plunged; the passionate dream of finding
in Philip of Spain deliverance from her evils, and food
for her woman's starving heart, did the rest. Gradual
symptoms of an intellect becoming unhinged began to
present themselves. There was no special mysticism in
Mary's religion that we can discern; no expectation of
miracles; no calling out for signs—in itself the sign of an
unbalanced mind—in her earlier years. The evil began
with the fantastic sermon of Harpsfield, chaplain to
Bishop Bonner, which he preached before the Parliament
in 1553, the sermon being an introduction to a controversy
between selected members of the Catholic and Reformed
Churches. Harpsfield compared Mary to Judith, to Esther,

to Deborah, to Mary of Bethany, who had chosen the
better part; finally, to the Virgin Mary, with whom she
might sing, "Behold, from henceforth all generations
shall call me blessed." The comparison, strange on the
lips of a Roman Catholic, sank into what was the latent
soaring enthusiasm of Mary's spirit, and found an echo
in the sympathetic souls of all highly strung enthusiastic
Roman Catholics. From that time there was a disposition, both in herself and in those who held her views,
to regard her as a woman with a divine mission, set apart,
to be distinguished by particular intimations of God's will
and marks of His favour—a conviction which, even when
it is held dispassionately, with no mixture of motives, or
of personal loves and hates, is perilously fraught with
danger to the reason.

Then Mary summoned Renard—who was neither an
enthusiast nor a man of religious principles—and, in the
presence of one of her ladies-in-waiting, made him approach the altar bearing the holy wafer, which she was
accustomed to speak of as " her protector, her guide, and
her adviser." She told her two companions how she had
spent her days and nights in tears and prayers before it,
"imploring God to direct her." " She flung herself on
her knees, with Renard and Lady Clarence at her side, and
the three together before the altar sang the ' Veni Creator.'
. . . As the chant died into silence, Mary rose from her
knees, as if inspired, and announced the Divine message.
The Prince of Spain was the chosen of heaven for the
Virgin Queen. If miracles were required to give him to
her, there was a stronger than man who would work them.
The malice of this world should not keep him from her;
she would cherish and love him, and him alone." On
another occasion Mary took Renard into her confidence,
when she swore, in his presence before the Host, that she
would marry Philip, and only Philip.

It was in a manner not altogether dissimilar that Mary's

great-grandmother, the venerable Margaret, had, in her
tender youth, risen from her little bed and sought the
direction of higher powers in her choice of a husband,
when, as the child believed, St. Nicholas appeared to her,
and bade her wed young Owen Tudor. But Margaret
was a simple, humble-minded child, who never dreamt
that she was different from other children, or that she
was appointed to redeem England, though it were by
fire and blood. From the date of that conviction a
strain of insanity, always increasing, was visible in Mary's
conduct.

Mary used the failure of Wyatt's rebellion to wring
from her Council and Parliament their consent to her
marriage with Philip of Spain. The Pope's dispensation
was procured in March, 1554. Count Egmont was again
in the country as the proxy of Philip, and was brought to
Whitehall by Lord Pembroke and Lord William Howard,
the commanders of the army and navy. On the 6th of
March, at three o'clock in the afternoon, in the presence
of her court and of the foreign ambassadors, Mary,
kneeling before the Sacrament in her Presence-room, gave
her hand to Egmont as Philip's representative, and the
marriage by proxy was accomplished. The next moment
the Queen fell on her knees and asked all present to join
in asking a blessing on the marriage. Egmont presented
her with a ring from Philip, which she showed to the
company. She sent the donor an affectionate message,
but declined to write, as he had not yet written to her, a
remissness which was one of the many indications of
Philip's inveterate dislike to the marriage into which
ambition and avarice, with his father, the Emperor, as
their exponent, forced him.

THE WIFE OF PHILIP II. OF SPAIN.

Every effort was made, in the examination of the prisoners taken in Wyatt's insurrection, to discover how far Elizabeth had been guilty in it. Nothing more came to light than the copy of her letter to Henry II. of France and Wyatt's letters to her, which were not enough to convict her. They were enough, however, to cause her to be brought before the Council, and to enable the Chancellor, Gardiner, to propose that she should be sent to the Tower. Stephen Gardiner, the head of the old Church party, had been Elizabeth's consistent enemy from the beginning of Mary's reign. Actuated by other motives than those which influenced Renard, the Emperor's ambassador, Gardiner had joined him in constantly warning Mary against her sister, and in pressing on the Queen, as her best policy, to hold Elizabeth at a distance, and get her out of the way.

The more just and liberal members of the Council opposed the proposal of Gardiner, who turned upon them and asked if any of them would be responsible for the safe keeping of the Princess, when every man shrank from the obligation. Elizabeth's attendants were removed, soldiers were picketed beneath the windows of her rooms in Whitehall, and on the following morning, the 17th of March, 1554, the Lords of Winchester and Sussex communicated to her the decision of the Council, and told her that a barge was in readiness to take her to the Tower.

Ominous as the words were, Elizabeth behaved with the utmost spirit. She asked time to write to the Queen, and Sussex promised on his knees to put the letter into Mary's hands. The letter still exists, and the writing is more than usually firm, in which Elizabeth, "with great force and lucidity," protested before God her innocence, and prayed Him to "confound her" if she was guilty. She pleaded for an interview with her sister.

Mary refused to grant the interview, and was indignant

with Sussex, who by his compliance with Elizabeth's request had caused such delay that the tide had turned, and the barge could not pass London Bridge till the following day. On the other hand, Mary durst not venture to send Elizabeth a prisoner through the streets in the sight of the citizens and populace, whose idol she was fast becoming. In the Queen's wrath she cried that Sussex would not have acted so in her father's time, and wished Henry were alive and among them for a month. On the next day Elizabeth passed by the Traitor's Gate into the Tower.

The Queen could not condemn her sister without a trial, and Parliament was assembled for the purpose of procuring a trial. In the meantime Wyatt on the scafford proclaimed, with a slight reserve, the innocence of Elizabeth and Courtenay. The condemned man said they were not privy to his rising *before it began*. The speech was regarded by the listeners as clearing the accused persons. The news spread like wildfire over the country. The judges refused to convict Elizabeth, and on their refusal it was impossible to detain her in the Tower. The difficulty was, what to do with her. There was more than one plan for sending her abroad by marrying her to a foreign prince. But she was the next heir to the throne, and would not readily consent to her own banishment; and Mary, on her side, refused to consider Anne Boleyn's daughter worthy of a princely alliance. Elizabeth was at last sent, still in disgrace and well guarded, to Woodstock, where she fretted in her confinement till she fell ill.

By Whit Sunday Mary was looking eagerly forward to Philip's arrival, and passing the interval in entering zealously into all the religious ceremonials of the season. "She marched day after day in procession, with canopies and banners, and bishops in silk slippers, round St. James's, round St. Martin's, round Westminster." She had masses said for the repose of her father's soul. The constant strain of excitement, the sense of hope deferred in the non-arrival of her longed-for bridegroom, the growing consciousness that she was losing the affections of her people, and that the turbulent spirits among them were learning to look upon her with hatred and scorn, preyed more and more on Mary's shattered nerves. She withdrew for quiet in the summer sunshine to the green shades of Richmond; but she carried an unquiet spirit with her. She grew irritable to such a degree that she was well-nigh distracted. She blamed every one, even her prince, who had neither written to her nor sent her a lover-like message. She questioned every sailor she came across as to Don Philip's movements, and the state of the Channel, where the English fleet might not protect his vessel from the French ships. She would start from her sleep in wild terror. But the sharpest pang of all was, that her prince did not love her, that she was beyond her prime while time was passing, and that she would never win his love.

As an excuse for Philip's reluctance to fulfil his pledge, one of Mary's historians has in fairness recalled the disheartening facts, that he was not allowed to bring more than a handful of Spanish noblemen in his suite; that he was advised to select these gentlemen because of their pacific tempers, that they might stand the insults they were likely to receive from the hostile and rude English people; that it would be wise to have disguised men-at-arms for lacqueys; and that the heir of the great Emperor ought to take the precaution of carrying his own cook along with him to lessen the risk of poison.

The sea was squally and unfriendly to Philip's Spanish fleet. Like his grand-aunt, Catherine, he had a rough passage, and was overwhelmed by sea-sickness. But when he arrived in Southampton Water on the 20th of July, 1554, a year from Mary's accession, he received a courteous, magnificent welcome. He was met by the Lords Arundel and Pembroke, Shrewsbury and Derby, and the great assemblage awaiting him knelt as he stepped on

shore. Mary was not able to present Philip with a crown
matrimonial as she had desired, but Lord Shrewsbury
invested him with the Order of the Garter, including a
gold and jewelled collar, and a mantle of blue velvet
fringed with gold and pearls—the whole so splendid that
it was valued at two thousand pounds. Mary also sent
her bridegroom a fine horse, which he mounted and rode
to the church of the Holy Rood, to return thanks for his
successful voyage.

The Queen had fixed to meet her bridegroom at Winchester, and to be married to him there by her Chancellor,
Bishop Gardiner, Cranmer, the Archbishop of Canterbury
being still in durance under the charge of heresy and
treason. As soon as Mary heard of the arrival of the
Spanish fleet she set out with a noble retinue for King
Arthur's old town, so dear to her grandfather, Henry VII.
But the day on which she arrived at the Bishop's palace
was wild and stormy with wind and rain. The same storm,
terminating in floods of rain, was the accompaniment of
Philip's ride to Winchester. As yet, during the day and
a half he had stayed at Southampton, the impression he
had given was favourable. He had made an effort to
overcome his natural "stiffness" and coolness, and was
courteous to Mary's subjects, though it was noticed that
when they were presented to him he did not put his hand
to his cap. He spoke to the English gentlemen in Latin,
and gravely drank some ale at the banquet, because ale
was the wine of the country in which he had come to
dwell, and he desired to live like an Englishman. There
was no fault to find with him personally, though in stature
he was rather short, while he was well-formed. Miss
Strickland describes his complexion as cane-coloured, and
his hair sandy; but a more complimentary chronicler of
his looks simply calls attention to his yellow hair and
beard, and has nothing to say against his heavily lidded
grey-blue eyes, or the hereditary gloom of his expression.

Certainly his dress set off such good looks as he possessed, and added to his dignity. In contrast to the grand and fantastic dress of the time, Philip almost always wore plain black velvet in doublet and trunk hose, with a small black velvet cap, which on this occasion had a lacing of fine gold chains and a little drooping feather. This was the picturesque outward garb of the man. In broad contrast to his romantic antecedents and appearance, he was a gross eater, over-indulging himself in the fat of bacon till he fell ill with the excess. He had also, like his sagacious father, a childish passion for pastry, which he gratified to the detriment of his health and temper. What was worse, he was absolutely cold-hearted and radically vicious.

Out of compliment to Spanish taste in dress, as it seems, the English gentlemen who escorted Don Philip wore black velvet in their turn. But the exigencies of that dismally rainy ride compelled the Prince to wrap himself in a red felt cloak, and to put on a broad hat. Indeed, so execrable was the weather, for the middle of summer, that poor Mary sent a messenger post-haste to beg her future husband not to come on to her—a message which was in danger of being misunderstood by the Spaniards, who went aside and consulted together in perplexity and dismay as to what could have happened, till one of the English lords volunteered a smiling explanation in French—" Our Queen, sire, loves your highness so tenderly that she would not have you come to her in such wretched weather."

Arrived at Winchester, Philip repaired first to the cathedral, kissed the crucifix, prayed before the altar, and sat in the choir listening to a *Te Deum laudamus* till he had to be conducted by torchlight to the Deanery. Having changed his dress for hose of white and silver, and a black velvet doublet bordered with diamonds, he was conducted, at ten o'clock in the evening, by a private passage from the Deanery to the Bishop's palace, where Mary awaited him. There was no need of an interpreter between them.

Mary conversed with Philip in Spanish, and one can guess how sweet her mother's tongue must have sounded on his lips. Philip too was gracious. He asked her to teach him enough of her English to enable him to astonish the English gentlemen who were to conduct him back to the Deanery by taking leave of them in English. With glad goodwill Mary gave the required lesson, and Philip was furnished with the necessary weapons to surprise the lords in attendance by being qualified to say, "Good night, my lords, all of you."

Mary's fond dream was realised, but woe's me for the awakening. It did not dawn on her for a brief season. She was permitted to be the happiest of the happy for a passing hour. Philip's natural reserve helped to conceal his utter indifference to the woman whom he had crossed the seas to marry. The rigid etiquette of his country prevented any betrayal of discourtesy to the Queen. But in the course of six weeks all the urgent remonstrances of the ambassador Renard, who had schemed and striven for the match, were wanted to keep the brutally heartless young man from abandoning his newly wedded wife and returning on any pretext to his beloved Spain.

Little did Mary dream of what was in store for her when she held her first grand court at Winchester the day after Philip's arrival, and the pair stood conversing together under the canopy of state in the presence of a crowd of courtiers.

The marriage took place on the 25th of July, the day dedicated to St. James, the patron saint of Spain. The Queen walked on foot from the palace to the Cathedral, her train borne by her cousin, Lady Margaret Douglas, now Countess of Lennox.

Philip was attended by sixty Spanish grandees, among them Alva and Egmont, whose names were to figure on such very different pages in their country's history. Mary was dressed in French fashion in a robe of gold brocade, a train edged with pearls and diamonds, and her large sleeves gathered up by clusters of the same jewels. Her coif was bordered with a double row of large diamonds. Her kirtle was of white satin embroidered with silver. On her breast she wore the great diamond sent to her by Philip on their betrothal. Scarlet shoes and a black velvet scarf completed the costume.

We have a life-like engraving from a fine picture of Mary, by Antoine More, in our mind's eye, as we find her in her fortieth year thus decked out for her ill-fated bridal. The rich formal dress of the period adds to the formality, if it also increases the dignity, of the figure. The face is naturally strong and sensible in spite of the distraction which was to convulse it. The forehead is large, the nose marked, the mouth firm, with the upper lip slightly pressed beneath the under. The expression is conscientious and good, notwithstanding the mountain load of curses which have rested for centuries on the unhappy Queen's head.

Philip's suit on his wedding day was hardly so picturesque and becoming, however splendid, as that which he wore on ordinary occasions. He too was in brocade bordered with pearls and diamonds. His trunk hose were of white satin worked with silver. His collar of the Order of the Golden Fleece was of beaten gold studded with diamonds, while round his knee was the jewelled riband of the Garter.

Mary was given away by the chief lords of her Council, Derby, Pembroke, &c. She chose to be married with a plain gold ring "like any other maiden." With the same loving deference, which was conceded by another and a later Mary, it was her will that Philip's name should take precedence of hers when they appeared in company. It was not to be "Mary and Philip," but "Philip and Mary."

The marriage ceremonial lasted from seven o'clock in the summer morning till three in the afternoon. It must have been an exhausting experience to Mary, whose head never failed to ache acutely under the influence of fatigue, excitement, and agitation. At the marriage banquet, when Mary and her husband sat side by side under a canopy, the service was of solid gold plate. The banquet was followed by a ball. Princess Elizabeth, sick and sorry under her banishment to Woodstock, with a somewhat hard jailor in Sir Henry Bedingfield, heard only the distant echoes of the rejoicing.

Philip and Mary went, the day after their marriage, to Basing House, where they were entertained by the Marquis of Winchester. They then proceeded to Windsor, and Philip presided at a festival of the Knights of the Garter to celebrate his installation. In August the royal couple removed to Richmond, and on the 28th of the month they entered London in state. Gog and Magog stood on London Bridge to receive Mary and her prince, and conducted themselves like well-behaved giants. But as it happened, a painting or effigy of Henry VIII. among the nine worthies round the turret at the conduit in Gracechurch Street, represented the King in the act of presenting a book, on which was inscribed, *Verbum Dei* (the "Word of God"), to his son King Edward. The significance of the inscription was unmistakable, and awoke the resentment of Mary. Some say the Queen, some say Gardiner, caused the book to be painted out and a pair of gloves substituted in its place. According to other authorities, what were supposed to be gloves were merely the blurred fingers of the hand, which the painter, sharply called to account, painting in his haste and trepidation, had nearly effaced. However, Philip had brought with him numerous chests of bullion, which were proudly displayed on their way to the Tower. These caused even his greatest enemies to forgive him for a time, so acceptable was the precious metal to an empty exchequer.

After a short stay at Whitehall, Mary retired with her husband to the privacy of Hampton Court, and there doubtless the first symptoms of his discontent and restlessness disturbed her woman's dream. If she, who was anxiously deferring to him in everything, and pressing her unwilling Council to grace him with still more substantial honours and powers, saw with aching suspicion and apprehension the signs of what was coming, the public were not permitted to witness them. Whether out of a concession to Spanish etiquette, or from wounded pride, or a sad sinking of heart which caused her to shrink from observation, the Queen ordained that the royal family and court, which had hitherto been in full view of the people, should withdraw behind closed gates at Hampton.

From her youth Mary had shown herself fond of children, and "she ardently desired an heir which should shut her contumacious, dissembling, heretical sister out of the succession." The passionate hope that her wishes were about to be fulfilled restored to Mary for a fleeting interval the first glow of the short-lived happiness which was fast fading. Here again the mystic, inflated, religious, and patriotic sentiments, which had been fostered in her after her accession, took possession of her. She might live to bear a child who should be the deliverer of his race and nation by restoring the faith which Henry and his son had subverted, and by giving back to the "Holy Father" in Rome the kingdom which had profanely cast off his yoke. The one point on which Mary could never have been disappointed in Philip was his punctilious observance of the rites of their Church. While his heart was like the nether millstone, and he was destitute of manly virtue, he was, after the fashion of Louis XI. of France, the most slavishly superstitious of men, so far apart may the letter be from the spirit, so widely severed profession from practice. It was a strong proof at once of Mary's fanaticism and of her infatuation where Philip was concerned, that a woman so honest, in the midst of her worse faults, did not see through and loathe this empty mask of religion.

At last Reginald Pole was permitted to return to England as the Pope's legate. He arrived at the palace stairs of Whitehall with the silver cross as his pennon at the bow of his barge. He was received with open arms by both Philip and Mary. Philip forgot his Spanish slowness and stateliness, and rushed from supper to embrace the Pope's representative. Mary went to the head of the great staircase to throw herself in her turn on the breast of the ambassador of peace from her spiritual sovereign. It was also the breast of her early companion, her mother's friend, and she cried out that his coming gave her as much joy as the possession of her kingdom.

Pole, with his rapt, handsome face, his hectically red lips apart, his dreamy eyes, and his burning enthusiasm, was as one-ideaed and transcendental as Mary, and in circumstances which brought out the qualities, as dogmatic and inhuman as Philip. Pole played his part unconsciously, without any intent to deceive, in farther mystifying and deluding Mary to the verge of frenzy. He hailed her with the " Ave Maria!" the salutation addressed to the Virgin.

The next act in the drama was Reginald Pole's appearance before Parliament, and the floridly eloquent speech in which he called on England to return to the jurisdiction of the representative of St. Peter. The die was cast ; both Houses of Parliament, with but two dissenting votes, agreed to renounce the principles of the Reformation as they had been established in England! On St. Andrew's Day, 30th March, 1554, Parliament again assembled at Whitehall, the Prince and Queen, with the legate, occupying three chairs beneath a golden canopy. Gardiner, the Chancellor, who had once stood up stoutly for the independence of the Church of England, announced the submission of the nation to Rome through their Parliament. The legate solemnly accepted it in the name of the Pope, and, while the whole assembly, with their Queen, knelt, pronounced their absolution and their reconciliation to the head of the Roman Catholic Church. Amidst the breathless silence the smothered sobs of the Queen could be heard. The imposing ceremony ended with the singing of the *Te Deum* in the Royal Chapel.

But instead of peace it was terrible internecine war, with the fire and faggot let loose in the land, of which that unqualified submission was the precursor. An awful ordeal was needed to awaken the minds and consciences of the people to what had been the true nature of their apostasy. It was the signal and the authority for the persecutions which, though God in His providence overruled them, so that the blood of the martyrs was indeed the seed of the Church, and Protestantism, in place of being ignobly crushed, was triumphantly re-established in England, stained Mary's reign with horrible cruelty, and loaded her memory with obloquy. It is one more reason for prayer against blindness of heart, that neither Mary nor Pole was cruel by nature; that they were morally among the purest - minded and most self - denying of human beings; and that in their private lives, as far as they saw, they were just, generous, and charitable. Self-will, and at the last vindictiveness, on the part of Mary, and on Pole's side extravagant self-reliance and self-conceit, which left him with the conviction that he was to be the saviour of his country, were their chief errors. Notwithstanding this fact the pair were, along with Bishop Gardiner, the instruments of the most hideous tyranny and barbarous outrages which have been committed in England since its annals were those of civilisation and Christianity. For it was the work of the legate and the Chancellor, supported by Mary, to see that the submission to Rome, and the absolution granted to England, were proclaimed and maintained in every parish in the country. Registers were drawn up of the parish adherents to the national submission, while the recusants who failed to record their names were immediately proceeded against with all the penalties of ecclesiastical law.

To those who, like Mary and Pole, were full of single-minded devotion to Rome, whose gratitude to the Pope was in proportion to their faith in his claims, nothing could seem so base as the unwillingness to accept his amnesty, and the persistent refusal to accord him homage in spite of his graciousness.

This is not the place to record the valiant deeds of the martyrs and their glorious faith. Their number amounted to between three and four hundred. It exceeded the number of those who had perished from the violent dealings of Henry's reign and during Somerset's Protectorate by nearly twenty to one. There was this great difference also, that while the vengeance of the earlier party in power struck, with a few exceptions, at those in high places, at men like Wolsey, More, and Surrey, the later persecution raged against great and small alike—slew the Primate of all England, his bishops and vicars, fell upon servants as well as masters, assailed simple women and ignorant boys and girls, whose sole distinction was their grand constancy in the grace given to them to endure to the end. They did not always go singly to their fiery death ; they perished in batches of three, six, and on one occasion thirteen, encouraging each other to remain steadfast, amidst the breathless admiration and sobbing sympathy of crowds of spectators.

Mary and Pole believed that this appalling holocaust was acceptable to God as freeing the country from heresy. But the sacrifice simply made and spread the Protestantism which the persecutors called heresy, and established it on such sure foundations, that the mass of the English people were and have been Protestant to the heart's core since those fearful days.

The wish to divide the blame, or to screen Mary from the extent to which she was accountable for it, has induced several writers on the subject to attribute the worst of the persecution to the influence of Philip and of the Emperor's ambassador. But there is no good ground for these assertions. Philip, indeed, showed himself in after years quite capable of a similar crusade in the Low Countries, but the circumstance that this persecution proceeded in England with as great activity in his absence as in his presence in the country, disposes largely of the argument. As for Renard, and his master the Emperor, there is abundant proof that from the beginning of Mary's reign their policy was contrary to religious persecution in England, and that they did their best to oppose the strong measures which Mary was disposed to take against the Reformers.

Elizabeth had been a little cheered in her captivity at Woodstock by a visit from her great-uncle and staunch friend, Lord William Howard, the brave commander of Mary's fleet. He had insisted, without the Queen's being able to baulk him, on personally inquiring into the condition of his young kinswoman. There was, indeed, no longer an apology for detaining the Princess at a distance from the court, and Mary not only permitted her sister's return, but consented to the personal interview which she had declined before. There seems some difficulty in ascertaining the date of this meeting, which is differently stated as having taken place in the autumn of 1554 and in the summer of 1555. If the last date is correct the sisters had not met, as Mr. Froude calculates, for almost two years. Elizabeth was brought to Hampton Court, where Lady Clarence, a trusted bed-chamber woman of the Queen's, was sent to conduct the Princess across the garden in the dusk and take her by a back staircase to Mary's rooms. Elizabeth knelt, but it was not to beg for mercy, it was to assert as positively and undauntedly as ever that she was the Queen's true sister and subject.

"You will not confess," Mary said gloomily. "You stand to your truth ; I pray God it may so fall out."

"If it does not," said Elizabeth, "I desire neither favour nor pardon at your hands."

"Well," Mary answered bitterly, "you persevere in your truth; belike you will not confess that you have been lawfully punished?"

"I must not say so to your Majesty," Elizabeth replied cautiously.

"Belike you will to others," said the Queen.

"No, please your Majesty," answered the Princess. "I have borne the burden—I must bear it;" and she again entreated the Queen to think her sister her true subject always.

The Queen did not answer her, but muttered in Spanish *Sabe Dios* (God knows).

There seems no trustworthy evidence for the tradition that Mary gave Elizabeth a ring in token of their reconciliation, and in remembrance of a former ring which the Queen had bestowed on the Princess on an earlier occasion as a talisman by which she was to appeal to her sovereign in case of their alienation. The tradition goes on to say that Elizabeth had sent the ring before she was taken to the Tower, but that the token had no effect. The story is too like other stories of the kind to deserve much credence, while so far as the gift of the second ring goes to establish proof of an entire reconciliation between the sisters, it is plain enough, from what is preserved of the conversation, that nothing of the kind occurred during this interview. Rumour made the half comical addition to the record of the scene that Philip hid behind the tapestry in order to see for the first time his sister-in-law, the people's idol. He was not then an enemy to Elizabeth. He is said to have been the great upholder of the proposal that she should be honourably disposed of in marriage to Philibbert, Prince of Savoy. But not even to please her husband would Mary consent that her sister should be restored to the full dignity of a princess by arranging such a marriage on her behalf.

Mary withdrew to Hampton Court for the birth of the child whom she vainly hoped to call her own. Litanies were sung, processions, in which Philip figured conspicuously, were undertaken, bonfires were piled ready in the streets of London to hail the happy event which never took place. Mary was mistaken in her expectations, and Philip, deprived of any chance of a regency, indifferent to his wife's sorrow, and to the wretched state of her health, altogether weary of the situation, chose that time of all others to leave her to her fate. He found a plea in his father's abdication of his throne and retirement into a monastery, to return to Spain.

Even before Mary knew of her husband's intention she would sit on the floor of her room in the sweet May weather, her features shrunk and haggard, her knees drawn up to her face. She had agonising pain in her head, which became much swollen, and constant attacks of hysteria—the outward signs of which she sought to suppress. She was persuaded that God was punishing her for some crime. She had already impoverished herself by restoring the Church lands which had fallen into her possession. She had given back her town house of St. John's to the monastic order from which it had been taken. She had vowed to rebuild, at her own expense, the abbeys and religious houses which her father had pulled down, or suffered to fall into ruins. What could be the sin which was causing God to hide His face from her, and inflict on her such misery, if it were not that of suffering heresy to exist in her dominions ?

So Mary wrote, or caused to be written, to her bishops, on whom their horrible work was palling, "rattling letters" to stir them up to fresh activity in the task.

As soon as the Queen's health enabled her to be moved she went to the country palace of Eltham, in Kent, where she recovered in part from the disease of dropsy. But so wretched was the half-frenzied woman that even Philip's hard heart was touched. He stooped to deceive her with regard to the length of his stay in Spain, and persuaded her that he would return to England very shortly. He encouraged her to accompany him to Greenwich, when her infirmities would not suffer her to be taken, as she wished, to Dover, to see him sail and there to await his return.

On the royal couple's way to the barge which was to convey them to Greenwich, Mary was carried through the City in an open litter, with Philip riding by her side. It was said this arrangement was made in order to show the people that their Queen was still alive, as there had been many reports of her death.

Philip's departure took place in September, 1555, a year and two months after his marriage. Mary remained behind to struggle with sickness, the cares of the State, and the ever-increasing hatred of her subjects, displayed against her in coarse libels and lampoons, which found their way into her very chamber, and shocked her proud modesty and rectitude. She did not cease to pray piteously for her husband's return in the words of the prayer which the legate had written for her, and to strive to rule according to his wishes, in so far as what she saw to be her duty to England would permit her. She tried to constrain her Council to bribe him to come back by bestowing on him the bauble of the crown of a king-consort. She even tried to work upon them to appoint him her successor to the throne in the room of her sister Elizabeth. When she could not obtain her ends she filled the palace chambers with her bootless weeping and wailing, or she spent her time in writing to Philip letters blotted with her burning tears.

For a time nothing shook Mary's steadfast regard for her husband—not the interception and making public by the French of the packet of Spanish letters in which Philip and his grandees expressed their dissatisfaction with the marriage, and betrayed their contempt for the Queen; not the tidings of his evil conduct when he was freed from the restraint of her presence, and had withdrawn from the virtuous atmosphere of her court; not his unblushing delay in returning to his duties as a husband.

Among Philip's injunctions to Mary, which she religiously observed, were particular directions to show care and kindness to Princess Elizabeth. His earnestness on this point has produced the impression that even then, in spite of his advocacy of the suit of Philibbert of Savoy, Philip proposed, in case of Mary's death, to become an aspirant for the hand of her beautiful and high-spirited sister, much better matched with him in years than poor Mary had been.

Accordingly Elizabeth remained at Greenwich during Mary's stay there, for the remainder of what was one in a succession of bad harvests and wet, stormy autumns, which reduced the oppressed, discontented people to the verge of starvation, and caused much dangerous and deadly sickness.

Mary appeared again in public in the spring of 1556, "pale as a corpse, and looking ten years older than before her illness." In private she was able to walk a little with her ladies to visit the poor cottagers in the neighbourhood of her country palaces, personally relieving the wants of the peasant families. She could work at her embroidery frame, and study when she had leisure. She kept up a show of courtesy to Elizabeth, though there was little love lost between the sisters. They exchanged visits, the Princess coming to Somerset House while Mary was in residence there, and the Queen returning the visit by going to Elizabeth's seat of Hatfield, where she was entertained with playing on the virginals, choir singing, &c. The period might have been comparatively tranquil but for the hapless Queen's sick longing for Philip, and the abortive plots against her which kept smouldering, breaking out and being quenched in blood. Such were two insurrections—the one led by a Dudley, a cousin of the late Duke of Northumberland, the other by a member of the Stafford family, a nephew of the legate's. Both plots were discovered in time, and severely punished, every effort being made, even to the use of the torture, in the examination of the prisoners to induce them to confess the names of all who were implicated in the treason. But though the old rallying cry of " Elizabeth and Courtenay " was still to be heard, no evidence could be found that they or their friends had in any way supported the *émeutes*. Indeed, the course of the weak, handsome Courtenay was all but run. He died of fever at Venice in 1556, while he was still in the prime of early manhood. As he left no direct descendant, one bugbear was removed from the thorny path of the sovereigns of England. No more was heard of a Courtenay as a pretender to the crown.

For the relentless punishment of the conspirators— mostly rash, restless young men, with allies who were exiles in France under the ostentatious patronage of Henry II.—Mary was certainly more or less accountable, just as she was more and not less responsible for the continued religious persecutions, which were exciting such a reaction of admiration for the faithful sufferers that the mobs, in place of hooting and reviling the heretics, encouraged them with warm words of sympathy, and to each of their dying prayers added a fervent Amen. Gardiner had largely withdrawn from the crusade—only the enthusiast and bigot Pole was with the Queen in it to the end.

In the spring of 1557, a year and a half after he had quitted England, Philip chose to return on a visit to his wife. The welcome news of his coming was brought to Mary by one of the sons of Northumberland whom she

had spared, Lord Robert Dudley; and Philip himself
arrived at Greenwich on March 20th. Mary received
him with open arms, heard mass with him, caused *Te
Deums* to be sung in every church in London, and all
the bells to be rung right merrily. She came with Philip
in state to the Tower, the sword of state and the sceptre
being borne before the couple. The City consented to
indulge in outward demonstrations of loyalty—not the
most insignificant motive for which was the new prospect
of trade with Russia, ratified by the presence of a Russian
ambassador in the form of a Duke of Muscovy.

The Queen was able to accompany her husband and
her priests in more than one religious procession round
the Westminster cloisters. But no faith was kept by
Philip in relation to the pledge which he had given on
his marriage, that England should not be drawn into the
Spanish wars with France that were chronic, for in June,
1557, war was proclaimed between England and France.
In the following July Philip, after a stay of between
three and four months, embarked again for Spain, having
taken his last farewell of his devoted wife. She had,
however, the satisfaction of hearing soon afterwards that
he had won the battle of St. Quintin. But the pleasure
was speedily followed by the bitter mortification, which
all England shared, when in 1558 the news arrived that
the Duke of Guise had wrested Calais from the English.
The whole nation regarded Calais as the gate of France,
and clung to it as the last memorial of the old glorious
conquests of the Black Prince and Henry V. How much
Mary took the loss to heart is indicated by the speech
ascribed to her, that if that heart were laid bare after
her death the word " Calais " would be found written
on it.

The beautiful Christina of Denmark, the widowed
Duchess of Lorraine, who at fifteen had been proposed
as a fit wife for Henry VIII., was Philip's cousin, as she

was Mary's, through their common ancestress, Isabella of Castile. She was in Philip's confidence to a degree that piqued Mary intensely. Christina came to England—the country over which she had once had the chance of reigning—as Philip's unofficial ambassadress in advocating the old scheme of Princess Elizabeth's marriage to Philibbert of Savoy, a scheme which Mary never favoured. In her exasperation at the envoy who was supposed to have a special feminine talent for conducting royal treaties and smoothing down royal objections, the Queen was guilty of the one act of personal violence attributed to her. She is reported to have cut to pieces with her own hand a portrait of Philip, which he had recently sent to her at her special request, because it represented him as she had never seen him, in complete armour, save for the helmet which he held in his hand.

Mary had lucid intervals in her idolatry of her unworthy husband, as when she said, in the presence of her ladies, with a significance which impressed them, that "God sent oft-times to good women bad husbands." And again, when she announced her too-short-lived intention to live quietly and contentedly among her ladies, as she had lived before her disastrous marriage. But these intervals were always followed by strong revulsions of feeling, which caused her to write the humblest letters to Philip, and to labour as far as she could, without being utterly false to her coronation oath, to further his objects. She had lost all her fine self-reliance and fearless confidence in her fellows. She was conscious, with a sharp pang, of the detestation she had inspired in the subjects for whom she had desired to do great things. Her very courage deserted her. She dreaded assassination, and would shut herself up with her women, and with one or two trusted gentlemen of her household, declining to go abroad, and remaining unseen for many weeks, so that the people could not tell whether she was alive or dead.

The last time she appeared before her Council and Parliament she was carried into the hall to preside over their doings, but had to resign the task, as she found herself incapable of conducting any business.

In the spring of the year 1558—a wet spring following on a wet autumn—Mary's chronic malady was increased by an attack of the prevailing fever or ague. At the same time death began to be busy with the few friends left of those she had prized most. She had already lost Stephen Gardiner, her first adviser when she came to the throne. Whatever his faults, he was a firm friend to Mary. In the course of this spring she heard of the death of her cousin, the great Emperor, in the convent to which he had retired on his abdication; and when the Queen's illness became more severe, and she had herself removed to the palace of St. James's, she learnt that the legate, Reginald Pole, who had been her youthful companion, was lying at the point of death also, and had declared his joy that he would not survive his Queen. The night was closing fast on her troubled day. In compliance with the last request of Philip, the Queen had appointed her sister Elizabeth her successor, and the courtiers were already flocking to Hatfield to hail the rising sun there, while Mary, aware of the fact, lay dying at St. James's.

In the early morning of the 17th of November, 1558, Mary met death with all the spirit of her earlier and happier years. She was more than resigned. She was cheerful in the conviction that the long, hard struggle was about to be ended at last. After receiving extreme unction she requested that mass might be said in her room. When the Host was raised she lifted her eyes to heaven, and at the benediction bowed her head and died.

It is customary to speak of Mary Tudor as an old woman at the time of her death; in reality she was only in her forty-fifth year. Her unhappy reign had not lasted much more than five years.

Mary had asked to be buried in the habit of a poor nun, and that no crown should be set on her head, but the title on her coffin was that of the " Queen of England, Ireland, France, Spain, and the Indies." The mortal remains of the real woman lay in her nun's dress in the coffin, but a conspicuous figure in the funeral procession was a waxen image made to resemble her as closely as possible, sumptuously attired in crimson velvet, with the fingers loaded with rings. The Queen's ladies were on horseback, with their black trains sweeping the ground. Many priests and monks followed in their order, already dreading the repetition under Elizabeth of Henry VIII.'s acts of dispersion and attainder. Philip's servants rode two and two in the line of march. There was a great display of royal standards and banners. The armour of a warrior—shield, helmet, &c.—was carried before the dead Queen, who had been supposed to wield the sword of state. The company of mourners was great, but the women of her household and her priests were the only true mourners of the woman who had meant so well, whose death was as eagerly welcomed as her accession had been. She was buried, according to the rites of her Church, in her grandfather Henry VII.'s chapel, after she had lain in her hearse in Westminster Abbey during the night of the 13th of December.

When the news of his wife's death reached Philip at Brussels, he had a requiem duly sung to her memory in the Cathedral of St. Gudule.

In her will, of which Philip was executor, Mary sought to found an hospital for poor soldiers. She left a sum of money for the re-founding of various convents, and of the Savoy Hospital for the relief of the poor. She had always been a greater benefactress to the Church and to the poor than to any seat of learning, though she was in her own person a scholar. She did, however, found the original schools for Oxford students. She had caused masses to be said for the souls of others, but she made no provision, by "ever-burning lamp" or "appointed pilgrimage," for her own soul's benefit.

Mary died a poor queen. She petitioned her successor to pay her debts as well as what remained of the debts of her father and brother, and she besought Elizabeth to maintain the Roman Catholic religion. The single personal boon which Mary craved was that the remains of her beloved mother, Queen Catherine, should be removed from Peterborough and placed near those of her daughter in Westminster Abbey. This prayer was not granted.

The magnificent diamonds presented to the Queen by Philip—the great table diamond in her ring of betrothal, and the diamonds in two other rings given to her by him, the golden collar set with diamonds and a ruby ring, which were likewise his offerings, were all restored to him at her request.

Few sovereigns have begun their reigns so enshrined in the respect and regard of their people as Mary began hers. None in England, unless it may be the base and mad King John, has ended life so universally hated and overwhelmed with reproaches. Yet good old Fuller wrote truly of her:—"She had been a worthy Princess if as little cruelty had been done under her as by her. She hated to equivocate, and always was what she was without dissembling her judgment or conduct for fear or flattery." Her fate was piteous to have so bright a beginning and so dark an ending; to stake all and lose all; to give her heart to be trampled upon and cast aside as a worthless offering; to labour for what she wrongly conceived was the eternal good of her subjects, and receive from them in return nothing save scorn and loathing; to shed rivers of innocent blood and yet be by nature an upright and humane woman. Alas! for human frailty.

She was wounded to the quick in a woman's tenderest feelings; she was mortified and shamed by the failure of her brightest and sweetest hopes; she was on the losing side in religion and politics; she died by inches of a wasting disease; she would have died for the honour of England, though her sympathies were mainly foreign, not English, and she lived to realise the loss in prestige no less than in possessions which England suffered in her reign, her heart aching as if she had been the most patriotic of monarchs. It was possible for her to guess that her name would descend to posterity with a nation's curse upon it. The lion spirit which she shared with Elizabeth supported her weak body through the slights and injuries inflicted on her youth, and the fierce strife of a disputed succession, but it failed at last before greater calamities. Her heart was broken and her reason tottered in the balance, ere lifelong disease laid her low. The English Mary, though she did not perish by a violent death, was hardly behind the Scotch Mary as a queen of sorrow. But the qualities which wrought Mary Tudor's ruin, and the penalties she paid, do not appeal to the popular imagination like the misfortunes and punishment of Mary Stuart.

If any of the readers of this book wish to realise for themselves the great tragedy of "Bloody Mary," let them turn to Tennyson's drama of *Queen Mary*, in which the poet has made her live again through her short-lived triumph and lasting desolation.

DATE DUE

DEC 22 '98		
MAY 5 '99		
SEP 14 '99		
Oct 4 '99		
JUL 24 '0		